POETRY

EXPLICATION

A Checklist of Interpretation since 1925 of

British and American Poems Past and Present

by Joseph M. Kuntz

Revised edition, 1962

Alan Swallow, Denver

CONTENTS

PREFACE TO FIRST EDITION   9

PREFACE TO SECOND EDITION   15

INTRODUCTION   17

CHECKLIST   19

MAIN SOURCES CONSULTED   317

POETRY

EXPLICATION

PREFACE TO THE FIRST EDITION

Believing as we do in the method of explication, as it is being practiced at its best, we have compiled this checklist. We hope that it will serve as a means of locating explications both for their use as such and for fuller perspective in this new aspect of criticism.

In our introductory essay we define explication as "an examination of a work of literature for a knowledge of each part, for the relation of these parts to each other, and for their relation to the whole." This definition makes one requirement (that of organic unity) and several exclusions (those of antiquarian identifications, influences, etc.) which have seemed to us essential marks of explication as distinguished from miscellaneous commentary.

In spite of the wide use of explication, there has been very little examination of its critical principles or of its place in the history of literary criticism. We chose 1925 as a starting point since it predates by a safe margin some of the earliest work in modern explication,* and since it follows immediately the publication of Richards' first critical vol-

---

* Riding and Graves, *A Survey of Modernist Poetry*, 1928; Richards, *Practical Criticism*, 1929; Empson, *Seven Types of Ambiguity*, 1930.

ume, *Principles of Literary Criticism.* This date should not suggest that we are unaware of explication that is earlier. But we have concluded that comparatively little of it in the modern sense exists.

Our checklist, then, is compiled under these two limitations of definition and chronology. Certain other omissions of potential material also occur: 1) We have generally limited ourselves to explications of poems of not more than five hundred lines. This limitation has kept us largely free from becoming entangled with the extensive bibliographies of Chaucer, Spenser, and Shakespeare. 2) We have omitted explications of poems by about thirty-five contemporary authors for whom general recognition does not yet exist. Our selection was based on recognition and not on merit, and for many of the poets not included we have a higher regard than for past and present poets who do appear. Occasionally, the importance of the explication has weighted our choice. 3) We have omitted commentary on poems which seemed less concerned with the poem as a whole than with a minor part of it. We have also omitted material on poems that relates exclusively to the sources and circumstances of composition. Yet we have inclined to include rather than exclude borderline explications. 4) Unless they show concern with the total effect of the poem, we have generally excluded paraphrase and metrical analysis. 5) We have not listed explications from books devoted to single authors. A person interested in Eliot will presumably know—or at least be able to acquaint himself with—such a separate publication as Elizabeth Drew's *T. S. Eliot: The Design of His Poetry.*

Primarily what we have done is to index the explications in a select group of volumes and literary periodicals.* Many of these will be in the personal libraries of those who use this checklist, and others are commonly available in public collections. Our choice of these has nearly always been

---

* See "Main Sources Consulted" below.

determined by the fact that they contain explications with sufficient frequency to make their indexing worthwhile. A few we have included because they are commonly credited with containing more explication than they do; and a few we regretfully omit because of practical difficulties in obtaining copies. Though every reader may be disappointed that a certain book or run of periodicals has not been indexed by us, we think that in most instances examination of the book or periodical will show that explication is so rare as to have made indexing of it less than an essential task—and a task which carried to its consistent conclusion would have made it impossible ever to complete this work. However, we have frequently consulted standard bibliographies, and when separate explications have come to our attention in books or periodicals not on our list, we have included them. Thus we hope that in spite of limitations use will prove that this book makes a just and reasonably complete listing of poetry explications published in the past twenty-five years.

We should hardly feel it necessary to say that the omissions do not imply lack of interest or respect, except that the comments of some readers of the manuscript show that we should. Within our purpose, the five kinds of omissions that we have itemized in an earlier paragraph were mostly made because our energies and time were limited. The same reasons apply to our not attempting to index explications of drama, of fiction, or of French, German, Italian, and Spanish poems. Certainly we believe that these three checklists ought to be made; but it was not a task that we assigned ourselves, even though we should be happy to encourage and advise those who wish to undertake it.

Though neither one of the compilers has read all the material of the entries listed, our collaboration has involved constant consultation. Both of us have read many entries in common, and the final preparation of the manuscript has been shared by both. It is fair to add that Mr. Arms began the compilation and that Mr. Kuntz, using his colleague's work as a starting point, systematized and extended it. Mr. Kuntz has carried the larger burden, and more than half the entries are directly attributable to him.

In this edition the checklist extends through 1949. We hope that if it serves its purpose well, later supplements or revisions will be issued. We should be grateful to receive corrected or additional entries from those who use it, and also to hear from them about improvements in the general basis and method of the project.

We wish to acknowledge with thanks the help of several groups: John P. Kirby, Louis G. Locke, and J. Edwin Whitesell, who as co-editors of *The Explicator* with Mr. Arms made suggestions and gave assistance when the checklist was begun in 1942; Roy P. Basler and Charles C. Walcutt, who since 1944 have compiled annual checklists for *The Explicator* that we have freely used;* T. M. Pearce, head of the Department of English at The University of New Mexico, and his secretary, Florence M. Shoemaker, for numerous favors; Helen Hefling, Helen L. McIntyre, Ruth Russell, and other librarians at The University of New Mexico for their help; and the Faculty Research Committee of The University of New Mexico for a grant to assist in the preparation of manuscript.

We also wish to thank a number of individuals who, having seen the manuscript in an early hectographed version or having seen the list of sources consulted, have made suggestions and supplied additional entries: Wilson O. Clough, Louis Filler, Brewster Ghiselin, William M. Gibson, Vernon Hall, Edwin Honig, Clay Hunt, Willis D. Jacobs, John P. Kirby, Lewis Leary, Robert D. Mayo, Josephine Miles, Deane

---

* The present list does not, however, duplicate the annual *Explicator* list for the years since 1944. The *Explicator* list includes fiction, drama, and long poems; and it also admits borderline explications rather more freely than we have wished to do.

Mowrer, William Van O'Connor, Ned Polsky, Desmond Powell, Mark Schorer, Arthur H. Scouten, Robert W. Stallman, Fred Stocking, Kester Svendsen, Alan Swallow, Jarvis Thurston, Charles C. Walcutt, T. Weiss, Ray West, Philip Wheelwright, Dudley Wynn, Ernest W. Baughman, Norton Crowell, Joaquin Ortega, and Hyatt Waggoner. Particularly we appreciate the especially generous help given by Mr. Stallman.

The introduction first appeared in *The Western Review*.

G. A. and J. M. K.

February, 1950
The University of New Mexico

PREFACE TO THE SECOND EDITION

The second edition of *Poetry Explication: A Checklist* incorporates explication published during the decade 1950-1959 with the first checklist, which was limited to publications appearing between 1925 and 1949. The present volume then is not so much a supplement to or a revision of the earlier work (though some errors and omissions have been rectified) but an extension. It presents a comprehensive index of poetry explications printed during the period 1925-1959, inclusive, compiled with the same aim, scope, and limitations set forth in the Preface to the first edition.

In the first edition an introduction undertook to define explication, but a similar essay no longer seems necessary in view of a great many critical studies that have since appeared. A more extensive treatment by Mr. Arms appears in *Contemporary Literature Scholarship,* ed. Lewis Leary (1958); my own reconsideration of the subject is contained in a recent University of Denver dissertation. I should also like to mention as particularly pertinent Monroe C. Beardsley, *Aesthetics: Problems in the Philosophy of Criticism* (1958); Murray Krieger, *The New Apologists for Poetry* (1956); Hyatt Howe Waggoner, "The Current Revolt Against the New Criticism," *Criticism,* I (Summer,

1959) ; William K. Wimsatt, Jr., "Explication as Criticism," *The Verbal Icon* (1954) ; William K. Wimsatt, Jr., and Cleanth Brooks, *Literary Criticism: A Short History* (1957).

Explication continues to hold a prominent position in modern critical method, for the number of new explications published during the last decade exceeds by some hundreds of items the number printed during the preceding twenty-five year period. There is no evidence to indicate that close reading of the text is on the decline in recent critical method; on the contrary, it has become the basis for most criticism. Although recent "schools" of criticism made explication a primary concern in their method and consequently popularized it, its presence in all kinds of critical writing attests to its basic values and usefulness.

Many of the individuals who helped in the compilation of the first edition also assisted in the preparation of the second. To this group may be added the names of Seymour Betsky, Stanley Cameron, Harvey Gross, Jane Kluckhohn, Harold M. Priest, Arvid Shulenberger, Dane Smith, William S. Ward, C. V. Wicker, John Williams; Marjorie Dick, Jay Ladd, Genevieve Porterfield, and other librarians of the University of New Mexico Library; Charles C. Walcutt, Chairman of the Committee for the Checklist of *The Explicator*. I wish to acknowledge with thanks their assistance.

George Arms has been most generous in advising me. The credit for the original plan of a checklist of poetry explications and for many of the entries contained in the first edition belongs to him. For the preparation of the manuscript, for the systemizing of the entries, for her encouragement at all times, I wish to thank my wife, Elizabeth. Her name should appear on the title page as co-author, but she has declined the offer.

JMK

November, 1960
The University of New Mexico

POETRY

EXPLICATION

CHECKLIST

AGEE, JAMES, "Sunday: Outskirts of Knoxville, Tenn."
DREW and SWEENEY, *Directions in Modern Poetry*, pp.
243-247.
DREW, *Poetry*, pp. 211-214.
AIKEN, "The Crystal"
JAMES DICKEY, "A Gold-Mine of Consciousness,"
Poetry, XCIV (April, 1959), 42-43.
AIKEN, "Sursum Corda"
DONALD A. STAUFFER, "Genesis, or the Poet as Maker,"
Poets at Work, pp. 72-76.
Reprinted Engle and Carrier, *Reading Modern
Poetry*, pp. 240-241.
AKENSIDE, "Ode on the Winter Solstice"
WILLIAM FROST, *English Masterpieces*, Vol. VI, *Ro-
mantic and Victorian Poetry*, pp. 3-4.
ANDERSON, PATRICK, "The Unfinished Hotel"
J. F. NIMS, *Poetry: A Critical Supplement*, March,
1948, p. 4-5.
ANONYMOUS, "Adam Lay Ibounden"
SAVAGE, *The Personal Principle*, pp. 48-49.
ANONYMOUS, "Alysoun"
ARTHUR K. MOORE, *The Secular Lyric in Middle
English*, pp. 68-69.
ANONYMOUS, "De Clerico et Puella"
ARTHUR K. MOORE, *The Secular Lyric in Middle
English*, pp. 70-72.

ANONYMOUS, "Edward"
> BROOKS, PURSER, WARREN, *An Approach to Literature,*
> pp. 435-437.
>
> Reprinted third edition, pp. 288-290.
>
> DANIELS, *The Art of Reading Poetry,* pp. 151-154.
>
> ARTHUR K. MOORE, "The Literary Status of the
> English Popular Ballad," *Comparative Literature,*
> X (Winter, 1958), 16.

ANONYMOUS, "Fowles in the Frith"
> DAICHES, *A Study of Literature,* pp. 151-152.

ANONYMOUS, "Frankie and Johnny"
> BROOKS, PURSER, WARREN, *An Approach to Literature,*
> pp. 431-432.
>
> Reprinted third edition, pp. 285-286.

ANONYMOUS, "Goosey-Goosey-Gander"
> ROBERT GRAVES, "Mother Goose's Lost Goslings,"
> *The Hudson Review,* IV (Winter, 1951), 590-591.

ANONYMOUS, "The Grand Old Duke of York"
> ROBERT GRAVES, "Mother Goose's Lost Goslings,"
> *The Hudson Review,* IV (Winter, 1951), 587.

ANONYMOUS, "Ich Am of Irlaunde"
> NORMAN HOLLAND, *The Explicator,* XV (June, 1957),
> 55.

ANONYMOUS, "Jacob and Joseph"
> OSCAR SHERWIN, "Art's Spring-Birth: The Ballad of
> Iacob and Iosep," *Studies in Philology,* XLII (Jan.,
> 1945), 1-18.

ANONYMOUS, "Johnie Armstrong"
> BROOKS and WARREN, *Understanding Poetry,* pp. 35-
> 39.
>
> Revised edition, pp 9-13.

ANONYMOUS, "The Lion and the Unicorn"
> ROBERT GRAVES, "Mother Goose's Lost Goslings,"
> *The Hudson Review,* IV (Winter, 1952), 591-592.

ANONYMOUS, "Little Jack Horner"
> ROBERT GRAVES, "Mother Goose's Lost Goslings,"
> *The Hudson Review,* IV (Winter, 1951), 588.

ANONYMOUS "Little Miss Muffet" (Mother Goose)
DANIELS, *The Art of Reading Poetry*, pp. 77-80.

ANONYMOUS, "London Lickpenny"
ARTHUR K. MOORE, *The Secular Lyric in Middle English*, pp. 164-165.

ANONYMOUS, "Lord Randall"
BROOKS and WARREN, *Understanding Poetry*, pp. 122-125.
Revised edition, pp. 48-51.
ARTHUR K. MOORE, "The Literary Status of the English Popular Ballad," *Comparative Literature*, X (Winter, 1958), 16.

ANONYMOUS, "Man in the Moon"
ARTHUR K. MOORE, *The Secular Lyric in Middle English*, pp. 95-97.

ANONYMOUS, "Nou Goth Sonne Under Wod"
JOHN L. CUTLER, *The Explicator*, IV (Oct., 1945), 7. Reprinted *Readings for Liberal Education*, II, 506-507.
STEPHEN MANNING, "Nou Goth Sonne under Wod," *MLN*, LXXIV (Nov., 1959), 578-581.
C. G. THAYER, *The Explicator*, XI (Feb., 1953), 25.

ANONYMOUS, "Nutbrowne Mayde"
ARTHUR K. MOORE, *The Secular Lyric in Middle English*, pp. 182-188.

ANONYMOUS, "The Parlement of the Three Ages"
JOHN SPEIRS, " 'Wynnere and Wastoure' and 'The Parlement of the Three Ages,' " *Scrutiny*, XVII (Autumn, 1950), 221-252.

ANONYMOUS, "Satire Against the Blacksmiths"
ARTHUR, K. MOORE, *The Secular Lyric nn Middle English*, pp. 98-99.

ANONYMOUS, "The Seafarer"
I. L. GORDON, "Traditional Themes in *The Wanderer* and *The Seafarer*," *Review of English Studies*, N. S., V (Jan. 1954), 1-13.
KENNETH SISAM, "Seafarer, Lines 97-102," *Review of English Studies*, XXI (Oct., 1945), 316-317.

ANONYMOUS, "Shoot False Love I Care Not"
MACDONALD EMSLIE, *The Explicator*, XIII (May, 1955), 44.

ANONYMOUS, "Sir Patrick Spens"
BROOKS, PURSER, WARREN, *An Approach to Literature*, pp. 429-431.
Reprinted third edition, pp. 283-284.
DANIELS, *The Art of Reading Poetry*, pp. 137-141.
FRANKENBERG, *Invitation to Poetry*, pp. 112-113.
ARTHUR K. MOORE, "The Literary Status of the English Popular Ballad," *Comparative Literature*, X (Winter, 1958), 11-13.
VAN DOREN, *Introduction to Poetry*, pp. 127-129.
Reprinted Locke, Gibson, Arms, *Introduction to Literature*, third edition, pp. 6-8.

ANONYMOUS, "Song of the Husbandman"
ARTHUR K. MOORE, *The Secular Lyric in Middle English*, pp. 85-87.

ANONYMOUS, "Summer Is Icumen In"
HUNTINGTON BROWN, *The Explicator*, III (Feb., 1945), 34.
THEODORE C. HOEPFNER, *The Explicator*, III (Dec., 1944), 18, and III (June, 1945), 59.
JOHN S. KENYON, *The Explicator*, III (March, 1945), 40.
STEPHEN MANNING, *The Explicator*, XVIII (Oct., 1959), 2.
ARTHUR K. MOORE, *The Secular Lyric in Middle English*, pp. 50-52.

ANONYMOUS, "Thirty Days Hath September"
THEODORE SPENCER, "How to Criticize a Poem," *The New Republic*, CIX (Dec. 6, 1943), 816-817. Reprinted *Readings for Liberal Education*, II, 340-342.
Reprinted Stallman and Watters, *The Creative Reader*, pp. 847-849.

ANONYMOUS, "Thomas Rymer"

DANIELS, *The Art of Reading Poetry*, pp. 144-147.

ANONYMOUS,   "The Three Ravens"

BROOKS and WARREN, *Understanding Poetry*, pp. 118-122.

Revised edition, pp. 45-48.

DANIELS, *The Art of Reading Poetry*, pp. 133-137. Reprinted *Readings for Liberal Education*, II, 363-366.

TYRUS HILLWAY, *The Explicator*, V (March, 1947), 36.

SEYMOUR LAINOFF, *The Explicator*, XVII (May, 1959), 55.

LOUIS G. LOCKE, *The Explicator*, IV (June, 1946), 54.

ROSENTHAL AND SMITH, *Exploring Poetry*, pp. 311-314.

ANONYMOUS,   "The Twa Corbies"

DANIELS, *The Art of Reading Poetry*, pp. 133-137. Reprinted *Readings for Liberal Education*, II, 363-366.

DREW, *Poetry*, pp. 93-94.

ARTHUR K. MOORE, "The Literary Status of the English Popular Ballad," *Comparative Literature*, X (Winter, 1958), 15-16.

ANONYMOUS,   "The Wanderer"

ROBERT O. BOWEN, *The Explicator*, XIII (Feb., 1955), 26.

I. L. GORDON, "Traditional Themes in *The Wanderer* and *The Seafarer*," *Review of English Studies*, N. S., V (Jan., 1954), 1-13.

STANLEY B. GREENFIELD, "*The Wanderer*: A Reconsideration of Theme and Structure," *Journal of English and Germanic Philology*, L (Oct., 1951), 451-465.

B. F. HUPPÉ, "*The Wanderer*: Theme and Structure," *Journal of English and Germanic Philology*, XLII (Oct., 1943), 516-538.

D. W. ROBERTSON, JR., "Historical Criticism," *English Institute Essays*, 1950, pp. 18-22.

THOMAS C. RUMBLE, "From *Eardstapa* to *Snotter On Mode:* The Structural Principle of 'The Wanderer,'" *Modern Language Quarterly*, XIX (Sept., 1958), 225-230.

SUSIE I. TUCKER, "Return to *The Wanderer*," *Essays in Criticism*, VIII (July, 1958), 229-237.

ANONYMOUS, "A Wayle Whyte ase Whalles Bon"

ARTHUR K. MOORE, *The Secular Lyric in Middle English*, pp. 64-65.

ANONYMOUS, "Western Wind, When Wilt Thou Blow"

BATESON, *English Poetry*, p. 81.

Abridged in *The Case for Poetry*, p. 13.

BROOKS AND WARREN, *Understanding Poetry*, revised edition, pp. 177-178.

CIARDI, *How Does a Poem Mean?* pp. 996-998.

WALTER GIERASCH, *The Explicator*, XIV (April, 1956), 43.

NAT HENRY, *The Explicator*, XVI (Oct., 1957), 5.

ARTHUR O. LEWIS, JR., *The Explicator*, XV (Feb., 1957), 28.

ARTHUR K. MOORE, *The Secular Lyric in Middle English*, pp. 29-30.

STAUFFER, *The Nature of Poetry*, p. 63.

Abridged in *The Case for Poetry*, p. 13.

PATRIC M. SWEENEY, *The Explicator*, XIV (Oct., 1955), 6.

UNGER AND O'CONNOR, *Poems for Study*, pp. 12-13.

R. P. WARREN, "Pure and Impure Poetry," *The Kenyon Review*, V (Spring, 1943), 233-235. Reprinted *Criticism*, p. 369, and *Critiques*, pp. 89-90.

Abridged in *The Case for Poetry*, p. 13.

Also reprinted West, *Essays in Modern Literary Criticism*, pp. 250-251.

Also reprinted *The Kenyon Critics*, pp. 22-24.

ANONYMOUS, "The Wife of Usher's Well"
BROOKS and WARREN, *Understanding Poetry*, pp. 42-45.
Revised edition, pp. 16-20.
ARTHUR K. MOORE, "The Literary Status of the English Popular Ballad," *Comparative Literature*, X (Winter, 1958), 13-14.

ANONYMOUS, "The Wind of the Moor"
D. W. ROBERTSON, JR., "Historical Criticism," *English Institute Essays, 1950*, pp. 26-27.

ANONYMOUS, "Wynnere and Wastoure"
JOHN SPEIRS, "'Wynnere and Wastoure' and 'The Parlement of the Three Ages,'" *Scrutiny*, XVII (Autumn, 1950), 221-252.

ARNOLD, "Dover Beach"
CLEANTH·BROOKS, "Irony and 'Ironic' Poetry," *The English Journal*, XXXVII (Feb., 1948), 59-60.
RODNEY DELASANTA, *The Explicator*, XVIII (Oct., 1950), 7.
DREW, *Poetry*, pp. 221-223.
FREDERICK L. GWYNN, *The Explicator*, VIII (April, 1960), 46.
WENDELL S. JOHNSON, "Some Functions of Poetic Form," *Journal of Aesthetics and Art Criticism*, XIII (June, 1955), 501.
J. P. KIRBY, *The Explicator*, I (April, 1943), 42. Reprinted *Readings for Liberal Education*, II, 524-525.
MURRAY KRIEGER, "'Dover Beach' and the Tragic Sense of Eternal Recurrence," *The University of Kansas City Review*, XXIII (Autumn, 1956), 73-79.
GENE MONTAGUE, *The Explicator*, XVIII (Nov., 1959), 15.

THEODORE MORRISON, "Dover Beach Revisited: A New Fable for Critics," *Harper's Magazine*, CLXXX (Feb. 1940), 235-244.
Reprinted Stallman and Watters, *The Creative Reader*, pp. 863-873.

F. A. POTTLE, *The Explicator*, II (April, 1944), 45.

NORMAN C. STAGEBERG, *The Explicator* (March, 1951), 34.

STAGEBERG AND ANDERSON. *Poetry as Experience,* p. 492.

ARNOLD,   "Empedocles on Etna"
KERMODE, *Romantic Image,* pp. 12-19.

ARNOLD,   "In Utrumque Paratus"
W. STACY JOHNSON, *The Explicator,* X (May, 1952), 46.

ARNOLD,   "Isolation"

DREW, *Poetry,* pp. 145-147.

STAUFFER, *The Nature of Poetry,* pp. 232-235.

ARNOLD,   "The Last Word"
DANIELS, *The Art of Reading Poetry,* p. 273.

ARNOLD,   "Memorial Verses"
BATESON, *English Poetry and the English Language,* pp. 106-108.

ARNOLD,   "Requiescat"
THOMAS and BROWN, *Reading Poetry,* p. 639.

ARNOLD,   "The Scholar Gipsy"
BROOKS and WARREN, *Understanding Poetry,* pp. 545-549.
Revised edition, pp. 416-420.

DOUGLAS, LAMSON, SMITH, *The Critical Reader,* pp. 46-49.

A. E. DYSON, "The Last Enchantments," *Review of English Studies,* VIII, n.s. (Aug., 1957), 257-265.

R. M. GAY, *The Explicator,* II (Feb., 1944), 28.

CLYDE K. HYDER, *The Explicator,* IX (Dec., 1950), 23.

JOHNSON, *The Alien Vision of Victorian Poetry,* pp. 199-202.

WILLIAM S. KNICKERBOCKER, *The Explicator,* VIII (May, 1950), 51.

G. WILSON KNIGHT, " 'The Scholar Gypsy': an Interpretation," *Review of English Studies,* VI, n.s. (Jan., 1955), 53-62.

GENE MONTAGUE, *The Explicator,* XVIII (Nov., 1959), 15.

LAURENCE PERRINE, *The Explicator*, XV (Feb., 1957), 33.

ARNOLD, "Shakespeare"
F. A. DUDLEY, *The Explicator*, IV (June, 1946), 57.
FRANKENBERG, *Invitation to Poetry*, pp. 93-94.
E. M. HALLIDAY and CARLTON F. WELLS, *The Explicator*, VI (Oct., 1947), 4.
LEAVIS, *Education and the University*, pp. 73-76.
F. A. PHILBRICK, *The Explicator*, V (Dec., 1946), 24.

ARNOLD, "Thyrsis"
JOHNSON, *The Alien Vision of Victorian Poetry*, pp. 202--204.
MICHAEL MACKLEM, "The Elegiac Theme in Housman," *Queens Quarterly*, LIX (Spring, 1952), 48.

ARNOLD, "To Marguerite"
KATHLEEN TILLOTSON, " 'Yes: in the Sea of Life,' " *Review of English Studies*, III, n.s. (Oct., 1952), 346-364.

AUDEN, "Address for a Prize-Day"
MONROE K. SPEARS, "Late Auden: The Satirist as Lunatic Clergyman," *The Sewanee Review*, LIX (Winter, 1951), 66.

AUDEN, "As I Walked Out One Evening"
ELLSWORTH MASON, *The Explicator*, XII (May, 1954), 43.
EDWARD C. MCALEER, "As Auden Walked Out," *College English*, XVIII (Feb., 1957), 271-272.

AUDEN, "Caliban to the Audience"
MONROE K. SPEARS, "Late Auden: The Satirist as Lunatic Clergyman," *The Sewanee Review*, LIX (Winter, 1951), 66-70.

AUDEN, "The Climbers"
MAYNARD MACK, LEONARD DEAN, and WILLIAM FROST, *English Masterpieces*, Vol. VII, *Modern Poetry*, pp. 21-22.

AUDEN, "Crisis"
HAROLD MORLAND, *The Explicator*, V (Nov., 1946), 17.
F. A. PHILBRICK, *The Explicator*, V (April, 1947), 45.

AUDEN, "The Dance of Death"
  BROOKS, *Modern Poetry and the Tradition*, pp. 133-135.
AUDEN, "Dear, Though the Night Is Gone"
  FRANKENBERG, *Invitation to Poetry*, p. 172.
AUDEN, "The Diaspora"
  ROBERT E. KNOLL, "The Style of Contemporary Poetry," *The Prairie Schooner*, XXIX (Summer, 1955), 122-124.
AUDEN, "Doom Is Dark and Deeper than any Sea-Dingle"
  MORTON W. BLOOMFIELD, "W. H. Auden and *Sawles Warde*," *MLN*, LXIII (Dec., 1948), 548-552.
AUDEN, "Family Ghosts" ("The Strings' Excitement")
  SISTER M. CLEOPHAS, *The Explicator*, VII (Oct., 1948), 1.
  Reprinted Engle and Carrier, *Reading Modern Poetry*, pp. 294-295.
AUDEN, "For the Time Being"
  MAYNARD MACK, LEONARD DEAN, and WILLIAM FROST, *English Masterpieces*, Vol. VII, *Modern Poetry*, pp. 22-24.
AUDEN, "Foxtrot from a Play"
  WILLIAM POWERS, *The Explicator*, XVI (March, 1958), 32.
AUDEN, "Fugal-Chorus"
  WILLIAM FROST, *The Explicator*, XI (Dec., 1952), 21.
  FREDERICK A. POTTLE, *The Explicator*, XI (April, 1953), 40.
AUDEN, "Get There If You Can and See the Land You Once Were Proud to Own" (Poem XII of *Poems*)
  SAVAGE, *The Personal Principle*, pp. 161-162.
AUDEN, "Have a Good Time"
  F. A. PHILBRICK, *The Explicator*, IV (Dec., 1945), 21.
AUDEN, "Horae Canonicae"
  ADAMS, *Strains of Discord*, pp. 125-127.
AUDEN, "In Memory of W. B. Yeats (d. Jan. 1939)"
  DREW, *Poetry*, pp. 267-270.
  ROBERT ROTH, "The Sophistication of W. H. Auden: A Sketch in Longinian Method," *Modern Philol-*

ogy, XLVIII (Feb., 1951), 198-202.

AUDEN, "It's No Use Raising a Shout"
GEORGE McFADDEN, *The Explicator*, XV (Nov., 1956), 12.
MARK ROWAN, *The Explicator*, XV (Nov., 1956), 12.
JOHN H. SUTHERLAND, *The Explicator*, XV (Nov., 1956), 12.

AUDEN, "Law Like Love"
UNGER and O'CONNOR, *Poems for Study*, pp. 647-649.

AUDEN, "Lay Your Sleeping Head, My Love"
STEPHEN SPENDER, "W. H. Auden and His Poetry," *Atlantic Monthly*, CXCII (July, 1953), 79.

AUDEN, "Letter to a Wound"
MONROE K. SPEARS, "Late Auden: The Satirist as Lunatic Clergyman," *The Sewanee Review*, LIX (Winter, 1951), 65-66.

AUDEN, "Memorial for the City"
MONROE K. SPEARS, "The Dominant Symbols of Auden's Poetry," *The Sewanee Review*, LIX (Summer, 1951), 416-417.

AUDEN, "New Year's Letter"
DEUTSCH, *Poetry in Our Time*, pp. 383-384, 399-400.
FRANKENBERG, *Pleasure Dome*, pp. 309-313.

AUDEN, "Now the Leaves Are Falling Fast"
DREW, *Poetry*, pp. 89-92.

AUDEN, ". . . The One Whose Past It Is to Lean" (Poem III of *Poems*)
SAVAGE, *The Personal Principle*, pp. 162-163.

AUDEN, "The Orators"
DAICHES, *Poetry and the Modern World*, pp. 220-227.
SAVAGE, *The Personal Principle*, pp. 165-169.

AUDEN, "Our Hunting Fathers Told the Story"
F. CUDWORTH FLINT, *The Explicator*, II (Oct., 1943), 28.
TATE, *Reason in Madness*, pp. 97-98. Reprinted *On the Limits of Poetry*, pp. 127-128.

AUDEN, "Oxford"
BATESON, *English Poetry*, pp. 240-245.

AUDEN, "Petition"
DEUTSCH, *Poetry in Our Time*, pp. 381-382.

AUDEN, "Pleasure Island"

R. MAYHEAD, "The Latest Auden," *Scrutiny*, XVIII (June, 1952), 316-318.

AUDEN, "Poem XX"

BROOKS, *Modern Poetry and the Tradition*, pp. 126-129.

AUDEN, "Prime"

R. MAYHEAD, "The Latest Auden," *Scrutiny*, XVIII (June, 1952), 315-316.

AUDEN, "Schoolchildren"

RICHARD A. LONG, *The Explicator*, VII (Feb., 1949), 32.

AUDEN, "September 1, 1939"

PHYLLIS BARTLETT and JOHN A. POLLARD, *The Explicator*, XIV (Nov., 1955), 8.

DAPHNE N. BENNETT, "Auden's 'September 1, 1939,' " *Quarterly Journal of Speech*, XLII (Feb., 1956), 4-13.

AUDEN, "Sir, No Man's Enemy, Forgiving All"

BROOKS, *Modern Poetry and the Tradition*, pp. 1-2.

WALLACE CABLE BROWN, *The Explicator*, III (March, 1945), 38.

D. A. ROBERTSON, JR., W. K. WIMSATT, JR., and HALLET SMITH, *The Explicator*, III (May, 1945), 51.

AUDEN, "Song for St. Cecilia's Day"

DEUTSCH, *Poetry in Our Time*, pp. 390-391.

AUDEN, "Spain"

DELMORE SCHWARTZ, "The Two Audens," *The Kenyon Review*, I (Winter, 1939), 43-44.

AUDEN, "Venus Will Now Say a Few Words"

DEUTSCH, *Poetry in Our Time*, pp. 380-381.

AUDEN, "Which Side Am I Supposed to Be On?" (or "Ode to My Pupils")

C. B. LeCOMPTE, JR., *The Explicator*, VIII (Dec., 1949), 21.

RICHARD A. LONG, *The Explicator*, VI (April, 1948), 39.

BAILEY, "Life's More Than Breath and the Quick Round of Blood" (from *Festus*)

I. A. RICHARDS, *Practical Criticism*, pp. 21-30.

BARKER, GEORGE, "The Amazons"

DAVID DAICHES, "The Lyricism of George Barker," *Poetry*, LXIX (March, 1947), 337-339.

BARKER, GEORGE, "The Seagull, Spreadeagled, Splayed on the Wind"

DAY LEWIS, *The Poetic Image*, pp. 128-130.

Reprinted Engle and Carrier, *Reading Modern Poetry*, pp. 248-249.

BENÉT, S. V., "Ode to Walt Whitman"

MORTON D. ZABEL, "The American Grain," *Poetry*, XLVIII (August, 1936), 279-281.

BERRYMAN, "The Disciple"

ROBERT FITZGERALD, "Poetry and Perfection," *The Sewanee Review*, LVI (Autumn, 1948), 690-691.

BERRYMAN, "The Dispossessed"

J. F. NIMS, *Poetry: A Critical Supplement*, April, 1948, pp. 1-5.

BERRYMAN, "World's Fair"

J. F. NIMS, *Poetry: A Critical Supplement*, April, 1948, p. 6.

BINYON, "The Supper"

JAMES G. SOUTHWORTH, "Laurence Binyon," *The Sewanee Review*, XLIII (July-Sept., 1935), 343-346.

BISHOP, ELIZABETH, "The Colder the Air"

KARL F. THOMPSON, *The Explicator*, XII (March, 1954), 33.

BISHOP, ELIZABETH, "The Map"

FRANKENBERG, *Pleasure Dome*, pp. 331-333.

Reprinted Engle and Carrier, *Reading Modern Poetry*, pp. 228-229.

BISHOP, JOHN PEALE, "Behavior of the Sun"

R. W. STALLMAN, *The Explicator*, V (Oct., 1946), 6.

R. W. STALLMAN, "The Poetry of John Peale Bishop," *Western Review*, XI (Autumn, 1946), 15-16.

BISHOP, "Divine Nativity"

JOSEPH FRANK, "Force and Form: A Study of John Peale Bishop," *The Sewanee Review,* LV (Winter, 1947), 97-98.

BISHOP, "O Let Not Virtue Seek"

JOSEPH FRANK, "Force and Form: A Study of John Peale Bishop," *The Sewanee Review,* LV (Winter, 1947), 91-93.

BISHOP, "Perspectives are Precipices"

R. W. STALLMAN, *The Explicator,* V (Nov., 1946), 8.

R. W. STALLMAN, "The Poetry of John Peale Bishop," *Western Review,* XI (Autumn, 1946), 17-19.

ALLEN TATE, "A Note on Bishop's Poetry," *The Southern Review,* I (Autumn, 1935), 362-363.

TATE, *Reactionary Essays on Poetry and Ideas,* pp. 60-62. Reprinted *On the Limits of Poetry,* pp. 244-246.

BISHOP, "The Return"

ALLEN TATE, "A Note on Bishop's Poetry," *The Southern Review,* I (Autumn, 1935), 361-362.

TATE, *Reactionary Essays on Poetry and Ideas,* pp. 58-60. Reprinted *On the Limits of Poetry,* pp. 243-244.

BISHOP, "The Saints"

JOSEPH FRANK, "Force and Form: A Study of John Peale Bishop," *The Sewanee Review,* LV (Winter, 1947), 95-96.

BISHOP, "Southern Pines"

R. W. STALLMAN, *The Explicator,* IV (April, 1946), 46.

R. W. STALLMAN, "The Poetry of John Peale Bishop," *Western Review,* XI (Autumn, 1946), 10-12.

BISHOP, "Speaking of Poetry"

DEUTSCH, *Poetry in Our Time,* pp. 191-193.

JOSEPH FRANK, "Force and Form: A Study of John Peale Bishop," *The Sewanee Review,* LV (Winter, 1947), 83-86.

BISHOP, "The Tree"

JOSEPH FRANK, "Force and Form: A Study of John Peale Bishop," *The Sewanee Review,* LV (Winter, 1947), 98-99.

BISHOP, "Twelfth Night"

JOSEPH FRANK, "Force and Form: A Study of John Peale Bishop," *The Sewanee Review*, LV (Winter, 1947), 79-80.

BLACKMUR, "Judas Priest," Sonnet III: "Judas, Not Pilate, Had a Wakened Mind"

ALLEN TATE, *Reason in Madness*, pp. 175-179.

BLACKMUR, "Missa Vocis"

DONALD A. STAUFFER, "Genesis, of the Poet As Maker," *Poets at Work*, pp. 43-52.

BLACKMUR, "The Spear"

ALLEN TATE, *Reason in Madness*, pp. 174-175.

BLAKE, "Ahania"

H. M. MARGOLIOUTH, "Notes on Blake," *Review of English Studies*, XXIV (Oct., 1948), 304.

BLAKE, "Ah! Sunflower!"

BOWRA, *The Romantic Imagination*, p. 45.

WOLF MANKOWITZ, "William Blake (2) *The Songs of Experience*," *Politics and Letters*, I (Winter-Spring, 1947), 20.

BLAKE, "America"

H. M. MARGOLIOUTH, "Notes on Blake," *Review of English Studies*, XXIV (Oct., 1948), 303-304.

BLAKE, "The Angel"

WOLF MANKOWITZ, "William Blake (2) *The Songs of Experience*," *Politics and Letters*, I (Winter-Spring, 1947), 19-20.

BLAKE, "Auguries of Innocence"

UNGER and O'CONNOR, *Poems for Study*, pp. 341-343.

BLAKE, "The Clod and the Pebble"

ARTHUR DICKSON, *The Explicator*, II (Nov., 1943), 12.

"OLYBRIUS," *The Explicator*, I (Feb., 1943), 32.

WOLF MANKOWITZ, "William Blake (2) *The Songs of Experience*," *Politics and Letters*, I (Winter-Spring, 1947), 18-19.

BLAKE, "Earth's Answer"

WOLF MANKOWITZ, "William Blake (2) *The Songs of*

Experience," *Politics and Letters,* I (Winter-Spring, 1947), 16-17.

BLAKE, "The Echoing Green"

TILLYARD, *Poetry Direct and Oblique,* pp. 9-12. Reprinted *Criticism,* pp. 286-288.

BLAKE, "Hear the Voice of the Bard"

BATESON, *English Poetry,* pp. 37-39.

BODKIN, *Archetypal Patterns in Poetry,* pp. 317-323.

BLAKE, "Holy Thursday"

ROBERT F. GLECKNER, "Point of View and Context in Blake's Songs," *New York Public Library Bulletin,* LXI (Nov., 1957), 534-535.

BLAKE, "I Asked a Thief"

ROSENTHAL and SMITH, *Exploring Poetry,* pp. 455-458.

BLAKE, "Infant Sorrow"

WOLF MANKOWITZ, *"William Blake* (2) The Songs *of Experience," Politics and Letters,* I (Winter-Spring, 1947), 21-22.

BLAKE, "Introduction" (*Songs of Experience*)

NORTHROP FRYE, "Blake's Introduction to Experience," *Huntington Library Quarterly,* XXI (Nov., 1957), 57-67.

ROBERT F. GLECKNER, "Point of View and Context in Blake's Songs," *New York Public Library Bulletin,* LXI (Nov., 1957), 535-537.

WOLF MANKOWITZ, "William Blake (2) *The Songs of Experience," Politics and Letters,* I (Winter-Spring, 1947), 15.

RENÉ WELLEK, "A Letter," *The Importance of Scrutiny,* pp. 24-25. First published in *Scrutiny,* 1937.

BLAKE, "Introduction" (*Songs of Innocence*)

WILLIAM R. BOWDEN, *The Explicator,* XI (April, 1953), 41.

FRANKENBERG, *Invitation to Poetry,* pp. 64-65.

MARGARET GIOVANNINI, *The Explicator,* VIII (Oct. 1949), 5.

HOWARD JUSTIN, *The Explicator*, XI (Oct., 1952), 1.

ARTHUR WORMHOUDT, *The Explicator*, VII (May, 1949), 55.

BLAKE, "The Lily"

WOLF MANKOWITZ, "William Blake (2) *The Songs of Experience*," *Politics and Letters*, I (Winter-Spring, 1947), 20.

BLAKE, "The Little Black Boy"

JACOB H. ADLER, "Symbol and Meaning in 'The Little Black Boy,'" *MLN*, LXXII (June, 1957), 412-415.

RALPH D. EBERLY, *The Explicator*, XV (April, 1957), 42.

LLOYD N. JEFFREY, *The Explicator*, XVII (Jan., 1959), 27.

VAN DOREN, *Introduction to Poetry*, pp. 111-115.

J. E. WHITESELL, *The Explicator*, V (April, 1947), 42.

BLAKE, "The Little Girl Lost and Found"

WOLF MANKOWITZ, "William Blake (2) *The Songs of Experience*," *Politics and Letters*, I (Winter-Spring, 1947), 20.

BLAKE, "The Little Vagabond"

ROBERT F. GLECKNER, "Point of View and Context in Blake's Songs," *New York Public Library Bulletin*, LXI (Nov., 1957), 534.

BLAKE, "London"

WILLIAM BLISSETT, "Poetic Wave and Poetic Particle," *The University of Toronto Quarterly*, XXIV (Oct., 1954), 5-6.

BOWRA, *The Romantic Imagination*, pp. 42-43.

BROOKS, PURSER, WARREN, *An Approach to Literature*, pp. 496-498.

Reprinted third edition, pp. 387-390.

ROSENTHAL and SMITH, *Exploring Poetry*, pp. 693-695.

Reprinted Locke, Gibson, and Arms, *Introduction to Literature*, third edition, p. 77.

WOLF MANKOWITZ, "William Blake (2) *The Songs of Experience,*" *Politics and Letters,* I (Winter-Spring, 1947), 21.

BLAKE,   "Mad Song"

H. J. C. GRIERSON, "Blake and Macpherson," *Times Literary Supplement,* April 7, 1945, p. 163.

GEOFFREY KEYNES, "Blake's 'Poetical Sketches'—I," *Times Literary Supplement,* March 10, 1945, p. 120.

BLAKE,   "Memory"

VIVANTE, *English Poetry,* p. 91.

BLAKE,   "Mental Traveller"

JOHN H. SUTHERLAND, "Blake's 'Mental Traveller,'" *Journal of English Literary History,* XXII (June, 1955), 136-147.

BLAKE,   "My Pretty Rose Tree"

ROBERT F. GLECKNER, *The Explicator,* XIII (May, 1955), 43.

ROBERT F. GLECKNER, "Point of View and Context in Blake's Songs," *New York Public Library Bulletin,* LXI (Nov., 1957), 531-532.

BLAKE,   "O Earth, O Earth, Return"

BOWRA, *The Romantic Imagination,* pp. 46-47.

BLAKE,   "A Poison Tree"

T. O. MABBOTT and EDWARD C. SAMPSON, *The Explicator,* VI (Dec., 1947), 19.

BLAKE,   "The Scoffers"

BROOKS and WARREN, *Understanding Poetry,* pp. 579-582.

Revised edition, pp. 423-427.

BLAKE,   "The Sick Rose"

BOWRA, *The Romantic Imagination,* p. 44.

Abridged in *The Case for Poetry,* p. 25.

BROWER, *The Fields of Light,* pp. 6-11.

DREW, *Poetry,* pp. 63-64.

F. R. LEAVIS, " 'Thought' and Emotional Quality," *Scrutiny,* XIII (Spring, 1945), 69-70.

WOLF MANKOWITZ, "William Blake (2) *The Songs of Experience,"* *Politics and Letters,* I (Winter-Spring), 17-18.

E. H. W. MEYERSTEIN, " 'A True Maid' and 'The Sick Rose,' " *Times Literary Supplement,* June 22, 1946, p. 295.

ROSENTHAL and SMITH, *Exploring Poetry,* pp. 501-502.

TILLYARD, *Poetry Direct and Oblique,* pp. 168-170.

Abridged in *The Case for Poetry,* p. 25.

BLAKE,   "Song: My Silks and Fine Array"

CLEANTH BROOKS, "Current Critical Theory and the Period Course," *CEA Critic,* XII (Oct., 1950), 1, 5-6.

BLAKE,   **"Stanzas from Milton"**

L. G. LOCKE, *The Explicator,* I (March, 1943), 38.

BLAKE,   **"The Tiger"**

BASLER, *Sex, Symbolism, and Psychology in Literature,* pp. 19-24.

ROBERT O. BOWEN, *The Explicator,* VII (June, 1949), 62.

BOWRA, *The Romantic Imagination,* pp. 47-49.

ELIZABETH DREW, *Discovering Poetry,* p. 160.

R. D. EBERLY, *The Explicator,* VIII (Nov., 1949), 12.

T. O. MABBOTT, *Notes and Queries,* CLXXXVIII (Nov. 17, 1945), 211-212.

WOLF MANKOWITZ, "William Blake (2) *The Songs of Experience,"* *Politics and Letters,* I (Winter-Spring, 1947), 22-23.

ELIZABETH NITCHIE, *The Explicator,* I (Feb., 1943), 34.

MARTIN K. NURMI, "Blake's Revisions of *The Tyger,"* *PMLA,* LXXI (Sept., 1956), 669-683.

FREDERICK A. POTTLE, *The Explicator,* VIII (March, 1950), 39.

ROSENTHAL and SMITH, *Exploring Poetry*, pp. 185-187.

GEORGE WINCHESTER STONE, JR., *The Explicator*, I (Dec., 1942), 19.

BLAKE, "To the Accuser Who Is the God of This World"

STAUFFER, *The Nature of Poetry*, pp. 53-54.

BLAKE, "To Spring"

VIVANTE, *English Poetry*, pp. 89-90.

W. K. WIMSATT, JR., "The Structure of Romantic Nature Imagery," *The Age of Johnson* (New Haven: Yale University Press, 1949), pp. 300-301. Reprinted *The Verbal Icon*, pp. 112-113.

BLAKE, "To the Muses"

VIVANTE, *English Poetry*, p. 92.

BLAKE, "Visions of the Daughters of Albion"

HENRY H. WASSER, "Notes on the *Visions of the Daughters of Albion,*" *Modern Language Quarterly*, IX (Sept., 1948), 292-297.

BLUNDEN, "A Summer's Fancy"

ROBERT PENN WARREN, *Poetry*, XLVIII (Feb., 1934), 287-288.

BLUNDEN, "Thomasine"

ANONYMOUS, "Menander's Mirror: Mr. Blunden's 'Thomasine,'" *Times Literary Supplement*, Jan. 20, 1945, p. 27.

BOGAN, "Solitary Observations . . ."

DANIELS, *The Art of Reading Poetry*, pp. 199-200.

BOWERS, "Dark Earth and Summer"

RICHARD G. STERN, "The Poetry of Edgar Bowers," *The Chicago Review*, XI (Autumn, 1957), 73-75.

BOWLES, "To the River Itchin"

W. K. WIMSATT, JR., "The Structure of Romantic Nature Imagery," *The Age of Johnson* (New Haven: Yale University Press, 1949), p. 294.

BRACKENRIDGE, "Poem on Divine Revelation"

Thomas Haviland, "The Miltonic Quality of Brackenridge's Poem on Divine Revelation," *PMLA*, LVI (June, 1941), 588-592.

BRIDGES, "Eros"

Rosenthal and Smith, *Exploring Poetry*, pp. 183-185.

Winters, *Primitivism and Decadence*, pp. 66-71. Also *In Defense of Reason*, pp. 77-82.

BRIDGES, "Low Barometer"

Yvor Winters, "The Poetry of Gerard Manley Hopkins (1)," *Hudson Review*, I (Winter, 1948), 458-460.

Reprinted *The Function of Criticism*, pp. 105-107.

BRIDGES, "Nightingales"

Brooks and Warren, *Understanding Poetry*, pp. 198-200.

Revised edition, pp. 95-97.

Daniels, *The Art of Reading Poetry*, p. 375.

BRIDGES, "Ode to Music"

Andrew J. Green, "Bridges' Odes for Music," *The Sewanee Review*, XLIX (Jan.-March, 1941), 30-38.

BRIDGES, "In the Summer House on the Mound"

Yvor Winters, "Traditional Mastery," *Hound and Horn*, V (Jan.-March, 1932), 324-325.

BRINNIN, "The Alps"

David Daiches, "Some Notes on Contemporary American Poetry," *Modern American Poetry*, B. Rajan, ed., pp. 113-114.

BRINNIN, "Goodnight, When the Door Swings"

David Daiches, "Some Notes on Contemporary American Poetry," *Modern American Poetry*, B. Rajan, ed., p. 114.

BRINNIN, "Views of the Favorite Colleges"

Sister Mary Humiliata, I.H.M., *The Explicator*, XIV (Jan., 1956), 20.

BRINNIN, "The Worm in the Whirling Cross"

J. F. Nims, *Poetry: A Critical Supplement*, Nov., 1947, pp. 1-15.

Reprinted in part in Friar and Brinnin, *Modern Poetry*, pp. 447-449.

JOHN THEOBALD, "The World in a Cross Word," *Poetry*, LXXI (Nov., 1947), 82-90.

BRONTE, EMILY, "Cold in the Earth"

F. R. LEAVIS, "Reality and Sincerity: Notes in the Analysis of Poetry," *Scrutiny*, XIX (Winter, 1952-3), 90-92, 93-94.

BROOKE, "The Soldier"

DANIELS, *The Art of Reading Poetry*, pp. 270-272.

BROOKS, GWENDOLYN, "The Children of the Poor"

HAYDEN CARRUTH, *A Critical Supplement to "Poetry,"* March, 1949, pp. 13-15.

BROOKS, GWENDOLYN, "A Light and Diplomatic Bird"

HAYDEN CARRUTH, *A Critical Supplement to "Poetry,"* March, 1949, pp. 16-18.

BROWN, HARRY, "Fourth Elegy: The Poet Compared to an Unsuccessful General"

HAYDEN CARRUTH, "The Poet with Wounds," *Poetry*, LXXI (Jan., 1948), 217-221.

J. F. NIMS, *Poetry: A Critical Supplement*, Jan., 1948, pp. 2-12.

BROWN, THOMAS EDWARD, "My Garden"

DANIELS, *The Art of Reading Poetry*, p. 261.

BROWNE, "Epitaph on the Countess Dowager of Pembroke"

TATE, *Reason in Madness*, pp. 95-96. Reprinted *On the Limits of Poetry*, p. 125.

TATE, "Understanding Modern Poetry," *College English*, I (April, 1940), 570.

BROWNING, E. B., "Sonnets from the Portuguese," XXII

ROBERT M. GAY, *The Explicator*, I (Dec., 1942), 24.

BROWNING, E. B., "Sonnets from the Portuguese," XLIII

WILLIAM T. GOING, *The Explicator*, XI (June, 1953), 58.

ROBERT B. HEILMAN, *The Explicator,* IV (Oct., 1945),
3. Reprinted *Readings for Liberal Education,* II,
213-214.
Reprinted Locke, Gibson, and Arms, *Introduction
to Literature,* third edition, pp. 116-117.

BROWNING,   "Abt Vogler"
LANGBAUM, *The Poetry of Experience,* pp. 140-143.
EMERSON R. MARKS, *The Explicator,* XVI (Feb.,
1958), 29.

BROWNING,   "Andrea del Sarto"
LANGBAUM, *The Poetry of Experience,* pp. 148-151,
152-155.

BROWNING,   "Bishop Blougram's Apology"
LANGBAUM, *The Poetry of Experience,* pp. 100-102.
WILLIAM O. RAYMOND, "Browning's Casuists," *Studies
in Philology,* XXXVII (Oct., 1940), 648-653.
C. E. TANZY, *Victorian Studies,* I (March, 1958), 255-
266.
C. N. WENGER, "The Masquerade in Browning's Dramatic Monologues," *College English,* III (Dec.,
1941), 228-229.

BROWNING,   "The Bishop Orders His Tomb at Saint
Praxed's Church"
DANIELS, *The Art of Reading Poetry,* pp. 99-101.

BROWNING,   "By the Fire-Side"
JEAN STIRLING LINDSAY, "The Central Episode of
Browning's 'By the Fire-Side,'" *Studies in Phi-
lology,* XXXIX (July, 1942), 571-579.

BROWNING,   "Caliban Upon Setebos"
E. K. BROWN, "The First Person in 'Caliban Upon
Setebos,'" *MLN,* LXVI (June, 1951), 392-395.

BROWNING,   "Childe Roland to the Dark Tower
Came"
GEORGE ARMS, " 'Childe Roland' and 'Sir Galahad,' "
College English, VI (Feb., 1945), 258-262.
DAVID V. ERDMAN, "Browning's Industrial Night-

mare," *Philological Quarterly*, XXXVI (Oct., 1957), 427-435.

R. E. HUGHES, "Browning's 'Child Roland' and the Broken Taboo," *Literature and Psychology*, IX (Spring, 1959), 18-19.

LANGBAUM, *The Poetry of Experience*, pp. 192-200.

LIONEL STEVENSON, "The Pertinacious Victorian Poets," *The University of Toronto Quarterly*, XXI (April, 1952), 239-240.

BROWNING, "Cleon"

EDWARD C. McALEER, "Browning's 'Cleon' and Auguste Comte," *Comparative Literature*, VIII (Spring, 1956), 143-145.

BROWNING, "Cristina"

CLYDE S. KILBY, *The Explicator*, II (Nov., 1943), 16.

BROWNING, "Count Gismond"

INA B. SESSIONS, "The Dramatic Monologue," *PMLA*, LXII (June, 1947), 510-511.

BROWNING, "Evelyn Hope"

INA B. SESSIONS, "The Dramatic Monologue," *PMLA*, LXII (June, 1947), 515.

BROWNING, "Fra Lippo Lippi"

C. M. HUDSON, JR., and EDWARD H. WEATHERLY, "The Survey Course at the University of Missouri," *College English*, VIII (March, 1947), 323-327.

MARGARET W. PEPPERDENE, *The Explicator*, XV (Feb., 1957), 34.

LAURENCE PERRINE, *The Explicator*, XVI (Dec., 1957), 18.

BROWNING, "The Glove"

LOUISE SCHUTZ BOAS, *The Explicator*, II (Nov., 1943), 13.

LOUIS S. FRIEDLAND, *The Explicator*, I (May, 1943), 54.

LOUIS S. FRIEDLAND, *The Explicator*, II (Feb., 1944), 30.

BENNETT WEAVER, "Primer Study in Browning's Satire," *College English*, XVI (Nov., 1952), 80.

R. W. WHIDDEN, *The Explicator*, II (Dec., 1943), 23.

BROWNING, "A Grammarian's Funeral"
J. MITCHELL MORSE, "Browning's Grammarian, Warts and All," *College English Association Critic,* XX (Jan., 1958), 1, 5.

BROWNING, "Holy-Cross Day"
BENNETT WEAVER, "Primer Study in Browning's Satire," *College English,* XVI (Nov., 1952), 79-80.

BROWNING, "Home-Thoughts, from the Sea"
FREDERICK L. GWYNN, *The Explicator,* XII (Nov., 1953), 12.
Reprinted Locke, Gibson, and Arms, *Introduction to Literature, third edition,* pp. 131-132.

BROWNING, "In a Balcony"
ELMER E. STOLL, "Browning's 'In a Balcony,'" *Modern Language Quarterly,* III (Sept., 1942), 407-415.

BROWNING, "The Inn Album"
J. T. FOSTER, *The Explicator,* X (Dec., 1951), 18.

BROWNING, "James Lee's Wife," VIII
G. ROBERT STANGE, *The Explicator,* XVII (Feb., 1959), 32.

BROWNING, "Karshish"
MAUREEN WRIGHT, *Times Literary Supplement* (May 1, 1953), p. 285.

BROWNING, "The Laboratory"
DANIELS, *The Art of Reading Poetry,* pp. 92-95.
LIONEL STEVENSON, "The Pertinacious Victorian Poets," *The University of Toronto Quarterly,* XXI (April, 1952), 243-244.

BROWNING, "La Saisiaz"
F. E. L. PRIESTLEY, "A Reading of 'La Saisiaz,'" *The University of Toronto Quarterly,* XXV (Oct., 1955), 47-59.

BROWNING, "Love Among the Ruins"
DAVID V. ERDMAN, "Browning's Industrial Nightmare," *Philological Quarterly,* XXXVI (Oct. 1957), 425-426.

BROWNING, "Master Hugues of Saxe-Gotha"

LANGBAUM, *The Poetry of Experience,* pp. 144-146.
BENNETT WEAVER, "A Primer Study in Browning's Satire," *College English,* XVI (Nov., 1952), 78-79.
BROWNING, "Meeting at Night"
RALPH W. CONDEE, *The Explicator,* XII (Feb., 1954), 23.
FRANKENBERG, *Invitation to Poetry,* p. 231.

WALTER GIERASCH, *The Explicator,* I (May, 1943), 55.
F. R. Leavis, "Imagery and Movement," *Scrutiny,* XIII (Sept., 1945), 130-131.
PERRINE, *Sound and Sense,* pp. 41-42.

BROWNING, "My Last Duchess"
BROOKS, PURSER, WARREN, *An Approach to Literature,* pp. 437-439.
Reprinted third edition, pp. 292-293.

LOUIS S. FRIEDLAND, "Ferrara and 'My Last Duchess,' " *Studies in Philology,* XXXIII (Oct., 1936), 656-684.
B. R. JERMAN, "Browning's Witless Duke," *PMLA,* LXXII (June, 1957), 488-493.
KIRK and McCUTCHEON, *An Introduction to the Study of Poetry,* pp. 17-24.
LANGBAUM, *The Poetry of Experience,* pp. 82-85.
LAURENCE PERRINE, "Browning's Shrewd Duke," *PMLA,* LXXIV (March, 1959), 157-159.
JOHN D. REA, "My Last Duchess," *Studies in Philology,* XXIX (Jan., 1932), 120-122.
INA B. SESSIONS, "The Dramatic Monologue," *PMLA,* LXII (June, 1947), 508-510.

LIONEL STEVENSON, "The Pertinacious Victorian Poets," *The University of Toronto Quarterly,* XXI (April, 1952), 240-242.
BROWNING, "My Star"
PERRINE, *Sound and Sense,* p. 66.
BROWNING, "Parting at Morning"
RALPH W. CONDEE, *The Explicator,* XII (Feb., 1954), 23.
BROWNING, "Pictor Ignotus, Florence, 15—"

PAUL F. JAMIESON, *The Explicator*, XI (Nov., 1952), 8.

BROWNING, "Popularity"
BENNETT WEAVER, "A Primer Study in Browning's Satire," *College English*, XIV (Nov., 1952), 78.

BROWNING, "Porphyria's Lover"
BROOKS, PURSER, WARREN, *An Approach to Literature*, pp. 4-7.

BROWNING, "Prospice"
GEORGE ARMS, *The Explicator*, II (May, 1944), 53.
HARRY M. CAMPBELL, *The Explicator*, III (Oct., 1944), 2.

BROWNING, "Respectability"
LAURENCE PERRINE, "Browning's 'Respectability,'" *College English*, XIV (March, 1953), 347-348.
BENNETT WEAVER, "A Primer Study in Browning's Satire," *College English*, XIV (Nov., 1952), 79.

BROWNING, "Saul"
JOSEPH E. BAKER, "Religious Implications in Browning's Poetry," *Philological Quarterly*, XXXVI (Oct., 1957), 440.

BROWNING, "A Serenade at the Villa"
ARTHUR DICKSON, *The Explicator*, IX (June, 1951), 57.
WALTER GIERASCH, *The Explicator*, VIII (March, 1950), 37.
T. O. MABBOTT, *The Explicator*, VIII (Dec., 1949), Q6.

BROWNING, "Sibrandus Schafnaburgensis"
BENNETT WEAVER, "Primer Study in Browning's Satire," *College English*, XVI (Nov., 1952), 77-78.

BROWNING, "Soliloquy of the Spanish Cloister"
INA B. SESSIONS, "The Dramatic Monologue," *PMLA*, LXII (June, 1947), 512.

BROWNING, "The Statue and the Bust"
R. P. BASLER, DUDLEY FITTS, and DeLANCEY FERGUSON, *The Explicator*, III (June, 1945), 62.

W. O. RAYMOND, "Browning's 'The Statue and the Bust,' " *The University of Toronto Quarterly*, XXVIII (April, 1959), 233-249.

BROWNING,   "St. Martin's Summer"
KENNETH LESLIE KNICKERBOCKER, "An Echo from Browning's Second Courtship," *Studies in Philology*, XXXII (Jan., 1935), 120-124.

BROWNING,   "A Toccata of Galuppi's"
ROY P. BASLER, *The Explicator*, II (June, 1944), 60.
ARTHUR DICKSON, *The Explicator*, III (Nov., 1944), 15.
EDGAR H. DUNCAN, *The Explicator*, V (Oct., 1946), 5.
WILLIM FROST, *English Masterpieces*, Vol. VI, Romantic and Victorian Poetry, pp. 13-14.
STAUFFER, *The Nature of Poetry*, p. 178.
WILLIAM D. TEMPLEMAN and FREDERICK A. POTTLE, *The Explicator*, II (Feb., 1944), 25.
BENNETT WEAVER, "Primer Study in Browning's Satire," *College English*, XVI (Nov., 1952), 80-81.

BROWNING,   "Transcendentalism"
RICHARD D. ALTICK, "Browning's 'Transcendentalism,' " *Journal of English and Germanic Philology*, LVIII (Jan., 1959), 24-28.

BROWNING,   "Two in the Campagna"
DAY LEWIS, *The Poetic Image*, pp. 78-80.

BROWNING,   "The Year's at the Spring"
            (Pippa's Song)
JOHN CROWE RANSOM, "The Concrete Universal, II," *The Kenyon Review*, XVII (Summer, 1955), 395.

BRYANT,   "The Evening Wind"
GEORGE ARMS, "William Cullen Bryant," *The University of Kansas City Review*, XV (Spring, 1949), 222-223.
Reprinted *The Fields Were Green*, p. 18.

BRYANT,   "Green River"
GEORGE ARMS, "William Cullen Bryant," *The Univer-*

sity of Kansas City Review, XV (Spring, 1949), 219.

Reprinted *The Fields Were Green,* p. 13.

BRYANT, "Hymn to Death"

GEORGE ARMS, "William Cullen Bryant," *The University of Kansas City Review,* XV (Spring, 1949), 220-221.

Reprinted *The Fields Were Green,* pp. 15-16.

BRYANT, "Inscription for the Entrance to a Wood"

G. GIOVANNINI and WALTER GIERASCH, *The Explicator,* IV (April, 1946), 40.

BRYANT, "The Prairies"

GEORGE ARMS, "William Cullen Bryant," *The University of Kansas City Review,* XV (Spring, 1949), 221.

Reprinted *The Fields Were Green,* p. 16.

RALPH N. MILLER, "Nationalism in Bryant's 'The Prairies,' " *American Literature,* XXI (May, 1949), 227-232.

BRYANT, "Thanatopsis"

GEORGE ARMS, "William Cullen Bryant," *The University of Kansas City Review,* XV (Spring, 1949), 220.

Reprinted *The Fields Were Green,* pp. 14-15.

BRYANT, "To a Waterfowl"

GEORGE ARMS, "William Cullen Bryant," *The University of Kansas City Review,* XV (Spring, 1949), 221-222.

Reprinted *The Fields Were Green,* pp. 17-18.

DONALD DAVIE, *Interpretations,* John Wain, ed., pp. 130-137.

BUCHANAN, ROBERT, "The Ballad of Judas Iscariot"

C. C. CUNNINGHAM, *Literature as a Fine Art: Analysis and Interpretation,* pp. 98-99.

BURKE, KENNETH, "Three Seasons of Love"

JOHN CIARDI, "The Critic of Love," *Nation,* CLXXXI (Oct. 8, 1955), 307.

BURNS, "Address to the Deil"

DAICHES and CHARVAT, *Poems in English*, pp. 688-689.

BURNS, "Death and Dr. Hornbook"
WILLIAM FROST, *English Masterpieces*, Vol. VI, *Romantic and Victorian Poetry*, pp. 13-14.

BURNS, "Holy Willie's Prayer"
DAICHES and CHARVAT, *Poems in English*, pp. 687-688.

BURNS, "John Anderson My Jo, John"
KILBY, *Poetry and Life*, pp. 19-25.

BURNS, "The Jolly Beggars"
ALLAN H. MACLAINE, "Burns' 'Jolly Beggars' — A Mistaken Interpretation," *Notes and Queries*, CXCVIII (Nov., 1953), 486-487.

BURNS, "Mary Morison"
VAN DOREN, *Introduction to Poetry*, pp. 9-12.

BURNS, "Tam O'Shanter"
ALLAN H. MACLAINE, Burns's Use of Parody in 'Tam O'Shanter,' " *Criticism*, I (Fall, 1959), 308-316.

BURNS, "To a Mouse"
CLEANTH BROOKS and ROBERT P. HEILMAN, *Understanding Drama* (New York: Henry Holt and Company, 1945), pp. 19-22.

BURNS, "Ye Flowery Banks o' Bonie Doon"
STAUFFER, *The Nature of Poetry*, pp. 164-166.
Reprinted Locke, Gibson, and Arms, *Introduction to Literature*, third edition, pp. 79-80.

BYNNER, "Eden Tree"
R. P. BLACKMUR, "Versions of Solitude," *Poetry*, XXXIX (Jan., 1932), 217-221.

BYRON, "The Destruction of Sennacherib"
OGDEN NASH, "Very Like a Whale," *The Face is Familiar* (Garden City, 1941), pp. 104-105.

BYRON, "On This Day I Complete My Thirty-Sixth Year"
ARTHUR DICKSON, *The Explicator*, V (Nov., 1946), 15.
FREDERICK L. JONES, "Byron's Last Poem," *Studies in*

Philology, XXXI (July, 1934), 487-489.
T. O. MABBOTT, *The Explicator,* IV (March, 1946), 36.

BYRON,   "The Vision of Judgment"
LEAVIS, *Revaluation,* pp. 148-153.

CAMPION,   "Now Winter Nights Enlarge"
YVOR WINTERS, "The Sixteenth Century Lyric in England," *Poetry,* LIV (April, 1939), 37.

CAMPION,   "When Thou Must Home to Shades of Under Ground"
TUVE, *Elizabethan and Metaphysical Imagery,* p. 16.

CAMPION,   "When to Her Lute Corinna Sings"
TUVE, *Elizabethan and Metaphysical Imagery,* pp. 15-16.

CANE,   "April Flurry"
MELVILLE CANE, "Snow: Theme with Variations," *The American Scholar,* XX (Winter, 1952-53), 101-102.

CANE,   "Deep in Wagon-Ruts"
MELVILLE CANE, "Snow: Theme with Variations," *The American Scholar,* XXII (Winter, 1952-53), 97.

CANE,   "Hither and Thither"
MELVILLE CANE, "Snow: Theme with Variations," *The American Scholar,* XXII (Winter, 1952-53), 99-101.

CANE,   "Hopkinson"
MELVILLE CANE, "Concerning 'Hopkinson," *The University of Kansas City Review,* XVII (Summer, 1951), 288-293.

CANE,   "January Garden"
MELVILLE CANE, "Snow: Theme with Variations," *The American Scholar,* XXII (Winter, 1952-53), 97-98.

CANE,   "Last Night It Snowed"
MELVILLE CANE, "Snow: Theme with Variations," *The American Scholar,* XXII (Winter, 1952-53), 98-99.

CANE, "Presence of Snow"
> MELVILLE CANE, "Snow: Theme with Variations,"
> *The American Scholar,* XXII (Winter, 1952-53),
> 104-105.

CANE, "Snow in April"
> MELVILLE CANE, "Snow: Theme with Variations,"
> *The American Scholar,* XXII (Winter, 1952-53),
> 102-104.

CANE, "White Fog"
> MELVILLE CANE, "Snow: Theme with Variations,"
> *The American Scholar,* XXII (Winter, 1952-53),
> 96-97.

CAREW, "Ask Me No More Where Jove Bestows"
> BROOKS, *Modern Poetry and the Tradition,* pp. 21-22.
> BROOKS, PURSER, WARREN, *An Approach to Literature,*
> pp. 486-488.
> Reprinted third edition, pp. 362-363.
> DANIELS, *The Art of Reading Poetry,* pp. 364-366.
>
> VAN DOREN, *Introduction to Poetry,* pp. 3-8.
> Reprinted Stallman and Watters, *The Creative
> Reader,* pp. 854-856.

CAREW, "Disdain Returned"
> DONALD C. BAKER, *The Explicator,* XI (June, 1953),
> 54.
> MACDONALD EMSLIE, *The Explicator,* XII (Oct.,
> 1953), 4.

CAREW, "A Divine Mistress"
> MILES, *The Primary Language of Poetry in the 1640's,*
> pp. 5-6.

CAREW, "To A.L.: Persuasions to Love"
> TUVE, *Elizabethan and Metaphysical Imagery,* p. 260.

CAREW, "To My Inconstant Mistress"
> Bateson, *English Poetry and the English Language,*
> pp. 60-62.
> DANIELS, *The Art of Reading Poetry,* pp. 349-351.

CAREW, "Upon the King's Sicknesse"
> ELSIE DUNCAN-JONES, *The Explicator,* XIII (Dec.,
> 1954), 19.

CARY, ALICE, "Make Believe"
COOPER and HOLMES, *Preface to Poetry*, pp. 211-213.
CHAPMAN, "The Shadow of Night"
ROY BATTENHOUSE, "Chapman's 'The Shadow of Night,'" *Studies in Philology*, XXXVIII (Oct., 1941), 584-608.
JANET SPENS, "Chapman's Ethical Thought," *Essays and Studies*, XI (1925), 163-166.
CHAPMAN, "The Tears of Peace"
JANET SPENS, "Chapman's Ethical Thought," *Essays and Studies*, XI (1925), 166-169.
CHAUCER, "The Complaint of Mars"
D. S. BREWER, "Chaucer's 'Complaint of Mars,'" *Notes and Queries*, I, n.s. (Nov., 1954), 462-463.
GEORGE WILLIAMS, "What is the Meaning of Chaucer's *Complaint of Mars?*" *Journal of English and Germanic Philology*, LVII (April, 1958), 167-176.
CHAUCER, "The Complaint Unto Pity"
MALCOLM PITTOCK, "Chaucer: 'The Complaint Unto Pity,'" *Criticism*, I (Spring, 1959), 160-168.
CHAUCER, "Envoy to Scogan"
WALTER H. FRENCH, "The Meaning of Chaucer's 'Envoy to Scogan,'" *PMLA*, XLVIII (March, 1933), 289-292.
CHAUCER, "Fortune: Balades de Visage Sanz Peinture"
MARGARET GALWAY, "Chaucer Among Thieves," *Times Literary Supplement*, April 20, 1946, p. 187.
EDNA RIDEOUT, "Chaucer's 'Beste Frend,'" *Times Literary Supplement*, Feb. 8, 1947, p. 79.
CHAUCER, "To Rosemounde"
HELGE KOKENTZ, "Chaucer's 'Rosemounde,'" *MLN*, LXIII (May, 1948), 310-318.
ARTHUR K. MOORE, *The Secular Lyric in Middle English*, pp. 132-133.
CHAUCER, "Womanly Noblesse"
ARTHUR K. MOORE, *The Secular Lyric in Middle English*, pp. 131-132.

CHESTERTON, "The Donkey"
STAUFFER, *The Nature of Poetry,* p. 77.

CHILDE, WILFRED ROWLAND, "Solemn and Gray, the Immense Clouds of Even" (from *Ivory Palaces*)
I. A. RICHARDS, *Practical Criticism,* pp. 155-161.

CHISHOLM, HUGH, "Lament of the Lovers"
LEONARD UNGER, "Seven Poets," *The Sewanee Review,* LVI (Winter, 1948), 169.

CHISHOLM, HUGH, "Notes on Progress"
LEONARD UNGER, "Seven Poets," *The Sewanee Review,* LVI (Winter, 1948), 169-170.

CHURCHILL, "The Apology"
WALLACE CABLE BROWN, "Charles Churchill: A Revaluation," *Studies in Philology,* XL (July, 1943), 405-406.

CHURCHILL, "Fragment of a Dedication to P. W. Warburton"
WALLACE C. BROWN, "Dramatic Tension in Neoclassic Satire," *College English,* VI (Feb., 1945), 268.

CHURCHILL, "Night"
WALLACE CABLE BROWN, "Charles Churchill: A Revaluation," *Studies in Philology,* XL (July, 1943), 421-423.

CIARDI, "Letter to Virginia Johnson"
HARVEY CURTIS WEBSTER, "Humanism as the Father Face," *Poetry,* LXX (June, 1947), 146-150.

CIARDI, "Metropolitan Ice Co."
HAYDEN CARRUTH and JOHN CIARDI, *A Critical Supplement to "Poetry,"* April, 1949, pp. 15-18.

CIARDI, "To Judith"
J. F. NIMS, *Poetry: A Critical Supplement,* Feb., 1948, pp. 10-16.

CIARDI, "To Judith Asleep"
HAYDEN CORRUTH, *A Critical Supplement to "Poetry,"* April, 1949, pp. 18-19.

CLARE, JOHN, "Badger"
ROSENTHAL and SMITH, *Exploring Poetry,* pp. 284-285.

CLARE, JOHN, "Schoolboys in Winter"
FRANKENBERG, *Invitation to Poetry,* p. 235.
CLARE, JOHN, "The Sorrows of Love"
IAN GREGOR, "The Last Augustan," *The Dublin Review,* CCXXIX (First Quarter, 1955), 46-48.
CLEVELAND, "Hecatomb to His Mistress'
H. M. RICHMOND, "The Intangible Mistress," *Modern Philology,* LVI (May, 1959), 221.
CLOUGH, "Blessed Are Those Who Have Not Seen"
BRUCE BERLIND, "A Curious Accomplishment," *Poetry,* LXXXII (April, 1953), 28-30.
CLOUGH, "Love and Reason"
FREDERICK MULHAUSER, JR., "Clough's 'Love and Reason,'" *Modern Philology,* XLII (Feb., 1945), 174-186.
CLOUGH, "Say Not the Struggle Naught Availeth"
COOPER and HOLMES, *Preface to Poetry,* pp. 177-181.
WILLIAM HOWARD, *The Explicator,* XV (March, 1957), 39.
MILLETT, *Reading Poetry,* pp. 17-18.
COLERIDGE, "Cristabel"
ROY P. BASLER, "Cristabel," *The Sewanee Review,* LI (Winter, 1943), 73-95.
BASLER, *Sex, Symbolism, and Psychology in Literature,* pp. 25-51.
WARREN G. FRENCH, *The Explicator,* XIII (June, 1955), 48.
KNIGHT, *The Starlit Dome,* pp. 83-84 *et passim.*
A. H. NETHERCOT, "Coleridge's 'Christabel' and LeFanu's 'Carmilla,'" *Modern Philology,* XLVII (August, 1949), 32-39.
CHARLES TOMLINSON, *Interpretations,* John Wain, ed., pp. 103-112.
WORMHOUDT, *The Demon Lover,* pp. 17-29, 42-47.
COLERIDGE, "Dejection: an Ode"
BOWRA, *The Romantic Imagination,* pp. 85-92 *passim.*
RICHARD H. FOGLE, "The Dejection of Coleridge's

Ode," *Journal of English Literary History,* XVII (March, 1950), 71-77.

R. M. GAY, *The Explicator,* II (Nov., 1943), 14.

KNIGHT, *The Starlit Dome,* pp. 105-107 *et passim.*

MORLEY J. MAYS, *The Explicator,* II (Feb., 1944), 27.

JAMES SMITH, "The Poetry of Coleridge," *Scrutiny,* VIII (March, 1940), 416-420.

NEWTON PHELPS STALLKNECHT, "The Doctrine of Coleridge's *Dejection* and Its Relation to Wordsworth's Philosophy," *PMLA,* XLIX (March, 1934), 196-207.

COLERIDGE, "The Destiny of Nations"

KNIGHT, *The Starlit Dome,* pp. 136-142.

COLERIDGE, "The Eolian Harp"

BURKE, *The Philosophy of Literary Form,* pp. 93-98.

RICHARD H. FOGLE, "Coleridge's Conversation Poems," *Tulane Studies in English,* V (1955), 108-109.

COLERIDGE, "Fears in Solitude"

KNIGHT, *The Starlit Dome,* pp. 130-131 *et passim.*

COLERIDGE, "Frost at Midnight."

RICHARD H. FOGLE, "Coleridge's Conversation Poems," *Tulane Studies in English,* V (1955), 110.

LANGBAUM, *The Poetry of Experience,* pp 45-46.

COLERIDGE, "The Garden of Boccaccio"

KNIGHT, *The Starlit Dome,* pp. 117-119.

COLERIDGE, "The Hymn before Sunrise, in the Vale of Chamouni"

KNIGHT, *The Starlit Dome,* pp. 107-109.

A. P. ROSSITER, "Coleridge's 'Hymn Before Sunrise, *Times Literary Supplement* (Sept., 28, 1951), p. 613.

A. P. ROSSITER, "Coleridge's 'Hymn Before Sunrise,' " *Times Literary Supplement* (Oct. 26, 1951), p. 677.

COLERIDGE, "Kubla Khan"

N. B. ALLEN, "A Note on Coleridge's 'Kubla Khan,'" *MLN*, LVII (Feb., 1942), 108-113.

BODKIN, *Archetypal Patterns in Poetry*, pp. 90-116.

BERNARD R. BREYER, "Towards an Interpretation of 'Kubla Khan,'" *English Studies in Honor of James Southall Wilson*, pp. 227-290.

BROOKS, PURSER, WARREN, *An Approach to Literature*, third edition, pp. 376-378.

RICHARD H. FOGLE, "The Romantic Unity of 'Kubla Khan,'" *College English*, XIII (Oct., 1951), 13-18.

FRANKENBERG, *Invitation to Poetry*, pp. 45-48.

KNIGHT, *The Starlit Dome*, pp. 90-97 *et passim*.

DOROTHY F. MERCER, "The Symbolism of 'Kubla Khan,'" *Journal of Aesthetics and Art Criticism*, XII (Sept., 1953), 44-65.

R. H. MILNER, "Coleridge's 'Sacred River,'" *Times Literary Supplement* (May 18, 1951), p. 309.

ELISABETH SCHNEIDER, "The 'Dream' of *Kubla Khan*," *PMLA*, LX (Sept., 1945), 784-801.

JAMES SMITH, "The Poetry of Coleridge," *Scrutiny*, VIII (March, 1940), 411-414.

CARL R. WOODRING, "Coleridge and the Khan," *Essays in Criticism*, IX (Oct., 1959), 361-368.

COLERIDGE,   "Lewti"

G. L. JOUGHIN, "Coleridge's *Lewti*: The Biography of a Poem," *Texas Studies in English, 1943* (Austin: The University of Texas Press, 1943), pp. 66-93.

COLERIDGE,   "Monody on the Death of Chatterton"

I. A. GORDON, "The Case-History of Coleridge's *Monody on the Death of Chatterton*," *Review of English Studies*, XVIII (Jan., 1942), 49-71.

COLERIDGE,   "Ode on the Departing Year"

LOUISE SCHUTZ BOAS, *The Explicator*, IX (Nov., 1950), 15.

ARTHUR DICKSON, *The Explicator*, IX (Nov., 1950), 15.

WALTER GIERASCH, *The Explicator*, VIII (March, 1950), 34.

F. H. HEIDBRINK, *The Explicator*, II (Dec., 1943), 21.
KNIGHT, *The Starlit Dome*, pp. 129-130.
ARTHUR H. NETHERCOT, *The Explicator*, I (June, 1943), 64.

COLERIDGE, "On Donne's Poetry"
FRANKENBERG, *Invitation to Poetry*, pp. 87-88.

COLERIDGE, "The Pang More Sharp than All"
KNIGHT, *The Starlit Dome*, pp. 120-121.

COLERIDGE, "The Picture"
KNIGHT, *The Starlit Dome*, pp. 116-117 *et passim*.

COLERIDGE, "Religious Musings"
KNIGHT, The Starlit Dome, pp. 131-132.

COLERIDGE, "The Rime of the Ancient Mariner"
BEACH, *A Romantic View of Poetry*, pp. 8-22.

MARIUS BEWLEY, "The Poetry of Coleridge," *The Importance of Scrutiny*, pp. 169-174. Published in *Scrutiny*, 1940.

LOUISE SCHUTZ BOAS, *The Explicator*, II (May, 1944), 52.

BODKIN, *Archetypal Patterns in Poetry*, pp. 26-89.

BOWRA, *The Romantic Imagination*, pp. 52-75.

Abridged in *The Case for Poetry*, pp. 63, 65.

BURKE, *The Philosophy of Literary Form*, pp. 22-25 *et passim*.

KENNETH BURKE, "Towards Objective Criticism," *Poetry*, LXX (April, 1947), 42-47.

CIARDI, *How Does a Poem Mean?* pp. 721-722.

ARTHUR DICKSON, *The Explicator*, VI (June, 1948), 52.

NEWELL F. FORD, "Kenneth Burke and Robert Penn Warren: Criticism by Obsessive Metaphor," *Journal of English and Germanic Philology*, LIII (April, 1954), 172-177.

D. W. HARDING, "The Rime of the Ancient Mariner," *The Importance of Scrutiny*, pp. 174-181. Published in *Scrutiny*, 1941.

LYNN H. HARRIS, *The Explicator*, VI (March, 1948), 32.

LEO KIRSCHBAUM, *The Explicator*, VII (Oct., 1948), 5.

KNIGHT, *The Starlit Dome*, pp. 84-90 *et passim*.

KREUZER, *Elements of Poetry*, pp. 18-21.

FLORENCE MARSH, "The Ocean-Desert: 'The Ancient Mariner' and 'The Waste Land,'" *Essays in Criticism*, IX (April, 1959), 126-133.

B. R. McELDERRY, JR., "Coleridge's Revision of 'The Ancient Mariner,'" *Studies in Philology*, XXIX (Jan., 1932), 68-94.

ELIZABETH NITCHIE, "The Moral of the *Ancient Mariner* Reconsidered," *PMLA*, XLVIII (Sept., 1933), 867-876.

OLSON, *Critics and Criticism*, Crane, ed., pp. 138-144. Abridged in *The Case for Poetry*, p. 67.

J. W. R. PURSER, "Interpretation of the *Ancient Mariner*," *Review of English Studies*, VIII, n.s. (Aug., 1957), 249-256.

SEWELL, *The Structure of Poetry*, pp. 178-182.

JAMES SMITH, "The Poetry of Coleridge," *Scrutiny*, VIII (March, 1940), 406-411.

LIONEL STEVENSON, "*The Ancient Mariner* as a Dramatic Monologue," *The Personalist*, XXX (Jan., 1949), 34-44.

Abridged in *The Case for Poetry*, pp. 67, 69.

E. E. STOLL, "Symbolism in Coleridge," *PMLA*, LXIII (March, 1948), 214-229.

TILLYARD, *Five Poems, 1470-1870*, pp. 66-86.

ROBERT PENN WARREN, "A Poem of Pure Imagination (Reconsiderations VI)," *The Kenyon Review*, VIII (Summer, 1946), 391-427.

Abridged in *The Case for Poetry*, pp. 65, 67.

WELLS, *The Ballad Tree*, pp. 313-314.

GEORGE WHALLEY, "The Mariner and the Albatross," *The University of Toronto Quarterly*, XVI (July, 1947), 381-398.

J. EDWIN WHITESELL, " 'The Rime of the Ancient Mariner,' line 142," *Notes and Queries*, III, n.s. (Jan., 1956), 34-35.

STEWART C. WILCOX, *The Explicator*, VII (Feb., 1949), 28.

STEWART C. WILCOX, "The Water Imagery of The Ancient Mariner," *The Personalist*, XXXV (Summer, 1954), 285-292.

WORMHOUDT, *The Demon Lover*, pp. 29-42.

COLERIDGE,   "This Lime-Tree Bower My Prison"
R. A. DURR, " 'This Lime-Tree Bower My Prison': and a Recurrent Action in Coleridge," *Journal of English Literary History*, XXVI (Dec., 1959), 515-530.

COLERIDGE,   "Time, Real and Imaginary"
F. H. HEIDBRINK, *The Explicator*, III (Oct., 1944), 4.
A. A. RAVEN, *The Explicator*, III (Feb., 1945), 33.

COLERIDGE,   " 'To the River Otter"
W. K. WIMSATT, JR., "The Structure of Romantic Nature Imagery," *The Age of Johnson* (New Haven: Yale University Press, 1949), pp. 296-298.

Reprinted *The Verbal Icon*, pp. 108-110.

COLLINS,   "Ode on the Poetical Character"
E. L. BROOKS, "William Collins's 'Ode on the Poetical Character,' " *College English*, XVII (April, 1956), 403-404.

UNGER and O'CONNOR, *Poems for Study*, pp. 325-329.

COLLINS,   "Ode to Evening"
DANIELS, *The Art of Reading Poetry*, pp. 360-364.

WILLIAM FROST, *English Masterpieces*, Vol. VI, *Romantic and Victorian Poetry*, p. 4.

CONGREVE,   "Song: False Though She Be to Me and Love"
BATESON, *English Poetry and the English Language*, pp. 62-63.

CORBET, RICHARD,   "The Fairies' Farewell"

CLEANTH BROOKS, "The New Criticism and Scholarship," *Twentieth Century English*, 1946, pp. 371-383.

COTTON,   "Bacon's Epitaph, Made by His Man"
ROY P. BASLER, *The Explicator*, II (Dec., 1943), 20.

COWLEY,   "Hymn: to Light"
ALLEN TATE, "Tension in Poetry," *The Southern Review*, IV (Summer, 1938), 105-108. Reprinted Tate, *Reason in Madness*, pp. 67-69; Tate, *On the Limits of Poetry*, pp. 78-81; *Critiques*, pp. 57-60.

Also reprinted West, *Essays in Modern Literary Criticism*, pp. 270-272.

COWLEY,   "The Request"
MILES, *The Primary Language of Poetry in the 1640's*, pp. 46-48.

COWLEY, MALCOLM,   "The Source"
J. F. NIMS, *Poetry: A Critical Supplement*, April, 1948, pp. 12-13.

COWPER,   "The Castaway"
LODWICK HARTLEY, *The Explicator*, V (Dec., 1946), 21.

COWPER,   "To Mary Unwin"
KILBY, *Poetry and Life*, pp. 19-25.

COXE, LOUIS O.,   "Gunner's Mate"
LEONARD UNGER, "Seven Poets," *The Sewanee Review*, LVI (Winter, 1948), 160-161.

CRABBE,   "Abel Keene"
IAN GREGOR, "The Last Augustan," *The Dublin Review*, CCXXIX (First Quarter, 1955), 43-46.

CRABBE,   "Procrastination"
IAN GREGOR, "The Last Augustan," *The Dublin Review*, CCXXIX (First Quarter, 1955), 49-50.

CRABBE,   "The Village"
IAN GREGOR, "The Last Augustan," *The Dublin Review*, CCXXIX (First Quarter, 1955), 38-42.

CRANE,   "The Air Plant"

O'Connor, *Sense and Sensibility in Modern Poetry,* p. 148.

CRANE, "And Yet This Great Wink of Eternity"
Drew, *Directions in Modern Poetry,* pp. 212-217.

CRANE, "At Melville's Tomb"
Brooks and Warren, *Understanding Poetry,* pp. 477-482.

Revised edition, pp. 333-336.

Hart Crane, quoted in *Hart Crane* by Brom Weber. Reprinted *The Critic's Notebook,* pp. 242-247.

Eastman, *The Literary Mind,* pp. 94-97.

Harriet Monroe and Hart Crane, "A Discussion with Hart Crane," *Poetry,* XXIX (Oct., 1926), 34-41.

Reprinted Locke, Gibson, and Arms, *Introduction to Literature,* third edition, pp. 229-234.

CRANE, "Atlantis"
Friar and Brinnin, *Modern Poetry,* pp. 453-455.

CRANE, "Ave Maria"
Friar and Brinnin, *Modern Poetry,* pp. 451-452.

CRANE, "The Bridge"
Joseph Warren Beach, "The Cancelling Out—A Note on Recent Poetry," *Accent,* VII (Summer, 1947), 245-246.

Stanley K. Coffman, "Symbolism in *The Bridge,*" *PMLA,* LXVI (March, 1951), 65-77.

Lawrence Dembo, "The Unfractioned Idiom of Hart Crane's *Bridge,*" *American Literature,* XXVII (May, 1955), 203-224.

Deutsch, *Poetry in Our Time,* pp. 322-328.

Deutsch, *This Modern Poetry,* pp. 141-148.

Joseph Frank, "Hart Crane: American Poet," *The Sewanee Review,* LVII (Winter, 1949), 156-158.

Brewster Ghiselin, "Bridge into the Sea," *Partisan Review,* XVI (July, 1949), 679-686.

Hoffman, *The Twenties,* pp. 229-239.

HOWARD MOSS, "Disorder as Myth: Hart Crane's *The Bridge,*" *Poetry,* LXII (April, 1943), 32-45.

O'CONNOR, *Sense and Sensibility in Modern Poetry,* pp. 19-25.

QUINN, *The Metamorphic Tradition,* pp. 147-165.

BERNICE SLOTE, "Structure of Hart Crane's *The Bridge,*" *The University of Kansas City Review,* XXIV (Spring, 1958), 225-238.

ALAN SWALLOW, "Hart Crane," *The University of Kansas City Review,* XVI (Winter, 1949), 114, 116-118.

TATE, *Reactionary Essays on Poetry and Ideas,* pp. 30-42.
Reprinted Zabel, *Literary Opinion in America,* revised edition, pp. 230-236.

TATE, *On the Limits of Poetry,* pp. 228-237. First published in *Hound and Horn* and *Poetry.*

WAGGONER, *The Heel of Elohim,* pp. 157-158, 171-190.

WELLS, *New Poets from Old,* pp. 116-128.

YVOR WINTERS, "The Progress of Hart Crane," *Poetry,* XXXVI (June, 1930), 153-165.

YVOR WINTERS, "The Significance of *The Bridge,* by Hart Crane," *In Defense of Reason,* pp. 577-603.

CRANE,   "The Bridge," V "Three Songs"

J. R. WILLINGHAM, " 'Three Songs' of Hart Crane's *The Bridge*: A Reconsideration," *American Literature,* XXVII (March, 1955), 64-68

CRANE,   "The Broken Tower"

MARIUS BEWLEY, "Hart Crane's Last Poem," *Accent,* XIX (Spring, 1959), 75-85.

FRIAR and BRINNIN, *Modern Poetry,* p. 449.

MURIEL RUKEYSER, *The Life of Poetry* (New York: A. A. Wyn, 1949), pp. 32-33.

CRANE,   "Cape Hatteras" (from "The Bridge")

KARL SHAPIRO, "The Meaning of the Discarded Poem," *Poets at Work,* pp. 111-118.

CRANE,   "Chaplinesque"

Deutsch, *Poetry in Our Time,* pp. 317-318.

CRANE, "The Dance" (from "The Bridge")
Winters, *Primitivism and Decadence,* pp. 30-32. Also
In Defense of Reason, pp. 44-45, 52, and *Criticism,*
pp. 295, 298.

CRANE, "For the Marriage of Faustus and Helen"
Joseph Frank, "Hart Crane: American Poet," *The
Sewanee Review,* LVII (Winter, 1949), 155-156.
Will C. Jumper, *The Explicator,* XVII (Oct., 1958),
8.
Savage, *The Personal Principle,* pp. 115-118.

CRANE, "The Harbor Dawn"
Friar and Brinnin, *Modern Poetry,* pp. 452-453.

CRANE, "Key West"
Kingsley Widmer, *The Explicator,* XVIII (Dec.,
1959), 17.

CRANE, "Lachrymae Christi"
Blackmur, *The Double Agent,* pp. 135-137.
Reprinted *Language as Gesture,* pp. 312-314.
Barbara Herman, "The Language of Hart Crane,"
The Sewanee Review, LVIII (Winter, 1950), 62-65.
Martin Staples Shockley, "Hart Crane's 'Lachrymae
Christi,'" *The University of Kansas City Review,*
XVI (Autumn, 1949), 31-36.
Reprinted Engle and Carrier, *Reading Modern
Poetry,* pp. 321-328.

CRANE, "O Carib Isle!"
Friar and Brinnin, *Modern Poetry,* pp. 449-450.

CRANE, "Paraphrase"
Ben W. Griffith, Jr., *The Explicator,* XIII (Oct.,
1954), 5.

CRANE, "Passage"
Gene Koretz, *The Explicator,* XIII (June, 1955),
47.
John R. Willingham and Virginia Moseley, *The
Explicator,* XIII (June, 1955), 47.

CRANE, "Possessions"

ALAN SWALLOW, "Hart Crane," *The University of Kansas City Review*, XVI (Winter, 1949), 113.

CRANE, "Praise for an Urn"

ALAN SWALLOW, "Hart Crane," *The University of Kansas City Review*, XVI (Winter, 1949), 115.

VAN DOREN, *Introduction to Poetry*, pp. 103-107.

CRANE, "The Return"

THOMAS E. SANDERS, *The Explicator*, X (Dec., 1951), 20.

CRANE, "To Brooklyn Bridge" (from "The Bridge")

FRIAR and BRINNIN, *Modern Poetry*, pp. 427-428, 450-451.

CRANE, "Voyages"

FRIAR and BRINNIN, *Modern Poetry*, pp. 455-456.

H. C. MORRIS, "Crane's 'Voyages' as a Single Poem," *Accent*, XIV (Autumn, 1954), 291-299.

CRANE, "Voyages," II

DEUTSCH, *Poetry in Our Time*, pp. 319-321.

O'CONNOR, *Sense and Sensibility in Modern Poetry*, pp. 73-75.

MAX F. SCHULZ, *The Explicator*, XIV (April, 1956), 46.

UNGER and O'CONNOR, *Poems for Study*, pp. 637-641.

CRANE, "Voyages," VI

CHARLES C. WALCUTT, *The Explicator*, IV (May, 1946), 53.

JAMES ZIGERELL, *The Explicator*, XIII (Nov., 1954), 7.

CRANE, "Wine Menagerie"

BLACKMUR, *The Double Agent*, pp. 130-134.

Reprinted *Language as Gesture*, pp. 309-312.

Also reprinted *The Critic's Notebook*, pp. 106-110.

CRAPSEY, "Triad"

DANIELS, *The Art of Reading Poetry*, p. 53.

CRASHAW, "An Apology for the Precedent Hymn"

A. F. ALLISON, "Crashaw and St. Francis de Sales," *Review of English Studies*, XXIV (Oct., 1948), 296-300.

CRASHAW,   "Blessed Be the Paps Which Thou Hast Sucked"

ROBERT M. ADAMS, "Taste and Bad Taste in Metaphysical Poetry: Richard Crashaw and Dylan Thomas," *The Hudson Review*, VIII (Spring, 1955), 68-69.

ADAMS, *Strains of Discord*, p. 136.

CRASHAW,   "The Flaming Heart"

A. F. ALLISON, "Crashaw and St. Francis de Sales," *Review of English Studies*, XXIV (Oct., 1948), 300-301.

CRASHAW,   "Hymn in the Nativity"

KERBY NEILL, "Structure and Symbol in Crashaw's *Hymn in the Nativity*," *PMLA*, LXIII (March, 1948), 101-113.

CRASHAW,   "A Hymn to the Name and Honor of the Admirable Saint Teresa"

UNGER and O'CONNOR, *Poems for Study*, pp. 171-175.

CRASHAW,   "In the Glorious Epiphany of Our Lord God"

MARTIN TURNELL, "Richard Crashaw After Three Hundred Years," *Nineteenth Century and After*, CXLVI (Aug., 1949), 110-113.

CRASHAW,   "In Memory of the Vertuous and Learned Lady Madre de Teresa. . ."

ROBERT G. COLLMER, "Crashaw's 'Death More Misticall and High,' " *Journal of English and Germanic Philology*, LV (July, 1956), 373-380.

CRASHAW,   "The Mother of Sorrows"

A. F. ALLISON, "Crashaw and St. Francis de Sales," *Review of English Studies*, XXIV (Oct., 1948), 301-302.

CRASHAW,   "Music's Duel"

WILLIAM G. MADSEN, "A Reading of 'Musicks Duell,'"
A Reading in Honor of John Wilcox, pp. 39-50.

CRASHAW, "On Our Crucified Lord, Naked and Bloody"

ROBERT M. ADAMS, "Taste and Bad Taste in Metaphysical Poetry: Richard Crashaw and Dylan Thomas," *The Hudson Review*, VIII (Spring, 1955), 67.

ADAMS, *Strains of Discord*, pp. 133-134.

CRASHAW, "On the Wounds of Our Crucified Lord"

ADAMS, *Strains of Discord*, pp. 134-135.

CRASHAW, "Prayer"

MARTIN TURNELL, "Richard Crashaw After Three Hundred Years," *Nineteenth Century and After*, CXLVI (Aug., 1949), 104-106.

CRASHAW, "The Tear"

MARTIN TURNELL, "Richard Crashaw After Three Hundred Years," *Nineteenth Century and After*, CXLVI (Aug., 1949), 106-107.

CRASHAW, "To the Name Above Every Name, the Name of Jesus"

MARTZ, *The Poetry of Meditation*, pp. 62-64; 338-352.

CRASHAW, "Upon the Bleeding Crucifix"

GEORGE W. WILLIAMS, "Textual Revision in Crashaw's 'Upon the Bleeding Crucifix,'" *Papers of the Bibliographical Society*, University of Virginia, I (1948-1949), 191-193.

CRASHAW, "The Weeper"

ROBERT M. ADAMS, "Taste and Bad Taste in Metaphysical Poetry: Richard Crashaw and Dylan Thomas," *The Hudson Review*, VIII (Spring, 1955), 66-67, 69-71.

ADAMS, *Strains of Discord*, pp. 131-133, 136-137.

STEPHEN MANNING, "The Meaning of 'The Weeper,'"

Journal of English Literary History, **XXII** (March, 1955), 34-47.

JOHN PETER, "Crashaw and 'The Weeper,' " *Scrutiny,* **XIX** (Oct., 1953), 259-273.

WINTERS, *The Anatomy of Nonsense,* pp. 209-210. Also *In Defense of Reason,* pp. 538-540.

CREELEY, ROBERT,   "The Kind of Act Of"
> CID CORMAN, "A Requisite Commitment," *Poetry* **LXXXIII** (March, 1954), 340-342.

CUMMINGS,   "among these red pieces of"
> JOHN ARTHOS, "The Poetry of E. E. Cummings," *American Literature,* **XIV** (Jan., 1943), 386-387.
> JOHN PEALE BISHOP, "The Poems and Prose of E. E. Cummings," *The Southern Review,* **IV** (Summer, 1938), 176-177.
> EASTMAN, *The Literary Mind,* pp. 59-62.
> RIDING and GRAVES, *A Survey of Modernist Poetry,* pp. 84-89.

CUMMINGS,   "anyone lived in a pretty how town"
> HERBERT C. BARROWS, JR., and WILLIAM R. STEINHOFF, *The Explicator,* **IX** (Oct., 1950), 1. Abridged in *The Case for Poetry,* p. 95.
> ARTHUR CARR, *The Explicator,* **XI** (Nov., 1952), 6. Abridged in *The Case for Poetry,* pp. 95-96.
> GEORGE HAINES, IV " : : 2 : 1—The World and E. E. Cummings," *The Sewanee Review,* **LIX** (Spring, 1951), 216-217.
> STALLMAN and WATTERS, *The Creative Reader,* pp. 886-887.

CUMMINGS,   ("applaws)"
> JOSEPH AXELROD, "Cummings and Phonetics," *Poetry,* **LXV** (Nov., 1944), 88-94.
> KARL SHAPIRO, "Prosody as the Meaning," *Poetry,* **LXXIII** (March, 1949), 338-340 *et passim.*

CUMMINGS,   "because you go away i give roses"
> RIDING and GRAVES, *A Survey of Modernist Poetry,* pp. 60-64.

CUMMINGS, "! blac"

S. V. Baum, "E. E. Cummings: The Technique of Immediacy," *South Atlantic Quarterly*, LIII (Jan., 1954) , 87-88.

CUMMINGS, "Buffalo Bill's Defunct"

Louis J. Budd, *The Explicator*, XI (June, 1953) , 55.

CUMMINGS, "Chansons Innocentes I: in just-spring"

Marvin Felheim, *The Explicator*, XIV (Nov., 1955) , 11.

R. D. Mayo, *English "A" Analyst*, No. 2, pp. 1-4.

Reprinted Engle and Carrier, *Reading Modern Poetry*, pp. 133-136.

CUMMINGS, "darling! because my blood can sing"

Frankenberg, *Invitation to Poetry*, pp. 281-282.

CUMMINGS, "death is more than certain"

Norman Friedman, "Diction, Voice, and Tone: The Poetic Language of E. E. Cummings," *PMLA*, LXII (Dec. 1957) , 1057-1058.

Riding and Graves, *A Survey of Modernist Poetry*, pp. 244-247.

CUMMINGS, "floatfloafloflf"

Richard Crowder, *The Explicator*, XVI (April, 1958) , 11.

CUMMINGS, "i will be / Mo ving in the Street of her"

Theodore Spencer, "Technique as Joy," *The Harvard Wake*, V (Spring, 1946), 25-27.

CUMMINGS, "if everything happens that can't be done"

Norman Friedman, "Diction, Voice, and Tone: The Poetic Language of E. E. Cummings," *PMLA*, LXII (Dec., 1957) , 1050-1051.

CUMMINGS, "A kike is the most dangerous . . ."

M. L. Rosenthal, "Cummings and Hayes: Mr. Joy and Mr. Gloom," *New Republic*, CXXIII (Sept. 18, 1950) , 18.

CUMMINGS, "lxl"
JACK STEINBERG, *The Explicator,* VIII (Dec., 1949), 17.

CUMMINGS, "Memorabilia"
BEN W. GRIFFITH, JR., *The Explicator,* XII (May, 1954), 47.
CLYDE S. KILBY, *The Explicator,* XII (Nov., 1953), 15.

CUMMINGS, "mortals)"
GEORGE HAINES, IV, " : : 2 : 1—The World and E. E. Cummings," *The Sewanee Review,* LIX (Spring, 1951), 218-221.

CUMMINGS, "My father moved through dooms of love"
GEORGE HAINES, IV, " : : 2 : 1—The World and E. E. Cummings," *The Sewanee Review,* LIX (Spring, 1951), 215-216.

CUMMINGS, "no man, if men are gods"
FRANKENBERG, *Invitation to Poetry,* p. 74

CUMMINGS, "no time ago"
NORMAN FRIEDMAN, "Diction, Voice, and Tone: The Poetic Language of E. E. Cummings," *PMLA,* LXII (Dec., 1957), 1058.

CUMMINGS, " (one!) "
GEORGE C. BRAUER, JR., *The Explicator,* XVI (Dec., 1957), 14.
LOUIS C. RUS, *The Explicator,* XV (March, 1957), 40.

CUMMINGS, "one's not half two"
NORMAN FRIEDMAN, "Diction, Voice, and Tone: The Poetic Language of E. E. Cummings," *PMLA,* LXII (Dec., 1957), 1041.

CUMMINGS, "o pr"
SHERIDAN BAKER, "Cummings and Catullus," *MLN,* LXXIV (March, 1959), 231-234.

CUMMINGS, "pity this busy monster, manunkind"
JOHN BRITTON, *The Explicator,* XVIII (Oct., 1959), 5.

CUMMINGS, "Poem" ("love's function is to fabricate unknownness")
GERALD LEVIN, *The Explicator*, XVII (Dec., 1958), 18.

CUMMINGS, "Portrait"
BROOKS and WARREN, *Understanding Poetry*, pp. 296-298.
Revised edition, pp. 158-160.

CUMMINGS, "r-p-o-p-h-e-s-s-a-g-r" (*Collected Poems*, 276)
SAM HYNES, *The Explicator*, X (Nov., 1951), 9.

CUMMINGS, "the sky was"
JOHN ARTHOS, "The Poetry of E. E. Cummings," *American Literature*, XIV (Jan., 1943), 383-385.

CUMMINGS, "so little he is"
FRANKENBERG, *Pleasure Dome*, pp. 176-177.

CUMMINGS, "Space being (don't forget to remember) Curved"
RICHARD B. VOWLES, *The Explicator*, IX (Oct., 1950), 3.

CUMMINGS, "Sunset"
RIDING and GRAVES, *A Survey of Modernist Poetry*, pp. 12-28.

CUMMINGS, "ta" (*Collected Poems*, 52)
S. V. BAUM, "E. E. Cummings: The Technique of Immediacy," *South Atlantic Quarterly*, LIII (Jan., 1954), 83-84.

CUMMINGS, "there childreen singing in a stone a"
NAT HENRY, *The Explicator*, XIII (June, 1955), 51.
EDWIN M. MOSELEY, *The Explicator*, IX (Oct., 1950), 2.

CUMMINGS, "a thrown a"
S. V. BAUM, "E. E. Cummings: The Technique of Immediacy," *South Atlantic Quarterly*, LIII (Jan., 1954), 85-86.

CUMMINGS, "up into the silence of the green"

JOHN ARTHOS, "The Poetry of E. E. Cummings" *American Literature,* XIV (Jan., 1943), pp. 385-386.
CUMMINGS, "what a proud dreamhorse pulling (smooth-loomingly) through"
FRANKENBERG, *Invitation to Poetry,* pp. 257-260.
CUMMINGS, "what if a much of a which of a wind"
STEPHEN E. WHICHER, *The Explicator,* XII (Nov., 1953), 14.
CUMMINGS, "who are these (wraith a clinging with a wraith) "
NORMAN FRIEDMAN, "Diction, Voice, and Tone: The Poetic Language of E. E. Cummings:" *PMLA,* LXII (Dec. 1957), 1047.
CUNNINGHAM, "The Chase"
JOHN WILLIAMS, "J. V. Cunningham: The Major and the Minor," *Arizona Quarterly,* VI (Summer, 1950), 140-141.
CUNNINGHAM, "Passion"
JOHN WILLIAMS, "J. V. Cunningham: The Major and the Minor," *Arizona Quarterly,* VI (Summer, 1950), 142-144.
CUNNINGHAM, "Timor Dei"
JOHN WILLIAMS, "J. V. Cunningham: The Major and the Minor," *Arizona Quarterly,* VI (Summer, 137-139.
DANIEL, "Are They Shadows That We See?"
FRANKENBERG, *Invitation to Poetry,* p. 378.
DANIEL, *"Delia,* Sonnet XL, "Delia! These Eyes That So Admireth Thine"
THEODORE C. HOEPFNER, *The Explicator,* X (April, 1952), 38.
DANIEL, *Delia,* Sonnet XLV, "Care-Charmer Sleep, Son of the Sable Night"
TUVE, *Elizabethan and Metaphysical Imagery,* pp. 167-168.
DANIEL, "To the Lady Margaret"
CECIL C. SERONSY, "Well-Languaged Daniel: A Re-

consideration," *Modern Language Review,* LII
(Oct., 1957) , 494-495.

DAVIDSON, DONALD, "The Tall Men"
Louis D. Rubin, Jr., "The Concept of Nature in
Modern Southern Poetry," *American Quarterly,*
IX (Spring, 1957) , 65-67.

DAVIES, "The Moon"
B. Rajan, "Georgian Poetry: A Retrospect," *The
Critic,* I (Autumn, 1947), 10-11.

DAVIES, "Thy Beauty Haunts Me Heart and Soul"
Daiches, *Poetry and the Modern World,* pp. 53-55.

DAVIES, w. h., "The Villain"
Perrine, *Sound and Sense,* p. 126.

DAY LEWIS, "Children Look Down Upon the Morning-
Gray"
Stageberg and Anderson, *Poetry as Experience,* pp.
86-87.

DAY LEWIS, "Come Live With Me and Be My Love"
Robert Stallman, *The Explicator,* II (April, 1944),
46.

DAY LEWIS, "From Feathers to Iron"
Tschumi, *Thought in Twentieth-Century English
Poetry,* pp. 209-218.

DAY LEWIS, "The Image"
Tschumi, *"Thought in Twentieth-Century English
Poetry,* pp. 238-239.

DAY LEWIS, "An Italian Visit"
C. Day Lewis, "Poetry as Reportage," *Times Literary
Supplement* (March 6, 1953) , p. 152.

DAY LEWIS, "The Magnetic Mountain"
Tschumi, *Thought in Twentieth-Century English
Poetry,* pp. 218-232.

DAY LEWIS, "Rest From Loving and Be Living"
William Elton, *The Explicator,* VI (Dec., 1947), 16;
VII (Dec., 1948), 25.
Walter Gierasch and David C. Sheldon, *The Expli-
cator,* VI (March, 1948), 34.

DAY LEWIS, "A Time to Dance"

DAICHES, *Poetry and the Modern World,* pp. 206-209.

DAY LEWIS, "Transitional Poem"

DAICHES, *Poetry and the Modern World,* pp. 195-199.

TSCHUMI, *Thought in Twentieth-Century English Poetry,* pp. 199-209.

DAY LEWIS, "Word over All"

TSCHUMI, *Thought in Twentieth-Century English Poetry,* pp. 236-237.

DE LA MARE, "The Ghost"

LEAVIS, *New Bearings in English Poetry,* pp. 53-54.

DE LA MARE, "The Listeners"

DELANCEY FERGUSON, *The Explicator,* IV (Nov., 1945), 15.

Abridged in *The Case for Poetry,* p. 99.

FRANKENBERG, *Invitation to Poetry,* p. 139.

FREDERICK GWYNN, and RALPH W. CONDEE, *The Explicator,* XII (Feb., 1954), 26.

Abridged in *The Case for Poetry,* pp. 99-100.

J. M. PURCELL, *The Explicator,* III (March, 1945), 42; IV (Feb., 1946), 31.

Abridged in *The Case for Poetry,* p. 99.

DE LA MARE, "Maerchen"

ELISABETH SCHNEIDER, *The Explicator,* IV (Feb., 1946), 29. Reprinted *Readings for Liberal Education,* II, 526.

Reprinted Locke, Gibson, and Arms, *Introduction to Literature,* third edition, p. 178.

DE LA MARE, "The Mocking Fairy"

DANIELS, *The Art of Reading Poetry,* pp. 57-59.

DE LA MARE, "Nostalgia"

E. K. BROWN, "The Epilogue to Mr. de la Mare's Poetry," *Poetry,* LXVIII (May, 1946), 90-92.

DENHAM, "Cooper's Hill"

WASSERMAN, *The Subtler Language,* pp. 45-88.

DENNEY, REUEL, "The Rememberer"

HAYDEN CARRUTH, *A Critical Supplement to "Poetry,"* April, 1949, pp. 11-14.

DEUTSCH, BABETTE, "Visit to the Zoo"
FRANK JONES, *A Critical Supplement to "Poetry,"* Nov., 1949, pp. 11-14.

DICKINSON, "After Great Pain a Formal Feeling Comes"
BROOKS and WARREN, *Understanding Poetry,* pp. 468-471.
Revised edition, pp. 325-327.
DREW, *Poetry,* pp. 124-125.

DICKINSON, "Apparently with No Surprise"
PERRINE, *Sound and Sense,* pp. 126-127.

DICKINSON, "As Imperceptibly as Grief"
WALTER BLAIR, *The Literature of the United States,* II, 751.

DICKINSON, "At Half Past Three, a Single Bird"
ROBERT W. RUSSELL, *The Explicator,* XVI (Oct., 1957), 3.

DICKINSON, "Because I Could Not Stop for Death"
WALTER BLAIR, *The Literature of the United States,* II, 750.
RICHARD CHASE, abridged in *The Case for Poetry,* pp. 105-106 from *Emily Dickinson* (New York: William Sloane Associates, 1951), pp. 249-251.
DAICHES and CHARVAT, *Poems in English,* p. 727.
EUNICE GLENN, "Emily Dickinson's Poetry: A Revaluation," *The Sewanee Review,* LI (Autumn, 1943), 585-588.
THEODORE HOEPFNER, " 'Because I Could Not Stop for Death,' " *American Literature,* XXIX (March, 1957), 96.
TATE, *Reactionary Essays on Poetry and Ideas,* pp. 13-16. Reprinted *On the Limits of Poetry,* pp. 205-208. Also reprinted *Readings for Liberal Education,* II, 173-174.
Abridged in *The Case for Poetry,* p. 105.
Also reprinted Feidelson and Brodtkorb, *Inter-*

pretations of American Literature, pp. 204-205.
Also reprinted Locke, Gibson, and Arms, *Introduction to Literature*, third edition, pp. 158-159.

TATE, *Reason in Madness*, pp. 14-15.

UNGER and O'CONNOR, *Poems for Study*, pp. 547-548.

WINTERS, *Maule's Curse*, pp. 154-156. Also *In Defense of Reason*, pp. 288-290.

Abridged in *The Case for Poetry*, p. 105.

DICKINSON,   "A Bird Came Down the Walk"

FREDERIC I. CARPENTER, "Emily Dickinson and the Rhymes of Dream," *The University of Kansas City Review*, XX (Winter, 1953), 119-120.

J. P. KIRBY, *The Explicator*, II (June, 1944), 61.

DICKINSON,   "A Clock Stopped — Not the Mantel's"

EARL ROY MINER, *The Explicator*, XIII (Dec., 1954), 18.

LAURENCE PERRINE, *The Explicator*, XIV (Oct., 1955), 4.

DICKINSON,   "Crumbling Is Not an Instant's Act"

CHARLES R. ANDERSON, "The Conscious Self in Emily Dickinson's Poetry," *American Literature*, XXXI (Nov., 1959), 297-298.

DICKINSON,   "Except the Smaller Size"

CHARLES R. ANDERSON, "The Conscious Self in Emily Dickinson's Poetry," *American Literature*, XXXI (Nov., 1959), 295-296.

DICKINSON,   "Farther in Summer Than the Birds"

FRÉDÉRIC I. CARPENTER, "Emily Dickinson and the Rhymes of Dream," *The University of Kansas City Review*, XX (Winter, 1953), 118.

FREDERICK I. CARPENTER, *The Explicator*, VIII (March, 1950), 33.

ROBERT H. ELIAS and HELEN L. ELIAS, *The Explicator*, XI (Oct., 1952), 5.

RENE RAPIN, *The Explicator*, XII (Feb., 1954), 24.

MARSHALL VAN DEUSEN, *The Explicator*, XIII (March, 1955), 33.

WINTERS, *Maule's Curse,* pp. 158-159. Also *In Defense of Reason,* pp. 292-293. Reprinted *The Literature of the United States,* II, 752.

DICKINSON,   "Go Not Too Near a House of Rose"
WARREN BECK, "Poetry's Chronic Disease," *The English Journal,* XXXIII (Sept., 1944), 362-363.
MACKLIN THOMAS, "Analysis of the Experience in Lyric Poetry," *College English,* IX (March, 1948), 320-321.

DAVID W. THOMPSON, "Interpretative Reading as Symbolic Action," *Quarterly Journal of Speech,* XLII (Dec., 1956), 395.

DICKINSON,   "The Harm of Years Is on Him"
CHARLES R. ANDERSON, "The Conscious Self in Emily Dickinson's Poetry," *American Literature,* XXXI (Nov., 1959), 296-297.

DICKINSON,   "He Put the Belt Around My Life"
EUNICE GLENN, "Emily Dickinson's Poetry: A Revaluation," *The Sewanee Review,* LI (Autumn, 1943), 580-582.

DICKINSON,   "The Heart Asks Pleasure First"
FREDERIC I. CARPENTER, "Emily Dickinson and the Rhymes of Dream," *The University of Kansas City Review,* XX (Winter, 1953), 115.

DICKINSON,   "Hope Is a Strange Invention"
CHARLES R. ANDERSON, "The Conscious Self in Emily Dickinson's Poetry," *American Literature,* XXXI (Nov., 1959), 301-302.

DICKINSON,   "I Can Wade Grief"
WILLIAM HOWARD, *The Explicator,* XIV (Dec., 1955), 17.

DICKINSON,   "I Cannot Live With You"
EUNICE GLENN, "Emily Dickinson's Poetry: A Revaluation," *The Sewanee Review,* LI (Autumn, 1943), 582-585.

DICKINSON,   "I Died for Beauty, but Was Scarce"
FREDERIC I. CARPENTER, "Emily Dickinson and the Rhymes of Dream," *The University of Kansas City Review*, XX (Winter, 1953), 116-117.

DICKINSON,   "I Dreaded That First Robin So"
RUSSELL ST. C. SMITH, *The Explicator*, V (Feb., 1947), 31.

DICKINSON,   "I Had Not Minded Walls"
VAN DOREN, *Introduction to Poetry*, pp. 13-16.

DICKINSON,   "I Heard a Fly Buzz When I Died"
JOHN CIARDI, *The Explicator*, XIV (Jan., 1956), 22.
GERHARD FRIEDRICH, *The Explicator*, XIII (April, 1955), 35.

DICKINSON,   "I Know Some Lonely Houses Off the Road"
MYRON OCHSHORN, *The Explicator*, XI (Nov., 1952), 12.

DICKINSON,   "I Like to See It Lap the Miles"
GEORGE ARMS, *The Explicator*, II (May, 1944), Q31.
F. J. HOFFMAN, "The Technological Fallacy in Contemporary Poetry," *American Literature*, XXI (March, 1949), 97.
Reprinted Stageberg and Anderson, *Poetry as Experience*, p. 460.

DICKINSON,   "I'll Tell You How the Sun Rose"
WILBUR SCOTT, *The Explicator*, VII (Nov., 1948), 14.

DICKINSON,   "Immured in Heaven!"
THOMAS H. JACKSON, *The Explicator*, XI (March, 1953), 36.

DICKINSON,   "I Never Hear the One Is Dead"
MYRON OCHSHORN, "In Search of Emily Dickinson," *New Mexico Quarterly Review*, XXIII (Spring, 1953), 101-102, 104.

DICKINSON,   "I Should Have Been Too Glad, I See"
MYRON OCHSHORN, "In Search of Emily Dickinson," *New Mexico Quarterly Review*, XXIII (Spring, 1953), 103-106.

DICKINSON, "I Started Early, Took My Dog"
KATE FLORES, *The Explicator*, IX (May, 1951), 47.
LAURENCE PERRINE, *The Explicator*, X (Feb., 1952), 28.

DICKINSON, "I Taste a Liquor Never Brewed"
WALLACE W. DOUGLAS, *English "A" Analyst*, No. 4, pp. 1-3.

DICKINSON, "I've Dropped My Brain—My Soul Is Numb"
CHARLES R. ANDERSON, "The Conscious Self in Emily Dickinson's Poetry," *American Literature*, XXXI (Nov., 1959), 299-301.

DICKINSON, "The Last Night That She Lived"
HARRY MODEAN CAMPBELL, *The Explicator*, VIII (May, 1950), 54.

DICKINSON, "More Life Went Out, When He Went"
R. P. BLACKMUR, "Emily Dickinson: Notes on Prejudice and Fact," *The Southern Review*, III (Autumn, 1937), 337-341.
BLACKMUR, *Expense of Greatness*, pp. 126-130.
Reprinted *Language as Gesture*, pp. 40-43.

DICKINSON, "My Life Had Stood — A Loaded Gun"
The Poetry Workshop, Columbus, Georgia, *The Explicator*, XV (May, 1957), 51.

DICKINSON, "My Wheel Is in the Dark!"
MABEL HOWARD, WILLIAM HOWARD, and EMILY HARVEY, *The Explicator*, XVII (Nov., 1958), 12.

DICKINSON, "No Rack Can Torture Me"
EUNICE GLENN, "Emily Dickinson's Poetry: A Revaluation," *The Sewanee Review*, LI (Autumn, 1943), 577-578.

DICKINSON, "One Need Not Be a Chamber — to Be Haunted"
CHARLES R. ANDERSON, "The Conscious Self in Emily Dickinson's Poetry," *American Literature*, XXXI (Nov., 1959), 304-305.

DICKINSON, "The Only News I Know"

RALPH MARCELLINO, "Emily Dickinson," *College English*, VII (Nov., 1945), 102-103.

DICKINSON, "Renunciation Is a Piercing Virtue"
R. P. BLACKMUR, "Emily Dickinson: Notes on Prejudice and Fact," *The Southern Review*, III (Autumn, 1937), 333-336.
BLACKMUR, *Expense of Greatness*, pp. 119-123.

DICKINSON, "A Route of Evanescence"
FRANK DAVIDSON, "A Note on Emily Dickinson's Use of Shakespeare," *New England Quarterly*, XVIII (Sept., 1945), 407-408.
GROVER SMITH, *The Explicator*, VII (May, 1949), 54. Abridged in *The Case for Poetry*, p. 109.
GEORGE F. WHICHER, Abridged in *The Case for Poetry*, p. 109 from *This Was a Poet* (New York: Charles Scribner's Sons, 1938), p. 262.

DICKINSON, "Safe in Their Alabaster Chambers"
MOTHER ANGELA CARSON, O.S.U., *The Explicator*, XVII (June, 1959), 62.
WILLIAM HOWARD, *The Explicator*, XVII (June, 1959), 62.

DICKINSON, "The Snow That Never Drifts"
RALPH MARCELLINO, *The Explicator*, XIII (April, 1955), 36.

DICKINSON, "The Soul Selects Her Own Society"
HENRY F. POMMER, *The Explicator*, III (Feb., 1945), 32.
VAN DOREN, *Introduction to Poetry*, pp. 39-42.

DICKINSON, "There Came a Day at Summer's Full"
CAROLINE HOGUE, *The Explicator*, XI (Dec., 1952), 17.
WILLIAM HOWARD, *The Explicator*, XII (April, 1954), 41.

DICKINSON, "There Is No Frigate Like a Book"
PERRINE, *Sound and Sense*, p. 32.

DICKINSON, "There's a Certain Slant of Light"
LAURENCE PERRINE, *The Explicator*, XI (May, 1953), 50.

DICKINSON, "These Are the Days When Birds Come Back"
GEORGE ARMS, *The Explicator,* II (Feb., 1944), 29.

MARSHALL VAN DEUSEN, *The Explicator,* XII (April, 1954), 40.

DICKINSON, "This Consciousness That Is Aware"
CHARLES R. ANDERSON, "The Conscious Self in Emily Dickinson's Poetry," *American Literature,* XXXI (Nov., 1959), 304-305.

DICKINSON, "Those Not Live Yet"
DOROTHY WAUGH, *The Explicator,* XV (Jan., 1957), 22.

DICKINSON, "Title Divine Is Mine"
EUNICE GLENN, "Emily Dickinson's Poetry: A Revaluation," *The Sewanee Review,* LI (Autumn, 1943), 578-580.

DICKINSON, "To Undertake Is to Achieve"
RICHARD B. SEWALL, *The Explicator,* VI (June, 1948), 51.

DICKINSON, " 'Twas Like a Maelstrom, with a Notch"
MYRON OCHSHORN, "In Search of Emily Dickinson," *New Mexico Quarterly Review,* XXIII (Spring, 1953), 103-106.

DICKINSON, "When I Hoped I Feared"
WILSON O. CLOUGH, *The Explicator,* X (Nov., 1951), 10.

CAROLINE HOGUE, *The Explicator,* X (May., 1952), 49.

DICKINSON, "Wonder Is Not Precisely Knowing"
FRIAR and BRINNIN, *Modern Poetry,* pp. 456-457.

DODGSON, "Jabberwocky"
CIARDI, *How Does a Poem Mean?* pp. 705-709.

DONNE, "Air and Angels"
WILLIAM EMPSON, "Donne the Space Man," *The Kenyon Review,* XIX (Summer, 1957), 381-389.
GARDNER, *The Business of Criticism,* pp. 62-75.

FRANK L. HUNTLEY, *The Explicator,* VI (June, 1948), 53.

KERBY NEILL, *The Explicator,* VI (Nov., 1947), 8.

MARTIN TURNELL, "John Donne and the Quest for Unity," *Nineteenth Century,* CXLVII (April, 1950), 266-267.

UNGER, *The Man in the Name,* pp. 64-67.
Reprinted from *Donne's Poetry and Modern Criticism* (Chicago: Regnery, 1950).

UNGER and O'CONNOR, *Poems for Study,* pp. 119-121.

GEORGE WILLIAMSON, "Textual Difficulties in the Interpretation of Donne's Poetry," *Modern Philology,* XXXVIII (August, 1940), 42-45.

DONNE,   "The Anniversary"
FRANK J. WARNKE, *The Explicator,* XVI (Nov., 1957), 12.

DONNE,   "The Apparition"
EMPSON, *Seven Types of Ambiguity,* pp. 184-186; (1947 ed.), pp. 146-147.

WILLIAM EVERSON, *The Explicator,* IV (June, 1946), 56.

ALLAN H. GILBERT, *The Explicator,* IV (June, 1946), 56.

C. WILLIAM MILLER and DAN S. NORTON, *The Explicator,* IV (Feb., 1946), 24.

DONNE,   "The Blossom"
BROOKS and WARREN, *Understanding Poetry,* revised edition, pp. 247-250.

TILLYARD, *The Metaphysicals and Milton,* pp. 14-20.

DONNE   "The Canonization"
CLEANTH BROOKS, "The Language of Paradox," *The Language of Poetry,* Allen Tate, ed., pp. 46-61. Reprinted *Criticism,* pp. 361-365.

BROOKS, *The Well Wrought Urn,* pp. 10-17. Reprinted *Critiques,* pp. 71-76.

Abridged in *The Case for Poetry,* p. 113.

Reprinted *American Literary Criticism,* pp. 523-538.

CARVEL COLLINS, *The Explicator,* XII (Oct., 1953), 3.

DAICHES and CHARVAT, *Poems in English,* pp. 657-658.

KRIEGER, *The New Apologists for Poetry,* pp. 13-18.

PIERRE LEGOUIS, abridged in *The Case for Poetry,* pp. 112-113 from *Donne The Craftsman* (Paris: Henry Didier, 1928), pp. 55-61.

WILLIAM J. ROONEY, " 'The Canonization' — the Language of Paradox Reconsidered," *Journal of English Literary History,* XXIII (March, 1956), 36-47.

UNGER, *The Man in the Name,* pp. 49-53. Reprinted from *Donne's Poetry and Modern Criticism* (Chicago: Regnery, 1950).

DONNE, "Community"

UNGER, *The Man in the Name,* pp. 63-64. Reprinted from *Donne's Poetry and Modern Criticism* (Chicago: Regnery, 1950).

ELIZABETH L. WIGGINS, "Logic in the Poetry of John Donne," *Studies in Philology,* XLII (Jan., 1945), 54, 58.

DONNE, "The Computation"

LEE BALL, JR., *The Explicator,* VIII (April, 1950), 44.

DONNE, "The Cross"

WILLIAM EMPSON, "Donne the Space Man," *The Kenyon Review,* XIX (Summer, 1957), 379-380.

GEORGE WILLIAMSON, "Textual Difficulties in the Interpretation of Donne's Poetry," *Modern Philology,* XXXVIII (August, 1940), 64-66.

DONNE, "The Ecstasy"

ADAMS, *Strains of Discord,* pp. 108-109.
BROWER, *The Fields of Light,* pp. 79-83.

FRANK A. DOGGETT, "Donne's Platonism," *The Sewanee Review,* XLII (July-Sept., 1934), 284-290.

WILLIAM EMPSON, "Donne the Space Man," *The*

Kenyon Review, XIX (Summer, 1957), 368-369.

EMPSON, *English Pastoral Poetry,* pp. 132-136.

JOHN MARSHALL, "The Extasie," *Hound and Horn,* III (Oct.-Dec., 1929), 121-124.

G. R. POTTER, "Donne's *Extasie,* Contra Legouis, "*Philological Quarterly,* XV (July, 1936), 247-253.

SPITZER, *A Method of Interpreting Literature,* pp. 5-21.

TILLYARD, *The Metaphysicals and Milton,* pp. 79-84.

MARTIN TURNELL, "John Donne and the Quest for Unity," *Nineteenth Century,* CXLVII (April, 1950), 267-268.

WHEELWRIGHT, *The Burning Fountain,* pp. 72-73.

GEORGE WILLIAMSON, "Textual Difficulties in the Interpretation of Donne's Poetry," *Modern Philology,* XXXVIII (August, 1940), 55-58.

DONNE, "Elegy on the L. C."

MILES, *The Primary Language of Poetry in the 1640's,* pp. 90-92.

DONNE, "Elegy on Mistress Boulstred"

TUVE, *Elizabethan and Metaphysical Imagery,* pp. 201-202.

DONNE, "Elegy on . . . Prince Henry"

RUTH C. WALLERSTEIN, "Rhetoric in the English Renaissance: Two Elegies," *English Institute Essays 1948,* pp. 166-170.

DONNE, "Elegy X: The Dream"

FREDSON T. BOWERS, "An Interpretation of Donne's Tenth Elegy," *MLN,* LIV (April, 1939), 280-282.

ARNOLD STEIN, "Structures of Sound in Donne's Verse," *The Kenyon Review,* XIII (Spring, 1951), 261-264.

DONNE, "Elegy XIX: Going to Bed"

WILLIAM EMPSON, "Donne the Space Man, *The Kenyon Review,* XIX (Summer, 1957), 362-367.

W. W. MAIN, *The Explicator,* X (Nov., 1951), 14.

DONNE, "Farewell to Love"

KATHERINE T. EMERSON, "Two Problems in Donne's 'Farewell to Love,' " *MLN*, LXXII (Feb., 1957), 93-95.

HELEN GARDNER, "A Crux in Donne," *Times Literary Supplement*, June 10, 1949, p. 381.

LESLIE HOTSON, "A Crux in Donne," *Times Literary Supplement*, April 16, 1949, p. 249.

J. C. MAXWELL, "A Crux in Donne," *Times Literary Supplement*, May 6, 1949, p. 297.

GEORGE WILLIAMSON, "Donne's 'Farewell to Love,' " *Modern Philology*, XXXVI (Feb., 1939), 301-303. Cf. *ibid.*, XXXVIII (August, 1940), 39-41.

DONNE,   "A Fever"

UNGER, *The Man in the Name*, pp. 74-75. Reprinted from *Donne's Poetry and Modern Criticism* (Chicago: Regnery, 1950).

DONNE,   "The First Anniversary"

MARIUS BEWLEY, "Religious Cynicism in Donne's Poetry," *The Kenyon Review*, XIV (Autumn, 1952), 621-635.

CRUTTWELL, *The Shakespearean Moment*, pp. 73-94.

LEONARD DEAN, *English Masterpieces*, Vol. III, *Renaissance Poetry*, p. 13.

L. L. MARTZ, "John Donne in Meditation," *English Literary History*, XIV (Dec., 1947), 248-262.

MARTZ, *The Poetry of Meditation*, pp. 221-231.

NICOLSON, *The Breaking of the Circle*, pp. 65-104.

I. A. RICHARDS, "The Interaction of Words," *The Language of Poetry*, Allen Tate, ed., pp. 75-87. Reprinted *Modern Literary Criticism*, pp. 85-93.

ELIZABETH L. WIGGINS, "Logic in the Poetry of John Donne," *Studies in Philology*, XLII (Jan., 1945), 52-54 *et passim*.

DONNE,   "The Flea"

TUVE, *Elizabethan and Metaphysical Imagery*, pp. 172-173.

UNGER, *The Man in the Name*, pp. 79-80.

Reprinted from *Donne's Poetry and Modern Criticism* (Chicago: Regnery, 1950).

DONNE,   "The Funeral"

ADAMS, *Strains of Discord*, p. 109.

J. E. V. CROFTS, "John Donne," *Essays and Studies*, XXII (1936), 141-142.

KILBY, *Poetry and Life*, p. 160.

STAUFFER, *The Nature of Poetry*, pp. 86-87.

ALLEN TATE, "Poetry and the Absolute," *The Sewanee Review*, XXXV (Jan., 1927), 41-48.

DONNE,   "Good-Friday, 1613, Riding Westward"

W. NELSON FRANCIS, *The Explicator*, XIII (Feb., 1955), 21.

GEORGE HERMAN, *The Explicator*, XIV (June, 1956), 60.

MARTZ, *The Poetry of Meditation*, pp. 54-56.

ROSENTHAL and SMITH, *Exploring Poetry*, pp. 479-483.

GEORGE WILLIAMSON, "Textual Difficulties in the Interpretation of Donne's Poetry," *Modern Philology*, XXXVIII (August, 1940), 66-69.

DONNE,   "The Good Morrow"

BROOKS, PURSER, WARREN, *An Approach to Literature*, third edition, pp. 374-376.

DAICHES and CHARVAT, *Poems in English*, pp. 656-657.

WILLIAM EMPSON, "Donne the Space Man," *The Kenyon Review*, XIX (Summer, 1957), 358-362.

JAMES SMITH, "On Metaphysical Poetry," *Scrutiny*, II (Dec., 1933), 229-230.

UNGER, *The Man in the Name*, pp. 46-49. Reprinted from *Donne's Poetry and Modern Criticism* (Chicago: Regnery, 1950).

DONNE,   "Growth"

ARNOLD STEIN, "Structures of Sound in Donne's Verse," *The Kenyon Review*, XIII (Spring, 1951), 260-261.

DONNE,   "His Picture"

HELEN L. GARDNER, "John Donne: A Note on Elegie V, 'His Picture,'" *Modern Language Review,* XXXIX (Oct., 1944), 333-337.

DONNE, "Holy Sonnets"

DOUGLAS L. PETERSON, "John Donne's *Holy Sonnets* and the Anglican Doctrine of Contrition," *Studies in Philology,* LVI (July, 1959), 504-518.

DONNE, "Holy Sonnets" I: "Thou Hast Made Me, and Shall Thy Work Decay?"

YVOR WINTERS, "The Poetry of Gerard Manley Hopkins (1)," *Hudson Review,* I (Winter, 1948), 457-460.

Reprinted *The Function of Criticism,* pp. 105-107.

DONNE, "Holy Sonnets" V: "I Am a Little World Made Cunningly"

EMPSON, *English Pastoral Poetry,* pp. 74-76.

WILLIAM EMPSON, "Donne the Space Man," *The Kenyon Review,* XIX (Summer, 1957), 374-379.

DONNE, "Holy Sonnets" VII: "At The Round Earth's Imagined Corners Blow"

BROWER, *The Fields of Light,* pp. 67-70.

Reprinted Locke, Gibson, and Arms, *Introduction to Literature,* third edition, pp. 29-32.

MARTZ, *The Poetry of Meditation,* pp. 50-52.

RICHARDS, *Practical Criticism,* pp. 42-51 *et passim.*

STAUFFER, *The Nature of Poetry,* pp. 139-140.

DONNE, "Holy Sonnets" IX: "If Poisonous Minerals, and If That Tree"

MARTZ, *The Poetry of Meditation,* p. 52.

DONNE, "Holy Sonnets" X: "Death Be Not Proud, Though Some Have Called Thee"

DANIELS, *The Art of Reading Poetry,* pp. 275-278.

ELIZABETH WARD, *English "A" Analyst,* No. 12, pp. 1-4.

DONNE, "Holy Sonnets" XI: "Spit in My Face you Jews, and Pierce My Side"

MARTZ, *The Poetry of Meditation,* pp. 49-50.

DONNE,   "Holy Sonnets" XII: "Why Are We by All
           Creatures Waited On?"
M. E. GRENANDER, *The Explicator*, XIII (May,
1955), 42.
MARTZ, *The Poetry of Meditation*, pp.53-54.

DONNE,   "Holy Sonnets" XIII: "What If This Present
Were the World's Last Night?"
EMPSON, *Seven Types of Ambiguity*, pp. 183-184;
(1947 ed.), pp. 145-146.

DONNE,   "Holy Sonnets" XIV: "Batter My Heart, Three
Person'd God; for, You"
DREW, *Poetry*, pp. 58-60.
GEORGE HERMAN, *The Explicator*, XII (Dec., 1953),
18.
GEORGE KNOX, *The Explicator*, XV (Oct., 1956), 2.
P. C. LEVENSON, *The Explicator*, XI (March, 1953),
31.
P. C. LEVENSON, *The Explicator*, XII (April, 1954),
36.
STAUFFER, *The Nature of Poetry*, pp. 135-136.

DONNE,   "Holy Sonnets" XVI: "Father, Part of His
Double Interest"
GEORGE WILLIAMSON, "Textual Difficulties in the In-
terpretation of Donne's Poetry," *Modern Philology*,
XXXVIII (August, 1940), 62-64.

DONNE,   "Holy Sonnets," XVII, "Since She Whom I
           Lov'd Hath Paid Her Last Debt"
HELEN GARDNER, "Another Note on Donne: 'Since
She Whom I Lov'd,'" *Modern Language Review*,
LII (Oct., 1957), 564-565.

DONNE,   "Hymn to God, My God, in My Sickness"
DON CAMERON ALLEN, "John Donne's 'Paradise and
Calvarie,'" *MLN*, LX (June, 1945), 398-400.
HARRY M. CAMPBELL, "Donne's 'Hymn to God, My
God, in My Sickness,'" *College English* V (Jan.,
1944), 192-196. Reprinted *Readings for Liberal
Education*, II, 500-504.

CONRAD HILBERRY, "The First Stanza of Donne's 'Hymne to God My God, In My Sicknesse'," *Notes and Queries,* IV, n.s. (Aug., 1957), 336-337.

DONNE, "A Hymn to God the Father"

KESTER SVENDSEN, *The Explicator,* II (June, 1944), 62.

DONNE, "A Hymn to the Saints and to Marquis Hamilton"

ELIZABETH L. WIGGINS, "Logic in the Poetry of John Donne," *Studies in Philology,* XLII (Jan., 1945), 44-45.

DONNE, "If Poisonous Minerals"

BROOKS and WARREN, *Understanding Poetry,* pp. 520-524.

Revised edition, pp. 380-386.

DONNE, "A Jet Ring Sent"

TUVE, *Elizabethan and Metaphysical Imagery,* pp. 290-291.

DONNE, "A Lecture upon the Shadow"

M. A. GOLDBERG, *The Explicator,* XIV (May, 1956), 50.

JOHN D. RUSSELL, *The Explicator,* XVII (Nov., 1958), 9.

UNGER, *The Man in the Name,* pp. 76-77. Reprinted from *Donne's Poetry and Modern Criticism* (Chicago: Regnery, 1950).

VAN DOREN, *Introduction to Poetry,* pp. 27-31.

DONNE, "Letter to the Lady Carey and Mrs. Essex Riche, from Amyens"

LAURENCE STAPLETON, "The Theme of Virtue in Donne's Verse Epistles," *Studies in Philology,* LV (April, 1958), 197-198.

DONNE, "Love's Alchemy"

LESLIE A. FIEDLER, "Archetype and Signature: A Study of the Relationship between Biography and Poetry," *The Sewanee Review,* LX (Spring, 1952), 265-266.

W. A. MURRAY, "Donne and Paracelsus: An Essay in

Interpretation," *Review of English Studies,* XXV (April, 1949), 115-118.

DONNE, "Love's Deity"
JOHN L. SWEENEY, "Basic in Reading," *Kenyon Review,* V (Winter, 1943), 55-59.

DONNE, "Love's Diet"
JOHN V. HAGOPIAN, *The Explicator,* XVII (Oct., 1958), 5.
UNGER, *The Man in the Name,* pp. 75-76. Reprinted from *Donne's Poetry and Modern Criticism* (Chicago: Regnery, 1950).

DONNE, "Love's Growth"
TUVE, *Elizabethan and Metaphysical Imagery,* pp. 174-175.

DONNE, "Lovers' Infiniteness"
STAUFFER, *The Nature of Poetry,* pp. 240-241.
TILLYARD, *The Metaphysicals and Milton,* pp. 30-35.
MARTIN TURNELL, "John Donne and the Quest for Unity," *Nineteenth Century,* CXLVII (April, 1950), 264.

DONNE, "Love's Usury"
MARIUS BEWLEY, "Religious Criticism in Donne's Poetry," *The Kenyon Review,* XIV (Autumn, 1952), 638-639.
ROBERT F. GLECKNER and GERALD SMITH, *The Explicator,* VIII (April, 1950), 43.
UNGER, *The Man in the Name,* p. 77. Reprinted from *Donne's Poetry and Modern Criticism* (Chicago: Regnery, 1950).

DONNE, "Negative Love"
WALTER GIERASCH, *The Explicator,* IX (Nov., 1950), 13.
H. M. RICHMOND, "The Intangible Mistress," *Modern Philology,* LVI (May, 1959), 219-220.

DONNE, "A Nocturnal upon S. Lucy's Day"
WILLIAM EMPSON, "Donne the Space Man," *The*

Kenyon Review, XIX (Summer, 1957), 390-391.

LEISHMAN, *The Metaphysical Poets,* pp. 56-58.

W. A. MURRAY, "Donne and Paracelsus: An Essay in Interpretation," *Review of English Studies,* XXV (April, 1949), 118-123.

RICHARD SLEIGHT, *Interpretations,* John Wain, ed., pp. 32-58.

TILLYARD, *The Metaphysicals and Milton,* pp. 20-22.

MARTIN TURNELL, "John Donne and the Quest for Unity," *Nineteenth Century,* CXLVII (April, 1950), 265-266.

UNGER, *The Man in the Name,* pp. 67-71. Reprinted from *Donne's Poetry and Modern Criticism* (Chicago: Regnery, 1950).

ELIZABETH L. WIGGINS, "Logic in the Poetry of John Donne," *Studies in Philology,* XLII (Jan., 1945), 51-52.

DONNE,   "The Perfume"

ARTHUR MINTON, *The Explicator,* IV (May, 1946), 50.

HENRY TEN EYCK, *The Explicator,* V (Nov., 1946), 10.

DONNE,   "The Primrose"

E. D. CLEVELAND, *The Explicator,* VIII (Oct., 1949), 4.

DONNE,   "The Progress of the Soul"

MARIUS BEWLEY, "Religious Cynicism in Donne's Poetry," *The Kenyon Review,* XIV (Autumn, 1952), 623.

JOHN P. WENDELL, "Two Cruxes in the Poetry of Donne," *MLN,* LXIII (Nov., 1948), 480-481.

DONNE,   "The Prohibition"

UNGER, *The Man in the Name,* pp. 61-63. Reprinted from *Donne's Poetry and Modern Criticism.* (Chicago: Regnery, 1950).

ELIZABETH L. WIGGINS, "Logic in the Poetry of John Donne," *Studies in Philology,* XLII (Jan., 1945), 58-60.

DONNE,   "The Relique"

ARNOLD STEIN, "Structures of Sound in Donne's Verse," *The Kenyon Review*, XIII (Spring, 1951), 264-267.

DONNE,   "Resurrection Imperfect"

RUTH E. FALK, *The Explicator*, XVII (Dec., 1958), 24.

DONNE,   "Satire I"

S. F. JOHNSON, *The Explicator*, XI (June, 1953), 53.

DONNE,   "Satire III"

ADAMS, *Strains of Discord*, pp. 11-13.

SMITH, *Elizabethan Poetry*, pp. 224-225.

DONNE,   "The Second Anniversary"

MARIUS BEWLEY, "Religious Cynicism in Donne's Poetry," *The Kenyon Review*, XIV (Autumn, 1952), 621-635.

CRUTTWELL, *The Shakespearean Moment*, pp. 73-94.

L. L. MARTZ, "John Donne in Meditation," *English Literary History*, XIV (Dec., 1947), 262-273.

MARTZ *The Poetry of Meditation*, pp. 236-248.

NICOLSON, *The Breaking of the Circle*, pp. 65-104.

ELIZABETH L. WIGGINS, "Logic in the Poetry of John Donne," *Studies in Philology*, XLII (Jan., 1945), 48-49 *et passim*.

DONNE,   "Show Me, Dear Christ"

BROWER, *The Fields of Light*, pp. 24-25.

DONNE,   "Holy Sonnets," XVII, "Since She Whom I Lov'd Hath Paid Her Last Debt"

TILLYARD, *The Metaphysicals and Milton*, pp. 4-7, 77-78.

DONNE,   "Song, Go and Catch a Falling Star"

L. G. LOCKE, *The Explicator*, I (Feb., 1943), 29.

Reprinted Stageberg and Anderson, *Poetry as Experience*, pp. 472-473.

M. L. ROSENTHAL, W. C. HUMMEL, V. E. LEICHTY, *Effective Reading* (Boston: Houghton Mifflin Company, 1944), pp. 406-413.

DONNE, "Sonnet. The Token"

FRANCIS MANLEY, "Chaucer's Rosary and Donne's Bracelet: Ambiguous Coral," *MLN*, LXXIV (May, 1959), 385-389.

DONNE, "The Storme"

EAIRD W. WHITLOCK, "Donne's 'First Letter,'" *Times Literary Supplement*, (Aug. 22, 1952), p. 556.

DONNE, "The Sun Rising"

GLENN J. CHRISTENSEN, *The Explicator*, VII (Oct., 1948), 3.

LEONARD DEAN, *English Masterpieces*, Vol. III, *Renaissance Poetry*, p. 11.

DREW, *Poetry*, pp. 199-200.

FRANKENBERG, *Invitation to Poetry*, p. 212.

ROBERT L. GALE, *The Explicator*, XV (Dec., 1956) 14.

WALTER GIERASCH, *The Explicator*, VI (May, 1948), 47.

ROSENTHAL and SMITH, *Exploring Poetry*, pp. 477-479.

MARTIN TURNELL, "John Donne and the Quest for Unity," *Nineteenth Century*, CXLVII (April, 1950), 263-264.

UNGER, *The Man in the Name*, pp. 60-61. Reprinted from *Donne's Poetry and Modern Criticism* (Chicago: Regnery, 1950).

DONNE, "To the Countess of Huntingdon"

ELIZABETH LEWIS WIGGINS, "Logic in the Poetry of John Donne," *Studies in Philology*, XLII (Jan., 1945), 49-50.

DONNE, "To Sir Rowland Woodward"

LAURENCE STAPLETON, "The Theme of Virtue in Donne's Verse Epistles," *Studies in Philology*, LV (April, 1958), 194-195.

DONNE, "Twicknam Garden"

JOHN BOAL DONDS, "Donne's Technique of Dissonance," *PMLA*, LII (Dec., 1937), 1052-1054, 1056-1057.

UNGER, *The Man in the Name*, pp. 53-59. Reprinted from *Donne's Poetry and Modern Criticism* (Chicago: Regnery, 1950).

DONNE,   "A Valediction: Forbidding Mourning"

ADAMS, *Strains of Discord, pp.* 109-111.

—— BROOKS, *The Well Wrought Urn*, pp. 222-223.

—— CIARDI, *How Does a Poem Mean?* pp. 873-875.

—— DANIELS, *The Art of Reading Poetry*, pp. 213-216.

EDGAR H. DUNCAN, *The Explicator*, I (June, 1943), 63.

WILLIAM EMPSON, "Donne the Space Man," *The Kenyon Review*, XIX (Summer, 1957), 391-394.

BROTHER JOSEPH, F.S.C., *The Explicator*, XVI (April, 1958), 43.

KREUZER, *Elements of Poetry*, pp. 84-86.

MILLETT, *Reading Poetry*, pp. 62-63.

JAMES SMITH, "On Metaphysical Poetry," *Determinations*, pp. 28-29.

—— JAMES SMITH, "On Metaphysical Poetry," *Scrutiny*, II (Dec., 1933), 230-231.

ARNOLD STEIN, "Structures of Sound in Donne's Verse," *The Kenyon Review*, XII (Spring, 1951), 267-268.

ALLAN TATE, "The Point of Dying: Donne's 'Virtuous Men,'" *The Sewanee Review*, LXI (Winter, 1953), 76-81.

Also reprinted West, *Essays in Modern Literary Criticism*, pp. 273-275.

ALLEN TATE, "Tension in Poetry," *The Southern Review*, IV (Summer, 1938), 109-111. Reprinted Tate, *Reason in Madness*, pp. 73-75, 90-91; Tate, *On the Limits of Poetry*, pp. 84-85; *Critiques*, pp. 61-62.

UNGER, *The Man in the Name*, pp. 73-74. Reprinted from *Donne's Poetry and Modern Criticism* (Chicago: Regnery, 1950).

WHEELWRIGHT, *The Burning Fountain*, pp. 103-104.

DONNE,   "A Valediction: Of the Book"
RHODES DUNLAP, "Donne As Navigator," *Times Literary Supplement,* Dec. 28, 1946, p. 643.

UNGER, *The Man in the Name,* pp. 77-78. Reprinted from *Donne's Poetry and Modern Criticism* (Chicago: Regnery, 1950).

DONNE,   "Valediction: Of My Name in the Window"
BROOKS, *Modern Poetry and the Tradition,* pp. 24-25.

UNGER, *The Man in the Name,* pp. 80-81. Reprinted from *Donne's Poetry and Modern Criticism* (Chicago: Regnery, 1950).

DONNE,   "A Valediction: Of Weeping"
J. E. V. CROFTS, "John Donne," *Essays and Studies,* XXII (1936), 142-143.

DANIELS, *The Art of Reading Poetry,* pp. 216-217.

EMPSON, *Seven Types of Ambiguity,* pp. 175-183; (1947 ed.), pp. 139-145.

ARNOLD STEIN, "Structures of Sound in Donne's Verse," *The Kenyon Review,* XIII (Spring, 1951), 264-265.

MARTIN TURNELL, "John Donne and the Quest for Unity," *Nineteenth Century,* CXLVII (April, 1950), 266.

DONNE,   "The Will"
DON A. KEISTER, *The Explicator,* VIII (May, 1950), 55.

T. O. MABBOTT, *The Explicator,* VIII (Feb., 1950), 30.

TUVE, *Elizabethan and Metaphysical Imagery,* pp. 170-171.

UNGER, *The Man in the Name,* pp. 78-79. Reprinted from *Donne's Poetry and Modern Criticism* (Chicago: Regnery, 1950).

DONNE,   "Woman's Constancy"
KREUZER, *Elements of Poetry,* pp. 145-146.

H.D.,   "Oread"

DANIELS, *The Art of Reading Poetry,* pp. 198-199.

WILLIS D. JACOBS, *The Explicator,* X (May, 1952), 45.

MACKLIN THOMAS, "Analysis of the Experience in Lyric Poetry," *College English,* IX (March, 1948), 320.

H.D.,   "The Pool"
DANIELS, *The Art of Reading Poetry,* pp. 196-197.
Reprinted Stageberg and Anderson, *Poetry as Experience,* p. 29.

RICHARDS, *Principles of Literary Criticism,* pp. 199-200.

H.D.,   "Red Roses For Bronze"
R. P. BLACKMUR, "The Lesser Satisfaction," *Poetry,* XLI (Nov., 1932), 94-100.

H.D.,   "The Walls Do Not Fall"
H. H. WATTS, "H. D. and the Age of Myth," *The Sewanee Review,* LVI (Spring, 1948), 287-303.

WATTS, *Hound and Quarry,* pp. 210-221.

DRAYTON,   "Agincourt"
DANIELS, *The Art of Reading Poetry,* pp. 163-168.

DRAYTON,   "Clear Anchor"
TUVE, *Elizabethan and Metaphysical Imagery,* pp. 62-63.

DRAYTON,   "Like an Adventurous Sea-Farer Am I"
TUVE, *Elizabethan and Metaphysical Imagery,* pp. 61-62.

DRAYTON,   "Since There's No Help, Come Let Us Kiss and Part"
LEONARD DEAN, *English Masterpieces,* Vol. III, *Renaissance Poetry,* p. 4.

DRYDEN,   "Epistle to Charleton"
WASSERMAN, *The Subtler Language,* pp. 15-33.

DRYDEN,   "Mac Flecknoe"
GOODMAN, *The Structure of Literature,* pp. 117-126.
MAYNARD MACK, *English Masterpieces,* Vol. V, *The Augustans,* pp. 5-6.

DRYDEN, "Ode: To the Pious Memory of Mrs. Anne Killigrew"

I. A. RICHARDS, "The Interaction of Words," *The Language of Poetry*, pp. 75-87.

Reprinted *Modern Literary Criticism*, pp. 85-93.

TILLYARD, *Five Poems, 1470-1870* pp. 49-65.

Reprinted West, *Essays in Modern Literary Criticism*, pp. 353-365.

DRYDEN, "To the Memory of Mr. Oldham"

WALLACE CABLE BROWN, "The 'Heresy' of the Didactic," *University of Kansas City Review*, XI (Spring, 1945), 182-184.

DANIELS, *The Art of Reading Poetry*, pp. 377-379.

VAN DOREN, *Introduction to Poetry*, pp. 93-98.

DRYDEN, "Upon the Death of the Lord Hastings"

MILES, *The Primary Language of Poetry in the 1640's*, pp. 92-94.

TUVE, *Elizabethan and Metaphysical Imagery*, pp. 318-319.

DRYDEN, "Zambra Dance" (*The Conquest of Granada*)

BETTY GAY COSHOW, *The Explicator*, XVI (Dec., 1957), 16.

BRUCE KING, *The Explicator*, XVIII (Dec., 1959), 18.

DUNBAR, "Meditation in Winter"

ARTHUR K. MOORE, *The Secular Lyric in Middle English*, pp. 207-209.

JOHN SPEIRS, "William Dunbar," *Scrutiny*, VII (June, 1938), 67-68.

DUNBAR, "My Heid Did Yak Yesternicht"

ARTHUR K. MOORE, *The Secular Lyric in Middle English*, pp. 205-207.

DUNBAR, "Petition of the Gray Horse"

ARTHUR K. MOORE, *The Secular Lyric in Middle English*, pp. 209-213.

DUNBAR, "To a Lady"

WALTER GIERASCH, *The Explicator*, VI (Dec., 1947), 21.

ARTHUR K. MOORE, *The Secular Lyric in Middle English*, pp. 201-203.

JOHN SPEIRS, "William Dunbar," *Scrutiny*, VII (June, 1938), 59.

DUNBAR,   "The Twa Mariit Weman and the Wedo"
JOHN SPEIRS, "William Dunbar," *Scrutiny*, VII (June, 1938), 59-61.

DURRELL, LAWRENCE,   "At Epidaurus"
FRIAR and BRINNIN, *Modern Poetry*, pp. 457-458.

DURRELL, LAWRENCE,   "To Argos"
FRIAR and BRINNIN, *Modern Poetry*, pp. 457-458.

EBERHART,   "From Letter I"
J. F. NIMS, *Poetry: A Critical Supplement,* April, 1948, p. 11.

EBERHART,   "The Fury of Aerial Bombardment"
CIARDI, *How Does a Poem Mean?* pp. 999-1002.

EBERHART,   "Grave Piece"
RICHARD EBERHART, *The Explicator*, VI (Feb., 1948), 23.
    Reprinted Engel and Carrier, *Reading Modern Poetry*, pp. 273-274.

EBERHART,   "The Groundhog"
AEROL ARNOLD, *The Explicator*, XV (Oct., 1956), 3.
DEUTSCH, *Poetry in Our Time*, pp. 216-217.
SYDNEY MENDEL, *The Explicator*, XVII (June, 1959), 64.
    M. L. ROSENTHAL, "Three Poets in Focus," *New Republic*, CXXV (Dec. 10, 1951), 27.

EBERHART,   "I Walked Out to the Graveyard to See the Dead"
RICHARD EBERHART in Friar and Brinnin, *Modern Poetry*, pp. 458-459.

EBERHART,   "Meditation"
J. L. SWEENEY and I. A. RICHARDS, [Letters], *Furioso*, I (Spring, 1940), 42-43.

EBERHART, "Ur Burial"

RICHARD F. BAUERLE, *The Explicator*, XVI (April, 1958), 38.

RICHARD EBERHART, *The Explicator*, XVI (May, 1958), 48.

EBERHART, "The Young Hunter"

RICHARD EBERHART, *The Explicator*, VI (Feb., 1948), 24.

ELIOT, GEORGE, "I Grant You Ample Leave"

BERNARD J. PARIS, "George Eliot's Unpublished Poetry," *Studies in Philology*, LVI (July, 1959), 551-554.

ELIOT, GEORGE, "In a London Drawing Room"

BERNARD J. PARIS, "George Eliot's Unpublished Poetry," *Studies in Philology*, LVI (July, 1959), 549-551.

ELIOT, "Ash Wednesday"

BLACKMUR, *The Double Agent*, pp. 190-196.

Reprinted *Language as Gesture*, pp. 168-171.

CLEANTH BROOKS and ROBERT PENN WARREN, "The Reading of Modern Poetry," *The American Review*, VII (Feb., 1937), 445-446.

SISTER M. CLEOPHAS, "*Ash Wednesday: The Purgatorio* in a Modern Mode," *Comparative Literature*, XI (Fall, 1959), 329-339.

DANIEL N. DWYER, S.J., *The Explicator*, IX (Oct., 1950), 5.

GENEVIEVE W. FOSTER, "Archetypal Imagery of T. S. Eliot," *PMLA*, LX (June, 1945), 580-582.

VINCENT FREIMARCK, *The Explicator*, IX (Oct., 1950), 6.

FRIAR and BRINNIN, *Modern Poetry*, pp. 465-472.

HUGH KENNER, "Eliot's Moral Dialectic," *The Hudson Review*, II (Autumn, 1949), 439-446.

LEAVIS, *New Bearings in English Poetry*, pp. 117-128.

THEODORE MORRISON, "*Ash Wednesday: A Religious History*," *New England Quarterly*, XI (June, 1938), 266-286.

POTTLE, *The Idiom of Poetry*, pp. 89-91; (1946 ed.), pp. 96-99.

ELEANOR M. SICKELS, *The Explicator*, IX (Oct., 1950), 4.

GORDON SYMES, "T. S. Eliot and Old Age," *Fortnightly*, CLXIX (March, 1951), 188-191.

ALLEN TATE, "Irony and Humility," *Hound and Horn*, IV (Jan.-March, 1931), 290-297.

TATE, *Reactionary Essays on Poetry and Ideas*, pp. 210-220. Reprinted *On the Limits of Poetry*, pp. 344-349.

TSCHUMI, *Thought in Twentieth-Century English Poetry*, pp. 144-146.

UNGER, *The Man in the Name*, pp. 141-166.

LEONARD UNGER, "Notes on *Ash Wednesday*," *The Southern Review*, IV (Spring, 1939), 745-770.

LEONARD UNGER, "T. S. Eliot's Rose Garden: a Persistent Theme," *The Southern Review*, VII (Spring, 1942), 675-676.

WILLIAM CARLOS WILLIAMS, "The Fatal Blunder," *Quarterly Review of Literature*, Vol. II, No. 2, 125-126.

ELIOT,   "The Boston Evening Transcript"

W. C. BROWN, " 'A Poem Should Not Mean But Be,' " *The University of Kansas City Review*, XV (Autumn, 1948), 61-62.

ELIOT,   "Burbank With a Baedeker: Bleistein With a Cigar"

ROBERT F. GOHEEN, " 'Burbank with a Baedeker': The Third Stanza," *The Sewanee Review*, LXI (Winter, 1953), 109-119.

L. G. LOCKE, *The Explicator*, III (May, 1945), 53.

RIDING and GRAVES, *A Survey of Modernist Poetry*, pp. 235-242.

THEODORE SPENCER, "The Poetry of T. S. Eliot," *Atlantic Monthly*, CLI (Jan., 1933), 61-62.

JANE WORTHINGTON, "The Epigraphs to the Poetry of T. S. Eliot," *American Literature*, XXI (March, 1949), 6-7.

ELIOT, "Burnt Norton"

C. A. BODELSEN, "Two 'Difficult' Poems by T. S. Eliot," *English Studies*, XXXIV (Feb., 1953), 17-21.

DAICHES and CHARVAT, *Poems in English*, pp. 741-742.

ELIZABETH DREW in Locke, Gibson, and Arms, *Introduction to Literature*, third edition, pp. 216-222. Reprinted from Drew, *T. S. Eliot: The Design of His Poetry* (New York: Charles Scribner's Sons, 1950), pp. 151-162.

DREW and SWEENEY, *Directions in Modern Poetry*, pp. 138-140.

FRIAR and BRINNIN, *Modern Poetry*, pp. 461-465.

HARVEY GROSS, "Music and the Analogue of Feeling: Notes on Eliot and Beethoven," *The Centennial Review*, III (Summer, 1959), 272-274.

F. R. LEAVIS, "Eliot's Later Poetry," *Scrutiny*, XI (Summer, 1942), 65-67.

LEAVIS, *Education and the University*, pp. 94-98.

A. O. LEWIS, JR., *The Explicator*, VIII (Nov., 1949), 9.

MAYNARD MACK, LEONARD DEAN, and WILLIAM FROST, *English Masterpieces*, Vol. VII, *Modern Poetry*, pp. 15-16.

MARK REISENBERG, "A Footnote to *Four Quartets*," *American Literature*, XXI (Nov., 1949), 342-344.

TSCHUMI, *Thought in Twentieth-Century English Poetry*, pp. 149-154.

LEONARD UNGER, "T. S. Eliot's Rose Garden: a Persistent Theme," *The Southern Review*, VII (Spring, 1942), 677-681.

UNGER, *The Man in the Name*, pp. 177-181.

PHILIP WHEELWRIGHT, "The Burnt Norton Trilogy," *Chimera*, I (1942), 7-18.

JANE WORTHINGTON, "The Epigraphs to the Poetry of T. S. Eliot," *American Literature*, XXI (March, 1949), 16-17.

ELIOT,   "A Cooking Egg"

DREW, *Discovering Poetry,* pp. 113-115.

RICHARDS, *Principles of Literary Criticism,* pp. 293-294.

SHERNA S. VINOGRAD, "The Accidental: A Clue to Structure in Eliot's Poetry," *Accent,* IX (Summer, 1949), 231-232.

JANE WORTHINGTON, "The Epigraphs to the Poetry of T. S. Eliot," *American Literature,* XXI (March, 1949), 9-10.

ELIOT,   "Coriolan"

DONALD F. THEALL, "Traditional Satire in Eliot's 'Coriolan,' " *Accent,* XI (Autumn, 1951), 194-206.

ELIOT,   "The Cultivation of Christmas Trees"

HUGH KENNER, "A Plea for Metrics," *Poetry,* LXXXVI (April, 1955), 42-45.

ELIOT,   "Dans le Restaurant"

FRANKENBERG, *Pleasure Dome,* pp. 72-76.

LEONARD UNGER, "T. S. Eliot's Rose Garden: a Persistent Theme," *The Southern Review,* VII (Spring, 1942), 669-671.

UNGER, *The Man in the Name,* pp. 169-171.

ELIOT,   "The Dry Salvages"

HARVEY GROSS, "Music and the Analogue of Feeling: Notes on Eliot and Beethoven," *The Centennial Review,* III (Summer, 1959), 277.

F. R. LEAVIS, "Eliot's Later Poetry," *Scrutiny,* XI (Summer, 1942), 68-71.

LEAVIS, *Education and the University,* pp. 99-103.

LEONARD UNGER, "T. S. Eliot's Rose Garden: a Persistent Theme," *The Southern Review,* VII (Spring, 1942), 687-689.

UNGER, *The Man in the Name,* pp. 186-188.

WAGGONER, *The Heel of Elohim,* pp. 91-99.

PHILIP WHEELWRIGHT, "The Burnt Norton Trilogy," *Chimera,* I (1942), 7-18.

ELIOT,   "East Coker"

CURTIS BRADSFORD, "Footnotes to *East Coker:* A Reading," *The Sewanee Review,* LII (Jan.-March, 1944), 169-175.

D. BOSLEY BROTMAN, "T. S. Eliot: The Music of Ideas," *The University of Toronto Quarterly,* XVIII (Oct., 1948), 22-29.

HARVEY GROSS, "Music and the Analogue of Feeling: Notes on Eliot and Beethoven," *The Centennial Review,* III (Summer, 1959), 274-275.

H. W. HAUSERMANN, " 'East Coker' and *The Family Reunion,*" *Life and Letters,* VIII (Oct., 1945), 32-38.

SCOTT, *Rehearsals of Discomposure,* pp 237-243.

F. J. SMITH, "A Reading of 'East Coker,' " *Thought,* XXI (June, 1946), 272-286.

JAMES JOHNSON SWEENEY, "East Coker: a Reading," *The Southern Review,* VI (Spring, 1941), 771-791.

LEONARD UNGER, "T. S. Eliot's Rose Garden: a Persistent Theme," *The Southern Review,* VII (Spring, 1942), 686-687.

UNGER, *The Man in the Name,* pp. 185-186.

ELIOT,   "La Figlia Che Piange"

J. H. HAGSTRUM, *English "A" Analyst,* No. 3, pp. 1-7.

VERNON HALL, JR., *The Explicator,* V (Nov., 1946), 16.

JANE WORTHINGTON, "The Epigraphs to the Poetry of T. S. Eliot," *American Literature,* XXI (March, 1949), 4-5.

ELIOT,   "Four Quartets"

JOSEPH BEAVER, *The Explicator,* XI (March, 1953), 37.

WILLIAM BISSETT, "The Argument of T. S. Eliot's *Four Quartets,*" *The University of Toronto Quarterly,* XV (Jan., 1946), 115-126.

R. P. BLACKMUR, "Unappeasable and Peregrine: Behavior and the 'Four Quartets,' " *Thought,* XXVI (Spring, 1951), 50-76.

BLACKMUR, *Language as Gesture,* pp. 193-220.

BOWRA, *The Creative Experiment,* pp. 22-23.

JOHN M. BRADBURY, *"Four Quartets*: The Structural Symbolism," *The Sewanee Review,* LIX (Spring, 1951), 254-270.

CURTIS B. BRADSFORD, "Journeys to Byzantium," *Virginia Quarterly Review,* XXV (Spring, 1949), 216-224.

DONALD DAVIE, "T. S. Eliot: The End of an Era," *Twentieth Century,* CLIX (April, 1956), 350-362.

DEUTSCH, *Poetry in Our Time,* pp. 164-167, 170-172, 177-180.

ARNOLD P. DREW, "Hints and Guesses in *Four Quartets,*" *The University of Kansas City Review,* XX (Spring, 1954), 171-175.

R. W. FLINT, "The 'Four Quartets' Reconsidered," *The Sewanee Review,* LVI (Winter, 1948), 69-81.

JOSEPH FRANK, "Force and Form: A Study of John Peale Bishop," *The Sewanee Review,* LV (Winter, 1947), 102-103.

FRANKENBERG, *Pleasure Dome,* pp. 98-117.

FRIAR and BRINNIN, *Modern Poetry,* pp. 426-427, 459-461.

B. H. FUSSELL, "Structural Methods in *Four Quartets,*" *Journal of English Literary History,* XXII (Sept., 1955), 212-241..

PAUL FUSSELL, JR., "The Gestic Symbolism of T. S. Eliot," *Journal of English Literary History,* XXII (Sept., 1955), 201-208.

HELEN L. GARDNER, " 'Four Quartets': A Commentary." Reprinted *Critiques,* pp. 181-197.

SISTER MARY GERARD, "Eliot of the Circle and John of Cross," *Thought,* XXXIV (Spring, 1959), 107-127.

HARVEY GROSS, "Music and the Analogue of Feeling: Notes on Eliot and Beethoven," *The Centennial Review,* III (Summer, 1959), 276-277, 282-288.

GEORGE A. KNOX, "Quest for the Word in Eliot's

Four Quartets," Journal of English Literary History, XVIII (Dec., 1951), 310-321.

JAMES E. MILLER, JR., "Whitman and Eliot: The Poetry of Mysticism," *Southwest Review*, XLIII (Spring, 1958), 114-123.

ARTHUR MIZENER, "To Meet Mr. Eliot," *The Sewanee Review*, LXV (Winter, 1957), 45-49.

DE SOLA PINTO, *Crisis in English Poetry*, pp. 180-184.

QUINN, *The Metamorphic Tradition*, pp. 143-147.

T. B. SHEPHERD, "The *Four Quartets* Re-examined," *The London Quarterly and Holborn Review*, CLXXV (July, 1950), 228-239.

GORDON SYMES, "T. S. Eliot and Old Age," *Fortnightly*, CLXIX (March, 1951), 192-193.

ROBERT D. WAGNER, "The Meaning of Eliot's Rose Garden," *PMLA*, LXIX (March, 1954), 22-33.

WATTS, *Hound and Quarry*, pp. 226-238.

MORRIS WEITZ, "T. S. Eliot: Time as a Mode of Salvation," *The Sewanee Review*, LX (Winter, 1952), 49-52, 55-64.

WHEELWRIGHT, *The Burning Fountain*, pp. 332-336, 350 364.

ELIOT,   "Gerontion"

R. P. BLACKMUR, "T. S. Eliot," *Hound and Horn*, I (March, 1928), 201-203.

ALEC BROWN, "The Lyric Impulse in the Poetry of T. S. Eliot," *Scrutinies*, II, 7-12.

ROBERT M. BROWN and JOSEPH B. YOKELSON, *The Explicator*, XV (Feb., 1957), 31.

TAYLOR CULBERT, *The Explicator*, XVII (Dec., 1958), 20.

DAICHES and CHARVAT, *Poems in English*, pp. 738-740.

DAVID DAICHES, "Some Aspects of T. S. Eliot," *College English*, IX (Dec., 1947), 117-120.

DOUGLAS, LAMSON, SMITH, *The Critical Reader*, pp. 125-130.

DREW and SWEENEY, *Directions in Modern Poetry,* pp. 42-44.

WILLIAM R. ESHELMAN, *The Explicator,* IV (April, 1946), 44.

FRANKENBERG, *Pleasure Dome,* pp. 51-56.

FRIAR and BRINNIN, *Modern Poetry,* pp. 497-498.

HARVEY GROSS, "*Gerontion* and the Meaning of History," *PMLA,* LXXIII (June, 1958), 299-304.

LEAVIS, *New Bearings on English Poetry,* pp. 79-87.

MAYNARD MACK, LEONARD DEAN, and WILLIAM FROST, *English Masterpieces,* Vol. VII, *Modern Poetry,* p. 22.

JOHN M. MAJOR, "Eliot's 'Gerontion' and *As You Like It,*" *MLN,* LXXIV (Jan., 1959), 29-31.

ARTHUR MIZENER, "To Meet Mr. Eliot," *The Sewanee Review,* LXV (Winter, 1957), 42-44.

MYRTLE P. POPE, *The Explicator,* VI (May, 1948), Q16.

FREDERICK A. POTTLE, *The Explicator,* IV (June, 1946), 55.

ROSENTHAL and SMITH, *Exploring Poetry,* pp. 638-644.

GROVER SMITH, *The Explicator,* VII (Feb., 1949), 26.

GORDON SYMES, "T. S. Eliot and Old Age," *Fortnightly,* CLXIX (March, 1951), 189-190.

LEONARD UNGER, "T. S. Eliot's Rose Garden: a Persistent Theme," *The Southern Review,* VII (Spring, 1942), 672-673.

UNGER, *The Man in the Name,* pp. 172-173.

SHERNA S. VINOGRAD, "The Accidental: A Clue to Structure in Eliot's Poetry," *Accent,* IX (Summer, 1949), 233-235.

WHEELWRIGHT, *The Burning Fountain,* pp. 336-338.

MERVYN W. WILLIAMSON, "T. S. Eliot's 'Gerontion,' " *University of Texas Studies in English,* XXXVI (1957), 111-126.

Jane Worthington, "The Epigraphs to the Poetry of T. S. Eliot," *American Literature*, XXI (March, 1949), 5-6.

ELIOT,   "Gus: The Theatre Cat"

Priscilla Preston, "A Note on T. S. Eliot and Sherlock Holmes," *Modern Language Review*, LIV (Oct., 1959), 399.

ELIOT,   "The Hippopotamus"

Herbert Marshall McLuhan, *The Explicator*, II (May, 1944), 50.

Christine Meyer, *The Explicator*, VIII (Oct., 1949), 6.

Francis Lee Utley, *The Explicator*, III (Nov., 1944), 10.

Jane Worthington, "The Epigraphs to the Poetry of T. S. Eliot," *American Literature*, XXI (March, 1949), 10-11.

ELIOT,   "The Hollow Men"

R. P. Blackmur, "T. S. Eliot," *Hound and Horn*, I (March, 1928), 203-205.

Drew and Sweeney, *Directions in Modern Poetry*, pp. 134-136.

Genevieve W. Foster, "Archetypal Imagery of T. S. Eliot," *PMLA*, LX (June, 1945), 576-578.

Paul Fussell, Jr., "The Gestic Symbolism of T. S. Eliot," *Journal of English Literary History*, XXII (Sept., 1955), 198-201, 203.

Robert S. Kinsman, *The Explicator*, VIII (April, 1950), 48.

Gordon Symes, "T. S. Eliot and Old Age," *Fortnightly*, CLXIX (March 1951), 191-192.

John B. Vickery, "Eliot's Poetry: The Quest and the Way," (Part I), *Renascence*, X (Autumn, 1957), 8-9.

Jane Worthington, "The Epigraphs to the Poetry of T. S. Eliot," *American Literature*, XXI (March, 1949), 14-15.

ELIOT,   "Journey of the Magi"

DREW, *Poetry*, pp. 237-240.

GENEVIEVE W. FOSTER, "Archetypal Imagery of T. S. Eliot," *PMLA*, LX (June, 1945), 578-580.

JOHN HOWARD WILLS, *The Explicator*, XII (March, 1954), 32.

ELIOT,   "Little Gidding"

F. O. MATTHIESSEN, "Eliot's Quartets," *The Kenyon Review*, V (Spring, 1943), 173-175.

ROSENTHAL and SMITH, *Exploring Poetry*, pp. 696-704.

JOHN SHAND, "Around 'Little Gidding,' " *The Nineteenth Century and After*, CXXXVI (Sept., 1944), 120-132.

JAMES JOHNSON SWEENEY, "Little Gidding: Introductory to a Reading," *Poetry*, LXII (July, 1943), 216-223.

ELIOT,   "The Love Song of J. Alfred Prufrock"

ADAMS, *Strains of Discord*, pp. 112-113.

RUSSELL AMES, "Decadence in the Art of T. S. Eliot," *Science and Society*, XVI (Summer, 1952), 198-221.

ROY P. BASLER, "Psychological Pattern in 'The Love Song of J. Alfred Prufrock,' " *Twentieth Century English*, 1946, pp. 384-400.

BASLER, *Sex, Symbolism, and Psychology in Literature*, pp. 203-221.

R.P. BLACKMUR, "T. S. Eliot," *Hound and Horn*, I (March, 1928), 209-212.

MARGARET MORTON BLUM, "The Fool in 'The Love Song of J. Alfred Prufrock,' " *MLN*, LXXII (June, 1957), 424-426.

BROOKS and WARREN, *Understanding Poetry*, pp. 589-596.

Revised edition, pp. 433-444.

Reprinted Stallman and Watters, *The Creative Reader*, pp. 881-885.

R. G. COLLINGWOOD, *The Principles of Art* (Oxford:

Oxford University Press, 1938), pp. 310-311.

DANIEL N. DWYER, S.J., *The Explicator,* IX (March, 1951), 38.

PAUL ENGLE, Engle and Carrier, *Reading Modern Poetry,* pp. 167-174.

PAUL ENGLE, "Why Modern Poetry," *College English,* XV (October, 1953), 8.

CLIFFORD J. FISH, *The Explicator,* VIII (June, 1950), 62.

FRANKENBERG, *Pleasure Dome,* pp. 40-42, 45-49.

HUGH KENNER, "Prufrock of St. Louis," *The Prairie Schooner,* XXXI (Spring, 1957), 24-30.

LANGBAUM, *The Poetry of Experience,* pp. 189-192, 197, 200-202.

JOSEPH MARGOLIS, *Interpretations,* John Wain, ed., pp. 183-193.

JOHN C. POPE, "Prufrock and Raskolnikov," *American Literature,* XVII (Nov., 1945), 213-230; XVIII (Jan., 1947), 319-321.

LYALL H. POWERS, *The Explicator,* XIV (March, 1956), 39.

ROSENTHAL and SMITH, *Exploring Poetry,* pp. 376-377.

C. M. SHANAHAN, "Irony in LaForgue, Corbière, and Eliot," *Modern Philology,* LIII (Nov., 1955), 119.

GORDON SYMES, "T. S. Eliot and Old Age," *Fortnightly,* CLXIX (March, 1951), 188-189.

THOMAS and BROWN, *Reading Poems: An Introduction to Critical Study,* pp. 698-700.

TSCHUMI, *Thought in Twentieth-Century English Poetry,* pp. 127-132.

W. A. TURNER, "The Not So Coy Mistress of J. Alfred Prufrock," *South Atlantic Quarterly,* LIV (Oct., 1955), 516-522.

JOHN VIRTUE, *The Explicator,* XIII (Nov., 1954), 10.

CHARLES C. WALCUTT, "Eliot's 'The Love Song of J. Alfred Prufrock,'" *College English,* XIX (Nov., 1957), 71-72.

ARTHUR E. WATERMAN, *The Explicator,* XVII (June, 1959), 67.

WEITZ, *Philosophy of the Arts,* pp. 94-107, 145.

MORRIS WEITZ, "T. S. Eliot: Time .as a Mode of Salvation," *The Sewanee Review,* LX (Winter, 1952), 53-54.

ARTHUR WORMHOUDT, "A Psychoanalytic Interpretation of 'The Love Song of J. Alfred Prufrock,'" *Perspective,* II (Winter, 1949), 109-117.

JANE WORTHINGTON, "The Epigraphs to the Poetry of T. S. Eliot," *American Literature,* XXI (March, 1949), 1-2.

ELIOT, "Macavity: The Mystery Cat"

PRISCILLA PRESTON, "A Note on T. S. Eliot and Sherlock Holmes," *Modern Language Review,* LIV (Oct., 1959), 398-399.

ELIOT, "Marina"

DAICHES and CHARVAT, *Poems in English,* p. 741.

DEUTSCH, *Poetry in Our Time,* p. 175.

GENEVIEVE W. FOSTER, "Archetypal Imagery of T. S. Eliot," *PMLA,* LX (June, 1945), 582-583.

LEAVIS, *New Bearings on English Poetry,* pp. 129-131.

F. R. LEAVIS, "Eliot's Later Poetry," Scrutiny, XI (Summer, 1942), 61-63.

LEAVIS, *Education and the University,* pp. 90-92.

JANE WORTHINGTON, "The Epigraphs to the Poetry of T. S. Eliot," *American Literature,* XXI (March, 1949), 15-16.

ELIOT, "Mr. Apollinax"

ALEC BROWN, "The Lyric Impulse in the Poetry of T. S. Eliot," *Scrutinies,* II, 29-31.

JANE WORTHINGTON, "The Epigraphs to the Poetry of T. S. Eliot," *American Literature,* XXI (March, 1949), 3-4.

ELIOT, "Mr. Eliot's Sunday Morning Service"

ORVID SHULENBERGER, *The Explicator,* X (Feb., 1952), 29.

JANE WORTHINGTON, "The Epigraphs to the Poetry of T. S. Eliot," *American Literature,* XXI (March, 1949), 11-12.

ELIOT,   "Portrait of a Lady"

RICHARD J. GIANNONE, "Eliot's 'Portrait of a Lady' and Pound's 'Portrait d'une Femme,'" *Twentieth Century Literature,* V (Oct., 1959), 131-134.

C. M. SHANAHAN, "Irony in LaForgue, Corbiére, and Eliot," *Modern Philology,* LIII (Nov., 1955), 123-124.

W. A. TURNER, "The Not So Coy Mistress of J. Alfred Prufrock," *South Atlantic Quarterly,* LIV (Oct., 1955), 517-518.

JANE WORTHINGTON, "The Epigraphs to the Poetry of T. S. Eliot," *American Literature,* XXI (March, 1949), 2-3.

ELIOT,   "Rhapsody on a Windy Night"

CLEANTH BROOKS and ROBERT PENN WARREN, "The Reading of Modern Poetry," *The American Review,* VII (Feb., 1937), 442-445.

ELIOT,   "A Song for Simeon"

HUGH KENNER, "Eliot's Moral Dialectic, " *The Hudson Review,* II (Autumn, 1949), 424-428.

ELIOT,   "Sweeney Agonistes"

MORRIS FREEDMAN, "Jazz Rhythms and T. S. Eliot," *South Atlantic Quarterly,* LI (July, 1952), 420-423, 428-432.

MORRIS FREEDMAN, "The Meaning of T. S. Eliot's Jew," *South Atlantic Quarterly,* LV (April, 1956), 200-201.

SEARS JAYNE, "Mr. Eliot's Agon," *Philological Quarterly,* XXXIV (Oct., 1955), 395-414.

ELIOT,   "Sweeney Among the Nightingales"

DEUTSCH, *Poetry in Our Time,* pp. 168-170.

ELIZABETH DREW, abridged in *The Case for Poetry,* pp. 133-135 from *T. S. Eliot: The Design of His Poetry* (New York: Charles Scribner's Sons, 1949), pp. 44-46.

ELIZABETH RUDISILL HOMANN, *The Explicator*, XVII (Feb., 1959) , 34.

CHARLES KAPLAN, "Eliot Among the Nightingales: Fair and Foul," *New Mexico Quarterly Review*, XXIV (Summer, 1954) , 228.

LEO KERSCHBAUM and ROY P. BASLER, *The Explicator*, II (Dec., 1943), 18.

STAUFFER, *The Nature of Poetry*, pp. 78-80. Abridged in *The Case for Poetry*, p. 135.

CHARLES C. WALCUTT, *The Explicator*, II (April, 1944), 48.

GEORGE WILLIAMSON, abridged in *The Case for Poetry*, p. 133 from *A Reader's Guide to T. S. Eliot* (New York: The Noonday Press, 1953) , pp. 97-98.

JANE WORTHINGTON, "The Epigraphs to the Poetry of T. S. Eliot," *American Literature*, XXI (March, 1949), 13.

ELIOT,   "Sweeney Erect"

ARTHUR MIZENER, "To Meet Mr. Eliot," *The Sewanee Review*, LXV (Winter, 1957) , 41-42.

JANE WORTHINGTON, "The Epigraphs to the Poetry of T. S. Eliot," *American Literature*, XXI (March, 1949), 7-9.

ELIOT,   "Triumphal March" (from the unfinished *Coriolan*)

DANIELS, *The Art of Reading Poetry*, pp. 406-409.

F. R. LEAVIS, "Eliot's Later Poetry," *Scrutiny*, XI (Summer, 1942), 63-64.

LEAVIS, *Education and the University*, pp. 92-93.

ELIOT,   "The Waste Land"

JOHN ROSS BAKER, *The Explicator*, XIV (Jan., 1956) , 27.

BELGION, *Reading for Profit*, pp. 258-286, *passim*.

A. F. BERINGAUSE, "Journey through *The Waste Land*," *South Atlantic Quarterly*, LVI (Jan., 1957) , 79-90.

R. P. BLACKMUR, "T. S. Eliot," *Hound and Horn,* I (March, 1928), 190-196.

BODKIN, *Archetypal Patterns in Poetry,* pp. 310-315.

BOWRA, *The Creative Experiment,* pp. 159-188.

CLEANTH BROOKS, JR., "The Waste Land: An Analysis," *The Southern Review,* III (Summer, 1937), 106-136.

Reprinted Brooks and Warren, *Understanding Poetry,* revised edition, pp. 645-667.

ALEC BROWN, "The Lyric Impulse in the Poetry of T. S. Eliot," *Scrutinies,* II, 34-48.

RICHARD CHASE, "The Sense of the Present," *The Kenyon Review,* VII (Spring, 1945), 225-231.

DAICHES, *The Place of Meaning in Poetry,* pp. 49-55.

ROBERT GORHAM DAVIS, *et al.,* "The New Criticism," *American Scholar,* XX (Spring, 1951), 225-226.

DEUTSCH, *Poetry in Our Time,* pp. 160-164.

DEUTSCH, *This Modern Poetry,* pp. 118-127.

DREW and SWEENEY, *Directions in Modern Poetry,* pp. 40-44 *et passim.*

GENEVIEVE W. FOSTER, "Archetypal Imagery of T. S. Eliot," *PMLA,* LX (June, 1945), 571-576.

D. C. FOWLER, "*The Wasteland*: Mr. Eliot's 'Fragments,'" *College English,* XIV (Jan., 1953), 234-235.

FRANKENBERG, *Pleasure Dome,* pp. 64-77.

FRIAR and BRINNIN, *Modern Poetry,* pp. 425-426, 472-497.

PAUL FUSSELL, JR., "The Gestic Symbolism of T. S. Eliot," *Journal of English Literary History,* XXII (Sept., 1955), 194-211, *passim.*

HOFFMAN, *The Twenties,* pp. 291-303.

LEAVIS, *New Bearings in English Poetry,* pp. 90-114.

MAYNARD MACK, LEONARD DEAN, and WILLIAM FROST, *English Masterpieces,* Vol. VII, *Modern Poetry,* p. 21.

FLORENCE MARSH, "The Desert-Ocean: 'The Ancient

Mariner' and 'The Waste Land,'" *Essays in Criticism,* IX (April, 1959), 126-133.

WILLIAM H. MARSHALL, *The Explicator,* XVII (March, 1959), 42.

GIORGIO MELCHIORI, "Echoes in *The Waste Land,*" *English Studies,* XXXII (Feb., 1951), 1-11.

CHARLES MOORMAN, "Myth and Organic Unity in *The Waste Land,*" *South Atlantic Quarterly,* LVII (Spring, 1958), 194-203.

L. K. MORRIS, "Marie, Marie, Hold on Tight," *Partisan Review,* XXI (March-April, 1954), 231-233.

PALMER, *Post-Victorian Poetry,* pp. 312-322.

DE SOLA PINTO, *Crisis in English Poetry,* pp. 170-174.

QUINN, *The Metamorphic Tradition,* pp. 130-142.

JOHN CROWE RANSOM, "The Inorganic Muses," *The Kenyon Review,* V (Spring, 1943), 298-300.

RIDING and GRAVES, *A Survey of Modernist Poetry,* pp. 50-58 *et passim.*

HARRY M. SCHWALB, *The Explicator,* XI (April, 1953), 46.

DELMORE SCHWARTZ, "T. S. Eliot as the International Hero," *Partisan Review,* XII (Spring, 1945), 200-206.

SCOTT, *Rehearsals of Discomposure,* pp. 203-225.

C. M. SHANAHAN, "Irony in LaForgue, Corbiére, and Eliot," *Modern Philology,* LIII (Nov., 1955), 125-127.

IRENE SIMON, "Echoes in 'The Waste Land,'" *English Studies,* XXXIV (April, 1953), 64-72.

THEODORE SPENCER, "The Poetry of T. S. Eliot," *Atlantic Monthly,* CLI (Jan., 1933), 64-65.

TATE, *On the Limits of Poetry,* pp. 299-302, 344-345. First published in *Hound and Horn* and *The American Review.*

THOMAS and BROWN, *Reading Poems: An Introduction to Critical Study,* pp. 716-731, 749-751.

TSCHUMI, *Thought in Twentieth-Century English Poetry,* pp. 132-144.

JOHN B. VICKERY, "Eliot's Poetry: The Quest and the Way," (Part I), *Renascence*, X (Autumn, 1957), 5-8.

HELEN WATSON-WILLIAMS, "The Blackened Wall: Notes on Blake's 'London' and Eliot's 'The Waste Land,'" *English*, X (Summer), 181-184.

WHEELWRIGHT, *The Burning Fountain*, pp. 338-351.

GEORGE WILLIAMSON, "The Structure of *The Waste Land*," *Modern Philology*, XLVII (Feb., 1950), 191-206.

EDMUND WILSON, *Axel's Castle*, pp. 104-111. Reprinted *Literary Opinion in America*, pp. 186-193.

Revised edition, pp. 213-218.

WINTERS, *The Anatomy of Nonsense*, pp. 162-167. Also *In Defense of Reason*, pp. 497-501.

JANE WORTHINGTON, "The Epigraphs to the Poetry of T. S. Eliot," *American Literature*, XXI (March, 1949), 13-14.

ELIOT,   "The Waste Land I, The Burial of the Dead"

LYMAN A. COTTEN, *The Explicator*, IX (Oct., 1950), 7.

LYLE GLAZIER, *The Explicator*, VIII (Feb., 1950), 26.

LYSANDER KEMP, *The Explicator*, VII (June, 1949), 60.

LYSANDER KEMP, *The Explicator*, VIII (Feb., 1950), 27.

ELEANOR M. SICKELS, *The Explicator*, IX (Oct., 1950), 4.

RAY SMITH, *The Explicator*, IX (Oct., 1950), 8.

WILLIE T. WEATHERS, *The Explicator*, IX (Feb., 1951), 31.

ELIOT,   "The Waste Land II, A Game of Chess"

ELIZABETH DREW, *Discovering Poetry*, pp. 119-120.

EMPSON, *Seven Types of Ambiguity* (1947 ed.), pp. 77-78.

ELEANOR M. SICKELS, *The Explicator*, VII (Dec., 1948), 20.

ELIOT,   "The Waste Land IV, Death by Water"

GROVER SMITH, "Observations on Eliot's 'Death by

Water,'" *Accent,* VI (Summer, 1946), 257-263.

ELIOT,   "The Waste Land V, What the Thunder Said"
R. P. BLACKMUR, "T. S. Eliot," *Hound and Horn,* I (March, 1928), 197-201.

ELIOT,   "Whispers of Immortality"
R. P. BLACKMUR, "T. S. Eliot," *Hound and Horn,* I (March, 1928), 207-208.
EMPSON, *Seven Types of Ambiguity,* (1947 ed.), pp. 78-79.
SISTER M. CLEOPHAS, R. S. M., *The Explicator,* VIII (Dec., 1949), 22.
VICTOR STRANDBERG, *The Explicator,* XVII (May, 1959), 53.
CHARLES C. WALCUTT, *The Explicator,* VII (Nov., 1948), 11.

EMERSON,   "The Bohemian Hymn"
RICHARD E. AMACHER, *The Explicator,* V (June, 1947), 55.
ERIC W. CARLSON, "Emerson's 'The Bohemian Hymn,'" *Emerson Society Quarterly,* VI (First Quarter, 1957), pp. 6-7.

EMERSON,   "Brahma"
ROBERT FROST, "A Poet, Too, Must Learn the Magic Way of Poetry," *N.Y. Times* (March 21, 1954), p. 1
RICHARD GREENLEAF, "Emerson and Wordsworth," *Science and Society,* XXII (Summer, 1958), 229.
VAN DOREN, *Introduction to Poetry,* pp. 90-93.

EMERSON,   "Concord Hymn"
GEORGE ARMS, *The Explicator,* I (Dec., 1942), 23.

EMERSON,   "Days"
GEORGE ARMS, *The Explicator,* IV (Nov., 1945), 8. Abridged in *The Case for Poetry,* p. 140.
EDWARD G. FLETCHER, *The Explicator,* V (April, 1947), 41.
SEYMOUR L. GROSS, "Emerson and Poetry," *South Atlantic Quarterly,* LIV (Jan., 1955), 93-94.
JOSEPH JONES, *The Explicator,* IV (April, 1946), 47.

Abridged in *The Case for Poetry,* p. 140.
KIRK and MCCUTCHEON, *An Introduction to the Study of Poetry,* pp. 35-36.
Abridged in *The Case for Poetry,* p. 139.
MATTHIESSEN, *American Renaissance,* pp. 59-60.
EMERSON,   "Each and All"
WALTER BLAIR and CLARENCE FAUST, "Emerson's Literary Method," *Modern Philology,* XLII (Nov., 1944), 89-91.
S. L. GROSS, "Emerson and Poetry," *South Atlantic Quarterly,* LIV (Jan., 1955), 89-91.
EMERSON,   "The Rhodora"
S. L. GROSS, "Emerson and Poetry," *South Atlantic Quarterly,* LIV (Jan., 1955), 91-93.
MATTHIESSEN, *American Renaissance,* pp. 49-50.
EMERSON,   "The Snow-Storm"
MATTHIESSEN, *American Renaissance,* pp. 138-139.
Reprinted Stageberg and Anderson, *Poetry as Experience,* pp. 485-486.
EMERSON,   "The Sphinx"
THOMAS R. WHITAKER, "The Riddle of Emerson's 'Sphinx,'" *American Literature,* XXVII (May, 1955), 179-195.
EMERSON,   "'Terminus"
AUGUST H. MASON, *The Explicator,* IV (March, 1946), 37.
EMERSON,   "Threnody"
WALTER BLAIR and CLARENCE FAUST, "Emerson's Literary Method," *Modern Philology,* XLII (Nov., 1944), 91-95.
N. A. BRITTIN, "Emerson and the Metaphysical Poets," *American Literature,* VIII (March, 1936), 15.
EMPSON,   "Flighting for Duck"
WILLIAM EMPSON in Friar and Brinnin, *Modern Poetry,* p. 499.
EMPSON,   "Four Legs, Two Legs, Three Legs"
WILLIAM EMPSON in Friar and Brinnin, *Modern*

Poetry, p. 499. Reprinted from *The Gathering Storm* (London: Faber and Faber, 1940), pp. 63-64
WILLIAM L. HEDGES, "The Empson Treatment," *Accent*, XVII (Autumn, 1957), 231-241.

EMPSON, "Let It Go"
ANONYMOUS, "Not Wrongly Moved . . ." *Times Literary Supplement* (Oct. 7, 1955), p. 588.

EMPSON, "Missing Dates"
DREW, *Poetry*, pp. 138-140.
WILLIAM EMPSON in Friar and Brinnin, *Modern Poetry*, pp. 498-499.
ROBERT D. SPECTOR, "Form and Content in Empson's 'Missing Dates,' " *MLN*, LXXIV (April, 1959), 310-311.

EMPSON, "The Teasers"
G. S. FRASER, *Interpretations*, John Wain, ed., pp. 225-234.

EMPSON, "This Last Pain"
RICHARD EBERHART, "Empson's Poetry," *Accent*, IV (Summer, 1944), 203-206.

EMPSON, "Legal Fiction"
DREW and SWEENEY, *Directions in Modern Poetry*, pp. 204-207.

EMPSON, "Note on Local Flora"
DREW and SWEENEY, *Directions in Modern Poetry*, pp. 81-83 (quoting Empson's own explanation).

EMPSON, "Ufa Nightmare"
RICHARD EBERHART, "Empson's Poetry," *Accent*, IV (Summer, 1944), 199-200.

FEARING, "The Face in the Bar Room Mirror"
J. F. NIMS, *Poetry: A Critical Supplement*, Oct., 1947, pp. 16-17.

FEARING, "Green Light"
MACHA ROSENTHAL, "The Meaning of Kenneth Fearing's Poetry," *Poetry*, LXIV (July, 1944), 211-212.

FEARING, "Obituary"

MACHA ROSENTHAL, "The Meaning of Kenneth Fearing's Poetry," *Poetry*, LXIV (July, 1944), 214.

FEARING,   "Radio Blues"
MACHA ROSENTHAL, "The Meaning of Kenneth Fearing's Poetry," *Poetry*, LXIV (July, 1944), 220.

FEARING,   "What if Mr. Jesse James Should Someday Die?"
MACHA ROSENTHAL, "The Meaning of Kenneth Fearing's Poetry," *Poetry*, LXIV (July, 1944), 214-215.

FEARING,   "Yes, the Serial Will Be Continued"
WALTER GIERASCH, "Reading Modern Poetry," *College English*, II (Oct., 1940), 34-35.

FERGUSSON,   "Auld Reekie"
DAVID DAICHES, "Eighteenth-Century Vernacular Poetry," *Scottish Poetry: A Critical Survey*, pp. 183-184.

FERGUSSON,   "The Daft-Days"
DAVID DAICHES, "Eighteenth-Century Vernacular Poetry,," *Scottish Poetry: A Critical Survey*, pp. 172-173.

FERGUSSON,   "The Farmer's Ingle"
DAVID DAICHES, "Eighteenth-Century Vernacular Poetry," *Scottish Poetry: A Critical Survey*, pp. 180-181.

FERGUSSON,   "The King's Birthday in Edinburgh"
DAVID DAICHES, "Eighteenth-Century Vernacular Poetry," *Scottish Poetry: A Critical Survey*, pp. 175-176.

FIELDS, JAMES T.,   "The Captain's Daughter"
DANIELS, *The Art of Reading Poetry*, pp. 85-88.

FINCH, ANNE, COUNTESS OF WINCHELSEA,   "An Affliction"
REUBEN A. BROWER, "Lady Winchelsea and the Poetic Tradition of the Seventeenth Century," *Studies in Philology*, XLII (Jan., 1945), 65-66.

FLETCHER, GILES,   "Christ's Victory and Triumph"
ROSENTHAL and SMITH, *Exploring Poetry*, pp. 507-509.

FRANCIS, ROBERT,   "The Big Tent"

J. F. Nims, *A Critical Supplement to "Poetry,"* Nov., 1948, pp. 17-18.

FRANKENBERG, "I Lazarus"
Nelson Algren, "Lloyd Frankenberg's Poems," *Poetry,* LVI (April, 1940), 47-48.

FRENEAU, "The Indian Burying Ground"
George Arms, *The Explicator,* II (May, 1944), 55.

FROST, frances, "Cradle Song"
John Cardi, "Sensitivity Without Discipline," *Nation,* CLXXIX (Dec. 4, 1954), 490-492.

FROST, "Acquainted with the Night"
Malcolm Brown, "The Sweet Crystalline Cry," *Western Review,* XVI (Summer, 1952), 266.

FROST, "After Apple Picking"
Brooks, *Modern Poetry and the Tradition,* pp. 114-116.

Brooks and Warren, *Understanding Poetry,* revised edition, pp. 389-397.

Cardwell, *Readings, from the Americas,* pp. 776-777.
Reginald L. Cook, "Frost as a Parablist," *Accent,* X (Autumn, 1949), 36.

FROST, "The Bear"
H. H. Watts, "Robert Frost and the Interrupted Dialogue," *American Literature,* XXVII (March, 1955), 76-77.

Winters, *The Function of Criticism,* pp. 166-167.

FROST, "Brown's Descent"
Walter Gierasch, *The Explicator,* XI (June, 1953), 60.

FROST, "Come In"
Deutsch, *Poetry in Our Time,* pp. 75-76.
Robert Ornstein, *The Explicator,* XV (June, 1957), 61.

FROST, "The Death of the Hired Man"
C. M. Bowra, "Reassessments I: Robert Frost," *Adelphi,* XXVII (Nov., 1950), 46-64.

Robert P. Tristram Coffin, (Review), *American Literature,* XIV (Jan., 1943), 438-439.

C. C. Cunningham, *Literature as a Fine Art: Analysis and Interpretation,* pp. 106-110.

Bess C. Hopkins, "A Study of 'The Death of the Hired Man,'" *The English Journal,* XLIII (April, 1954), 175-176.

Charles C. Walcutt, *The Explicator,* III (Oct., 1944), 7.

FROST,   "The Demiurge's Laugh"

Walter Blair, *The Literature of the United States,* II, 933.

FROST,   "Desert Places"

R. P. Blackmur, "The Instincts of a Bard," *Nation,* CXLII (June 24, 1936), 819.

Brooks and Warren, *Understanding Poetry,* pp. 193-194.

Revised edition, pp. 87-88.

W. C. Brown, "'A Poem Should Not Mean But Be,'" *The University of Kansas City Review,* XV (Autumn, 1948), 62-63.

FROST,   "Design"

Drew, *Poetry,* pp. 186-188.

Randall Jarrell, "To the Laodiceans," *The Kenyon Review,* XIV (Autumn, 1952), 543-545.

FROST,   "Devotion"

Walter Gierasch, *The Explicator,* X (May, 1952), 50.

FROST,   "Directive"

James M. Cox, "Robert Frost and the Edge of the Clearing," *Virginia Quarterly Review,* XXXV (Winter, 1959), 85-87.

Deutsch, *Poetry in Our Time,* p. 75.

Drew, *Poetry,* pp. 229-233.

Mildred E. Hartsock, *The Explicator,* XVI (April, 1958), 42.

FROST,   "The Discovery of the Madeiras"

YVOR WINTERS, "Robert Frost: Or, The Spiritual Drifter as Poet," *The Sewanee Review*, LVI (Autumn, 1948), 593-594.

Reprinted *The Function of Criticism*, pp. 184-185.

FROST,   "The Egg and the Machine"
YVOR WINTERS, "Robert Frost: Or, The Spiritual Drifter as Poet," *The Sewanee Review*, LVI (Autumn, 1948), 577-578.

Reprinted *The Function of Criticism*, pp. 170-171.

Reprinted Zabel, *Literary Opinion in America*, revised edition, pp. 425-426.

FROST,   "For Once, Then, Something"
DAN G. HOFFMAN, *The Explicator*, IX (Nov., 1950), 17.

FROST,   "The Gift Outright"
KREUZER, *Elements of Poetry*, pp. 154-155.

FROST,   "The Grindstone"
REGINALD L. COOK, "Frost as Parablist," *Accent*, X (Autumn, 1949), 37-38.

FROST,   "Happiness Makes up in Height"
W. G. O'DONNELL, "Robert Frost and New England: A Revaluation," *Yale Review*, XXXVII (Summer, 1948), 698-712.

FROST,   "The Last Mowing"
WALTER GIERASCH, *The Explicator*, X (Feb., 1952), 25.

YVOR WINTERS, "Robert Frost: Or, The Spiritual Drifter as Poet," *The Sewanee Review*, LVI (Autumn, 1948), 589-590.

Reprinted *The Function of Criticism*, pp. 181-182.

Reprinted Zabel, *Literary Opinion in America*, revised edition, pp. 434-435.

FROST,   "The Lesson for Today"
YVOR WINTERS, "Robert Frost: Or, The Spiritual Drifter as Poet," *The Sewanee Review*, LVI (Autumn, 1948), 585-586.

Reprinted *The Function of Criticism,* pp. 177-178.
Reprinted Zabel, *Literary Opinion in America,* revised edition, pp. 431-432.

FROST, "A Lone Striker"

FREDERICK L. GWYNN, "Poetry Crisis at Corning," *College English Association Critic,* XV (Dec., 1953), 1, 3.

HAROLD H. WATTS, "Robert Frost and the Interrupted Dialogue," *American Literature,* XXVII (March, 1955), 77-78.

FROST, "The Lovely Shall Be Choosers"

ELIZABETH NITCHIE, *The Explicator,* XIII (April, 1955), 39.

EDWARD SCHWARTZ, *The Explicator,* XIII (Oct., 1954), 3.

W. L. WERNER, *The Explicator,* XIII (April, 1955), 39.

FROST, "A Masque of Mercy"

SISTER MARY JEREMY FINNEGAN, O.P., "Frost's *Masque of Mercy,*" *Catholic World,* CLXXXVI (Feb., 1958), 358-361.

FROST, "Meeting and Passing"

THOMAS SHALVEY, S.J., "Valery and Frost: Two Views of Subjective Reality," *Renascence,* XI (Summer, 1959), 188.

FROST, "Mending Wall"

JOSEPH WARREN BEACH, "Robert Frost," *Yale Review,* XLIII (Winter, 1953), 210-211.

JOHN C. BRODERICK, *The Explicator,* XIV (Jan., 1956), 24.

DEUTSCH, *This Modern Poetry,* pp. 42-44.

MARION MONTGOMERY, "Robert Frost and His Use of Barriers: Man vs. Nature Toward God," *South Atlantic Quarterly,* LVII (Summer, 1958), 349-350.

ROSENTHAL and SMITH, *Exploring Poetry,* pp. 5-6.

THOMAS SHALVEY, S.J., "Valery and Frost: Two Views

of Subjective Reality," *Renascence*, XI (Summer, 1959), 187.

FROST,   "The Most of It"

THOMAS SHALVEY, S.J., "Valery and Frost: Two Views of Subjective Reality," *Renascence*, XI (Summer, 1959), 188.

YVOR WINTERS, "Robert Frost: Or, The Spiritual Drifter as Poet," *The Sewanee Review*, LVI (Autumn, 1948), 591-592.

Reprinted *The Function of Criticism*, pp. 182-183.

Reprinted Zabel, *Literary Opinion in America*, revised edition, pp. 435-436.

FROST,   "Nature's First Green Is Gold"

SOUTHWORTH, *Some Modern American Poets*, pp. 84-85.

FROST,   "The Need of Being Versed in Country Things"

BROOKS, PURSER, WARREN, *An Approach to Literature*, third edition, pp. 346-347.

FROST,   "Neither Out Far Nor in Deep"

HAROLD H. CORBIN, JR., and CECILIA HENNEL HENDRICKS, *The Explicator*, I (May, 1943), 58.

RANDALL JARRELL, "To the Laodiceans," *Kenyon Review*, XIV (Autumn, 1952), 539-540.

LAURENCE PERRINE, *The Explicator*, VII (April, 1949), 46.

R. W. STALLMAN, "The Position of Poetry Today," *The English Journal*, XLVI (May, 1957), 247-248.

FROST,   "Nothing Gold Can Stay"

WARREN BECK, "Poetry's Chronic Disease," *The English Journal*, XXXIII (Sept., 1944), 363.

WALTER SUTTON, "The Contextualist Dilemma—or Fallacy?" *Journal of Aesthetics and Art Criticism*, XVII (Dec., 1958), 225-226.

FROST,   "October"

SOUTHWORTH, *Some Modern American Poets*, pp. 69-71.

FROST, "Once by the Pacific"
VAN DOREN, *Introduction to Poetry*, pp. 77-80.

FROST, "The Oven Bird"
VAN DOREN, *Introduction to Poetry*, pp. 73-77.

FROST, "The Pasture"
ROD. W. HORTON and LAWRENCE THOMPSON, *The CEA Critic*, XI (Feb., 1949), 4-5.
WILLIAM S. LONG, "Frost," *The CEA Critic*, X (Nov., 1948), 4.

FROST, "Provide, Provide"
RANDALL JARRELL, "To the Laodiceans," *The Kenyon Review*, XIV (Autumn, 1952), 541-542.

FROST, "The Road Not Taken"
DANIELS, *The Art of Reading Poetry*, pp. 347-349.
BEN W. GRIFFITH, JR., *The Explicator*, XII (June, 1954), 55.
SOUTHWORTH, *Some Modern American Poets*, pp. 74-75.

FROST, "The Runaway"
MARK VAN DOREN, "The Permanence of Robert Frost," *American Scholar*, V (Spring, 1936), 190-198.

FROST, "Sand Dunes"
LAURENCE PERRINE, *The Explicator*, XIV (March, 1956), 38.
R. W. STALLMAN, "The Position of Poetry Today," *The English Journal*, XLVI (May, 1957), 246-247.

FROST, "Sitting by a Bush in Broad Sunlight"
HARRY MODEAN CAMPBELL, *The Explicator*, V (Dec., 1946), 18.

FROST, "The Span of Life"
CIARDI, *How Does a Poem Mean?* pp. 994-995.

FROST, "Stopping by Woods on a Snowy Evening"
BLAIR and GERBER, *Better Reading 2: Literature*, pp. 156-157.
CIARDI, *How Does a Poem Mean?* pp. 671-676.

JOHN CIARDI, "Robert Frost: The Way to a Poem," *The Saturday Review,* XLI (April 12, 1958), 13-15, 65. Reprinted *Harbrace College Reader.* Mark Schorer, Phylip Durham, Everett L. Jones, eds., (New York: Harcourt, Brace and Co., 1959), pp. 444-456.

COOPER and HOLMES, *Preface to Poetry,* pp. 605-607. Reprinted *Readings for Liberal Education,* II, 510-512.

Reprinted Stallman and Watters, *The Creative Reader,* pp. 840-842.

Reprinted Engle and Carrier, *Reading Modern Poetry,* pp. 1-4.

Reprinted Locke, Gibson, and Arms, *Introduction to Literature,* third edition, pp. 182-184.

JAMES M. COX, "Robert Frost and the Edge of the Clearing," *Virginia Quarterly Review,* XXXV (Winter, 1959), 82-84.

DANIELS, *The Art of Reading Poetry,* pp. 16-18.

Reprinted Stallman and Watters, *The Creative Reader,* pp. 875-878.

CHARLES A. MCLAUGHLIN, "Two Views of Poetic Unity," *The University of Kansas City Review,* XXII (Summer, 1956), 312-315.

UNGER and O'CONNOR, *Poems for Study,* pp. 597-600.

CHARLES CHILD WALCUTT, "Interpreting the Symbol," *College English,* XIV (May, 1953), 450.

FROST,   "The Subverted Flower"
HOWARD MUNFORD, *The Explicator,* XVII (Jan., 1959), 31.

DONALD B. STAUFFER, *The Explicator,* XV (March, 1957), 38.

FROST,   "To Earthward"
WILBUR S. SCOTT, *The Explicator,* XVI (Jan., 1958), 23.

FROST,   "Tree at My Window"
R. W. STALLMAN, "The Position of Poetry Today," *The English Journal,* XLVI (May, 1957), 248-249.

FROST, "Tuft of Flowers"
 THOMAS SHALVEY, S.J., "Valery and Frost: Two Views of Subjective Reality," *Renascence*, XI (Summer, 1959), 187-188.

FROST, "Two Tramps in Mud-Time"
 WALTER BLAIR, *The Literature of the United States*, II, 940.

 BROOKS, *Modern Poetry and the Tradition*, pp. 112-113.

 CHARLES KAPLAN, *The Explicator*, XII (June, 1954), 51.

 GEORGE F. WHICHER, "Frost at Seventy," *The American Scholar*, XIV (Autumn, 1945), 412-414.

FROST, "The Vanishing Red"
 C. M. BOWRA, "Reassessments I: Robert Frost," *Adelphi*, XXVII (Nov., 1950), 46-64.

FROST, "West-Running Brook"
 JOSEPH WARREN BEACH, "Robert Frost," *Yale Review*, XLIII (Winter, 1953), 212.

 RICHARD D. LORD, "Frost and Cyclicism," *Renascence*, X (Autumn, 1957), 20-25, 31.

 H. H. WATTS, "Robert Frost and the Interrupted Dialogue," *American Literature*, XXVII (March, 1955), 70-74 *passim*.

 H. T. WEBSTER, *The Explicator*, VIII (Feb., 1950), 32.

FROST, "The Woodpile"
 BROOKS, *Modern Poetry and the Tradition*, pp. 113-114.

 BROOKS, PURSER, WARREN, *An Approach to Literature*, pp. 453-454.

 Reprinted third edition, pp. 305-307.

FRY, CHISTOPHER, "Venus Observed"
 ROBERT C. FOX, *The Explicator*, XVI (May, 1958), 47.

GARRIGUE, "Dialog for Belvedere"
 JOSEPH WARREN BEACH, "The Cancelling Out—A

Note on Recent Poetry," *Accent,* VII (Summer, 1947), 246-248.

GASCOIGNE, "Gascoigne's Woodmanship"
YVOR WINTERS, "The 16th Century Lyric in England: Part I," *Poetry,* LIII (Feb., 1939), 269-272.

GASCOIGNE, "Good Morrow"
MALCOLM M. ROSS, "History and Poetry: Decline of the Historical Concrete," *Thought,* XXVI (Autumn, 1951), 437-438.

GASCOYNE, DAVID, "Winter Garden"
DAY LEWIS, *The Poetic Image,* pp. 130-131.

GAY, "Saturday" (*The Shepherd's Week*)
JOHN R. MOORE, "Gay's Burlesque of Sir Richard Blackmore's Poetry," *Journal of English and Germanic Philology,* L (Jan., 1951), 83-89.

GHISELIN, "Bath of Aphrodite"
BREWSTER GHISELIN, "The Birth of a Poem," *Poetry,* LXIX (Oct., 1946), 30-43.

Reprinted Locke, Gibson, and Arms, *Introduction to Literature,* third edition, pp. 239-246.

GHISELIN, "Gull in the Great Basin"
RAY B. WEST, *Writing in the Rocky Mountains* (Lincoln: Unversity of Nebraska Press, 1947), pp. 58-59.

GIBBS, BARBARA, "Dry Canyon, September"
HAYDEN CARRUTH, *A Critical Supplement to "Poetry,"* Jan., 1949, p. 16.

GIBBS, BARBARA, "In a Garden, I and II"
HAYDEN CARRUTH, *A Critical Supplement to "Poetry,"* Jan., 1949, pp. 14-16.

GIBSON, WALKER, "Billiards"
ABBE, *You and Contemporary Poetry,* pp. 40-41.

GIBSON, WALKER, "Thaw"
ABBE, *You and Contemporary Poetry,* p. 39.

GOLDSMITH, "The Deserted Village"
HOWARD J. BELL, JR., "*The Deserted Village* and Goldsmith's Social Doctrines," *PMLA,* LIX (Sept., 1944), 747-772.

DONALD DAVIE, *"The Deserted Village*: Poem as Virtual History," *Twentieth Century*, CLVI (Aug., 1954), 168-174.

MORRIS GOLDEN, "The Broken Dream of *The Deserted Village*," *Literature and Psychology*, IX (Summer & Fall, 1959), 41-44.

DESMOND PACEY, "The Goldsmith's and their Villages," *University of Toronto Quarterly*, XXI (Oct., 1951), 27-38.

GRAHAM, "The White Threshold"

LEONIE ADAMS, "First Poems of Celebration," *Poetry*, LXXXII (Aug., 1953), 275-276.

GRAVES, "The Return of the Goddess Artemis"

ROBERT GRAVES, *Poetry: A Critical Supplement*, April, 1948, pp. 18-21.

J. F. NIMS, *Poetry: A Critical Supplement*, Oct., 1947, pp. 14-16.

GRAVES, "To Juan at the Winter Solstice"

ROBERT GRAVES in Friar and Brinnin, *Modern Poetry*, pp. 500-501.

GRAY, "Elegy Written in a Country Churchyard"

BATESON, *Ennglish Poetry*, pp. 181-193.

BROOKS, *The Well Wrought Urn*, pp. 96-113.

Abridged in *The Case for Poetry*, pp. 157-159.

DAICHES and CHARVAT, *Poems in English*, p. 684.

A. E. DYSON, "The Ambivalence of Gray's 'Elegy, " *Essays in Criticism*, VII (July, 1957), 257-261.

FRANK H. ELLIS, "Gray's Elegy: The Biographical Problem in Literary Criticism," *PMLA*, LXVI (Dec., 1951), 984-1008. Abridged in *The Case for Poetry*, pp. 161-163.

EMPSON, *English Pastoral Poetry*, p. 4. Reprinted BROOKS and WARREN, *Understanding Poetry*, pp. 514-515.

WILLIAM EMPSON, "Thy Darling in an Urn," *The Sewanee Review*, LV (Oct.-Dec., 1957), 692. Abridged in *The Case for Poetry*, p. 159.

WILLIAM FROST, *English Masterpieces*, Vol. VI, *Romantic and Victorian Poetry*, pp. 19-20.

LYLE GLAZIER, "Gray's Elegy: 'The Skull Beneath the Skin,'" *The University of Kansas City Review*, XIX (Spring, 1953), 174-180.

E. D. MACKERNESS, "Thomas Gray," *The Contemporary Review*, CLXXIV (Sept., 1948), 168-169.

RENE RAPIN, *The Explicator*, IX (Nov., 1950), 14.

STAGEBERG and ANDERSON, *Poetry as Experience*, pp. 195-197.

HERBERT W. STARR, "'A Youth to Fortune and to Fame Unknown': A Re-Estimation," *Journal of English and Germanic Philology*, XLVIII (Jan., 1949), 97-107.

VIVANTE, *English Poetry*, pp. 80-82.

GRAY, "Ode on the Death of a Favorite Cat Drowned in a Tub of Gold Fishes"

EMPSON, *Seven Types of Ambiguity*, pp. 97-99, 154-155; (1947 ed.), pp. 77, 121-123.

GRAY, "Ode on a Distant Prospect of Eton College"

KARL F. THOMPSON, *The Explicator*, IX (Feb., 1951), 28.

GRAY, "The Progress of Poesy"

ARTHUR DICKSON, *The Explicator*, IX (May, 1951), 49.

GREENE, "Sweet Are the Thoughts"

GEORGE ARMS and L. G. LOCKE, *The Explicator*, III (Feb., 1945), 27.

GREGORY, "Under the Stone I Saw Them Flow" (from *Chorus for Survival*)

WALTER GIERASCH, "Reading Modern Poetry," *College English*, II (Oct., 1940), 33-34.

WALTER GIERASCH, *The Explicator*, III (June, 1945), 63.

GREVILLE, Sonnet LXXXVII, "When as Man's Life, the Light of Human Lust"

De Mourgues, *Metaphysical Baroque & Precieux Poetry*, pp. 24-25.

HARDY,   "According to the Mighty Working"
John Crowe Ransom, "Honey and Gall," *The Southern Review*, VI (Summer, 1940), 10-11.

HARDY,   "After a Journey"
F. R. Leavis, "Reality and Sincerity: Notes in the Analysis of Poetry," *Scrutiny*, XIX (Winter, 1953), 92-98.

HARDY,   "An Ancient to Ancients"
Deutsch, *Poetry in Our Time*, pp. 7-8.

HARDY,   "Channel Firing"
Brooks and Warren, *Understanding Poetry*, pp. 309-311.
Revised edition, pp. 164-166.
Deutsch, *Poetry in Our Time*, pp. 9-10.

HARDY,   "A Commonplace Day"
F. R. Leavis, "Hardy the Poet," *The Southern Review*, VI (Summer, 1940), 95-97.

HARDY,   "The Convergence of the Twain"
Brooks, Purser, Warren, *An Approach to Literature*, pp. 490-491.
Reprinted third edition, pp. 380-382.
Wendell S. Johnson, "Some Functions of Poetic Form," *Journal of Asethetics and Art Criticism*, XIII (June, 1955), 503-504.
Donat O'Donnell, "Poetry, Inspiration, and Criticism," *Spectator*, CXCV (July 8, 1955), 53.
Paul N. Siegel, *The Explicator*, XI (Nov., 1952), 13.

HARDY,   "A Drizzling Easter Morning"
Delmore Schwartz, "Poetry and Belief in Thomas Hardy," *The Southern Review*, VI (Summer, 1940), 73-74. Reprinted *Critiques*, p. 342.
Also reprinted in part *The Critic's Notebook*, pp. 201-203. Also reprinted *Modern Literary Criticism*, pp. 347-348.

HARDY,   "Drummer Hodge"

Van Doren, *Introduction to Poetry*, pp. 99-102.

HARDY, "During Wind and Rain"
Kreuzer, *Elements of Poetry*, pp. 162-164.

HARDY, "The Fallow Deer at the Lonely House"
Kilby, *Poetry and Life*, pp. 5-6

HARDY, "Friends Beyond"
John Crowe Ransom, "Hardy—Old Poet," *New Republic*, CXXVI (May 12, 1952), 30-31.

HARDY, "The Garden Seat"
John Crowe Ransom, "Honey and Gall," *The Southern Review*, VI (Summer, 1940), 7-9.

HARDY, "George Meredith"
Richards, *Practical Criticism*, pp. 146-153 *et passim*.

HARDY, "He Abjures Love"
V. H. Collins, "The Love Poetry of Thomas Hardy," *Essays and Studies*, XXVIII (1942), 71-72.

HARDY. "Her Father"
Lawrence Richard Holmes, *The Explicator*, XIV (May, 1956), 53.

HARDY, "In the Days of Crinoline"
Blackmur, *Expense of Greatness*, pp. 62-64.
Reprinted *Language as Gesture*, pp. 70-71.

HARDY, "In Tenebris, I"
Walter Gierasch, *The Explicator*, IV (April, 1946), 45.

HARDY, "In Time of 'The Breaking of Nations' "
DeLancey Ferguson, *The Explicator*, IV (Feb., 1946), 25.

HARDY, "The Lacking Sense"
Gilbert Neiman, "Was Hardy Anthropomorphic?" *Twentieth Century Literature*, II (July, 1956), 86-91.

HARDY, "Last Words to a Dumb Friend"
Blackmur, *Expense of Greatness*, pp. 68-72 *et passim*.
Reprinted *Language as Gesture*, pp. 76-78.

HARDY, "The Man He Killed"
Perrine, *Sound and Sense*, pp. 21-22.

HARDY,   "The Masked Face"
DELMORE SCHWARTZ, "Poetry and Belief in Thomas
Hardy," *The Southern Review*, VI (Summer, 1940),
71-72. Reprinted *Critiques*, pp. 340-341.
Also reprinted, *Modern Literary Criticism*, pp.
345-346. Also reprinted in part *The Critic's Note-
book*, pp. 202-203.
HARDY,   "The Moth-Signal"
R. D. BLACKMUR, "The Shorter Poems of Thomas
Hardy," *The Southern Review*, VI (Summer, 1940),
36-38.
BLACKMUR, *The Expense of Greatness*, pp. 59-61.
Reprinted *Language as Gesture*, pp. 68-69.
HARDY,   "Nature's Questioning"
ALLEN TATE, "Hardy's Philosophic Metaphors," *The
Southern Review*, VI (Summer, 1940), 104-107.
TATE, *Reason in Madness*, pp. 125-129. Reprinted
On the Limits of Poetry, pp. 191-194, and *Criticism*,
pp. 185-186.
HARDY,   "Neutral Tones"
BROOKS, PURSER, WARREN, *An Approach to Literature*,
pp. 460-461.
Reprinted third edition, pp. 329-331.
JOHN CROWE RANSOM, "Hardy—Old Poet," *New
Republic*, CXXVI (May 12, 1952), 16, 30.
HARDY,   "Nobody Comes"
UNGER and O'CONNOR, *Poems for Study*, pp. 574-575.
HARDY,   "On an Invitation to the United States"
BROOKS, PURSER, WARREN, *An Approach to Literature*,
pp. 464-467.
Reprinted third edition, pp. 337-340.
HARDY,   "On the Departure Platform"
WALTER GIERASCH, *The Explicator*, IV (Nov., 1945),
10.
HARDY,   "The Oxen"
DEUTSCH, *Poetry in Our Time*, p. 11.

DELMORE SCHWARTZ, "Poetry and Belief in Thomas Hardy," *The Southern Review,* IV (Summer, 1940), 70-71. Reprinted *Critiques,* pp. 339-340. Also reprinted *Modern Literary Criticism,* pp. 344-345.

HARDY,   "The Roman Road"
VAN DOREN, *Introduction to Poetry,* pp. 107-110.

HARDY,   "The Sacrilege"
RICHARD L. PURDY, *The Explicator,* III (Feb., 1945), 28.

HARDY,   "Seen by the Waits"
BLACKMUR, *The Expense of Greatness,* pp. 61-62.
Reprinted *Language as Gesture,* pp. 69-70.

HARDY,   "She to Him"
R. P. BLACKMUR, "The Shorter Poems of Thomas Hardy," *The Southern Review,* VI (Summer, 1940), 25-27.

HARDY,   "The Telegram"
BLACKMUR, *The Expense of Greatness,* pp. 56-59.
Reprinted *Language as Gesture,* pp. 66-67.

HARDY,   "To An Unborn Pauper Child"
DAY LEWIS, *The Poetic Image,* pp. 150-153.
Reprinted Engle and Carrier, *Reading Modern Poetry,* pp. 48-50.

HARDY,   "The Voice"
LEAVIS, *New Bearings on English Poetry,* pp. 59-60.

HART, RICHARD,   "Letter from Madrid"
J. F. NIMS, *Poetry: A Critical Supplement,* Jan., 1948, p. 13.

HARVEY,   "Gloss"
HALE MOORE, "Gabriel Harvey's References to Marlowe," *Studies in Philology,* XXIII (July, 1926), 343-357.

HARVEY,   "Sonnet: Gorgon, or the Wonderful Year"
HALE MOORE, "Gabriel Harvey's References to Marlowe," *Studies in Philology,* XXIII (July, 1926), 343-357.

HARVEY, "A Stanza Declarative: To the Lovers of Admirable Works"

HALE MOORE, "Gabriel Harvey's References to Marlowe," *Studies in Philology*, XXIII (July, 1926), 343-357.

HARVEY, "The Writer's Postscript: Or a Friendly *Caveat* to the Second Shakerley of Powles"

HALE MOORE, "Gabriel Harvey's References to Marlowe," *Studies in Philology*, XXIII (July, 1926), 343-357.

HAY, "Jim Bludso"

DANIELS, *The Art of Reading Poetry*, pp. 88-92.

HAYES, ALFRED, "The Shrunken Head"

J. F. NIMS, *A Critical Supplement to "Poetry,"* Nov., 1948, pp. 7-8.

HENLEY, "Invictus"

HERBERT MARSHALL MCLUHAN, *The Explicator*, III (Dec., 1944), 22.

Reprinted Stallman and Watters, *The Creative Reader*, pp. 874-875.

J. M. PURCELL, *The Explicator*, IV (Nov., 1945), 13.

HENLEY, "The Ways of Death"

RAY L. ARMSTRONG, *The Explicator*, XIV (Jan., 1956), 21.

DANIELS, *The Art of Reading Poetry*, pp. 268-269.

HENRYSON, ROBERT, "Robene and Makyne"

ARTHUR K. MOORE, *The Secular Lyric in Middle English*, pp. 188-194.

HERBERT, "Affliction, I"

EMPSON, *Seven Types of Ambiguity* (1947 ed.), pp. 183-184.

L. C. KNIGHTS, "George Herbert (1)," *Scrutiny*, XII (Spring, 1944), 180-183.

KNIGHTS, *Explorations*, pp. 141-144.

HERBERT, "The Agony"

MARTZ, *The Poetry of Meditation*, pp. 84-85.

HERBERT,   "The Banquet"
MALCOLM M. ROSS, "A Note on the Metaphysicals,"
    The Hudson Review, VI (Spring, 1953), 111.
HERBERT,   "Business'
ROBERT G. COLLMER, *The Explicator,* XVI (Nov.,
    1957), 11.
HERBERT,   "Church-Monuments"
MARTZ, *The Poetry of Meditation,* pp. 141-143.
HERBERT,   "The Church-Porch"
MARTZ, *The Poetry of Meditation,* pp. 290-292.
HERBERT,   "The Collar"

G. P. V. AKRIGG, "George Herbert's 'Collar,' " *Notes
    and Queries,* I, n.s. (Jan., 1954), 17.

JACK M. BICKHAM, *The Explicator,* X (Dec., 1951),
    17.

DAY LEWIS, *The Poetic Image,* pp. 80-81.

T. O. MABBOTT, *The Explicator,* III (Nov., 1944), 12.

DAN S. NORTON, *The Explicator,* II (April, 1944), 41.

DAN S. NORTON, *The Explicator,* III (April, 1945),
    46.

HERBERT,   "The Cross"
MARTZ, *The Poetry of Meditation,* pp. 134-135.
HERBERT,   "Discipline"
JACOB H. ADLER, "Form and Meaning in Herbert's
    'Discipline,' " *Notes and Queries,* V. n.s. (June,
    1958), 240-243.
HERBERT,   "Dooms Day"
CONRAD HILBERRY, *The Explicator,* XVI (Jan., 1958),
    24.
HERBERT,   "The Flower"
L. C. KNIGHTS, "George Herbert (1)," *Scrutiny,* XII
    (Spring, 1944), 185-186.
KNIGHTS, *Explorations,* pp. 146-147.
VAN DOREN, *Introduction to Poetry,* pp. 70-73.
HERBERT,   "The Holy Communion"
MALCOLM M. ROSS, "A Note on the Metaphysicals,"
    The Hudson Review, VI (Spring, 1953), 110-111.

HERBERT,   "I Gave to Hope a Watch of Mine"
  EMPSON, *Seven Types of Ambiguity,* pp. 150-153;
  (1947 ed.), pp. 118-120.
HERBERT,   "Jordan"
  FRANCES ELDREDGE, *The Explicator,* XI (Oct., 1952),
  3.
HERBERT,   "Jordan I"
  MACDONALD EMSLIE, *The Explicator,* XII (April,
  1954), 35.
HERBERT,   "Life"
  MARTZ, *The Poetry of Meditation,* pp. 58-59.
HERBERT,   "Love"
  ADAMS, *Strains of Discord,* pp. 123-124.

  BROWER, *The Fields of Light,* pp. 28-30.
  DREW, *Poetry,* pp. 245-247.
HERBERT,   "Man"
  MARTZ, *The Poetry of Meditation,* pp. 59-61.
HERBERT,   "The Pearl"
  STEPHEN MANNING, *The Explicator,* XIV (Jan.,
  1956), 25.
HERBERT,   "Pilgrimage"

  EMPSON, *Seven Types of Ambiguity,* pp. 163-165;
  (1947 ed.), pp. 129-131.
  KNIGHTS, *Explorations,* pp. 135-137.
  MARTZ, *The Poetry of Meditation,* pp. 304-306.
HERBERT,   "Prayer"
  DANIELS, *The Art of Reading Poetry,* pp. 201-205.
  MARTZ, *The Poetry of Meditation,* pp. 298-300.
HERBERT,   "The Pulley"
  DANIELS, *The Art of Reading Poetry,* pp. 208-210.
  D. S. MEAD, *The Explicator,* IV (Dec., 1945), 17.
HERBERT,   "Redemption"
  BERNARD KNIEGER, *The Explicator,* XI (Feb., 1953),
  24.
HERBERT,   "Sacrifice"
  WILLIAM EMPSON, "George Herbert and Miss Tuve,"

The Kenyon Review, XII (Autumn, 1950), 735-738.

MARTZ, *The Poetry of Meditation,* pp. 91-96.

ROSAMOND TUVE, "On Herbert's 'Sacrifice,'" *The Kenyon Review,* XII (Winter, 1950), 51-75.

HERBERT,   "They Did Accuse Me of Great Villainy"

EMPSON, *Seven Types of Ambiguity,* pp. 286-295; (1947 ed.), pp. 226-233.

HERBERT,   "To All Angels and Saints"

MARTZ, *The Poetry of Meditation,* pp. 97-98.

HERBERT,   "Trinity Sunday"

JOSEPH H. SUMMERS, *The Explicator,* X (Feb., 1952), 23.

HERBERT,   "A True Hymn"

FRANKENBERG, *Invitation to Poetry,* p. 63.

HERBERT,   "Virtue"

EDWIN B. BENJAMIN, *The Explicator,* IX (Nov., 1950), 12.

HERBERT MARSHALL MCLUHAN, *The Explicator,* II (Oct., 1943), 4. Reprinted *Readings for Liberal Education,* II, 534-535.

ROSENTHAL and SMITH, *Exploring Poetry,* pp. 416-417.

HERBERT,   "The Windows"

BROWER, *The Fields of Light,* pp. 45-47.

HERRICK,   "Another Grace for a Child"

ANNA JEAN MILL, *The Explicator,* III (June, 1945), 61.

HERRICK,   "The Apparition of His Mistress Calling Him to Elysium"

ROSENTHAL and SMITH, *Exploring Poetry,* pp. 251-252.

HERRICK,   "The Argument of His Book"

EDWARD L. HIRSH, *The Explicator,* II (Nov., 1943), 11.

HERRICK,   "The Bracelet: To Julia"

KILBY, *Poetry and Life,* p. 15.

HERRICK,   "Cherry-Ripe"

DAICHES, *A Study of Literature,* pp. 148-150.

HERRICK,   "The Coming of Good Luck"
BATESON, *English Poetry,* pp. 82-83.

HERRICK,   "Corinna's Going A-Maying"
BROOKS, *The Well Wrought Urn,* pp. 62-73.

Reprinted West, *Essays in Modern Literary Criticism,* pp. 327-335.

ROY HARVEY PEARCE, " 'Pure' Criticism and the History of Ideas," *Journal of Aesthetics and Art Criticism,* VII (Dec., 1948), 126-129.

HERRICK,   "Delight in Disorder"
F. W. BATESON, *English Poetry and the English Language,* pp. 42-43. Reprinted Brooks and Warren, *Understanding Poetry,* p. 328.

Reprinted Unger and O'Connor, *Poems for Study,* p. 147.

DREW, *Poetry,* pp. 78-79.

KILBY, *Poetry and Life,* pp. 14-15.

HERRICK,   "The Funeral Rites of the Rose"
EMPSON, *Seven Types of Ambiguity* (1947 ed.), pp. 162-163.

T. R. WHITAKER, "Herrick and the Fruits of the Garden," *Journal of English Literary History,* XXII (March, 1955), 16-23.

HERRICK,   "His Winding-Sheet"
T. R. WHITAKER, "Herrick and the Fruits of the Garden," *Journal of English Literary History,* XXII (March, 1955), 26-29.

HERRICK,   "Julia's Petticoat"
TUVE, *Elizabethan and Metaphysical Imagery,* p. 93.

HERRICK,   "The Mad Maid's Song"
WILLIAM VAN O'CONNOR, "Tension and Structure of Poetry," *The Sewanee Review,* LI (Oct.-Dec., 1943), 557-558.

UNGER and O'CONNOR, *Poems for Study,* p. 145.

HERRICK, "The Night Piece, to Julia"
DOUGLAS, LAMSON, SMITH, *The Critical Reader*, pp. 83-86.

HERRICK, "To Anthea Lying in Bed"
TUVE, *Elizabethan and Metaphysical Imagery*, pp. 11-12.

HERRICK, "To Blossoms"
BROOKS and WARREN, *Understanding Poetry*, pp. 368-370, 374.
Revised edition, pp. 246-247.

HERRICK, "To Daffodils"
THOMAS and BROWN, *Reading Poems: An Introduction to Critical Study*, pp. 650-651, 695-697.

HERRICK, "To Electra"
HENNIG COHEN, *The Explicator*, XVII (March 1959), 44.

HERRICK, "To Live Merrily and to Trust to Good Verses"
FRANKENBERG, *Invitation to Poetry*, pp. 49-50.

HERRICK, "To Meadows"
VAN DOREN, *Introduction to Poetry*, pp. 66-69.

HERRICK, "To the Virgins"
GEORGE ARMS, *The Explicator*, I (Oct., 1942), 2.
TILLYARD, *The Metaphysicals and Milton*, pp. 53-57.

HERRICK, "Upon Julia's Clothes"
BATESON, *English Poetry*, p. 46.
MONTGOMERY BELGION, "The Poetic Name," *The Sewanee Review*, LIV (Oct.-Dec., 1946), 643-644.
EARL DANIELS, *The Explicator*, I (March, 1943), 35.
Reprinted Stallman and Watters, *The Creative Reader*, pp. 852-853.
Abridged in *The Case for Poetry*, p. 175.
NAT HENRY, *The Explicator*, V (April, 1947), 46.
NAT HENRY, *The Explicator*, XIV (Dec., 1955), 15.
C. S. LEWIS, "The Personal Heresy in Criticism," *Essays and Studies*, XIX (1933), 9-11 *et passim*.

C. S. Lewis, "An Open Letter to Dr. Tillyard," *Essays and Studies,* XXII (1936), 160-161.

Elisabeth Schneider, *The Explicator,* XIII (March, 1955), 30.

Stauffer, *The Nature of Poetry,* pp. 162-163.

E. M. W. Tillyard, "The Personal Heresy in Criticism: A Rejoinder," *Essays and Studies,* XX (1934), 17-20.

Abridged in *The Case for Poetry,* p. 175.

HERRICK,   "Upon Julia's Voice"
Perrine, *Sound and Sense,* p. 171.

HERRICK,   "Upon Sylvia"
Tuve, *Elizabethan and Metaphysical Imagery,* p. 129.

HERRICK,   "The Vision"
Tuve, *Elizabethan and Metaphysical Imagery,* pp. 87-88.

HODGSON, ralph,   "February"
Darrell Abel, "How to Teach Students to Read a Poem," *College English,* XVI (Nov., 1955), 90-92.

HODGSON, ralph,   "The Muse and the Mastiff"
Anonymous, "Ralph Hodgson: A Poet's Journey in Time," *Times Literary Supplement,* (Feb., 13, 1959), p. 78.

HODGSON, ralph,   "The Skylark"
Anonymous, "Ralph Hodgson: A Poet's Journey in Time," *Times Literary Supplement,* (Feb. 13, 1959), p. 77.

HODGSON, ralph,   "Time"
Anonymous, "Ralph Hodgson: A Poet's Journey in Time," *Times Literary Supplement,* (Feb. 13, 1959), p. 78.

HODGSON, ralph,   "To Deck a Woman"
Anonymous, "Ralph Hodgson: A Poet's Journey in Time," *Times Literary Supplement,* (Feb. 13, 1959), pp. 77-78.

HODGSON, william noel,   "By All the Glories of the Day"

PALMER, *Post-Victorian Poetry*, pp. 229-231.

HOLMES, "The Chambered Nautilus"
GEORGE ARMS, *The Explicator*, IV (June, 1946), 51.
GEORGE ARMS, *The Fields Were Green*, pp. 108-110.

HOLMES, "The Deacon's Masterpiece"
GEORGE ARMS, *The Fields Were Green*, pp. 112-113.

HOLMES, "The Living Temple"
GEORGE ARMS, *The Explicator*, II (Nov., 1943), 15.
GEORGE ARMS, *The Fields Were Green*, pp. 104-105.

HOLMES, "The Peau de Chagrin of State Street"
GEORGE ARMS, *The Fields Were Green*, p. 102.

HOLMES, "Two Sonnets: Harvard"
GEORGE ARMS, *The Fields Were Green*, pp. 113-114.

HOLMES, "The Two Streams"
GEORGE ARMS, *The Fields Were Green*, pp. 97-99.

GEORGE ARMS, " 'To Fix the Image All Unveiled and Warm,' " *New England Quarterly*, XIX (Dec., 1946), 534-537.

HOOD, "Autumn"
AUDREY JENNINGS, "Hood's 'Autumn,' " *Times Literary Supplement* (June 26, 1953), p. 413.

HOPKINS, "As Kingfishers Catch Fire, Dragonflies Draw Flame"
HARTMAN, *The Unmediated Vision*, pp. 58-59.

HOPKINS, "The Blessed Virgin Compared to the Air We Breathe"
TAD W. GUZIE, "Are Modern Poets Morbid?" *Catholic World*, CLXXXV (April, 1957), 27-32.

HOPKINS, "The Caged Skylark"
FRIAR and BRINNIN, *Modern Poetry*, pp. 503-504.
MARGARET GIOVANNINI, *The Explicator*, XIV (March, 1956), 35.
MAYNARD MACK, LEONARD DEAN, and WILLIAM FROST, *English Masterpieces*, Vol. VII, *Modern Poetry*, pp. 20-21.

HOPKINS, "The Candle Indoors"

Denis Donoghue, "Technique in Hopkins," *Studies,* XLIV (Winter, 1955) , 452.

HOPKINS,   "Carrion Comfort"

Friar and Brinnin, *Modern Poetry,* p. 502.

Leavis, *New Bearings on English Poetry,* pp. 190-191.

Wells, *New Poets from Old,* pp. 153-154.

HOPKINS,   "Duns Scotus's Oxford"

Yvor Winters, "The Poetry of Gerard Manley Hopkins (2)," *Hudson Review,* II (Spring, 1949), 64. Reprinted *The Function of Criticism,* pp. 126-127.

HOPKINS,   "God's Grandeur"

Tad W. Guzie, "Are Modern Poets Morbid?" *Catholic World,* CLXXXV (April, 1957) , 27-32.

Rosenthal and Smith, *Exploring Poetry,* pp. 94-97.

Brooks Wright, *The Explicator,* X (Oct., 1951) , 5.

HOPKINS,   "The Habit of Perfection"

Boyd Litzinger, *The Explicator,* XVI (Oct., 1957), 1.

HOPKINS,   "Harry Ploughman"

Day Lewis, *The Poetic Image,* pp. 125-128.

Stageberg and Anderson, *Poetry as Experience,* pp. 222-229.

HOPKINS,   "Heaven-Haven"

Anonymous, "Poet and Priest," *Times Literary Supplement,* June 10, 1944, p. 282.

HOPKINS,   "Hurrahing in Harvest"

Friar and Brinnin, *Modern Poetry,* p. 504.

HOPKINS,   "I Wake and Feel the Fell of Dark, Not Day"

Alexander W. Allison, *The Explicator,* XVII (May, 1959) , 54.

Friar and Brinnin, *Modern Poetry,* pp. 502-503.

S. C. Pepper, *The Basis of Criticism in the Arts* (Cambridge: Harvard University Press, 1945), pp. 127-140.

HOPKINS,   "The Leaden Echo and the Golden Echo"

Leavis, *New Bearings on English Poetry,* pp. 172-175.

HOPKINS, "Margaret Clitheroe"
R. J. SCHOECK, "Peine Forte et Dure and Hopkins' 'Margaret Clitheroe,'" *MLN*, LXXIV (March, 1959), 220-225.

HOPKINS, "My Own Heart Let Me More Have Pity on"
ELISABETH SCHNEIDER, *The Explicator*, V (May, 1947), 51; and VII (May, 1949), 49.

HOPKINS, "No Worst, There Is None"
ROBERT A. DURR, *The Explicator*, XI (Nov., 1952), 11.
FRIAR and BRINNIN, *Modern Poetry*, p. 502.
SISTER MARCELLA M. HOLLOWAY, C.S.J., *The Explicator*, XIV (May, 1956), 51.
SISTER MARY HUMILIATA, "Hopkins and the Prometheus Myth," *PMLA*, LXX (March, 1955), 58-68.
YVOR WINTERS, "The Poetry of Gerard Manley Hopkins (1)," *Hudson Review*, I (Winter, 1948), 460-466.
Reprinted *The Function of Criticism*, pp. 107-113.

HOPKINS, "On a Piece of Music"
YVOR WINTERS, "The Poetry of Gerard Manley Hopkins (2)," *Hudson Review*, II (Spring, 1949), 87-88.
Reprinted *The Function of Criticism*, pp. 137-138, 152-153.

HOPKINS, "Pied Beauty"
JOHN BRITTON, S.J., " 'Pied Beauty' and the Glory of God," *Renascence*, XI (Winter, 1959), 72-75.
FRANKENBERG, *Invitation to Poetry*, pp. 294-296.
SAMUEL KLIGER, "God's 'Plenitude' in the Poetry of Gerard Manley Hopkins," *MLN*, LIX (June, 1944), 408-410.

HOPKINS, "Sonnet to St. Alphonsus Rodriguez"
HERBERT MARSHALL MCLUHAN, "The Analogical Mirrors," *The Kenyon Review*, VI (Summer, 1944), 329-330.

HOPKINS, "Soul, Self; Come, Poor Jackself, I Do Advise"

RIDING and GRAVES, *A Survey of Modernist Poetry*, pp. 90-94.

HOPKINS, "Spelt from Sibyl's Leaves"

DENIS DONOGHUE, "Technique in Hopkins," *Studies*, XLIV (Winter, 1955), 454.

FRIAR and BRINNIN, *Modern Poetry*, p. 503.

LEAVIS, *New Bearings on English Poetry*, pp. 182-186.

I. A. RICHARDS, "Gerard Hopkins," *The Dial*, LXXXI (Sept., 1926), 199-201.

WILLIAM J. ROONEY, " 'Spelt from Sibyl's Leaves'— a Study in Contrasting Methods of Evaluation," *Journal of Aesthetics and Art Criticism*, XIII (June, 1955), 507-519.

RAYMOND V. SCHODER, "Spelt from Sibyl's Leaves," *Thought*, XIX (Dec., 1944), 634-648.

II. C. SHERWOOD, *The Explicator*, XV (Oct., 1956), 5.

SISTER THERESE, S.N.D., *The Explicator*, XVII (April, 1959), 45.

HOPKINS, "Spring and Fall: To a Young Child"

DEUTSCH, *Poetry in Our Time*, p. 294.

DREW, *Poetry*, pp. 107-109.

EMPSON, *Seven Types of Ambiguity*, pp. 187-188; (1947 ed.), pp. 148-149.

RICHARDS, *Practical Criticism*, pp. 80-91 *et passim*.

HOPKINS, "The Starlight Night"

YVOR WINTERS, "The Poetry of Gerard Manley Hopkins (2)," *Hudson Review*, II (Spring, 1949), 63.

Reprinted *The Function of Criticism*, pp. 125-126.

HOPKINS, "That Nature Is a Heraclitean Fire and of the Comfort of the Resurrection"

FRIAR and BRINNIN, *Modern Poetry*, pp. 501-502.

HOPKINS, "Thee, God, I Come From, to Thee Go"

DENIS DONOGHUE, "Technique in Hopkins," *Studies*, XLIV (Winter, 1955), 451-453.

HOPKINS,   "Thou Art Indeed Just, Lord, If I Contend"
BROWER, *The Fields of Light,* pp. 26-27.
DREW, *Poetry,* pp. 140-141.

HOPKINS,   "Tom's Garland"
DEUTSCH, *This Modern Poetry,* pp. 178-180.
HENRY SILVERSTEIN, "On 'Tom's Garland,'" *Accent,* VII (Winter, 1947), 67-81.

HOPKINS,   "To R. B."
WILLIAM M. GIBSON, *The Explicator,* VI (Nov., 1947), 12.
STAUFFER, *The Nature of Poetry,* pp. 40-41.

HOPKINS,   "The Windhover, to Christ Our Lord"

ANONYMOUS, "Difficult Poetry," *Times Literary Supplement* (June 24, 1955), p. 349.
ANONYMOUS, "Hopkinsiana," *Times Literary Supplement* (Oct. 29, 1954), p. 689.
ANONYMOUS, "Passionate Science," *Times Literary Supplement* (March 18, 1955), p. 165.
ANONYMOUS, " 'Pied Beauty' in Spanish," *Times Literary Supplement* (Aug. 13, 1954), p. 510.
ANONYMOUS, "Poet and Priest," *Times Literary Supplement,* June 10, 1944, p. 282.
ROBERT W. AYERS, "Hopkins' 'The Windhover': A Further Simpification," *MLN,* LXXI (Dec., 1956), 577-584.
DEUTSCH, *Poetry in Our Time,* pp. 295-300.
DENIS DONOGHUE, "The Bird as Symbol: Hopkins' Windhover," *Studies,* XLIV (Autumn, 1955), 291-299.
DREW, *Poetry,* pp. 248-252.
WILLIAM EMPSON, "Hopkinsiana," *Times Literary Supplement* (Oct. 1, 1954), p. 625.
EMPSON, *Seven Types of Ambiguity,* pp. 284-286.
WILLIAM EMPSON, " 'The Windhover,'" *Times Literary Supplement* (May 20, 1955), p. 269.
FRIAR and BRINNIN, *Modern Poetry,* p. 504.

W. H. GARDNER, "The Religious Problem in G. M. Hopkins," *Scrutiny*, VI (June, 1937), 35-38. Reprinted *Critiques*, pp. 349-353.
Reprinted Engle and Carrier, *Reading Modern Poetry*, pp. 337-341.

W. H. GARDNER, "'The Windhover,'" *Times Literary Supplement* (June 24, 1955), p. 349.

FREDERICK L. GWYNN, "Hopkins' 'The Windhover': A New Simplification," *MLN*, LXVI (June, 1951), 366-370.

HARTMAN, *The Unmediated Vision*, pp. 49-67, 162.

ARCHIBALD A. HILL, "An Analysis of 'The Windhover': An Experiment in Structural Method," *PMLA*, LXX (Dec., 1955), 968-978.

JOHN D. HOWARD, "Letter to the Editor," *College English*, XIX (April, 1958), 312.

KILBY, *Poetry and Life*, pp. 208-209.

LANGBAUM, *The Poetry of Experience*, pp. 66-69.

F. N. LEES, "Hopkinsiana," *Times Literary Supplement* (Sept. 3, 1954), p. 557.

F. N. LEES, "Hopkinsiana," *Times Literary Supplement* (Oct. 22, 1954), p. 673.

F. N. LEES, "'The Windhover,'" *Scrutiny*, XVII (Spring, 1950), 32-38.

PETER LISCA, "The Return of 'The Windhover,'" *College English*, XIX (Dec., 1957), 124-126.

HERBERT MARSHALL McLUHAN, "The Analogical Mirrors," *The Kenyon Review*, VI (Summer, 1944), 326-329.

ARTHUR MIZENER, "Victorian Hopkins," *The Kenyon Review*, VI (Autumn, 1944), 604.

EDWIN MORGAN, "A Hopkins Phrase," *Times Literary Supplement*, May 27, 1949, p. 347.

B. DE BEAR NICOL, "A Hopkins Phrase," *Times Literary Supplement*, May 13, 1949, p. 313.

GERALD L. NOLAN, "'The Windhover,'" *Times Literary Supplement* (June 24, 1955), p. 349.

I. A. RICHARDS, "Gerard Hopkins," *The Dial,* LXXXI (Sept., 1926), 197-199.

JEAN GEORGES RITZ, " 'The Windhover,' " *Times Literary Supplement* (May 6, 1955), p. 237.

CLIVE SANSOM, "A Hopkins Phrase," *Times Literary Supplement,* May 20, 1949, p. 329.

STAGEBERG and ANDERSON, *Poetry as Experience,* pp. 493-496.

STAUFFER, *The Nature of Poetry,* pp. 41-42 *et passim.*

DENNIS WARD, *Interpretations,* John Wain, ed., pp. 138-151.

WINTERS, *The Function of Criticism,* pp. 127-135.

CARL R. WOODRING, "Once More 'The Windhover,' " *The Western Review,* XV (Autumn, 1950), 61-64.

HOPKINS,   "The Wreck of the Deutschland"

DEUTSCH, *Poetry in Our Time,* pp. 290-292.

DENIS DONOGHUE, "Techniques in Hopkins," *Studies,* XLIV (Winter, 1955), 449.

W. H. GARDNER, "The Wreck of the Deutschland," *Essays and Studies,* XXI (1935), 124-152.

LEAVIS, *New Bearings on English Poetry,* pp. 175-180.

F. R. LEAVIS, "Gerard Manley Hopkins," *Scrutiny,* XII (Spring, 1944), 82-93.

BOYD LITZINGER, *The Explicator,* XVIII (Dec., 1959), 19.

ARTHUR MIZENER, "Victorian Hopkins," *The Kenyon Review,* VI (Autumn, 1944), 603-606.

BROTHER ADELBERT SCHEVE, F.S.C., *The Explicator,* XVII (June, 1959), 60.

ELISABETH SCHNEIDER, *The Explicator,* XVI (May, 1958), 46.

FRANCIS B. THORNTON, "Essays on 'The Wreck of the Deutschland,' " *The Catholic World,* CLX (Oct., 1944), 41-46.

HOSKINS,   "Absence"

CLEANTH BROOKS, JR., "Three Revolutions in Poetry," *The Southern Review,* I (Autumn, 1935), 330.

Brooks, *Modern Poetry and the Tradition,* pp. 22-24.

HOUSMAN, "Bredon Hill" (*Shropshire Lad,* 21)

Cleanth Brooks, "Alfred Edward Housman," *Anniversary Lectures,* 1959, pp. 46-48.

HOUSMAN, "The Chestnut Casts His Flambeaux" (*Last Poems,* 9)

F. A. Philbrick, *The Explicator,* IV (Dec., 1945), 20.

Warren Taylor, *The Explicator,* III (June, 1945), 64.

HOUSMAN, "Crossing Alone the Nighted Ferry" (*More Poems,* 23)

Randall Jarrell, "Texts from Housman," *The Kenyon Review,* I (Summer, 1939), 261-266.

HOUSMAN, "Eight O'Clock" (*Last Poems,* 15)

Cleanth Brooks, "Alfred Edward Housman," *Anniversary Lectures, 1959,* pp. 42-43.

Richard H. Fogle, "Empathic Imagery in Keats and Shelley," *PMLA,* LXI (March, 1946), 169-170.

Rosenthal and Smith, *Exploring Poetry,* pp. 69-71.

HOUSMAN, "1887" (*Shropshire Lad,* 1)

Cleanth Brooks, "Alfred Edward Housman," *Anniversary Lectures 1959,* pp. 48-51.

T. S. K. Scott-Craig, Charles C. Walcutt and Cleanth Brooks, Jr., *The Explicator,* II (March, 1944), 34.

Charles Child Walcutt, "Housman and the Empire: An Analysis of '1887,'" *College English,* V (Feb., 1944), 255-258. Reprinted *Readings for Liberal Education,* II, 418-423.

Reprinted Engle and Carrier, *Reading Modern Poetry,* pp. 20-26.

W. L. Werner, "Housman's '1887'—No Satire," *College English,* VI (Dec., 1944), 165-166.

HOUSMAN, "Epitaph on an Army of Mercenaries" (*Last Poems,* 37)

Cleanth Brooks, "Alfred Edward Housman," *Anniversary Lectures 1959,* pp. 40-41.

VINCENT FREIMARCK, "Further Notes on Housman's Use of the Bible," *MLN,* LXVII (Dec., 1952) , 549-550.

W. L. WERNER, *The Explicator,* II (March, 1944), 38.

HOUSMAN, "Farewell to Barn and Stack and Tree" *(Shropshire Lad,* 8)

GEORGE ARMS, *The Explicator,* I (April, 1943), Q29.

WILBUR S. SCOTT, *The Explicator,* V (Nov., 1946), 11.

FRANK SULLIVAN, *The Explicator,* II (March, 1944), 36.

HOUSMAN, "Hell Gate" *(Last Poems,* 31)

JOHN HAWLEY ROBERTS, *The Explicator,* V (April, 1947), 44.

HOUSMAN, "Her Strong Enchantments Failing" *(Last Poems,* 3)

CLYDE K. HYDER, *The Explicator,* IV (Nov., 1945), 11.

HOUSMAN, "Here in the Beechen Forest"

TOM B. HABER, "A Poem of Beeches from the Notebooks of A. E. Housman," *Dalhousie Review,* XXXI (Autumn, 1951) , 196-197.

HOUSMAN, "I Hoed and Trenched and Weeded," *(Shropshire Lad,* 63)

DONALD A. STAUFFER, "Genesis, or the Poet as Maker," *Poets at Work,* pp. 41-43.

HOUSMAN, "The Immortal Part" *(Shropshire Lad,* 43)

LOUISE SCHUTZ BOAS, *The Explicator,* II (March, 1944), 37.

CLEANTH BROOKS, "Alfred Edward Housman," *Anniversary Lectures 1959,* pp. 45-46.

BROOKS and WARREN, *Understanding Poetry,* revised edition, pp. 617-622.

HOUSMAN, "Into My Heart an Air that Kills" *(Shropshire Lad,* 40)

STAUFFER, *The Nature of Poetry,* pp. 22-24, 156-157, 158-159, *et passim.*

HOUSMAN, "It Nods and Curtseys and Recovers" *(Shropshire Lad,* 16)

RANDALL JARRELL, "Texts from Housman," *The Kenyon Review*, I (Summer, 1939), 266-270.

HOUSMAN, "The Lent Lily" *(Shropshire Lad, 29)*
MICHAEL MACKLEM, "The Elegiac Theme in Housman," *Queens Quarterly*, LIX (Spring, 1952), 50-51.

HOUSMAN, "Loveliest of Trees" *(Shropshire Lad, 2)*
GEORGE ARMS, *The Explicator*, I (May, 1943), 57.
WINIFRED LYNSKEY, *The Explicator*, IV (June, 1946), 59.
MICHAEL MACKLEM, "The Elegiac Theme in Housman," *Queens Quarterly*, LIX (Spring, 1952), 41.
WILLIAM L. WERNER, *The Explicator*, I (June, 1943), 69.
W. L. WERNER, *The Explicator*, V (Oct., 1946), 4.

HOUSMAN, "The Merry Guide" *(Shropshire Lad, 42)*
LOUISE SCHUTZ BOAS, *The Explicator*, III (Oct., 1944), 6.

HOUSMAN, "The Night Is Freezing Fast" *(Last Poems, 20)*
CLEANTH BROOKS, "Alfred Edward Housman," *Anniversary Lectures, 1959*, pp. 44-45.
KREUZER, *Elements of Poetry*, pp. 220-221.

HOUSMAN, "Now Hollow Fires Burn Out to Black"
TOM BURNS HABER, *The Explicator*, XI (March, 1953), 35.

HOUSMAN, "On Wenlock Edge" *(Shropshire Lad, 31)*
DeLANCEY FERGUSON, *The Explicator*, IV (Nov., 1945), 15.
SPIRO PETERSON, *The Explicator*, XV (April, 1957), 46.
ROBERT WOOSTER STALLMAN, *The Explicator*, III (Feb., 1945), 26.

HOUSMAN, "The Oracles" *(Last Poems, 25)*
BREWSTER GHISELIN, *The Explicator*, IV (March, 1946), 33.
CLYDE K. HYDER, *The Explicator*, IV (Oct., 1945), 5.

HOUSMAN, "Reveille" (*Shropshire Lad,* 8)

> F. R. LEAVIS, "Imagery and Movement," *Scrutiny,* XIII (Sept., 1945), 132-134.
>
> STAUFFER, *The Nature of Poetry,* pp. 140-147.

HOUSMAN, "Revolution" (*Last Poems,* 36)

> F. A. PHILBRICK and RALPH P. BOAS, *The Explicator,* II (March, 1944), 35 (cf. also "Announcements," April, 1944).
>
> JOHN W. STEVENSON, "The Martyr as Innocent: Housman's Lonely Lad," *South Atlantic Quarterly,* LVII (Winter, 1958), 78-79.

HOUSMAN, "Tell Me Not Here; It Needs Not Saying" (*Last Poems,* 40)

> CLEANTH BROOKS, "Alfred Edward Housman," *Anniversary Lectures 1959,* pp. 53-56.

HOUSMAN, "Terence, This Is Stupid Stuff" (*Shropshire Lad,* LXII)

> JOHN W. STEVENSON, "The Pastoral Setting in the Poetry of A. E. Housman," *South Atlantic Quarterly,* LV (Oct., 1956), 494-496.

HOUSMAN, "To an Athlete Dying Young" (*Shropshire Lad,* 19)

> WILLIAM BACHE, *The Explicator,* X (Oct., 1951), 6.
>
> BROOKS and WARREN, *Understanding Poetry,* pp. 385-387.
>
> Revised edition, pp. 267-269.
>
> C. R. B. COMBELLACK, *The Explicator,* X (March, 1952), 31.
>
> NAT HENRY, *The Explicator,* XII (May, 1954), 48.
>
> WALTER L. MEYERS, *The Explicator,* XI (Feb., 1953), 23.
>
> CHARLES CHILD WALCUTT, "Interpreting the Symbol," *College English,* XIV (May, 1953), 449-451.

HOUSMAN, "The True Lover" (*Shropshire Lad,* 53).

> DARREL ABEL, *The Explicator,* VIII (Dec., 1949), 23.
>
> BROOKS, PURSER, WARREN, *An Approach to Literature,* pp. 442-443.
>
> Reprinted third edition, pp. 296-297.

MAUDE M. HAWKINS, *The Explicator*, VIII (June, 1950) , 61.

HOUSMAN, "We'll to the Woods No More" (*Last Poems*, preface) ·
ELISABETH SCHNEIDER, *Aesthetic Motive*, pp. 97-103.
Reprinted in part *The Critic's Notebook*, p. 225.

HOUSMAN, "When Israel Out of Egypt Came" (*More Poems*, 2)
L. G. LOCKE, *The Explicator*, II (March, 1944), 39.

HOUSMAN, "When Smoke Stood up from Ludlow" (*Shropshire Lad*, 7)
STAUFFER, *The Nature of Poetry*, pp. 217-218.

HOUSMAN, "White in the Moon the Long Road Lies"
KREUZER, *Elements of Poetry*, pp. 132-134.

HOUSMAN, "With Rue My Heart Is Laden" (*Shropshire Lad*, 54)
WINIFRED LYNSKEY, "A Critic in Action: Mr. Ransom," *College English*, V (Feb., 1944), 239-242.
JOHN CROWE RANSOM, "Honey and Gall," *The Southern Review*, VI (Summer, 1940), 7-8.
THOMAS and BROWN, *Reading Poems: An Introduction to Critical Study*, pp. 754-756.

HOUSMAN, "With Seed The Sowers Scatter" (*More Poems*, 32)
WILLIAM EMPSON, "Emotions in Words Again," *The Kenyon Review*, X (Autumn, 1948), 587-589.
Reprinted *The Kenyon Critics*, pp. 133-135.

HOWES, BARBARA, "The Heart of Europe"
HAYDEN CARRUTH, *A Critical Supplement to "Poetry,"* Feb., 1949, pp. 7-8.

HOWES, BARBARA, "In the Cold Country"
HAYDEN CARRUTH, *A Critical Supplement to "Poetry,"* Feb., 1949, pp. 3-7.

HOWES, BARBARA, "Portrait of an Artist"
HAYDEN CARRUTH, *A Critical Supplement to "Poetry,"* Feb., 1949, p. 9.

HUMPHRIES, "Little Fugue"
HAROLD E. COOK, *The Explicator*, XIV (Dec., 1955) , 14.

HUNT,   "Abou Ben Adhem"
   Ernest E. Leisy, *The Explicator*, V (Nov., 1946), 9.
   T. O. Mabbott, *The Explicator,* V (March, 1947), 39.
HUXLEY,   "In the Chaos of the Moon's" (unpublished)
   Rudolf Arnheim, "Psychological Notes on the Poetical Process," *Poets at Work,* pp. 144-146.
HUXLEY,   "Leda"
   Arthur Minton, *The Explicator*, VII (Feb., 1949), 31.
JARRELL, randall,   "The Black Swan"
   Quinn, *The Metamorphic Tradition,* pp. 186-188.
JARRELL, randall,   "Burning the Letters"
   Quinn, *The Metamorphic Tradition,* pp. 198-199.
JARRELL, randall,   "A Camp in a Prussian Forest"
   W. S. Graham, "It All Comes Back to Me Now," *Poetry*, LXXII (Sept., 1948), 306.
   Stephen Spender, "Randall Jarrell's Landscape," *Nation*, CLXVI (May 1, 1948), 476.
JARRELL, randall,   "The Death of the Ball Turret Gunner"
   Isabel C. Hungerland, "The Interpretation of Poetry," *Journal of Aesthetics and Art Criticism,* XIII (March, 1955), 353-354.
   Kreuzer, *Elements of Poetry,* pp. 146-148.
   Rosenthal and Smith, *Exploring Poetry,* pp. 547-549.
JARREL, randall,   "Eighth Air Force"
   Cleanth Brooks, "Irony as a Principle of Structure," *Literary Opinion in America*, M. D. Zabel, ed., revised edition, pp. 738-741.
   Books, Purser, Warren, *An Approach to Literature,* third edition, pp. 397-399.
JARRELL, randall,   "The Emancipators"
   Mordecai and Erin Marcus, *The Explicator*, XVI (Feb., 1958), 26.
JARRELL, randall,   "The Girl Dreams That She Is Giselle"
   Quinn, *The Metamorphic Tradition,* pp. 188-191.
JARRELL, randall,   "Hohensalzburg"

HAYDEN CARRUTH, *A Critical Supplement to "Poetry,"* April, 1949, pp. 1-10.

QUINN, *The Metamorphic Tradition,* pp. 174-175, 178-181.

JARRELL, RANDALL, "King's Hunt"
QUINN, *The Metamorphic Tradition,* pp. 192-193.

JARRELL, RANDALL, "Love in Its Separate Being"
JOSEPH WARREN BEACH, "The Cancelling Out—A Note on Recent Poetry," *Accent,* VII (Summer, 1947), 248-249.

JARRELL, RANDALL, "The Metamorphosis"
QUINN, *The Metamorphic Tradition,* pp. 200-201.

JARRELL, RANDALL, "The Night Before the Night Before Christmas"
QUINN, *The Metamorphic Tradition,* pp. 182-185.

JARRELL, RANDALL, "A Quilt-Pattern"
QUINN, *The Metamorphic Tradition,* pp. 193-195.

JARRELL, RANDALL, "A Rhapsody on Irish Themes"
QUINN, *The Metamorphic Tradition,* p. 191.

JARRELL, RANDALL, "The Sleeping Beauty: Variation of the Prince"
QUINN, *The Metamorphic Tradition,* pp. 175-177.

JARRELL, RANDALL, "Soul"
QUINN, *The Metamorphic Tradition,* pp. 172-173.

JARRELL, RANDALL, "The Venetian Blind"
QUINN, *The Metamorphic Tradition,* pp. 191-192.

JEFFERS, "Christmas Card"
DEUTSCH, *Poetry in Our Time,* pp. 21-22.

JEFFERS, "Fire on the Hills"
GEORGE ARMS, *The Explicator,* I (May, 1943), 59.

JEFFERS, "Give Your Heart to the Hawks"
FRAJAM TAYLOR, "The Enigma of Robinson Jeffers: II, The Hawk and the Stone," *Poetry,* LV (Oct., 1939), 39-44.

JEFFERS, "Greater Grandeur"
J. F. NIMS, *Poetry: A Critical Supplement,* Oct., 1947, pp. 5-6.

JEFFERS, "Margrave"
WAGGONER, *The Heel of Elohim,* pp. 121-129.

JEFFERS,   "Meditation on Saviours"
    W. S. Johnson, "The 'Savior' in the Poetry of Robinson Jeffers," *American Literature*, XV (May, 1943), 163-164.
JEFFERS,   "Science"
    Delmore Schwartz, "The Enigma of Robinson Jeffers: I, Sources of Violence," *Poetry*, LV (Oct., 1939), 34-38.
JEROME,   "Aubade"
    Judson Jerome, "Rivalry with Madmen," *Yale Review*, XLVIII (March, 1959), 345-350.
JEROME,   "From Beowulf to Thomas Hardy"
    Judson Jerome, "Rivalry with Madmen," *Yale Review*, XLVIII (March, 1959), 352-353.
JOHNSON, lionel,   "By the Statue of King Charles at Charing Cross"
    F. R. Leavis, " 'Thought' and Emotional Quality," *Scrutiny*, XIII (Spring, 1945), 62-66.
JOHNSON,   "Comely and Calm He Rides"
    H. P. Collins, "A Note on the Classical Principle in Poetry," *The Criterion*, III (April, 1925), 391-394.
JOHNSON, lionel,   "The Dark Angel"
    Iain Fletcher, *Interpretations*, John Wain, ed., pp. 155-178.
JOHNSON, lionel,   "Oxford"
    Bateson, *English Poetry*, pp. 235-239.
JOHNSON,   "On the Death of Dr. Robert Levet"
    Susie I. Tucker, and Henry Gifford, *The Explicator*, XV (April, 1957), 45.
JOHNSON,   "The Vanity of Human Wishes"
    Anonymous, *"Vanity of Human Wishes, lines 15-20,"* *Notes and Queries*, IV, n.s. (Aug., 1957), 353-354.
    Wallace C. Brown, "Dramatic Tension in Neoclassic Satire," *College English*, VI (Feb., 1945), 266-267.
    Macdonald Emslie, *The Explicator*, XII (Nov., 1953), 8.
    Henry Gifford, " 'The Vanity of Human Wishes,' "

Review of English Studies, VI, n.s. (April, 1955), 157-165.

SUSIE I. TUCKER, " 'The Steeps of Fate' *Vanity of Human Wishes,* I, 125," *Notes and Queries,* IV, n.s. (Aug., 1957), 354.

SUSIE I. TUCKER and HARRY GIFFORD, "Johnson's Poetic Imagination," *Review of English Studies,* VIII, n.s. (Aug., 1957), 241-248.

UNGER and O'CONNOR, *Poems for Study,* pp. 308-312.

JONSON,   "An Epistle Mendicant"

GEORGE B. JOHNSTON, " 'An Epistle Mendicant' by Ben Jonson," *Notes and Queries,* I, n.s. (Nov., 1954), 471.

JONSON,   "It Was a Beauty That I Saw"

DANIELS, *The Art of Reading Poetry,* pp. 200-201.

JONSON,   "On a Lover's Dust Made Sand for an Hour Glass"

MILES, *The Primary Language of Poetry in the 1640's,* pp. 67-68.

JONSON,   "Pan's Anniversary"

EMPSON, *Seven Types of Ambiguity,* pp. 35-36; (1947 ed.), p. 27.

JONSON,   "To Celia: Drink to Me Only with Thine Eyes"

A. D. FITTON BROWN, "Drink to Me, Celia," *Modern Language Review,* LIV (Oct., 1959), 554-557.

GERALD BULLETT, "Drink to me only. . . ," *Times Literary Supplement* (June 1, 1956), p. 329.

EMPSON, *Seven Types of Ambiguity,* pp. 306-307; (1947 ed.), pp. 242-243.

E. A. HORSMAN, "Drink to me only . . .," *Times Literary Supplement* (June 8, 1956), p. 345.

GERALD SANDERS and RALPH P. BOAS, *The Explicator,* I (Feb., 1943), 28.

MARSHALL VAN DEUSEN, "Criticism and Ben Jonson's 'To Celia,' " *Essays in Criticism,* VII (Jan., 1957), 96-103.

JONSON, "A Fit of Rime Against Rime"
George Hemphill, *The Explicator*, XII (June, 1954), 50.

JONSON, "Inviting a Friend to Supper"
Leonard Dean, *English Masterpieces*, Vol. III, *Renaissance Poetry*, p. 14.

JONSON, "The Pattern of Piety"
Percy Simpson, "A Westminster Schoolboy and Ben Jonson," *Times Literary Supplement* (Nov. 27, 1953), p. 761.

JONSON, "To John Donne"
Frederick M. Combellack, *The Explicator*, XVII (Oct., 1958), 6.

JOYCE, "Alone"
Frankenberg, *Invitation to Poetry*, p. 171.

JOYCE, "Ecce Puer"
Marvin Fisher, "James Joyce's 'Ecce Puer,'" *The University of Kansas City Review*, XXV (Summer, 1959), 265-271.
Lawrence Richard Holmes, *The Explicator*, XIII (Nov., 1954), 12.
Richard M. Kain, *The Explicator*, XIV (Feb., 1956), 29.

KAVANAGH, patrick, "Primrose"
Dudley Fitts, *New York Times Book Review*, August 24, 1947, p. 10.

KEATS, "Bright Star"
Bateson, *English Poetry*, pp. 10-11.
Brooks, Purser, Warren, *An Approach to Literature*, pp. 481-482.
Reprinted third edition, pp. 358-359.
Knight, *The Starlit Dome*, pp. 304-305.

KEATS, "Epistle to Charles Cowden Clarke"
Ciardi, *How Does an Poem Mean?* p. 783.

KEATS, "The Eve of St. Agnes"
Roy P. Basler, *The Explicator*, III (Oct., 1944), 1.
Arthur Carr, "John Keats' Other 'Urn,'" *The Uni-*

versity of Kansas City Review, XX (Summer, 1954), 237-242.

CIARDI, *How Does a Poem Mean?*" pp. 772-774.

R. H. FOGLE, "A Reading of Keats's 'Eve of St. Agnes,'" *College English*, VI (March, 1945), 325-328.

WILLIAM J. GRACE, "Teaching Poetic Appreciation Through Quantitative Analysis," *College English*, I (Dec., 1939), 224-226.

ELMO HOWELL, *The Explicator*, XIV (Feb., 1956), 28.

KNIGHT, *The Starlit Dome*, pp. 279-280.

KREUZER, *Elements of Poetry*, pp. 14-16, 125-132.

W. S. WARD, "A Device of Doors in *The Eve of St. Agnes*," *MLN*, LXXIII (Feb., 1958), 90-91.

REGINALD R. WHIDDEN, *The Explicator*, I (June, 1943), 66.

J. E. WHITESELL, *The Explicator*, I (Nov., 1942), 13.

WORMHOUDT, *The Demon Lover*, pp. 71-77.

HERBERT G. WRIGHT, "Has Keats's 'Eve of St. Agnes' a Tragic Ending?" *Modern Language Review*, XL (April, 1945), 90-94.

KEATS,   "Eve of St. Mark"

WALTER E. HOUGHTON, "The Meaning of Keats' 'Eve of St. Mark,'" *English Literary History*, XIII (March, 1946), 64-78.

KEATS,   "Fairy's Song"

J. BURKE SEVERS, *The Explicator*, XIV (Oct., 1955), 3.

KEATS,   "The Fall of Hyperion"

HERBERT READ, "The True Voice of John Keats," *The Hudson Review*, VI (Spring, 1953), 98-104.

BRIAN WICKER, "The Disputed Lines in *The Fall of Hyperion*," *Essays in Criticism*, VII (Jan., 1957), 28-41.

KEATS,   "Hyperion"

JAMES RALSTON CALDWELL, "The Meaning of *Hyperion*," *PMLA*, LI (Dec., 1936), 1080-1097.

PAUL DE MAN, "Keats and Holderlin," *Comparative Literature,* VIII (Winter, 1956), 37-45.

HUNGERFORD, *Shores of Darkness,* pp. 137-162.

HERBERT READ, "The True Voice of John Keats," *The Hudson Review,* VI (Spring, 1953), 94-99.

JOHN HAWLEY ROBERTS, "Poetry of Sensation or of Thought?" *PMLA,* XLV (Dec., 1930), 1134-1137.

MARTHA HALE SHACKFORD, "Hyperion," *Studies in Philology,* XXII (Jan., 1925), 48-60.

KEATS,   "Isabella; or the Pot of Basil"

KNIGHT, *The Starlit Dome,* pp. 280-282.

KEATS,   "La Belle Dame Sans Merci"

BERNARD BREYER, *The Explicator,* VI (Dec., 1947), 18.

H. E. BRIGGS, "Keats, Robertson, and 'That Most Hateful Land,'" *PMLA,* LIX (March, 1944), 195-197.

DANIELS, *The Art of Reading Poetry,* pp. 157-160.

DON A. KEISTER, *The Explicator,* V (Feb., 1947), 29.

L. G. LOCKE, *The Explicator,* V (Oct., 1946), 1.

T. O. MABBOTT, *The Explicator,* V (May, 1947), 50.

MILLET, *Reading Poetry,* pp. 64-65.

FRANCIS L. UTLEY, "The Infernos of Lucretius and of Keats's 'La Belle Dame Sans Merci,'" *Journal of English Literary History,* XXV (June, 1958), 105-121..

WORMHOUDT, *The Demon Lover,* pp. 75-76.

KEATS,   "Lamia"

ADAMS, *Strains of Discord,* pp. 62-63.

BEACH, *A Romantic View of Poetry,* pp. 123-131.

D. B. HARDISON, JR., "The Decorum of *Lamia,*" *Modern Language Quarterly,* XIX (March, 1958), 33-42.

WORMHOUDT, *The Demon Lover,* pp. 77-82.

KEATS,   "Nebuchadnezzar's Dream"

AILEEN WARD, "Keats's Sonnet, 'Nebuchadnezzar's Dream,'" *Philological Quarterly,* XXXIV (April, 1955), 177-188.

KEATS, "Ode on a Grecian Urn"

M. H. ABRAMS, "Belief and Disbelief," *The University of Toronto Quarterly*, XXVII (Jan., 1958), 124-127.

ROBERT M. ADAMS, *"Trompe-L'Oeil* in Shakespeare and Keats," *The Sewanee Review*, LXI (Spring, 1953), 251-253.

ADAMS, *Strains of Discord*, pp. 68-71.

ROY P. BASLER, *The Explicator*, IV (Oct., 1945), 6.

BATESON, *English Poetry*, pp. 217-222.

ROBERT BERKELMAN, "Keats and the Urn," *South Atlantic Quarterly*, LVII (Summer, 1958), 354-358. Reprinted *A Grammar of Motives*, pp. 447-463. Also reprinted West, *Essays in Modern Literary Criticism*, pp. 396-411.

MARIUS BEWLEY, "Kenneth Burke as a Literary Critic," *Scrutiny*, XV (Dec., 1948), 270-273.

BOWRA, *The Romantic Imagination*, pp. 126-148.

CLEANTH BROOKS, JR., "History Without Footnotes: An Account of Keats' Urn," *The Sewanee Review*, LII (Winter, 1944), 89-101.

BROOKS, *The Well Wrought Urn*, pp. 139-152.

KENNETH BURKE, "Symbolic Action in a Poem by Keats," *Accent*, IV (Autumn, 1943), 30-42.

WILLIAM EMPSON, "Thy Darling in an Urn," *The Sewanee Review*, LV (Oct.-Dec., 1947), 693-697.

WILLIAM EMPSON, "Emotions in Words Again," *The Kenyon Review*, X (Autumn, 1948), 580-581.

EMPSON, *The Structure of Complex Words*, pp. 368-374.

RICHARD H. FOGLE, "Empathic Imagery in Keats and Shelley," *PMLA*, LXI (March, 1946), 184-187.

NEWELL F. FORD, "Keats, Empathy, and the 'Poetical Character,'" *Studies in Philology*, XLV (July, 1948), 488-489.

ROBERT C. FOX, *The Explicator*, XIV (June, 1956), 58.

T. S. GREGORY, "John Keats and Apocalypse," *The Dublin Review*, CCXXV (Third Quarter, 1951), 28-37.

K. M. HAMILTON, "Time and the Grecian Urn," *The Dalhousie Review*, XXXIV (Autumn, 1954), 246-254.

VICTOR M. HAMM, *The Explicator*, III (May, 1945), 56.

R. D. HAVENS, "Concerning the 'Ode on a Grecian Urn,'" *Modern Philology*, XXIV (Nov., 1926), 209-214.

KNIGHT, *The Starlit Dome*, pp. 294-296.

ALICE FOX KORNBLUTH, *The Explicator*, XVI (June, 1958), 56.

F. R. LEAVIS, "Keats (Revaluations IX)," *Scrutiny*, IV (March, 1936), 384-388.

CHARLES I. PATTERSON, "Passion and Performance in Keats' 'Ode on a Grecian Urn," *Journal of English Literary History*, XXI (Sept., 1954), 208-220.

R. C. PETTIGREW, *The Explicator*, V (Nov., 1946), 13.

ROYALL SNOW, "Heresy Concerning Keats," *PMLA*, XLIII (Dec., 1928), 1142-1149.

R. W. STALLMAN, "Keats the Apollinian," *The University of Toronto Quarterly*, XVI (Jan., 1947), 155-156.
Reprinted in part, *The Critic's Notebook*, pp. 188-189.

WYLIE SYPHER, "Portrait of the Artist as John Keats," *Virginia Quarterly Review*, XXV (Summer, 1949), 422-423.

ALLEN TATE, "A Reading of Keats (II)," *American Scholar*, XV (Spring, 1946), 194-197. Reprinted *On the Limits of Poetry*, pp. 177-180.

THOMAS and BROWN, *Reading Poems: An Introduction to Critical Study*, p. 660.

UNGER and O'CONNOR, *Poems for Study*, pp. 457-459.

VIVANTE, *English Poetry*, pp. 196-203.

JACOB D. WIGOD, Keats's Ideal in the *Ode on a Grecian Urn,*" *PMLA,* LXII (March, 1957), 113-121.

STEWART C. WILCOX, *The Explicator,* VI (Oct., 1947), 2; and VII (April, 1949), 47.

STEWART C. WILCOX, "The Unity of 'Ode on a Grecian Urn,'" *Personalist,* XXXI (Spring, 1950), 149-156.

KEATS,   "Ode on Indolence"

KNIGHT, *The Starlit Dome,* p. 296.

KEATS,   "Ode on Melancholy"

M. RAY ADAMS, *The Explicator,* XIV (May, 1956), 49.

BEACH, *A Romantic View of Poetry,* pp. 91-94.

BROOKS, PURSER, WARREN, *An Approach to Literature,* pp. 479-481.

Reprinted third edition, pp. 355-358.

RICHARD D. EBERLY, *The Explicator,* VI (April, 1948), 38.

Reprinted Stallman and Watters, *The Creative Reader,* pp. 857-858.

EMPSON, *Seven Types of Ambiguity,* pp. 272-275; (1947 ed.), pp. 214-217.

KNIGHT, *The Starlit Dome,* pp. 296-298.

F. R. LEAVIS, "Keats (Revaluations IX)," *Scrutiny,* IV (March, 1936), 390-393.

LEAVIS, *Revaluation,* pp. 260-262.

KEATS,   "Ode to a Nightingale"

ROBERT M. ADAMS, "*Trompe-L'Oeil* in Shakespeare and Keats," *The Sewanee Review,* LXI (Spring, 1953), 248-251.

ADAMS, *Strains of Discord,* pp. 65-68.

E. H. AUDEN and N. H. PEARSON, *Poets of the English Language, IV* (New York: The Viking Press, 1950), XIX-XX.

HARRY BELSHAW, "Keats on the Mount of Transfiguration," *The London Quarterly and Holborn Review,* CLXXV (October, 1950), 320-324.

BLAIR and CHANDLER, *Approaches to Poetry*, pp. 552-556.

BOWRA, *The Romantic Imagination*, pp. 136-137.

BROOKS, *Modern Poetry and the Tradition*, p. 31.

BROOKS and WARREN, *Understanding Poetry*, pp. 409-415.

Revised edition, pp. 338-345.

DANIELS, *The Art of Reading Poetry*, pp. 366-372.

DREW, *Poetry*, pp. 178-179.

R. H. FOGLE, "Keats's *Ode to a Nightingale*," *PMLA*, LXVIII (March, 1953), 211-222.

R. H. FOGLE, "A Note on Keats's *Ode to a Nightingale*," *Modern Language Quarterly*, VIII (March, 1947), 81-84.

NEWELL F. FORD, "Keats, Empathy, and the 'Poetical Character,'" *Studies in Philology*, XLV (July, 1948), 489-490.

ALBERT GUERARD, JR., "Prometheus and the Aeolian Lyre," *Yale Review*, XXXIII (Spring, 1944), 495-496.

KNIGHT, *The Starlit Dome*, pp. 298-300.

F. R. LEAVIS, "Keats (Revaluations IX)," *Scrutiny*, IV (March, 1936), 378-384.

LEAVIS, *Revaluation*, pp. 244-252.

HERBERT MARSHALL MCLUHAN, "Aesthetic Pattern in Keats' Odes," *University of Toronto Quarterly*, XII (Jan., 1943), 167-179.

LOWRY NELSON, JR., "The Rhetoric of Ineffability: Toward a Definition of Mystical Poetry," *Comparative Literature*, VIII (Fall, 1956), 332-335.

S. M. PITCHER, *The Explicator*, III (March, 1945), 39.

W. O. RAYMOND, " 'The Mind's Internal Heaven' in Poetry," *The University of Toronto Quarterly*, XX (April, 1951), 229-230.

ROSENTHAL and SMITH, *Exploring Poetry*, pp. 505-507.

WYLIE SYPHER, "Portrait of the Artist as John Keats,"

Virginia Quarterly Review, XXV (Summer, 1949), 425.

ALLEN TATE, "A Reading of Keats (II)," *American Scholar*, XV (Spring, 1946), 189-194. Reprinted *On the Limits of Poetry*, pp. 171-177 *et passim*.

THOMAS and BROWN, *Reading Poems: An Introduction to Critical Study*, pp. 658-660.

DOROTHY VAN GHENT, "The Passion of the Groves," *The Sewanee Review*, LII (Spring, 1944), 226-246.

VIVANTE, *English Poetry*, pp. 193-195.

KEATS,   "Ode to Psyche"

ROBERT M. ADAMS, "*Trompe-L'Oeil* in Shakespeare and Keats," *The Sewanee Review*, LXI (Spring, 1953) , 247-248.

ADAMS, *Strains of Discord*, pp. 63-65.

KENNETH ALLOTT, "Keats's 'Ode to Psyche,' " *Essays in Criticism*, VI (July, 1956) , 278-301.

KNIGHT, *The Starlit Dome*, pp. 301-304.

HENRY PETTIT, "Scientific Correlatives of Keats' 'Ode to Psyche,' " *Studies in Philology*, XL (Oct., 1943), 560-566.

WYLIE SYPHER, "Portrait of the Artist as John Keats," *Virginia Quarterly Review*, XXV (Summer, 1949), 425-426.

GEORGE YOST, JR., "An Identification in Keats' 'Ode to Psyche,' " *Philological Quarterly*, XXVI (Oct., 1957) , 496-499.

KEATS,   "On First Looking into Chapman's Homer"

JOSEPH WARREN BEACH, "Keats's Realms of Gold," *PMLA*, XLIX (March, 1934), 246-257.

H. E. BRIGGS, "Swift and Keats," *PMLA*, LXI (Dec., 1946), 1104-1105.

DANIELS, *The Art of Reading Poetry*, pp. 210-212.

B. IFOR EVANS, "Keats's Approach to the Chapman Sonnet," *Essays and Studies*, XVI (1930), 26-52.

G. GIOVANNINI, "Keats' Elysium of Poets," *MLN*, LXIII (Jan., 1948), 19-25.

LYNN H. HARRIS, *The Explicator*, IV (March, 1946), 35.

T. O. MABBOTT, *The Explicator*, V (Dec., 1946), 22.

DOUGALD M. MACEACHEN, "Letter to the Editor," *College English*, XVIII (Oct., 1956), 56.

J. MIDDLETON MURRY, "When Keats Discovered Homer," *Hibbert Journal*, XXVII (Oct., 1928), 93-110, and *Bookman*, LXVIII (Dec., 1928), 391-401.

R. W. STALLMAN, "Keats the Apollinian," *The University of Toronto Quarterly*, XVI (Jan., 1947), 153-154.

STAUFFER, *The Nature of Poetry*, pp. 36-38.

WYLIE SYPHER, "Portrait of the Artist as John Keats," *Virginia Quarterly Review*, XXV (Summer, 1949), 423-424.

CHARLES C. WALCUTT, *The Explicator*, V (June, 1947), 56.

C. V. WICKER, "Cortez—Not Balboa," *College English*, XVII (April, 1956), 383-387.

KEATS,   "On Visiting the Tomb of Burns"

GEORGE YOST, JR., "A Source and Interpretation of Keats's Minos," *Journal of English and Germanic Philology*, LVII (April, 1958), 220-229.

KEATS,   "Sleep and Poetry"

KNIGHT, *The Starlit Dome*, pp. 265-267 *et passim*.

ARCHIBALD LAMPMAN, "The Character of the Poetry of Keats," *The University of Toronto Quarterly*, XV (July, 1946), 361-363.

JOHN HAWLEY ROBERTS, "Poetry of Sensation or of Thought?" *PMLA*, XLV (Dec., 1930), 1129-1130.

KEATS,   "To Autumn"

BROWER, *The Fields of Light*, pp. 39-41.

ROBERT DANIEL and MONROE C. BEARDSLEY, "Reading Takes a Whole Man," *College English*, XVII (Oct., 1955), 31-32.

NORMAN HAMPSON, "Keats and Ourselves," *Times Literary Supplement*, Dec. 22, 1945, p. 607.

KNIGHT, *The Starlit Dome*, pp. 300-301.

F. R. LEAVIS, "Keats (Revaluations IX)," *Scrutiny*, IV (March, 1936), 392-393.

LEAVIS, *Revaluation*, pp. 262-264.

ANNA JEAN MILL, "Keats and Ourselves," *Times Literary Supplement*, Feb. 2, 1946, p. 55.

LEONARD UNGER, "Keats and the Music of Autumn," *Western Review*, XIV (Summer, 1950), 275-284. Reprinted *The Man in the Name*, pp. 18-29.

UNGER and O'CONNOR, *Poems for Study*, pp. 454-456.

KEATS,   "To——: What Can I Do to Drive Away Remembrance from My Eyes"

A. D. ATKINSON, "Lines to Fanny," *Times Literary Supplement*, Nov. 25, 1949, p. 771.

HAROLD E. BRIGGS, "Keats, Robertson, and 'That Most Hateful Land,'" *PMLA*, LIX (March, 1944), 184-195.

JOHN R. MOORE, "Lines to Fanny," *Times Literary Supplement*, Dec. 23, 1949, p. 841.

J. MIDDLETON MURRY, "Lines to Fanny," *Times Literary Supplement*, Nov. 18, 1949, p. 751.

KEATS,   "When I Have Fears That I May Cease to Be"

THOMAS E. CONNOLLY, *The Explicator*, XIII (Dec., 1954), 14.

DANIEL GIBSON and MORLEY J. HAYS, *The Explicator*, I (April, 1943), 47.

M. A. GOLDBERG, "The 'Fears' of John Keats," *Modern Language Quarterly*, XVIII (June, 1957), 125-131.

KEES, WELDON,   "The Locusts, the Plaza, the Room"

J. F. NIMS, *Poetry: A Critical Supplement*, Oct., 1947, pp. 10-11.

KENNEDY, REV. G. A. STUDDERT   ("Woodbine Willie")

"There Was Rapture of Spring in the Morning (*More Rough Rhymes of a Padre*)

I. A. RICHARDS, *Practical Criticism*, pp. 53-61, 262-266.

KILMER,   "Trees"

BROOKS and WARREN, *Understanding Poetry*, pp. 387-391.

Revised edition, pp. 274-278.

JEFFREY FLEECE, "Further Notes on a 'Bad' Poem," *College English*, XII (March, 1951), 314-320.

KING, HENRY, "The Exequy"
ROBERT F. GLECKNER, *The Explicator*, XII (May, 1954), 46.

KING, HENRY, "The Labyrinth"
TUVE, *Elizabethan and Metaphysical Imagery*, p. 357.

KINNELL, GALWAY, "First Song"
GENE H. KORETZ, *The Explicator*, XV (April, 1957), 43.

MELVIN WALKER LaFOLLETTE, *The Explicator*, XIV (April, 1956), 48.

KIPLING, "Danny Deever"
LOUIS S. FRIEDLAND, *The Explicator*, II (Oct., 1943), 9.

KIPLING, "M'Andrew's Hymn"
DEUTSCH, *Poetry in Our Time*, p. 29.

KUNITZ, "Among the Gods"
GEORGE P. ELLIOTT, "The Poetry of Stanley Kunitz," *Accent*, XVIII (Autumn, 1958), 270.

KUNITZ, "Careless Love"
GEORGE P. ELLIOT, "The Poetry of Stanley Kunitz," *Accent*, XVIII (Autumn, 1958), 268-269.

LAMB, "The Old Familiar Faces"
LEO SPITZER, *The Southern Review*, VI (Winter, 1941), 586-588.

LANDOR, "Mild Is the Parting Year and Sweet"
MARY ELLEN RICKEY, *The Explicator*, XIII (Oct., 1954), 2.

LANDOR, "Proud Word You Never Spoke"
KIRK and McCUTCHEON, *An Introduction to the Study of Poetry*, pp. 15-16.

LANDOR, "Rose Aylmer"
BROOKS and WARREN, *Understanding Poetry*, pp. 270-273.
Revised edition, pp. 145-147.

R. H. SUPER, *The Explicator*, III (Feb., 1945), 31.

ROBERT PENN WARREN, "Pure and Impure Poetry," *The Kenyon Review*, V (Spring, 1943), 235-237. Reprinted *Criticism*, pp. 369-370, and *Critiques*, pp. 90-92.

Also reprinted *The Kenyon Critics*, pp. 24-26.

Also reprinted West, *Essays in Modern Literary Criticism*, pp. 251-253.

LANIER, "The Marshes of Glynn"

PHILIP GRAHAM, "Sidney Lanier and the Pattern of Contrast," *American Quarterly*, XI (Winter, 1959), 506-507.

ALLEN TATE, *New Republic*, LXXVI (August 30, 1933), 67-70.

R. P. WARREN, "The Blind Poet: Sidney Lanier," *The American Review*, II (Nov., 1933), 42-45.

LANIER, "My Springs"

BROOKS and WARREN, *Understanding Poetry*, pp. 442-445.

Revised edition, pp, 299-302.

LANIER, "Night and Day"

EDD W. PARKS, "Lanier's 'Night and Day,' " *American Literature*, XXX (March, 1958), 117-118.

LANIER, "Sunrise"

PHILIP GRAHAM, "Sidney Lanier and the Pattern of Contrast," *American Quarterly*, XI (Winter, 1959), 506.

LANIER, "The Symphony"

ELISABETH J. HOGENES, *The Explicator*, XVI (Oct., 1957), 4.

LAWRENCE, "Corot"

BLACKMUR, *The Double Agent*, pp. 112-115.

Reprinted *Language as Gesture*, pp. 294-295.

LAWRENCE, "End of Another Home Holiday"

SAVAGE, *The Personal Principle*, pp. 135-136.

LAWRENCE, "The Enkindled Spring"

SKELTON, *The Poetic Pattern*, pp. 104-105.

LAWRENCE, "Gipsy"
> BLACKMUR, *The Double Agent,* pp. 108-109.
>> Reprinted *Language as Gesture,* pp. 290-291.

LAWRENCE, "Lotus and Frost"
> SKELTON, *The Poetic Pattern,* pp. 103-104.

LAWRENCE, "Piano"
> F. R. LEAVIS, " 'Thought' and Emotional Quality," *Scrutiny,* XIII (Spring, 1945), 55-58.
>
> RICHARDS, *Practical Criticism,* pp. 104-117 *et passim.*
>
> MACKLIN THOMAS, "Analysis of the Experience in Lyric Poetry," *College English,* IX (March, 1948), 318-319.

LAWRENCE, "Snake"
> DEUTSCH, *Poetry in Our Time,* pp. 89-91.

LAWRENCE, "Song of a Man Who Has Come Through"
> ROBERT HOGAN, *The Explicator,* XVII (April, 1959), 51.

LAWRENCE, "Whether or Not"
> DEUTSCH, *Poetry in Our Time,* pp. 5-6.

LAWRENCE, "The Wild Common"
> BLACKMUR, *The Double Agent,* pp. 110-111.
>> Reprinted *Language as Gesture,* pp. 291-292.

LEAR, EDWARD, "The Dong with a Luminous Nose"
> DAICHES, *A Study of Literature,* pp. 201-202.
>
> A. E. DYSON, "Method in Madness: A Note on Edward Lear," *English,* X (Autumn, 1955), 221.

LEAR, EDWARD, "Jumblies"
> A. E. DYSON, "Method in Madness: A Note on Edward Lear," *English,* X (Autumn, 1955), 222-223.

LEWIS, ALUN, "Ha, Ha! Among the Trumpets"
> RALPH HOUSTON, "The Broken Arch: A Study of the Poetry of Alun Lewis," *Adelphi,* XXVIII (Fourth Quarter, 1951), 403-413.

LEWIS, ALUN, "Raider's Dawn"
> RALPH HOUSTON, "The Broken Arch: A Study of the Poetry of Alun Lewis," *Adelphi,* XXVIII (Fourth Quarter, 1951), 403-413.

LEWIS, JAMES FRANKLIN,   "Dawn in the Study"
MARY GRAHAM LUND, *The Explicator*, XVIII (Nov., 1959), 12.

LINDSAY,   "The Congo"
A. J. BADER, "Lindsay Explains 'The Congo,'" *Philological Quarterly*, XXVII (April, 1948), 190-192.
WALTER BLAIR, *The Literature of the United States*, II, 946.
AUSTIN WARREN, "The Case of Vachel Lindsay," *Accent*, VI (Summer, 1946), 237-239.

LINDSAY,   "General William Booth Enters into Heaven"
WALTER BLAIR, *The Literature of the United States*, II, 944.
AUSTIN WARREN, "The Case of Vachel Lindsay," *Accent*, VI (Summer, 1946), 237.

LINDSAY,   "The Santa Fe Trail"
RICHARD E. AMACHER, *The Explicator*, V (March, 1947), 33.
RICHARD E. AMACHER, "Off 'The Santa Fe Trail,'" *American Literature*, XX (Nov., 1948), 337.
A. L. BADER, "Vachel Lindsay and 'The Santa Fe Trail,'" *American Literature*, XIX (Jan., 1948), 360-362.

LODGE,   "Satire 5" (from *A Fig for Momus*)
SIDNEY H. ATKINS, "Dyer at Woodstock," *Times Literary Supplement*, Feb. 3, 1945, p. 55.

LONGFELLOW,   "Aftermath"
ARMS, *The Fields Were Green*, pp. 213-214.

LONGFELLOW,   "The Cross of Snow"
ROBERT A. DURR, *The Explicator*, XIII (March, 1955), 32.

LONGFELLOW,   "Divina Commedia," Sonnet I
GEORGE ARMS, *The Explicator*, II (Oct., 1943), 7.
ARMS, *The Fields Were Green*, p. 211.

LONGFELLOW,   "The Falcon of Ser Federigo"
ARMS, *The Fields Were Green*, pp. 218-219.

LONGFELLOW,   "The Fire of Drift-Wood"
ARMS, *The Fields Were Green,* p. 212.

LONGFELLOW,   "Hymn to the Night"
GEORGE ARMS, *The Explicator,* I (Oct., 1942), 7.

LONGFELLOW,   "In the Churchyard at Cambridge"
ARMS, *The Fields Were Green,* pp. 208-209.

RICHARDS, *Practical Criticism,* pp. 162-178 *et passim.*

LONGFELLOW,   "Jugurtha"
RICHARD E. AMACHER, *The Explicator,* VI (Feb., 1948), 29.

GEORGE ARMS, *The Fields Were Green,* p. 215.

LONGFELLOW,   "Killed at the Ford"
ARMS, *The Fields Were Green,* pp. 221-222.

LONGFELLOW,   "My Lost Youth"
GEORGE ARMS, "The Revision of 'My Lost Youth,'"
MLN, LXI (June, 1946), 389-392.

LONGFELLOW,   "Paul Revere's Ride"
N. H. PEARSON, "Both Longfellows," *The University of Kansas City Review,* XVI (Summer, 1950), 247.

LONGFELLOW,   "Seaweed"
ARMS, *The Fields Were Green,* pp. 209-211.

LONGFELLOW,   "Serenade"
ARMS, *The Fields Were Green,* pp. 220-221.

LONGFELLOW,   "Snow-Flakes"
ARMS, *The Fields Were Green,* pp. 207-208.

N. H. PEARSON, "Both Longfellows," *The University of Kansas City Review,* XVI (Summer, 1950), 252-253.

LOVELACE,   "A Black Patch on Lucasta's Face"
C. F. WILLIAMSON, "Two Notes on the Poems of Richard Lovelace," *Modern Language Review,* LII (April, 1957), 229.

LOVELACE,   "The Grasshopper"
DON CAMERON ALLEN, "An Explication of Lovelace's 'The Grass-Hopper,'" *Modern Language Quarterly,* XVIII (March, 1957), 35-43.

LOVELACE,   "La Bella Bona-Roba"

MARIUS BEWLEY, "The Colloquial Mode of Byron," *Scrutiny*, XVI (March, 1949), 12-14.

LOVELACE, "Song: No, No, Fair Heretic. It Needs Must Be"

KREUTZER, *Elements of Poetry*, p. 153.

LOVELACE, "To Althea, from Prison"

EMPSON, *Seven Types of Ambiguity*, pp. 266-267; (1947 ed.), pp. 209-211.

LOVELACE, "To Lucasta"

KIRK and McCUTCHEON, *An Introduction to the Study of Poetry*, pp. 12-14.

NORMAN HOLMES PEARSON, *The Explicator*, VII (June, 1949), 58.

Reprinted Locke, Gibson, and Arms, *Introduction to Literature*, third edition, pp. 48-49.

VAN DOREN, *Introduction to Poetry*, pp. 22-26.

LOVELACE, "To My Dear Friend Mr. E. R."

C. F. WILLIAMSON, "Two Notes on the Poems of Richard Lovelace," *Modern Language Review*, LII (April, 1957), 227-228.

LOWELL, AMY, "Night Clouds"

COOPER and HOLMES, *Preface to Poetry*, pp. 141-142.

LOWELL, AMY, "Patterns"

BROOKS and WARREN, *Understanding Poetry*, pp. 139-143.

Revised edition, pp. 58-61.

LOWELL, AMY, "Sunshine"

DANIELS, *The Art of Reading Poetry*, pp. 196-197.

LOWELL, JAMES RUSSELL, "Agassiz"

ARMS, *The Fields Were Green*, 124-126.

LOWELL, JAMES RUSSELL, "Auspex"

RICHARD E. AMACHER, *The Explicator*, IX March, 1951), 37.

ARMS, *The Fields Were Greeen*, pp. 133-134.

LOWELL, JAMES RUSSELL, "The Cathedral"

ARMS, *The Fields Were Green*, pp. 135-138.

LOWELL, JAMES RUSSELL, "Fitz Adam's Story"

ARMS, *The Fields Were Green,* pp. 130-132.

LOWELL, JAMES RUSSELL, "Ode Recited at the Harvard Commemoration"

ARMS, *The Fields Were Green,* pp. 138-140.

LOWELL, JAMES RUSSELL, "To the Dandelion"

ARMS, *The Fields Were Green,* pp. 132-133.

LOWELL, ROBERT, "After Surprising Conversions"

JOHN AKEY, *The Explicator,* IX (June, 1951), 53.

G. GIOVANNINI, *The Explicator,* IX (June, 1951), 53.

ROY HARVEY PEARCE, *The Explicator,* IX (June, 1951), 53.

LOWELL, ROBERT, "As a Plane Tree by the Water"

DE SALES STANDERWICK, "Notes on Robert Lowell," *Renascence,* VIII (Winter, 1955), 80.

LOWELL, ROBERT, "At the Indian Killer's Grave"

DE SALES STANDERWICK, "Notes on Robert Lowell," *Renascence,* VIII (Winter, 1955), 78-79.

AUSTIN WARREN, "A Double Discipline," *Poetry,* LXX (August, 1947), 265.

LOWELL, ROBERT, "Between the Porch and the Altar"

MARIUS BEWLEY, "Aspects of Modern American Poetry," *Scrutiny,* XVII (March, 1951), 345-347.

LOWELL, ROBERT, "Mother Marie Therese"

DE SALES STANDERWICK, "Notes on Robert Lowell," *Renascence,* VIII (Winter, 1955), 81-82.

LOWELL, ROBERT, "Napoleon Crosses the Berezina"

DE SALES STANDERWICK, "Notes on Robert Lowell," *Renascence,* VIII (Winter, 1955), 79.

LOWELL, ROBERT, "A Prayer for My Grandfather to Our Lady"

MARIUS BEWLEY, "Aspects of Modern American Poetry," *Scrutiny,* XVII (March, 1951), 344-345.

LOWELL, ROBERT, "The Quaker Graveyard in Nantucket"

PAUL ENGLE, "Five Years of Pulitzer Poets," *The English Journal,* XXXVIII (Feb., 1949), 64.

FRIAR and BRINNIN, *Modern Poetry,* pp. 520-521.

DESALES STANDERWICK, "Notes on Robert Lowell,"

Renascence, VIII (Winter, 1955), 76-78.

LOWELL, ROBERT, " 'Sunthin' in the Pastoral Line"
JOHN C. BRODERICK, "Lowell's 'Sunthin' in the Pastoral Line,' " *American Literature,* XXXI (May, 1959), 163-172.

LOWELL, ROBERT, "Where the Rainbow Ends"
MARIUS BEWLEY, "Aspects of Modern American Poetry," *Scrutiny,* XVII (March, 1951), 343-344.

RANDALL JARRELL, "From the Kingdom of Necessity," *Nation,* CLXIV (Jan., 18, 1947), 74-75.
Reprinted *Mid-Century American Poets,* pp. 160-161.

DE SALES STANDERWICK, "Notes on Robert Lowell," *Renascence,* VIII (Winter, 1955), 80-81.

LUCE, G. H., "Climb Cloud, and Pencil all the Blue"
I. A. RICHARDS, *Practical Criticism,* pp. 131-144 *et passim.*

MacDIARMID, "The Eemis Stane"
DAVID DAICHES, "Hugh MacDiarmid and Scottish Poetry," *Poetry,* LXXII (July, 1948), 206-207.

MacDIARMID, HUGH, "Lourd on My Hert as Winter Lies"
DAVID DAICHES, "Hugh MacDiarmid and Scottish Poetry," *Poetry,* LXXII, (July, 1948), 209-210.

MacDIARMID, HUGH, "Moonstruck"
DAVID DAICHES, "Hugh MacDiarmid and Scottish Poetry," *Poetry* LXXII (July, 1948), 211.

MacDIARMID, HUGH, "Yet Ha'e I Silence Left, the Croon o' A' "
DAVID DAICHES, "Hugh MacDiarmid and Scottish Poetry," *Poetry,* LXXII (July, 1948), 210.

MacLEISH, ". . . & Forty-Second Street"
IVAR L. MYHR, *The Explicator,* III (April, 1945), 47.

MacLEISH, "Ars Poetica"
VICTOR P. STAUDT, " 'Ars Poetica' and the Teacher," *College English,* XIX (Oct., 1957), 28-29.
STAUFFER, *The Nature of Poetry,* pp. 121-125.

Reprinted Engle and Carrier, *Reading Modern Poetry*, pp. 99-101.

MacLEISH, " 'Dover Beach' — A Note to That Poem"
KREUZER, *Elements of Poetry*, pp. 183-189, 191-192.
JAMES ZIGERELL, *The Explicator*, XVII (March, 1959), 38.

MacLEISH, "Einstein"
HOFFMAN, *The Twenties*, pp. 287-288.
WAGGONER, *The Heel of Elohim*, pp. 143-146.

MacLEISH, "Eleven"
DEUTSCH, *Poetry in Our Time*, p. 147.

MacLEISH "Epistle to Be Left in the Earth"
WAGGONER, *The Heel of Elohim*, pp. 146-148.

MacLEISH, "The Hamlet of A. MacLeish"
WAGGONER, *The Heel of Elohim*, pp. 141-143.

MacLEISH, "Hyprocrite Auteur"
NICHOLAS JOOST, *The Explicator*, XI (May, 1953), 47.

MacLEISH, "L 'An Trentiesme de Mon Eage"
RICHARD E. AMACHER, *The Explicator*, VI (April, 1948), 42.

MacLEISH, "Lines for an Interment"
KREUZER, *Elements of Poetry*, pp. 141-143.

MacLEISH, "Memorial Rain"
BROOKS, *Modern Poetry and the Tradition*, pp. 122-124.

MacLEISH, "Men"
BROOKS, *Modern Poetry and the Tradition*, pp. 117-118.

MacLEISH, "Pony Rock"
GERALD SANDERS, *The Explicator*, II (Oct., 1943), 8.

MacLEISH, "You, Andrew Marvell"
BROOKS, *Modern Poetry and the Tradition*, p. 122.
GUY A. CARDWELL, *Readings from the Americas* (New York: Ronald Press Co., 1947), pp. 790-791.
DREW, *Poetry*, pp. 104-105.
PERRINE, *Sound and Sense*, pp. 68-69.

MacNEICE, "Autumn Journal"
S. G. BROWN, "Some Poems of Louis MacNeice," *The*

Sewanee Review, LI (Winter, 1943), 68-72.
MacNEICE, "Entirely"
DONALD A. STAUFFER, "Genesis, or the Poet as Maker," *Poets at Work*, pp. 70-72.
MacNEICE, "Leaving Barra"

S. G. BROWN, "Some Poems of Louis MacNeice," *The Sewanee Review*, LI (Winter, 1943), 64-66.
MacNEICE, "Les Sylphides"
DREW and SWEENEY, *Directions in Modern Poetry*, pp. 247-249.
MacNEICE, "Perseus"
DREW and SWEENEY, *Directions in Modern Poetry*, pp. 87-88 (quoting MacNeice's explanation).
MacNEICE, "Prayer Before Birth"
DEUTSCH, *Poetry in Our Time*, pp. 365-366.
MacNEICE, "Snow"
MARIE BARROFF, "What a Poem Is: For Instance 'Snow,'" *Essays in Criticism*, VIII (Oct., 1958), 393-404.
SISTER M. MARTIN BARRY, O. P., *The Explicator*, XVI (Nov., 1957), 10.
DREW, *Poetry*, pp. 226-228.
MacNEICE, "The Sunlight on the Garden"
THOMAS and BROWN, *Reading Poems: An Introduction to Critical Study*, pp. 686 697.
MacNEICE, "These Days Are Misty"
STAGEBERG and ANDERSON, *Poetry as Experience*, pp. 216-221.
MacNEICE, "You Who Will Soon Be Unrecapturable"
S. G. BROWN, "Some Poems of Louis MacNeice," *The Sewanee Review*, LI (Winter, 1943), 66-67.
MAGEE, J. G., "High Flight"
STAGEBERG and ANDERSON, *Poetry as Experience*, p. 4.
MAHONY, "The Bells of Shandon"
BROOKS and WARREN, *Understanding Poetry*, pp. 222-224.
Revised edition, pp. 114-116.

MALLALIEU, H. B., "Lines from Europe"
J. F. NIMS, *Poetry: A Critical Supplement,* April, 1947, pp. 14-16.

MANIFOLD, JOHN, "Fife Tune"
ROSENTHAL and SMITH, *Exploring Poetry,* pp. 549-550.

MARKHAM, "The Man With the Hoe"
LYNN H. HARRIS, *The Explicator,* III (March, 1945), 41.

MARLOWE, "The Passionate Shepherd to His Love"
BOULTON, *The Anatomy of Poetry,* pp. 160-163.

MARVELL, "Damon the Mower"
JOSEPH H. SUMMERS, "Marvell's 'Nature,'" *Journal of English Literary History,* XX (June, 1953), 128.

MARVELL, "Daphnis and Chloe"
M. C. BRADBROOK and M. G. FLOYD THOMAS, "Marvell and the Concept of Metamorphosis," *The Criterion,* XVIII (Jan., 1939), 237-238.

MARVELL, "The Definition of Love"
BROOKS and WARREN, *Understanding Poetry,* pp. 437-440.
Revised edition, pp. 294-297.
DENNIS DAVISON, "Marvell's 'The Definition of Love,'" *Review of English Studies,* VI, n.s. (April, 1955), 141-146.
DREW, *Poetry,* pp. 201-203.

GEOFFREY WALTON, "The Poetry of Andrew Marvell: A Summing Up," *Politics and Letters,* I (Summer, 1948), 27-28.

MARVELL, "A Dialogue Between the Soul and Body"
F. R. LEAVIS, "The Responsible Critic: Or the Function of Criticism at Any Time," *Scrutiny,* XIX (Spring, 1953), 163-170.

TUVE, *Elizabethan and Metaphysical Imagery,* pp. 207-208 *et passim.*

MARVELL, "Eyes and Tears"
EMPSON, *Seven Types of Ambiguity,* pp. 217-220; (1947 ed.), pp. 171-173.

MARVELL, "The First Anniversary"
JAMES WINNY, "A Marvell Emendation," *Times Literary Supplement* (Oct. 2, 1953), p. 626.
MARVELL, "The Garden"
M. C. BRADBROOK and M. G. FLOYD THOMAS, "Marvell and the Concept of Metamorphosis," *The Criterion,* XVIII (Jan., 1939), 236-244.
DAICHES and CHARVAT, *Poems in English,* pp. 662-663.
DANIELS, *The Art of Reading Poetry,* pp. 261-264.
DOUGLAS, LAMSON, SMITH, *The Critical Reader,* pp. 68-72.
WILLIAM EMPSON, "Marvell's 'Garden,'" *Determinations,* pp. 46-56.
WILLIAM EMPSON, "Marvell's 'Garden,'" *Scrutiny,* I (Dec., 1932), 236-240.
EMPSON, *English Pastoral Poetry,* pp. 119-132. Reprinted *Criticism,* pp. 342-352.
Also reprinted West, *Essays in Modern Literary Criticism,* pp. 335-353.
LAWRENCE W. HYMAN, "Marvell's 'Garden,'" *Journal of English Literary History,* XXV (March, 1958), 13-22.
DON A. KEISTER, *The Explicator,* X (Feb., 1952), 24.
MILTON KLONSKY, "A Guide Through the Garden," *The Sewanee Review,* LVIII (Winter, 1950), 16-35.
JOHN MCCHESNEY, *The Explicator,* X (Oct., 1951), 4.
MAREN-SOFIE ROSTVIG, "Andrew Marvell's 'The Garden': A Hermetic Poem," *English Studies,* XL (April, 1959), 65-77.
JOHN CROWE RANSOM, "Mr. Empson's Muddles," *The Southern Review,* IV (Autumn, 1938), 331-334.
JOSEPH H. SUMMERS, "Marvell's 'Nature,'" *Journal of English Literary History,* XX (June, 1953), 125.
UNGER, *The Man in the Name,* pp. 126-128.
VAN DOREN, *Introduction to Poetry,* pp. 61-65.
GEOFFREY WALTON, "The Poetry of Andrew Marvell:

A Summing Up," *Politics and Letters,* I (Summer, 1948), 30-31.

MARVELL,   "An Horatian Ode"

CLEANTH BROOKS, "Criticism and Literary History: Marvell's 'Horatian Ode,'" *The Sewanee Review,* LV (April-June, 1947), 199-222.

CLEANTH BROOKS, "Literary Criticism," *English Institute Essays 1946,* pp. 127-158.

CLEANTH BROOKS, "A Note on the Limits of 'History' and the Limits of 'Criticism,'" *The Sewanee Review,* LXI (Winter, 1953), 129-133.

BROOKS and WARREN, *Understanding Poetry,* revised edition, pp. 667-682.

L. D. LERNER, *Interpretations,* John Wain, ed., pp. 62-74.

GEOFFREY WALTON, "The Poetry of Andrew Marvell: A Summing Up," *Politics and Letters,* I (Summer, 1948), 32-33.

MARVELL,   "The Mower Against Gardens"

MARCIA E. ALLENTUCK, "Marvell's 'Pool of Air,'" *MLN,* LXXIV (Nov., 1959), 587-589.

JOSEPH H. SUMMERS, "Marvell's 'Nature,'" *Journal of English Literary History,* XX (June, 1953), 125-126.

MARVELL,   "The Mower to the Glow-worms"

TILLYARD, *The Metaphysicals and Milton,* pp. 32-35.

MARVELL,   "The Mower's Song"

JOSEPH H. SUMMERS, "Marvell's 'Nature,'" *Journal of English Literary History,* XX (June, 1953), 127.

MARVELL,   "The Nymph Complaining for the Death of Her Faun"

DON CAMERON ALLEN, "Marvell's 'Nymph,'" *Journal of English Literary History,* XXIII (June, 1956), 92-111.

M. C. BRADBROOK and M. G. FLOYD THOMAS, "Marvell and the Concept of Metamorphosis," *The Criterion,* XVIII (Jan., 1939), 252-253.

RUEL E. FOSTER, "A Tonal Study: Marvell," *The University of Kansas City Review*, XXII (Autumn, 1955), 73-78.

EDWARD S. LECOMTE, "Marvell's 'The Nymph Complaining for the Death of Her Faun,'" *Modern Philology*, L (Nov., 1952), 97-101.

LEO SPITZER, "Marvell's 'Nymph Complaining for the Death of Her Faun': Sources Versus Meaning," *Modern Language Quarterly*, XIX (Sept., 1958), 231-243.

MARVELL, "On a Drop of Dew"

EMPSON, *Seven Types of Ambiguity* (1947 ed.), p. 80.

MARVELL, "The Picture of Little T. C. in a Prospect of Flowers"

ELSIE DUNCAN-JONES, "T. C. of A Prospect of Flowers,'" *Times Literary Supplement* (Oct. 30, 1953), p. 693.

JOSEPH H. SUMMERS, "Marvell's 'Nature,'" *Journal of English Literary History*, XX (June, 1953), 130-134.

TILLYARD, *Poetry Direct and Oblique*, pp. 203-206.

MARVELL, "To His Coy Mistress"

RUSSELL AMES, "Decadence in the Art of T. S. Eliot," *Science and Society*, XVI (Summer, 1952), 198-221.

BATESON, *English Poetry*, p. 9.

M. C. BRADBROOK and M. G. FLOYD THOMAS, "Marvell and the Concept of Metamorphosis," *The Criterion*, XVIII (Jan., 1939), 245-246.

BROOKS, PURSER, WARREN, *An Approach to Literature*, pp. 504-506.

Reprinted third edition, pp. 393-395.

JOHN J. CARROLL, "The Sun and the Lovers in 'To His Coy Mistress,'" *MLN*, LXXIV (Jan., 1959), 4-7

ROBERT DANIEL, *The Explicator*, I (March, 1943), 37.

FREDERICK L. GWYNN, *The Explicator*, XI (May, 1953), 49.

JOHN CROWE RANSOM, *The New Criticism*, pp. 311-313.

JOHN HAWLEY ROBERTS, *The Explicator,* I (Dec., 1942), 17. Reprinted *Readings for Liberal Education,* II, 516-517.

LAWRENCE A. SASEK, *The Explicator,* XIV (April, 1956), 47.

ROGER SHARROCK, "The Date of Marvell's 'To His Coy Mistress,'" *Times Literary Supplement* (Jan. 16, 1959), p. 33.

W. A. TURNER, "The Not So Coy Mistress of J. Alfred Prufrock," *South Atlantic Quarterly* LIV (Oct., 1955), 520.

GEOFFREY WALTON, "The Poetry of Andrew Marvell: A Summing Up," *Politics and Letters,* I (Summer, 1948), 28-29.

WHEELWRIGHT, *The Burning Fountain,* pp. 112-113.

MARVELL, "Upon the Death of the Lord Hastings"

EMPSON, *Seven Types of Ambiguity,* pp. 212-217; (1947 ed.), pp. 168-171.

MASEFIELD, "Cargoes"

GEORGE ARMS, *The Explicator,* I (Nov., 1942), 15.

BLAIR and GERBER, *Better Reading 2: Literature,* pp. 176-177.

ARTHUR DICKSON, *The Explicator,* II (Nov., 1943), 12.

ROGER P. MCCUTCHEON, *The Explicator,* II (Feb., 1944), 31.

CLIFFORD A. NAULT, JR., *The Explicator,* XVI (Feb., 1958), 31.

MASEFIELD, "C. L. M."

WALTER GIERASCH, *The Explicator,* XIII (Feb., 1955), 25.

MASEFIELD, "The Racer"

COOPER and HOLMES, *Preface to Poetry,* pp. 170-173.

MASEFIELD, "Sea Fever"

C. C. CUNNINGHAM, *Literature as a Fine Art: Analysis and Interpretation,* pp. 160-164.

FRANCIS V. LLOYD, JR., *The Explicator,* III (March, 1945), 36.

MASTERS, "The Lost Orchard"
RICHARD E. AMACHER, *The Explicator*, VII (March, 1949), 38.
MARY B. DEATON, *The Explicator*, VIII (Nov., 1949), 16.

MELVILLE, "The Apparition: A Retrospect"
ROBERT PENN WARREN, "Melville the Poet," *The Kenyon Review*, VIII (Spring, 1946), 216-218.

MELVILLE, "Art"
LEO HAMALIAN, *The Explicator*, VIII (March, 1950), 40.

MELVILLE, "Commemorative of a Naval Victory"
BROOKS, PURSER, WARREN, *An Approach to Literature*, third edition, pp. 344-345.

MELVILLE, "The Conflict of Convictions"
ROBERT PENN WARREN, "Melville the Poet," *The Kenyon Review*, VIII (Spring, 1946), 213-214 *et passim*.

MELVILLE, "In a Bye-Canal"
ROBERT PENN WARREN, "Melville the Poet," *The Kenyon Review*, VIII (Spring, 1946), 209-211.

MELVILLE, "The Maldive Shark"
ROBERT PENN WARREN, "Melville the Poet," *The Kenyon Review*, VIII (Spring, 1946), 218 *et passim*.

MELVILLE, "A Rail Road Cutting Near Alexandria in 1855"
THOMAS O. MABBOTT, *The Explicator*, IX (June, 1951), 55.

MEREDITH, "Dirge in the Woods"
STAGEBERG and ANDERSON, *Poetry as Experience*, pp. 9-10.

MEREDITH, "In the Woods"
NORMAN FRIEDMAN, "The Jangled Harp: Symbolic Structure in *Modern Love*." *Modern Language Quarterly*, XVIII (March, 1957), 16-17.

MEREDITH, "Lucifer in Starlight"
WALTER BLAIR, *Manual of Reading* (Chicago: Scott,

Foresman and Company, 1943), pp. 145-147.

Brooks and Warren, *Understanding Poetry,* pp. 492-499.

Revised edition, pp. 367-373.

MEREDITH, "Meditation Under Stars"

R. W. Whidden and J. P Kirby, *The Explicator,* IV (Dec., 1945), 19.

MEREDITH, "Modern Love" XXXI: "This Golden Head Has Wit in It. I Live"

Carl H. Ketcham, *The Explicator,* XVII (Oct., 1958), 7.

MEREDITH, "Thus Piteously Love Closed What He Begat" (*Modern Love,* 50)

Day Lewis, *The Poetic Image,* pp. 83-85.

MEREDITH, "Youth in Memory"

Norman Friedman, "The Jangled Harp: Symbolic Structure in *Modern Love,*" *Modern Language Quarterly,* XVIII (March, 1957), 24-25.

MEREDITH, william, "Battlewagon"

Dudley Fitts, "Meredith's Second Volume," *Poetry,* LXXIII (Nov., 1948), 114-115.

MEREDITH, william, "Wedding Song"

Dudley Fitts, "Meredith's Second Volume," *Poetry,* LXXIII (Nov., 1948), 111-113.

MERTON, "St. Malachy"

Hayden Carruth, *A Critical Supplement to "Poetry,"* Feb., 1949, pp. 10-13.

MILLAY, "Euclid Alone Has Looked on Beauty Bare"

Bradford A. Booth, *The Explicator,* VI (Oct., 1947), 5.

Cooper and Holmes, *Preface to Poetry,* pp. 46-53.

Arthur Dickson, *The Explicator,* III (Dec., 1944), 23.

Arthur Dickson, *The Explicator,* VI (May, 1948), 49.

Drew and Sweeney, *Directions in Modern Poetry,*

pp. 207-208. Reprinted Douglas, Lamson, Smith, *The Critical Reader,* pp. 110-111.

CARL A. NIEMEYER and ROBERT M. GAY, *The Explicator,* I (Nov., 1942), 16.

MILLAY,   "Memorial to D. C.: Elegy"

WALTER GIERASCH, *The Explicator,* II (May, 1944), 23.

MILLAY,   "Oh, Sleep Forever in the Latmian Cave"

JOHN CROWE RANSOM, "The Poet as Woman," *The Southern Review,* II (Spring, 1937), 788-790.

RANSOM, *The World's Body,* pp. 83-86.

MILLAY,   "The Return"

JOHN CROWE RANSOM, "The Poet as Woman," *The Southern Review,* II (Spring, 1937), 804-806.

RANSOM, *The World's Body,* pp. 107-110.

MILLAY,   "What's This of Death, from You Who Never Will Die?"

WILLIAM ELTON, *The Explicator,* VII (March, 1949), 37.

RICHARDS, *Practical Criticism,* pp. 62-79 *et passim.*

MILTON,   "L'Allegro"

P. B. TILLYARD, "What is a Beck?" *Times Literary Supplement* (July 25, 1952), p. 485.

MILTON,   "L'Allegro" and "Il Penseroso"

LAWRENCE BABB, "The Background of 'Il Penseroso,' " *Studies in Philology,* XXXVII (April, 1940), 257-273.

BROOKS, *The Well Wrought Urn,* pp. 47-61.

NAN COOKE CARPENTER, "The Place of Music in *L'Allegro* and *Il Penseroso,*" *The University of Toronto Quarterly,* XXII (July, 1953), 354-367.

T. S. ELIOT, "A Note on the Verse of John Milton," *Essays and Studies,* XXI (1935), 34-35.

KNIGHT, *The Burning Oracle,* pp. 59-63.

PHYLLIS MACKENZIE, "Milton's Visual Imagination: An Answer to T. S. Eliot," *The University of Toronto Quarterly,* XV (Oct., 1946), 18-20.

Kester Svendsen, *The Explicator,* VIII (May, 1950), 49.

MILTON,   "I Did But Prompt the Age to Quit Their Clogs"

W. R. Parker, *The Explicator,* VIII (Oct., 1949), 3.

MILTON,   "Lawrence of Virtuous Father Virtuous Son"

Fraser Nieman, "Milton's Sonnet XX," *PMLA,* LXIV (June, 1949), 480-483.

MILTON,   "Lycidas"

Richard P. Adams, "The Archetypal Pattern of Death and Rebirth in Milton's *Lycidas,*" *PMLA,* LXIV (March, 1949), 183-188.

J. B. Broadbent, "Milton's Rhetoric," *Modern Philology,* LVI (May, 1959), 224-242.

Daiches, *A Study of Literature,* pp. 170-195.

Robert C. Fox, *The Explicator,* IX (June, 1951), 54.

J. Milton French, "The Digressions in Milton's 'Lycidas,'" *Studies in Philology,* L (July, 1953), 485-490.

John Edward Hardy, "Reconsideration I: Lycidas," *The Kenyon Review,* VII (Winter, 1945), 99-113.

Ralph E. Hone, "The Pilot of the Galilean Lake," *Studies in Philology,* LVI (Jan., 1959), 55-62.

Leon Howard, " 'That Two-Handed Engine' Once More," *Huntington Library Quarterly,* XV (Feb., 1952), 173-184.

R. E. Hughes, " 'That Two-Handed Engine'—Again," *Notes and Queries,* II, n.s. (Feb., 1955), 58-59.

Winifred Lynskey, "A Critic in Action: Mr. Ransom," *College English,* V (Feb., 1944), 242-243.

Maynard Mack, *English Masterpieces,* Vol. IV, *Milton,* pp. 9-11.

Michael Macklem, "The Elegiac Theme in Housman," *Queens Quarterly,* LIX (Spring, 1952), 46-47.

Emerson R. Marks, *The Explicator,* IX (April, 1951), 44.

CAROLINE W. MAYERSON, "The Orpheus Image in *Lycidas*," *PMLA*, LXIV (March, 1949), 189-207.

MILES, *The Primary Language of Poetry in the 1640's* pp. 88-90.

PAUL ELMER MORE, "How to Read 'Lycidas,'" *The American Review*, VII (May, 1936), 140-158. Reprinted *Criticism*, pp. 539-545.

Also reprinted Zabel, *Literary Opinion in America*, revised edition, pp. 146-156.

JOHN CROWE RANSOM, "A Poem Nearly Anonymous," *The American Review*, I (May, Sept., 1933), 179-203, 444-467. Reprinted *Criticism*, pp. 333-342.

RANSOM, *The World's Body*, pp. 1-54.

HARRY F. ROBINS, "Milton's 'Two-Handed Engine at the Door' and St. Matthew's Gospel," *Review of English Studies*, VI, n.s. (Jan., 1954), 25-36.

MALCOLM M. ROSS, "Milton and the Protestant Aesthetic: The Early Poems," *The University of Toronto Quarterly*, XVII (July, 1948), 358-360.

J. W. SAUNDERS, "Milton, Diomede, and Amaryllis," *Journal of English Literary History*, XXII (Dec., 1955), 255-256, 260-261.

WAYNE SHUMAKER, "Flowerets and Sounding Seas: A Study of the Affective Structure of *Lycidas*," *PMLA*, LXVI (June, 1951), 485-494.

THOMAS and BROWN, *Reading Poems: An Introduction to Critical Study*, pp. 692-694.

TILLYARD, *Poetry Direct and Oblique*, pp. 208-213.

W. ARTHUR TURNER, "Milton's Two-Handed Engine," *Journal of English and Germanic Philology*, XLIX (Oct., 1950), 562-565.

EDWARD WAGENKNECHT, "Milton in 'Lycidas,'" *College English*, VII (April, 1946), 393-397.

RUTH C. WALLERSTEIN, "Rhetoric in the English Renaissance: Two Elegies," *English Institute Essays 1948*, pp. 170-178.

MILTON,   "Methought I Saw My Late Espoused Saint"
EDWARD S. LE COMTE, "The Veiled Face of Milton's
Wife," *Notes and Queries*, I, n.s., (June, 1954),
245-246.
TILLYARD, *The Metaphysicals and Milton*, pp. 7-11.
VIVANTE, *English Poetry*, pp. 73-74.

MILTON,   "On His Blindness"
COOPER and HOLMES, *Preface to Poetry*, pp. 231-234.
DANIELS, *The Art of Reading Poetry*, pp. 34-36.
Abridged in *The Case for Poetry*, pp. 273-274.
DONALD C. DORIAN, *The Explicator*, X (Dec., 1951),
16. Abridged in *The Case for Poetry*, p. 274.
GOODMAN, *The Structure of Literature*, pp. 204-215.
J. L. JACKSON and W. E. WEESE, "'... Who Only
Stand and Wait': Milton's Sonnet 'On His Blind-
ness,'" *MLN*, LXXII (Feb., 1957), 91-93.
LYSANDER KEMP, "On a Sonnet by Milton," *Hopkins
Review*, VI (Fall, 1952), 80-83.
Abridged in *The Case for Poetry*, pp. 274-275.
WILLIAM R. PARKER, "The Dates of Milton's Sonnets
on His Blindness," *PMLA*, LXXIII (June, 1958),
199-200.
HARRY R. ROBINS, "Milton's First Sonnet on His
Blindness," *Review of English Studies*, VII, n.s.
(Oct., 1956), 362-366.

MILTON,   "On the Death of a Fair Infant Dying of a
Cough"
HUGH N. MACLEAN, "Milton's 'Fair Infant'," *Journal
of English Literary History*, XXIV (Dec., 1957),
296-305.

MILTON,   "On His Having Arrived at the Age of
Twenty-Three"
D. C. DORIAN, *The Explicator*, VIII (Nov., 1949), 10.
KESTER SVENDSEN, *The Explicator*, VII (May, 1949),
53.

MILTON,   "On the Late Massacre in Piedmont"

David S. Berkeley, *The Explicator*, XV (June, 1957), 58.

Kester Svendson, "Milton's Sonnet on the Massacre in Piedmont," *The Shakespeare Association Bulletin*, XX (Oct., 1945), 147-155.

Van Doren, *Introduction to Poetry*, pp. 121-123.

MILTON,   "On The Lord General Fairfax, at the Siege of Colchester"

John T. Shawcross, "Milton's 'Fairfax' Sonnet," *Notes and Queries*, II, n.s. (May, 1955), 195-196.

MILTON,   "On the Morning of Christ's Nativity"

Daiches and Charvat, *Poems in English*, pp. 665-667.

Knight, *The Burning Oracle*, pp. 59, 61.

Maynard Mack, *English Masterpieces*, Vol. IV, *Milton*, pp. 5-7.

Ivar L. Myhr, *The Explicator*, IV (Dec., 1945), 16.

Malcolm M. Ross, "Milton and the Protestant Aesthetic: The Early Poems," *The University of Toronto Quarterly*, XVII (July, 1948), 349-352.

Laurence Stapleton, "Milton and the New Music," *The University of Toronto Quarterly*, XXIII (April, 1954), 217-236.

MILTON,   "To Mr. Lawrence"

Van Doren, *Introduction to Poetry*, pp. 123-125.

MONRO,   "The Garden"

Stephen Spender, (Review), *The Criterion*, XII (July, 1933), 681-682.

MONROE, harold,   "Trees"

Skelton, *The Poetic Pattern*, pp. 122-128.

MOODY,   "Ode in Time of Hesitation"

R. P. Blackmur, "Moody in Retrospect," *Poetry*, XXXVIII (Sept., 1931), 334-335.

MOORE, marianne,   "Bird-Witted"

Lloyd Frankenberg, "The Imaginary Garden," *Quarterly Review of Literature*, IV, No. 2, 210-212.

FRANKENBERG, *Pleasure Dome,* pp. 137-141.

MOORE, MARIANNE, "Black Earth"

BLACKMUR, *The Double Agent,* pp. 150-154.

CHARLES TOMLINSON, "Abundance, Not Too Much: The Poetry of Marianne Moore," *The Sewanee Review,* LXV (Autumn, 1957), 677-682.

MOORE, MARIANNE, "Elephants"

CLEANTH BROOKS, "Miss Marianne Moore's Zoo," *Quarterly Review of Literature,* IV, No. 2, 179-181.

WALLACE FOWLIE, "Under the Equanimity of Language," *Quarterly Review of Literature,* IV, No. 2, 175-176.

MOORE, MARIANNE, "The Fish"

VIVIENNE KOCH, "The Peaceable Kingdom of Marianne Moore," *Quarterly Review of Literature,* IV, No. 2, 163-164.

Reprinted Stageberg and Anderson, *Poetry as Experience,* p. 499.

WILLIAM A. SYLVESTER, *The Explicator,* VII (Feb., 1949), 30.

ZABEL, *Literary Opinion in America,* pp. 433-434. Revised edition, pp. 390-391.

MOORE, MARIANNE, "He 'Digesteth Harde Yron' "

JOHN CROWE RANSOM, "On Being Modern with Distinction," *Quarterly Review of Literature,* IV, No. 2, 140-141.

WALLACE STEVENS, "About One of Marianne Moore's Poems," *Quarterly Review of Literature,* IV, No. 2, 143-147.

STEVENS, *The Necessary Angel,* pp. 93-103.

MOORE, MARIANNE, "The Icosasphere'

MARIE BORROFF, *The Explicator,* XVI (Jan., 1958), 21.

MOORE, MARIANNE, "In Distrust of Merits"

MARCIA EPSTEIN ALLENTUCK, *The Explicator,* X (April, 1952), 42.

WALLACE FOWLIE, "Under the Equanimity of Language," *Quarterly Review of Literature*, IV, No. 2, 176-177.

LLOYD FRANKENBERG, "The Imaginary Garden," *Quarterly Review of Literature*, IV, No. 2, 221-222.

FRANKENBERG, *Pleasure Dome*, pp. 153-155.

MOORE, MARIANNE,   "The Jerboa"

CLEANTH BROOKS, "Miss Marianne Moore's Zoo," *Quarterly Review of Literature*, IV, No. 2, 182-183.

LLOYD FRANKENBERG, "The Imaginary Garden," *Quarterly Review of Literature*, IV, No. 2, 202-203.

FRANKENBERG, *Pleasure Dome*, pp. 132-133.

PHILIP LEGLER, "Marianne Moore and the Idea of Freedom," *Poetry*, LXXXIII (Dec., 1953), 158-167.

MOORE, MARIANNE,   "Marriage"

VIVIENNE KOCH, "The Peaceable Kingdom of Marianne Moore," *Quarterly Review of Literature*, IV, No. 2, 167.

MOORE, MARIANNE,   "The Mind Is an Enchanting Thing"

FRANKENBERG, *Invitation to Poetry*, pp. 389-390.

MOORE, MARIANNE,   "The Monkeys"

BLACKMUR, *The Double Agent*, pp. 166-167.

Reprinted *Language as Gesture*, p. 281.

MOORE, MARIANNE,   "Nevertheless"

LLOYD FRANKENBERG, "The Imaginary Garden," *Quarterly Review of Literature*, IV, No. 2, 195-196.

FRANKENBERG, *Pleasure Dome*, p. 125.

MOORE, MARIANNE,   "Novices"

VIVIENNE KOCH, "The Peaceable Kingdom of Marianne Moore," *Quarterly Review of Literature*, IV, No. 2, 157.

MOORE, MARIANNE,   "The Past Is the Present"

BLACKMUR, *The Double Agent*, pp. 142-149.

MOORE, MARIANNE,   "Poetry"

LLOYD FRANKENBERG, "The Imaginary Garden," *Quarterly Review of Literature*, IV, No. 2, 207-209.

FRANKENBERG, *Pleasure Dome*, pp. 137-141.

MOORE,MARIANNE, "Roses Only"
BROWER, *The Fields of Light,* pp. 48-50.
MOORE, MARIANNE, "See in the Midst of Fair Leaves"
DAN G. HOFFMAN, *The Explicator,* X (March, 1952),
34. Reprinted Locke, Gibson, and Arms, *Intro-
duction to Literature,* third edition, pp. 203-204.
MOORE, MARIANNE, "Silence"
BLACKMUR, *The Double Agent,* pp. 154-160.

Reprinted *Language as Gesture,* pp. 271-276.
MOORE, MARIANNE, "Snakes, Mongooses, Snake-charm-
er and the Like"
ROSENTHAL and SMITH, *Exploring Poetry,* pp. 250-251.
MOORE, MARIANNE, "The Steeple-Jack"
LOUISE BOGAN, "Reading Contemporary Poetry," *Col-
lege English,* XIV (Feb., 1953), 257-260.
DENIS DONOGHUE, "Technique in Hopkins," *Studies*
XLIV (Winter, 1955), 452.
CHARLES TOMLINSON, "Abundance, Not Too Much:
The Poetry of Marianne Moore," *The Sewanee
Review,* LXV (Autumn, 1957), 677-682.
MOORE, MARIANNE, "Tom Fool at Jamaica"
MARIE BORROFF, " 'Tom Fool at Jamaica' by Mari-
anne Moore: Meaning and Structure," *College Eng-
lish* XVII (May, 1956), 466-469.
ELDER OLSON, "The Poetry of Marianne Moore,"
The Chicago Review, XI (Spring, 1957), 103-104.
MOORE, MARIANNE, "What Are Years?"
O'CONNOR, *Sense and Sensibility in Modern Poetry,*
pp. 229-230 (quoting Lloyd Frankenberg, *The Sat-
urday Review of Literature,* XXXIX [March 23,
1946]).
MOORE, MARIANNE, "The Wood-Weasel"
CLEANTH BROOKS, "Miss Marianne Moore's Zoo,"
Quarterly Review of Literature, IV, No. 2, 182.
MOORE, MERRILL, "Granny Weeks"
DUDLEY FITTS, "The Sonnets of Merrill Moore," *The
Sewanee Review,* XLVII (April-June, 1939), 278-
279.

MOORE, MERRILL, "The Gun Barrel Looked at Him With Love in Its Single Eyehole"
> DUDLEY FITTS, "The Sonnets of Merrill Moore," *The Sewanee Review,* XLVII (April-June, 1939), 274-275.

MOORE, MERRILL, "The Sound of Time Hangs Heavy in My Ears"
> DUDLEY FITTS, "The Sonnets of Merrill Moore," *The Sewanee Review,* XLVII (April-June, 1939), 291-292.

MOORE, NICHOLAS, "Alteration"
> JOHN BERRYMAN, *A Critical Supplement to "Poetry,"* Dec., 1949, pp. 11-12.

MOORE, NICHOLAS, "Unity Quitbread at Eltham"
> JOHN BERRYMAN, *A Critical Supplement to "Poetry,"* Dec., 1949, pp. 10-11.

MOORE, ROSALIE, "The Grasshopper Man"
> J. F. NIMS and ROSALIE MOORE, *A Critical Supplement to "Poetry,"* May, 1949, pp. 1-11.

MOORE, T. STURGE, "Love's Faintness Accepted"
> FREDERICK L. GWYNN, *The Explicator,* VII (April, 1949), 45.

MOORE, T. STURGE, "To Silence"
> WINTERS, *Primitivism and Decadence,* pp. 86-89. Also *In Defense of Reason,* pp. 96-99.
>
> Reprinted West, *Essays in Modern Literary Criticism,* pp. 224-225.

MOORE, THOMAS, "The Song of Fionnuala"
> BRENDAN P. O HEHIR, *The Explicator,* XV (Jan., 1957), 23.

MORDAUNT, "Sound, Sound the Clarion"
> GEORGE ARMS, *The Explicator,* I (Dec., 1942), 20.

MORRIS, WILLIAM, "The Chapel in Lyoness"
> CURTIS DAHL, "Morris's 'The Chapel in Lyoness': An Interpretation," *Studies in Philology,* LI (July, 1954), 482-491.

MORRIS, "The Nymph's Song to Hylas"

(*The Life and Death of Jason,* Book 4)
PAUL F. JAMISON, *The Explicator,* XIV (March, 1956), 36.
ANDREW RUTHERFORD, *The Explicator,* XIV (March, 1956), 36.
MOSS, HOWARD, "The City Lion"
J. F. NIMS, *A Critical Supplement to "Poetry,"* Nov., 1948, p. 9.
MUIR, EDWIN, "The Days"
RALPH J. MILLS, JR., "Edwin Muir: A Speech from Darkness Grown," *Accent,* XIX (Winter, 1959), 66-67.
MUIR, EDWIN, "Dialogue"
TSCHUMI, *Thought in Twentieth-Century English Poetry,* pp. 113-114.
MUIR, EDWIN, "The Gate"
KIMON FRIAR, "The Circular Route," *Poetry,* LXXX-IV (April, 1954), 29.
MUIR, EDWIN, "The Grove"
RALPH J. MILLS, JR., "Edwin Muir: A Speech from Darkness Grown," *Accent,* XIX (Winter, 1959), 60-62.
MUIR, EDWIN, "The Horses"
RALPH J. MILLS, JR., "Edwin Muir: A Speech from Darkness Grown," *Accent,* XIX (Winter, 1959), 68-69.
MUIR, EDWIN, "The Human Fold"
TSCHUMI, *Thought in Twentieth-Century English Poetry,* pp. 105-106.
MUIR, EDWIN, "The Labyrinth"
RALPH J. MILLS, JR., "Edwin Muir: A Speech from Darkness Grown," *Accent,* XIX (Winter, 1959), 64-65.
MUIR, EDWIN, "The Narrow Place"
TSCHUMI, *Thought in Twentieth-Century English Poetry,* pp. 106-107..
MUIR, EDWIN, "Outside Eden"
RALPH J. MILLS, JR., "Edwin Muir: A Speech from

Darkness Grown," *Accent,* XIX (Winter, 1959),
67-68.
MUIR, EDWIN, "The Recurrence"
TSCHUMI, *Thought in Twentieth-Century English
Poetry,* pp. 107-108.
MUIR, EDWIN, "The Three Mirrors"
TSCHUMI, *Thought in Twentieth-Century English
Poetry,* pp. 115-118.
MUIR, EDWIN, "To J. F. H."
TSCHUMI, *Thought in Twentieth-Century English
Poetry,* pp. 98-100.
MUIR, EDWIN, "Twice-Done, Once-Done"
TSCHUMI, *Thought in Twentieth-Century English
Poetry,* pp. 111-113.
MUIR, EDWIN, "Variations on a Time Theme"
RALPH J. MILLS, JR., "Edwin Muir: A Speech from
Darkness Grown," *Accent,* XIX (Winter, 1959),
54-56.
MUIR, EDWIN, "The Voyage"
RALPH J. MILLS, JR., "Edwin Muir: A Speech from
Darkness Grown," *Accent,* XIX (Winter, 1959),
62-64.
MUIR, EDWIN, "The Wheel"
TSCHUMI, *Thought in Twentieth-Century English
Poetry,* pp. 109-111.
MUIR, "The Window"
KIMON FRIAR, "The Circular Route," *Poetry,* LXXX-
IV (April, 1954), 28.
TSCHUMI, *Thought in Twentieth-Century English
Poetry,* pp. 114-115.
NASH, "Literary Reflection"
WARREN BECK, "Boundaries of Poetry," *College Eng-
lish,* IV (March, 1943), 347.
NASH, OGDEN, "The Turtle"
PERRINE, *Sound and Sense,* pp. 135-136.
NASHE, "Litany in Time of Plague"
EMPSON, *Seven Types of Ambiguity,* pp. 32-35, 145-
147; (1947 ed.), pp. 25-27, 115-116.

NEWMAN, "Dream of Gerontius"
ESTHER R. B. PESE, "A Suggested Background for Newman's *Dream of Gerontius*," *Modern Philology*, XLVII (Nov., 1949), 108-116.

NEWMAN, "Lead, Kindly Light"
PAULL F. BAUM, "The Road to Palermo," *South Atlantic Quarterly*, LV (April, 1956), 192-197.

NEWMAN, "The Pillar of the Cloud"
COOPER and HOLMES, *Preface to Poetry*, pp. 278-281.

NICHOLS, ROBERT, "Sunrise Poem"
ROBERT NICHOLS, "The Birth of a Poem," in Rosamond E. M. Harding, *An Anatomy of Inspiration* (3rd ed.; Cambridge: W. Heffer & Sons, 1948), pp. 147-168.

NIMS, "The Magical View of Nature"
WILLIAM ELTON, *A Critical Supplement to "Poetry,"* Oct., 1949, pp. 10-12.

NIMS, "Penny Arcade"
ROBERT SHELLEY, "A Palmtree of Steel," *Western Review*, XV (Winter, 1951), 141-142.

NIMS, "Winter in the Park"
ROBERT SHELLEY, "A Palmtree of Steel," *Western Review*, XV (Winter, 1951), 140.

NOYES, "For the Eightieth Birthday of George Meredith"
RICHARDS, *Practical Criticism*, pp. 118-129 *et passim*.

O'DONNELL, GEORGE MARION, "Return"
JOHN CROWE RANSOM, "The Making of a Modern," *The Southern Review*, I (Spring, 1936), 869-870.

OLSON, LAWRENCE, "Great Abaco"
MACHA ROSENTHAL, "Sailing for Great Abaco," *Poetry*, LXXII (April, 1948), 51-53.

OWEN, WILFRED, "Anthem for Doomed Youth"
SAMUEL J. HAZO, "The Passion of Wilfred Owen," *Renascence*, XI (Summer, 1959), 205-206.

OWEN, WILFRED, "Dulce et Decorum Est"
SAMUEL J. HAZO, "The Passion of Wilfred Owen," *Renascence*, XI (Summer, 1959), 202.

OWEN, WILFRED, "Greater Love"
SAMUEL J. HAZO, "The Passion of Wilfred Owen," *Renascence*, XI (Summer, 1959), 204-205.

OWEN, WILFRED, "The Show"
JOSEPH COHEN, *The Explicator*, XVI (Nov., 1957), 8.

OWEN, WILFRED, "Strange Meeting"
SAMUEL J. HAZO, "The Passion of Wilfred Owen," *Renascence*, XI (Summer, 1959), 206-208.
ROSENTHAL and SMITH, *Exploring Poetry*, pp. 546-547.
D. S. SAVAGE, "Two Prophetic Poems," *Western Review*, XIII (Winter, 1949), 67-78.
SKELTON, *The Poetic Pattern*, pp. 113-114.

PARKER, DOROTHY, "The Actress"
DANIELS, *The Art of Reading Poetry*, pp. 353-354.

PARNELL, "Hymn to Contentment"
RAYMOND D. HAVENS, "Parnell's 'Hymn to Contentment,'" *MLN*, LIX (May, 1944), 320-331.

PATMORE, "Amelia"
THEODORE MAYNARD, "Coventry Patmore's Doctrine of Love," *Thought*, XX (Sept., 1945), 505-506.

PATMORE, "The Angel in the House"
THEODORE MAYNARD, "Coventry Patmore's Doctrine of Love," *Thought*, XX (Sept., 1945), 503-518.

PATMORE, "The Victories of Love"
THEODORE MAYNARD, "Coventry Patmore's Doctrine of Love," *Thought*, XX (Sept., 1945), 508-509.

PEACOCK, "War Song"
EMPSON, *Seven Types of Ambiguity*, pp. 28-30; (1947 ed.), p. 22.

PEELE, "Bathsheba's Song" (*The Love of King David and Fair Bethsabe*)
VAN DOREN, *Introduction to Poetry*, pp. 31-33.

PELLEW, J. D. C., "The Temple"
I. A. RICHARDS, *Practical Criticism*, pp. 93-102, 212-213.

POE, "Al Aaraaf"
R. C. and M. M. PETTIGREW, "A Reply to Floyd Sto-

vall's Interpretation of 'Al Aaraaf,'" *American Literature,* VIII (Jan., 1937), 439-445.

FLOYD STOVALL, "An Interpretation of Poe's 'Al Aaraaf,'" *Studies in English* (Austin: University of Texas, 1929), IX, 106-133.

POE,   "Annabel Lee"

BRADFORD BOOTH, "The Identity of Annabel Lee," *College English,* VII (Oct., 1945), 17-19.

WALLACE C. BROWN, "The English Professor's Dilemma," *College English,* V (April, 1944), 380-382.

POE,   "The Bells"

ARTHUR E. DU BOIS, "The Jazz Bells of Poe," *College English,* II (Dec., 1940), 230-244.

POE,   "The City in the Sea"

ROY P. BASLER, *The Explicator,* IV (Feb., 1946), 30.

BASLER, *Sex, Symbolism, and Psychology in Literature,* pp. 192-195.

BOWRA, *The Romantic Imagination,* pp. 183-184.

T. O. MABBOTT, *The Explicator,* IV (Oct., 1945), 1.

POE,   "Dream-Land"

J. O. BAILEY, "The Geography of Poe's 'Dream-Land' and 'Ulalume,'" *Studies in Philology,* XLV (July, 1948), 517-518.

POE,   "Eldorado"

O. S. COAD, "The Meaning of Poe's 'Eldorado,'" *MLN,* LIX (Jan., 1944), 59-61.

T. O. MABBOTT, "The Sources of Poe's 'Eldorado,'" *MLN,* LX (June, 1945), 312-314.

W. STEPHEN SANDERLIN, JR., "Poe's 'Eldorado' Again," *MLN,* LXXI (March, 1956), 189-192.

POE,   "For Annie"

BOWRA, *The Romantic Imagination,* pp. 188-189.

POE,   "The Haunted Palace"

RICHARD WILBUR, "The House of Poe," *Anniversary Lectures 1959,* pp. 26-28.

POE,   "Israfel"

T. O. MABBOTT, *The Explicator,* II (June, 1944), 57.

W. L. WERNER, *The Explicator*, II (April, 1944), 44.

POE, "The Lake: To ———"

ROBERT MORRISON, *The Explicator*, VII (Dec., 1948), 22.

POE, "The Raven"

HOWARD MUMFORD JONES, "Poe, 'The Raven,' and the Anonymous Young Man," *Western Humanities Review*, IX (Spring, 1955), 132-138.

POE, "The Sleeper"

W. B. HUNTER, JR., "Poe's 'The Sleeper' and *Macbeth*," *American Literature*, XX (March, 1948), 55-57.

T. O. MABBOTT, "Poe's 'The Sleeper' Again," *American Literature*, XXI (Nov., 1949), 339-340.

POE, "To Helen"

BOWRA, *The Romantic Imagination*, pp. 185-186, 192.

WALLACE C. BROWN, "The English Professor's Dilemma," *College English*, V (April, 1944), 382-385.

ROBERT A. COLBY, "Poe's Philosophy of Composition," *The University of Kansas City Review*, (Spring, 1954), 211-214.

DREW, *Poetry*, p. 209.

T. O. MABBOTT, *The Explicator*, I (June, 1943), 60. Reprinted *Readings for Liberal Education*, II, 209-210.

ROSENTHAL and SMITH, *Exploring Poetry*, pp. 603-604.

POE, "To One in Paradise"

R. P. BASLER, "Byronism in Poe's 'To One in Paradise,'" *American Literature*, IX (May, 1937), 232-236.

POE, "Ulalume"

J. O. BAILEY, "The Geography of Poe's 'Dream-Land' and 'Ulalume,'" *Studies in Philology*, XLV (July, 1948), 518-523.

ROY P. BASLER, *The Explicator*, II (May, 1944), 49.

BASLER, *Sex, Symbolism, and Psychology in Literature*, pp. 184-187.

Reprinted Stallman and Watters, *The Creative Reader,* pp. 861-862.

J. M. BLUMENFELD, "Poe's 'Ulalume,' Line 43," *Notes and Queries,* CXCVII (March 29, 1952), 147.

BROOKS and WARREN, *Understanding Poetry,* Revised Edition, pp. 197-201.

ERIC W. CARLSON, *The Explicator,* XI (June, 1953), 56.

J. P. KIRBY, *The Explicator,* I (Oct., 1942), 8.

LEWIS LEARY, *The Explicator,* VI (Feb., 1948), 25.

T. O. MABBOTT, *The Explicator,* I (Feb., 1943), 25.

T. O. MABBOTT, *The Explicator,* VI (June, 1948), 57. Reprinted Stallman and Watters, *The Creative Reader,* pp. 860-861.

JAMES E. MILLER, JR., " 'Ulalume' Resurrected," *Philological Quarterly,* XXXIV (April, 1955), 197-205.

UNGER and O'CONNOR, *Poems for Study,* pp. 468-472.

YVOR WINTERS, "A Crisis in the History of American Obscurantism," *American Literature,* VIII (Jan., 1937), 394-395. Reprinted *Maule's Curse,* pp. 112-113. Also *In Defense of Reason,* pp. 252-253.

POE,   "The Valley of Unrest"

ROY P. BASLER, *The Explicator,* V (Dec., 1946), 25.

BASLER, *Sex, Symbolism, and Psychology in Literature,* pp. 197-200.

Reprinted Locke, Gibson, and Arms, *Introduction to Literature,* third edition, pp. 121-122.

POPE,   "The Dunciad"

KNIGHT, *The Burning Oracle,* pp. 174-182.

F. R. LEAVIS, "The Dunciad," *Scrutiny,* XII (Winter, 1943), 74-80.

GEORGE SHERBURN, "The *Dunciad,* Book IV," *Studies in English 1944* (Austin: The University of Texas Press, 1944), pp. 174-190.

POPE,   "The Dunciad," III, 340.

DANIEL P. DENEAU, "Pope's 'Iv'ry Gate': *The Dun-*

ciad, III, 340," *MLN,* LXXIV (March, 1959) , 208-212.

POPE, "The Dunciad, IV, 501-504"

F. R. LEAVIS, "The Responsible Critic: Or the Function of Criticism at Any Time," *Scrutiny,* XIX (Spring, 1953) , 171-172.

POPE, "Elegy to the Memory of an Unfortunate Lady"

CHRISTOPHER GILLIE, *Interpretations,* John Wain, ed., pp. 77-85.

F. R. LEAVIS, "The Poetry of Pope (Revaluations II)," *Scrutiny,* II (Dec., 1933), 269-274, 276-277. Reprinted *Revaluation,* pp. 69-73, 80-81.

POPE, "Eloisa to Abelard"

KNIGHT, *The Burning Oracle,* pp. 148-155.

LANGBAUM, *The Poetry of Experience,* p. 146-148.

MILES, *Major Adjectives in English Poetry,* pp. 341, 345-346.

HENRY PETTIT, "Pope's 'Eloisa to Abelard': An Interpretation," *University of Colorado Studies in Language and Literature,* No. 4 (July, 1953) , 72-79.

POPE, "Epilogue to the Satires, Dialogue I"

MAYNARD MACK, *English Masterpieces,* Vol. V, *The Augustans,* pp. 32-34.

REBECCA PRICE PARKIN, "The Quality of Alexander Pope's Humor," *College English,* XIV (Jan., 1953) , 200-201.

POPE, "Epistle to Dr. Arbuthnot"

WALLACE BROWN, "Dramatic Tension in Neoclassic Satire," *College English,* VI (Feb., 1945), 265-266.

MAYNARD MACK, *English Masterpieces,* Vol. V, *The Augustans,* pp. 30-32.

ELDER OLSON, "Rhetoric and the Appreciation of Pope," *Modern Philology,* XXXVII (August, 1939), 21-35.

POPE, "Essay on Criticism"

JOHN M. ADEN, " 'First Follow Nature': Strategy and Stratification in *An Essay on Criticism," Journal of English and Germanic Philology*, LV (Oct., 1956) , 604-617.

EMPSON. *The Structure of Complex Words*, pp. 84-100.

WILLIAM EMPSON, "Wit in the 'Essay on Criticism,' " *The Hudson Review*, II (Winter, 1950) , 559-577.

MAYNARD MACK, *English Masterpieces*, Vol. V, *The Augustans*, pp. 20-23.

REBECCA P. PARKIN, "Alexander Pope's Use of the Implied Dramatic Speaker," *College English*, XI (Dec., 1949), 140-141.

REBECCA PRICE PARKIN, "The Quality of Alexander Pope's Humor," *College English*, XIV (Jan., 1953) , 197-199.

JAMES EDWARD TOBIN, "Alexander Pope, 1744-1944," *Thought*, XIX (June, 1944), 250-261.

POPE,   "Essay on Man"

J. M. CAMERON, "Doctrinal to an Age: Notes Towards a Revaluations of Pope's *Essay on Man," The Dublin Review*, CCXXV (Second Quarter, 1951) , 54-69.

BROTHER ROLAND FALEY, T O R, *The Explicator*, IX (May, 1951) , 51.

WILLIAM FROST, *The Explicator*, VI (Nov., 1947), 11.

R. E. HUGHES, "Pope's *Essay on Man*: The Rhetorical Structure of Epistle I," *MLN*, LXXX (March, 1955) , 177-181.

J. P. KIRBY, *The Explicator*, I (Nov., 1942), 12.

KNIGHT, *The Burning Oracle*, pp. 159-174.

JOHN LAIRD, "Pope's *Essay on Man," Review of English Studies*, XX (Oct., 1944), 286-298.

MAYNARD MACK, *English Masterpieces*, Vol. V, *The Augustans*, pp. 26-29.

MAYNARD MACK, "On Reading Pope," *College English*, VII (Feb., 1946), 271-272.

Francis Manley, *The Explicator*, XV (April, 1957), 44.

Miles, *Major Adjectives in English Poetry*, pp. 340-345.

Berna Moran, "Pope and Thomas Vaughan," *Times Literary Supplement* (May 4, 1951), p. 277.

Rebecca P. Parkin, "Alexander Pope's Use of the Implied Dramatic Speaker," *College English*, XI (Dec., 1949), 139-140.

Rebecca Price Parkin, "The Quality of Alexander Pope's Humor," *College English*, XIV (Jan., 1953), 199-200.

James Edward Tobin, "Alexander Pope, 1744-1944," *Thought*, XIX (June, 1944), 259.

POPE,   "Moral Essays, Epistle II"
Douglas, Lamson, Smith, *The Critical Reader*, pp. 25-31.
Reprinted Locke, Gibson, and Arms, *Introduction to Literature*, third edition, pp. 68-72.
Maynard Mack, *English Masterpieces*, Vol. V, *The Augustans*, pp. 29-30.
Unger and O'Connor, *Poems for Study*, pp. 254-262.

POPE,   "Moral Essays, Epistle III"
Maynard Mack, "On Reading Pope," *College English*, VII (Feb., 1946), 269-271.

POPE,   "Moral Essays, Epistle IV," ("Of the Use of Riches")
Brower, *The Fields of Light*, pp. 144-163.
F. R. Leavis, "The Poetry of Pope (Revaluations II)," *Scrutiny*, II (Dec., 1933), 274-276. Reprinted *Revaluation*, pp. 77-80, 92-100.

POPE,   "Moral Essays, Epistle V"
Thomas O. Mabbott, *The Explicator*, X (Nov., 1951), 11.

POPE,   "Ode on Solitude"
Stauffer, *The Nature of Poetry*, pp. 160-162.

POPE,   "The Rape of the Lock"

CLEANTH BROOKS, "The Case of Miss Arabella Fermor: a Re-Examination," *The Sewanee Review*, LI (Autumn, 1943), 505-524.

BROOKS, *The Well Wrought Urn*, pp. 74-95.

ARTHUR E. CASE, "The Game of Ombre in 'The Rape of the Lock,' " *Studies in English, 1944* (Austin: The University of Texas Press, 1944), pp. 191-196.

KNIGHT, *The Burning Oracle*, pp. 136-148.

MAYNARD MACK, *English Masterpieces*, Vol. V, *The Augustans*, pp. 23-26.

REBECCA PRICE PARKIN, "The Quality of Alexander Pope's Humor," *College English*, XIV (Jan., 1953), 199.

HUGO M. REICHARD, "The Love Affair in Pope's *Rape of the Lock*," *PMLA*, LXIX (Sept., 1954), 887-902.

AUSTIN WARREN, "The Mask of Pope," *The Sewanee Review*, LIV (Winter, 1946), 27-31.

WARREN, *Rage for Order*, pp. 46-49.
Reprinted *Modern Literary Criticism*, pp 333-335.
Reprinted West, *Essays in Modern Literary Criticism*, pp. 371-373.

POPE,   "Windsor Forest"

KNIGHT, *The Burning Oracle*, pp. 131-136.

MAYNARD MACK, "On Reading Pope," *College English*, VII (Feb., 1946), 264-268.

POTTLE, *The Idiom of Poetry*, pp. 113-122; (1946 ed.), pp. 121-129.

WASSERMAN, *The Subtler Language*, pp. 101-168.

POUND,   "The Ballad of the Goodly Fere"

RIDING and GRAVES, *A Survey of Modernist Poetry*, pp. 140-142.

POUND,   "Fan Piece for Her Imperial Lord"

EARL MINER, "Pound, *Haiku* and the Image," *The Hudson Review*, IX (Winter, 1957), 580-581.

POUND,   "The Garden"

VAN DOREN, *Introduction to Poetry*, pp. 46-49.

POUND,   "Homage to Sextus Propertius"

R. P. Blackmur, "Masks of Ezra Pound," *Hound and Horn*, VII (Jan.-March, 1934), 184-191.

Reprinted *Language as Gesture*, pp. 130-136.

John Speirs, "Mr. Pound's Propertius," *Scrutiny*, III (Sept., 1934), 409-418.

POUND,   "Hugh Selwyn Mauberley"

R. P. Blackmur, "Masks of Ezra Pound," *Hound and Horn*, VII (Jan.-March, 1934), 180-184.

Reprinted *Language as Gesture*, pp. 126-130.

Thomas E. Connolly, "Further Notes on *Mauberley,*" *Accent*, XVI (Winter, 1956), 59-67.

Deutsch, *This Modern Poetry*, pp. 115-118.

Macdonald Emslie, *The Explicator*, XIV, (Jan., 1956), 26.

Friar and Brinnin, *Modern Poetry*, pp. 527-531.

G. Giovannini, *The Explicator*, XVI (March, 1958), 35.

Hoffman, *The Twenties*, pp. 37-46.

Leavis, *New Bearings on English Poetry*, pp. 141-143.

Richard A. Long, *The Explicator*, X (June, 1952), 56.

POUND,   "In a Station of the Metro"

Warren Beck, "Boundaries of Poetry," *College English*, IV (March, 1943), 346-347.

Brooks and Warren, *Understanding Poetry*, pp. 175-176.

Revised edition, pp. 78-80.

John J. Espy, *The Explicator*, XI (June, 1953), 59. Abridged in *The Case for Poetry*, p. 287.

Thomas A. Hanzo, *The Explicator*, XI (Feb., 1953), 26. Abridged in *The Case for Poetry*, p. 287.

Rosenthal and Smith, *Exploring Poetry*, pp. 157-158.

POUND,   "Near Perigord"

Thomas E. Connolly, Ezra Pound's 'Near Perigord': The Background of a Poem," *Comparative Literature*, VIII (Spring, 1956), 110-116.

POUND,   "Papyrus"

Daniels, *The Art of Reading Poetry*, p. 9.

CHRISTOPHER M. DAWSON, *The Explicator,* IX (Feb., 1951), 30.

GILBERT HIGHET, *The Classical Tradition* (New York: Oxford University Press, 1949), p. 517.

POUND, "Portrait d'une Femme"
RICHARD J. GIANNONE, "Eliot's 'Portrait of a Lady' and Pound's 'Portrait d'une Femme,'" *Twentieth Century Literature,* V (Oct., 1959), 131-134.

POUND, "The Return"
ANONYMOUS, "Experiment in Verse," *Times Literary Supplement* (Aug. 17, 1956), (Special Number), iii.

DEUTSCH, *Poetry in Our Time,* pp. 124-125.

PRIOR, "The Lady Who Offers Her Looking Glass to Venus"
BATESON, *English Poetry,* pp. 83-84.

PRIOR, "An Ode"
VAN DOREN, *Introduction to Poetry,* pp. 17-21.

PRIOR, "Written in the Beginning of Mezeray's History of France"
DAICHES, *A Study of Literature,* pp. 168-170.

PROCTOR, "The Pilgrims"
BROOKS and WARREN, *Understanding Poetry,* pp. 334-336.
Revised edition, pp. 181-183.

PUTNAM, "Ballad of a Strange Thing"
F. O. MATTHIESSEN, "Phelps Putnam (1894-1948)," *The Kenyon Review,* XI (Winter, 1949), 80-82.
Reprinted *The Responsibilities of the Critic,* pp. 274-276.

PUTNAM, "The Five Seasons"
MORTON D. ZABEL, "Phelps Putnam and America," *Poetry,* XL (Sept., 1932), 335-344.

PUTNAM, "Hasbrouck and the Rose"
F. O. MATTHIESSEN, "Phelps Putnam (1894-1948)," *The Kenyon Review,* XI (Winter, 1949), 78-80.
Reprinted *The Responsibilities of the Critic,* pp. 273-274.

RAINE, KATHLEEN,   "The Invisible Spectrum"
DUDLEY FITTS, "In Minute Particulars," *New Republic*, CXXVII (Oct. 6, 1952), 27-28.
RAINE, KATHLEEN,   "Pythoness"
DUDLEY FITTS, "In Minute Particulars," *New Republic*, CXXVII (Oct. 6, 1952), 27.
RAINE, KATHLEEN,   "Winter Fire"
DUDLEY FITTS, "In Minute Particulars," *New Republic*, CXXVII (Oct. 6, 1952), 28.
RALEGH,   "The Lie"
GEORGE ARMS and R. W. WHIDDEN, *The Explicator*, III (April, 1945), 50.
UNGER and O'CONNOR, *Poems for Study*, pp. 99-100.
RALEGH,   "The Pilgrimage"
MELVIN W. ADKEW, *The Explicator*, XIII (Nov., 1954), 9.
RALEGH,   "Walsingham"
O. C. WILLIAMS, *The Explicator*, IX (Feb., 1951), 27.
RANSOM,   "Amphibious Crocodile"
RICHMOND C. BEATTY, "John Crowe Ransom as Poet," *The Sewanee Review*, LII (Summer, 1944), 362-363.
RANSOM,   "Antique Harvesters"
VIVIENNE KOCH, "The Achievement of John Crowe Ransom," *The Sewanee Review*, LVIII (Spring, 1950), 252-255.
VIVIENNE KOCH, "The Poetry of John Crowe Ransom," *Modern American Poetry*, B. Rajan, ed., pp. 58-61.
F. O. MATTHIESSEN, "Primarily Language," *The Sewanee Review*, LVI (Summer, 1948), 394-395.
Reprinted *The Responsibilities of the Critic*, pp. 43-44.
LOUIS D. RUBIN, JR., "The Concept of Nature in Modern Poetry, "*The American Quarterly*, IX (Spring, 1957), 69-70.
RANSOM,   "Bells for John Whiteside's Daughter"
ROBERT B. HEILMAN, "Poetic and Prosiac: Program

Notes on Opposite Numbers," *Pacific Spectator,*
V (Autumn, 1951), 458-460. Abridged in *The
Case for Poetry,* p. 293.

VIVIENNE KOCH, "The Poetry of John Crowe Ransom," *Modern American Poetry,* B. Rajan, ed., pp.
43-44.

DONALD A. STAUFFER, "Portrait of the Critic Poet as
Equilibrist," *The Sewanee Review,* LVI (Summer,
1948), 430.

R. P. WARREN, "John Crowe Ransom: A Study in
Irony," *Virginia Quarterly Review,* XI (Jan., 1935),
106.

Abridged in *The Case for Poetry,* p. 293.

R. P. WARREN, "Pure and Impure Poetry," *The Kenyon Review,* V (Spring, 1943), 237-240. Reprinted
Criticism, pp. 370-372, and *Critiques,* 92-94.

Also reprinted *The Kenyon Critics,* pp. 26-29.

Reprinted Engle and Carrier, *Reading Modern
Poetry,* pp. 69-71.

Also reprinted West, *Essays in Modern Literary
Criticism,* pp. 253-255.

RANSOM,   "Blackberry Winter"

G. P. WASSERMAN, "The Irony of John Crowe Ransom," *The University of Kansas City Review,* XX-
III (Winter, 1956), 154-155.

RANSOM,   "Blue Girls"

CIARDI, *How Does a Poem Mean?* pp. 802-803.

VIVIENNE KOCH, "The Achievement of John Crowe
Ransom," *The Sewanee Review,* LVIII (Spring,
250-252.

VIVIENNE KOCH, "The Poetry of John Crowe Ransom," *Modern American Poetry,* B. Rajan, ed., pp.
56-58.

HOWARD NEMEROV, "Summer's Flare and Winter's
Flaw," *The Sewanee Review,* LVI (Summer, 1948),
418.

HYATT H. WAGGONER, *The Explicator,* XVIII (Oct.,
1959), 6.

RANSOM, "Captain Carpenter"
BROOKS, *Modern Poetry and the Tradition,* pp. 35-37.
RIDING and GRAVES, *A Survey of Modernist Poetry,*
pp. 103-109.
RANSOM, "Conrad in Twilight"
DELMORE SCHWARTZ, "Instructed of Much Mortality,"
The Sewanee Review, LIV (Summer, 1946), 445-
446.
RANSOM, "Dead Boy"
VIVIENNE KOCH, "The Achievement of John Crowe
Ransom," *The Sewanee Review,* LVIII (Spring,
1950), 239.
VIVIENNE KOCH, "The Poetry of John Crowe Ran-
som," *Modern American Poetry,* B. Rajan, ed., p.
46.
F. O. MATTHIESSEN, "Primarily Language," *The
Sewanee Review,* LVI (Summer, 1948), 398-400.
Reprinted *The Responsibilities of the Critic,* pp.
47-49.
STAGEBERG and ANDERSON, *Poetry as Experience,* pp.
26-27.
G. P. WASSERMAN, "The Irony of John Crowe Ran-
som," *The University of Kansas City Review,*
XXIII (Winter, 1956), 157-158.
RANSOM, "The Equilibrists"
RICHMOND C. BEATTY, "John Crowe Ransom as Poet,"
The Sewanee Review, LII (Summer, 1944), 359-360.
DREW and SWEENEY, *Directions in Modern Poetry,*
pp. 208-211.
HOWARD NEMEROV, "Summer's Flare and Winter's
Flaw," *The Sewanee Review,* LVI (Summer, 1948),
419-420.
G. P. WASSERMAN, "The Irony of John Crowe Ran-
som," *The University of Kansas City Review,*
XXIII (Winter, 1956), 158-159.
RANSOM, "The First Travels of Max"
VIVIENNE KOCH, "The Achievement of John Crowe

Ransom," *The Sewanee Review,* LVIII (Spring, 1950), 237.

VIVIENNE KOCH, "The Poetry of John Crowe Ransom," *Modern American Poetry,* B. Rajan, ed., pp. 44-45.

RANSOM, "Grace"

RICHMOND C. BEATTY, "John Crowe Ransom as Poet," *The Sewanee Review,* LII (Summer, 1944), 347-348.

G. P. WASSERMAN, "The Irony of John Crowe Ransom," *The University of Kansas City Review,* XXIII (Winter, 1956), 152-153.

RANSOM, "Here Lies a Lady"

WILLIAM BLEIFUSS, *The Explicator,* XI (May, 1953), 51.

JOHN M. BRADBURY, "Ransom as Poet," *Accent,* XI (Winter, 1951), 52-54.

KILBY, *Poetry and Life,* pp. 16-17.

F. H. STOCKING and ELLSWORTH MASON, *The Explicator,* VIII (Oct., 1949), 1.

RANSOM, "Janet Waking"

BROOKS, *Modern Poetry and the Tradition,* pp. 92-93.

DEUTSCH, *Poetry in Our Time,* pp. 206-207.

VIVIENNE KOCH, "The Achievement of John Crowe Ransom," *The Sewanee Review,* LVIII (Spring, 1950), 249-250.

VIVIENNE KOCH, "The Poetry of John Crowe Ransom," *Modern American Poetry,* B. Rajan, ed., pp. 55-56.

O'CONNOR, *Sense and Sensibility in Modern Poetry,* pp. 140-141.

ROSENTHAL and SMITH, *Exploring Poetry,* pp. 7-8.

G. P. WASSERMAN, "The Irony of John Crowe Ransom," *The University of Kansas City Review,* XXIII (Winter, 1956), 155-156.

RANSOM, "Lady Lost"

VIVIENNE KOCH, "The Achievement of John Crowe Ransom," *The Sewanee Review,* LVIII (Spring, 1950), 247-249.

VIVIENNE KOCH, "The Poetry of John Crowe Ransom," *Modern American Poetry*, B. Rajan, ed., pp. 54-55.

RANSOM, "Miller's Daughter"

RICHMOND C. BEATTY, "John Crowe Ransom as Poet," *The Sewanee Review*, LII (Summer, 1944), 357-358.

RANSOM, "Miriam Tazewell"

ROBERT FLYNN, *The Explicator*, XII (May, 1954), 45.

VIVIENNE KOCH, "The Achievement of John Crowe Ransom," *The Sewanee Review*, LVIII (Spring, 1950), 239-240.

VIVIENNE KOCH, "The Poetry of John Crowe Ransom," *Modern American Poetry*, B. Rajan, ed., pp. 46-47.

G. P. WASSERMAN, "The Irony of John Crowe Ransom," *The University of Kansas City Review*, XXIII (Winter, 1956), 156-157.

RANSOM, "Night Voices"

RICHMOND C. BEATTY, "John Crowe Ransom as Poet," *The Sewanee Review*, LII (Summer, 1944), 354-355.

RANSOM, "Noonday Grace"

RICHMOND C. BEATTY, "John Crowe Ransom as Poet," *The Sewanee Review*, LII (Summer, 1944), 345-346.

RANSOM, "Old Mansion"

VIVIENNE KOCH, "The Achievement of John Crowe Ransom," *The Sewanee Review*, LVIII (Spring, 1950), 245-247.

VIVIENNE KOCH, "The Poetry of John Crowe Ransom," *Modern American Poetry*, B. Rajan, ed., pp. 52-53.

RANSOM, "Painted Head"

RICHMOND C. BEATTY, "John Crowe Ransom as Poet," *The Sewanee Review*, LII (Summer, 1944), 365-366.

JOHN M. BRADBURY, "Ransom as Poet," *Accent*, XI (Winter, 1951), 55-56.

BROOKS, *Modern Poetry and the Tradition*, pp. 94-95.

VIVIENNE KOCH, "The Poetry of John Crowe Ransom," *Modern American Poetry*, B. Rajan, ed., pp. 62-64.

CHARLES MOORMAN, *The Explicator*, X (Dec., 1951), 15.

VIRGINIA WALLACK, *The Explicator*, XIV (April, 1956), 45.

RANSOM,   "Philomela"

DELMORE SCHWARTZ "Instructed of Much Mortality," *The Sewanee Review*, LIV (Summer, 1946), 443-444.

RANSOM,   "Prelude to an Evening"

CLEANTH BROOKS, "The Doric Delicacy," *The Sewanee Review*, LVI (Summer, 1948), 412-414.

VIVIENNE KOCH, "The Poetry of John Crowe Ransom," *Modern American Poetry*, B. Rajan, ed., pp. 62-64.

RANSOM,   "The School"

RICHMOND C. BEATTY, "John Crowe Ransom as Poet," *The Sewanee Review*, LII (Summer, 1944), 350.

RANSOM,   "Spectral Lovers"

RICHMOND C. BEATTY, "John Crowe Ransom as Poet," *The Sewanee Review*, LII (Summer, 1944), 353-354.

CLEANTH BROOKS, "The Doric Delicacy," *The Sewanee Review*, LVI (Summer, 1948), 410-412.

VIVIENNE KOCH, "The Achievement of John Crowe Ransom," *The Sewanee Review*, LVIII (Spring, 1950), 240-243.

VIVIENNE KOCH, "The Poetry of John Crowe Ransom," *Modern American Poetry*, B. Rajan, ed., pp. 47-50.

RANSOM,   "Spiel of the Three Mountebanks"

HOWARD NEMEROV, "Summer's Flare and Winter's Flaw," *The Sewanee Review*, LVI (Summer, 1948), 422.

RANSOM,   "The Swimmer"

RICHMOND C. BEATTY, "John Crowe Ransom as Poet," *The Sewanee Review*, LII (Summer, 1944), 345.

RANSOM, "The Tall Girl"

VIVIENNE KOCH, "The Achievement of John Crowe Ransom," *The Sewanee Review,* LVIII (Spring, 1950), 245.

VIVIENNE KOCH, "The Poetry of John Crowe Ransom," *Modern American Poetry,* B. Rajan, ed., pp. 51-52.

RANSOM, "Two in August"

RICHMOND C. BEATTY, "John Crowe Ransom as Poet," *The Sewanee Review,* LII (Summer, 1944), 359.

RANSOM, "Vaunting Oak"

CLEANTH BROOKS, "The Doric Delicacy," *The Sewanee Review,* LVI (Summer, 1948), 406-408.

F. O. MATTHIESSEN, "Primarily Language," *The Sewanee Review,* LVI (Summer, 1948), 394-395.

Reprinted *The Responsibilities of the Critic,* pp. 47-49.

RANSOM, "Winter Remembered"

RIDING and GRAVES, *A Survey of Modernist Poetry,* pp. 229-230.

READ, HERBERT, "The Analysis of Love"

TSCHUMI, *Thought in Twentieth-Century English Poetry,* pp. 181-182.

READ, HERBERT, "Beata l'Alma"

TSCHUMI, *Thought in Twentieth-Century English Poetry,* pp. 182-183.

READ, HERBERT, "The End of a War"

TSCHUMI, *Thought in Twentieth-Century English Poetry,* pp. 169-170.

READ, HERBERT, "Equation a+b+c= X"

TSCHUMI, *Thought in Twentieth-Century English Poetry,* p. 175.

READ, HERBERT, "John Donne Declines a Benefice"

TSCHUMI, *Thought in Twentieth-Century English Poetry,* pp. 179-180.

READ, HERBERT, "The Lament of St. Denis"

TSCHUMI, *Thought in Twentieth-Century English Poetry,* pp. 190-192.

READ, HERBERT, "Love and Death"
SKELTON, *The Poetic Pattern,* pp. 146-150.

READ, HERBERT, "Mutations of the Phoenix"
TSCHUMI, *Thought in Twentieth-Century English Poetry,* pp. 186-190.

READ, HERBERT, "The Narrow Labyrinth Has Light"
HERBERT READ, "Surrealism and the Romantic Principle," *Criticism,* 110-112.

READ, HERBERT, "Nuncio"
TSCHUMI, *Thought in Twentieth-Century English Poetry,* pp. 192-193.

READ, HERBERT, "The Retreat"
TSCHUMI, *Thought in Twentieth-Century English Poetry,* pp. 183-185.

READ, HERBERT, "A World Within a War"
HERBERT READ in Friar and Brinnin, *Modern Poetry,* p. 533.
TSCHUMI, *Thought in Twentieth-Century English Poetry,* pp. 173-174.

REED, HENRY, "Naming of Parts"
RICHARD A. CONDON, *The Explicator,* XII (June, 1954), 54.

REXROTH, "The Homestead Called Damascus"
LAWRENCE LIPTON, "Notes Toward an Understanding of Kenneth Rexroth with Special Attention to 'The Homestead Called Damascus,'" *Quarterly Review of Literature,* IX, (1957), 2, 37-46.

RICHARDS, I. A., "Not No"
ANONYMOUS, "The Poems of a Sage," *Times Literary Supplement* (May 1, 1959), p. 256.

ROBINSON, "Amaryllis"
WILLIAM C. CHILDERS, *The Explicator,* XIV (Feb., 1956), 34.

ROBINSON, "Cassandra"
YVOR WINTERS, "Religious and Social Ideas in the Didactic Work of E. A. Robinson," *The Arizona Quarterly,* I (Spring, 1945), 79-80.

ROBINSON, "The Clerks"

Louis O. Cope, "E. A. Robinson: The Lost Tradition," *The Sewanee Review,* LXII (Spring, 1954), 259-261.

ROBINSON, "Demos"

Yvor Winters, "Religious and Social Ideas in the Didactic Work of E. A. Robinson," *The Arizona Quarterly,* I (Spring, 1945), 80-81.

ROBINSON, "Dionysus in Doubt"

Yvor Winters, "Religious and Social Ideas in the Didactic Work of E. A. Robinson," *The Arizona Quarterly,* I (Spring, 1945), 82-84.

ROBINSON, "En Passant"

Bernice Slote, *The Explicator,* XV (Feb., 1957), 27.

ROBINSON, "Eros Turannos"

Louis Cope, "E. A. Robinson: The Lost Tradition," *The Sewanee Review,* LXII (Spring, 1954), 252-259.

Laurence Perrine, *The Explicator,* VIII (Dec., 1949), 20.

ROBINSON, "The Field of Glory"

Richard Crowder, *The Explicator,* VIII (Feb., 1950), 31.

ROBINSON, "Flammonde"

Millett, *Reading Poetry,* p. 64.

ROBINSON, "For a Dead Lady"

Richard Crowder, *The Explicator,* V (Dec., 1946), 19.

W. H. French, *The Explicator,* X (May, 1952), 51.

E. S. Fussell, *The Explicator,* IX (March, 1951), 33.

R. H. Super, *The Explicator,* III (June, 1945), 60.

R. H. Super, *The Explicator,* V (June, 1947), 60.

ROBINSON, "The Gift of God"

Louis O. Cope, "E. A. Robinson: The Lost Tradition," *The Sewanee Review,* LXII (Spring, 1954), 261-265.

ROBINSON, "Luke Havergal"

RICHARD CROWDER, *The Explicator,* VII (Nov., 1948), 15.

WALTER GIERASCH, *The Explicator,* III (Oct., 1944), 8.

Abridged in *The Case for Poetry,* p. 297.

MATHILDE M. PARLETT, *The Explicator,* III (June, 1945), 57.

A. A. RAVEN, *The Explicator,* III (Dec., 1944), 24.

ROBINSON,   "Lost Anchors"

CELESTE TURNER WRIGHT, *The Explicator,* XI (June, 1953), 57.

ROBINSON,   "The Man Against the Sky"

RICHARD CROWDER, " 'Man Against the Sky,' " *College English,* XIV (Feb., 1953), 269-276.

WINFIELD TOWNLEY SCOTT, "To See Robinson," *New Mexico Quarterly Review,* XXVI (Summer, 1956), 169.

WAGGONER, *The Heel of Elohim,* pp. 29-36.

YVOR WINTERS, "Religious and Social Ideas in the Didactic Work of E. A. Robinson," *The Arizona Quarterly,* I (Spring, 1945), 74-75 *et passim.*

ROBINSON,   "The Man Who Died Twice"

RICHARD CROWDER, "E. A. Robinson's Symphony: 'The Man Who Died Twice,' " *College English,* XI (Dec., 1949), 141-144.

ROBINSON,   "Mr. Flood's Party"

CIARDI, *How Does a Poem Mean?* p. 712.

WILLIS D. JACOBS, "E. A. Robinson's 'Mr. Flood's Party,' " *College English,* XII (Nov., 1950), 110.

E. SYDNOR OWNBEY, *The Explicator,* VIII (April, 1950), 47.

ROBINSON,   "New England"

RICHARD E. AMACHER, *The Explicator,* X (March, 1952), 33.

H. H. WAGGONER, *The Explicator,* X (March, 1952), 33.

ROBINSON,   "An Old Story"
RICHARD CROWDER, *The Explicator*, IV (Dec., 1945),
22.
ROBINSON,   "On the Way"
YVOR WINTERS, "Religious and Social Ideas in the
Didactic Work of E. A. Robinson," *The Arizona
Quarterly*, I (Spring, 1945), 81-82.
ROBINSON,   "Richard Cory"
HARRY R. GARVIN, "Poems Pickled in Anthological
Brine," *College English Association Critic*, XX
(Oct., 1958), 4.
STAGEBERG and ANDERSON, *Poetry as Experience*, pp.
189-192.
ROBINSON,   "The Sheaves"
RICHARD CROWDER, *The Explicator*, IV (March,
1946), 38.
ROBINSON,   "Sonnet: Oh for a Poet"
M. N. O., *The Explicator*, V (May, 1947), Q21.
ROBINSON,   "Veteran Sirens"
LAURENCE PERRINE, *The Explicator*, VI (Nov., 1947),
13.
ROBINSON,   "The Whip"
HENRY PETTIT, *The Explicator*, I (April, 1943), 50.
ROETHKE,   "The Big Wind"
KENNETH BURKE, "The Vegetal Radicalism of Theo-
dore Roethke," *The Sewanee Review*, LVIII (Win-
ter, 1950), 70-71.
ROETKE,   "Bring the Day"
HILTON KRAMER, "The Poetry of Theodore Roethke,"
The Western Review, XVIII (Winter, 1954), 137.
ROETHKE,   "The Dance"
CARROLL ARNETT, "Minimal to Maximal: Theodore
Roethke's Dialectic," *College English*, XVIII (May,
1957), 415-416.
ROETHKE,   "A Field of Light"
KENNETH BURKE, "The Vegetal Radicalism of Theo-
dore Roethke," *The Sewanee Review*, LVIII (Win-
ter, 1950), 94-95.

HILTON KRAMER, "The Poetry of Theodore Roethke," *The Western Review*, XVIII (Winter, 1954), 141-142.

ROETHKE,   "Give Way, Ye Gates"
HILTON KRAMER, "The Poetry of Theodore Roethke," *The Western Review*, XVIII (Winter, 1954), 138.

ROETHKE,   "The Long Alley"
KENNETH BURKE, "The Vegetal Radicalism of Theodore Roethke," *The Sewanee Review*, LVIII (Winter, 1950), 85-86, 93-94.

ROETHKE,   "The Lost Son"
CARROLL ARNETT, "Minimal to Maximal: Theodore Roethke's Dialectic," *College English*, XVIII (May, 1957), 415.

KENNETH BURKE, "The Vegetal Radicalism of Theodore Rothke," *The Sewanee Review*, LVIII (Winter, 1950), 87-93.

DEUTSCH, *Poetry in Our Time*, pp. 184-185.

HILTON KRAMER, "The Poetry of Theodore Roethke," *The Western Review*, XVIII (Winter, 1954), 138-141.

THEODORE ROETHKE, "Open Letter," *Mid-Century American Poets*, pp. 68-72.

ROETHKE,   "My Papa's Waltz"
CIARDI, *How Does a Poem Mean?* pp. 1003-1004.

ROETHKE,   "The Shape of Fire"
KENNETH BURKE, "The Vegetal Radicalism of Theodore Roethke," *The Sewanee Review*, LVIII, (Winter, 1950), 95-97, 100.

ROETHKE,   "The Visitant"
KENNETH BURKE, "The Vegetal Radicalism of Theodore Roethke," *The Sewanee Review*, LVIII (Winter, 1950), 71-72.

ROETHKE,   "Where Knock Is Open Wide"
KENNETH BURKE, "The Vegetal Radicalism of Theodore Roethke," *The Sewanee Review*, LVIII (Winter, 1950), 105-107.

HILTON KRAMER, "The Poetry of Theodore Roeth-

ke," *The Western Review*, XVIII (Winter, 1954),
135-136.

ROSSETTI, CHRISTINA, "Eve"

BOWRA, *The Romantic Imagination*, pp. 251-254.

ROSSETTI, CHRISTINA, "The Goblin Market"

WENDELL S. JOHNSON, "Some Functions of Poetic
Form," *Journal of Aesthetics and Art Criticism*,
(June, 1955), 504-505.

LONA M. PACKER, "Symbol and Reality in Christina
Rossetti's 'Goblin Market,'" *PMLA*, LXXIII (Sept.,
1958), 375-385.

ROSSETTI, CHRISTINA, "Rest"

KREUTZER, *Elements of Poetry*, pp. 17-18.

THOMAS and BROWN, *Reading Poems: An Introduction to Critical Study*, pp. 638-639.

ROSSETTI, CHRISTINA, "Spring Quiet"

RICHARDS, *Practical Criticism*, pp. 32-41 *et passim*.

ROSSETTI, D. G., "The Blessed Damozel"

C. C. CUNNINGHAM, *Literature as a Fine Art: Analysis
and Interpretation*, pp. 142-147.

K. L. KNICKERBOCKER, "Rossetti's 'The Blessed Damozel,'" *Studies in Philology*, XXIX (July, 1932),
485-504.

ROSSETTI, D. G., "Nuptial Sleep"

BOWRA, *The Romantic Imagination*, 212-213.

ROSSETTI, D. G., "A Sonnet Is a Moment's Monument"

STAUFFER, *The Nature of Poetry*, pp. 236-237.

RUKEYSER, "Boy with His Hair Cut Short"

WALTER GIERASCH, "Reading Modern Poetry," *College English*, II (Oct., 1940), 32-33.

ROSENTHAL and SMITH, *Exploring Poetry*, 285-287.

RUKEYSER, "The Childless Years Alone Without a
House"

J. F. NIMS, *Poetry: A Critical Supplement*, Jan., 1948,
pp. 15-17.

RUKEYSER, "They Came to Me and Said, 'There Is a
Child'"

J. F. NIMS, *Poetry: A Critical Supplement,* Jan., 1948, pp. 17-18.

RUSSELL ("A. E."),   "Self Discipline"

J. P. KIRBY, *The Explicator,* II (Dec., 1943), 22.

SANDBURG,   "Broken-Face Gargoyles"
BERNARD S. OLDSEY, *The Explicator,* VII (May, 1949), 50.

SANDBURG,   "Caboose Thoughts"
RICHARD CROWDER, *The Explicator,* IV (June, 1946), 52.

SANDBURG,   "Chicago"
CHARLES ALLEN, "Cadenced Free Verse," *College English,* IX (Jan., 1948), 197-198.
WALTER BLAIR, *Literature of the United States,* II, 962.

SANDBURG,   "Cool Tombs"
DANIEL G. HOFFMAN, *The Explicator,* IX (May, 1951), 46.

SANDBURG,   "Early Lynching"
RALPH P. BOAS, *The Explicator,* I (June, 1943), 67.

SANDBURG,   "Fog"
THOMAS and BROWN, *Reading Poems: An Introduction to Critical Study,* pp. 646-647.

SANDBURG,   "Nocturne in a Deserted Brickyard"
CHARLES ALLEN, "Cadenced Free Verse," *College English,* IX (Jan., 1948), 195-197.

SANDBURG,   "Number Man"
J. F. NIMS, *Poetry: A Critical Supplement,* Oct., 1947, pp. 1-4.

SANDBURG,   "On a Flimmering Flume You Shall Ride"
J. F. NIMS, *Poetry: A Critical Supplement,* Oct., 1947, pp. 4-5.

SANDBURG,   "To the Ghost of John Milton"
PAUL ENGLE, Engle and Carrier, *Reading Modern Poetry,* pp. 32-34.

SANTAYANA,   "I Sought on Earth a Garden of Delight"

PHILIP BLAIR RICE, "George Santayana," *The Kenyon Review,* II (Autumn, 1940), 469-471.

SASSOON,   "Acceptance"
C. E. MAGUIRE, "Harmony Unheard: The Poetry of Siegfried Sassoon," *Renascence,* XI (Spring, 1959), 119.

SASSOON,   "Everyone Sang"
SKELTON, *The Poetic Pattern,* pp. 142-143.

SASSOON,   "The Imperfect Lover"
C. E. MAGUIRE, "Harmony Unheard: The Poetry of Siegfried Sassoon," *Renascence,* XI (Spring, 1959), 119.

SASSOON,   "The Messenger"
C. E. MAGUIRE, "Harmony Unheard: The Poetry of Siegfried Sassoon," *Renascence,* XI (Spring, 1959), 122-123.

SCOTT, EVELYN,   "The Winter Alone"
DUDLEY FITTS, "The Verse of Evelyn Scott," *Poetry,* XXXVI (Sept., 1930), 338-343.

SCOTT, WALTER,   "County Guy"
DON A. KEISTER, *The Explicator,* IV (May, 1946), 49.

SCOTT, WALTER,   "Proud Maisie"
GEORGE ARMS and J. P. KIRBY, *The Explicator,* IV (Nov., 1945), 14.

SEDLEY, SIR CHARLES,   "Child and Maiden"
DENIS DONOGHUE, "Notes Towards a Critical Method," *Studies,* XLIV (Summer, 1955), 182-183.

SHAKESPEARE,   "But When I Came Alas to Wive" (*Twelfth Night*)
LESLIE HOTSON, "Twelfth Night," *Times Literary Supplement,* July 12, 1947, p. 351.
J. DOVER WILSON, "Twelfth Night," *Times Literary Supplement,* July 26, 1947, p. 379.

SHAKESPEARE,   "Doubt Thou the Stars are Fire" (*Hamlet,* II, ii, 116-119)
FRANK DOGGETT, *The Explicator,* XVI (Jan., 1958), 25.

SHAKESPEARE,   "Fear No More the Heat o' the Sun"
(*Cymbeline*)

W. W. MAIN, *The Explicator,* IX (March, 1951), 36.

EDWARD F. NOLAN, *The Explicator,* XI (Oct., 1952), 4.

GEORGE L. PHILLIPS, *The Explicator,* XII (Oct., 1953), 2.

WHEELWRIGHT, *The Burning Fountain,* pp. 149-150.

SHAKESPEARE,   "The Phoenix and the Turtle"

A. ALVAREZ, *Interpretations,* John Wain, ed., pp. 1-16.

RONALD BATES, "Shakespeare's 'The Phoenix and the Turtle,'" *Shakespeare Quarterly,* VI (Winter, 1955), 19-30.

M. C. BRADBROOK, "'The Phoenix and the Turtle,'" *Shakespeare Quarterly,* VI (Summer, 1955), 356-358.

CLEANTH BROOKS, "The Language of Paradox," *The Language of Poetry,* Allen Tate, ed., pp. 59-61. Reprinted *Criticism,* pp. 365-366.

BROOKS, *The Well Wrought Urn,* pp. 17-20. Reprinted *Critiques,* pp. 76-77.

Reprinted *American Literary Criticism,* pp. 529-531.

J. V. Cunningham, "'Essence' and the *Phoenix and the Turtle,*" *Journal of English Literary History,* XIX (Dec., 1952), 265-276.

W. J. ONG, "Metaphor and the Twinned Vision (*The Phoenix and the Turtle*)," *The Sewanee Review,* LXIII (Spring, 1955), 199-201.

SHAKESPEARE,   Sonnet II, "When Forty Winters Shall Besiege Thy Brow"

M. M. MAHOOD, "The Fatal Cleopatra: Shakespeare and the Pun," *Essays in Criticism,* I (July, 1951), 193-207.

SHAKESPEARE,   Sonnet V, "Those Hours, That with Gentle Work Did Frame"

PAUL ELMAN, "Shakespeare's Gentle Hours," *Shakespeare Quarterly,* IV (July, 1953), 301-309.

SHAKESPEARE, Sonnet VIII, "Music to Hear, Why Hear'st Thou Music Sadly?"
THEODORE H. BANKS, "Shakespeare's Sonnet No. 8," *MLN*, LXIII (Dec., 1948), 541-542.

SHAKESPEARE, Sonnet XV, "When I Consider Everything That Grows"
KIRK and McCUTCHEON, *An Introduction to the Study of Poetry*, pp. 39-41.

SHAKESPEARE, Sonnet XVI, "But Wherefore Do Not You a Mightier Way"
EMPSON, *Seven Types of Ambiguity*, pp. 70-74; (1947 ed.), pp. 54-57.

SHAKESPEARE, Sonnet XVIII, "Shall I Compare Thee to a Summer's Day"
SMITH, *Elizabethan Poetry*, p. 178.

SHAKESPEARE, Sonnet XXIX, "When In Disgrace with Fortune and Men's Eyes"
MALCOLM BROWN, "The Sweet Crystalline Cry, *1 ne Western Review*, XVI (Summer, 1952), 264-265.
FRANKENBERG, *Invitation to Poetry*, p. 239.

SHAKESPEARE, Sonnet XXX, "When to the Sessions of Sweet Silent Thought"
LEONARD DEAN, *English Masterpieces*, Vol. III, *Renaissance Poetry*, p. 9.
L. C. KNIGHTS, "Shakespeare's Sonnets," *Scrutiny*, III (Sept., 1934), 153.
KNIGHTS, *Explorations*, pp. 74-75.
KREUZER, *Elements of Poetry*, pp. 67-70.
S. C. PEPPER, *The Basis of Criticism in the Arts* (Cambridge: Harvard University Press, 1945), pp. 115-127.
Abridged in *The Case for Poetry*, pp. 307-309.
Reprinted in part Stageberg and Anderson, *Poetry as Experience*, p. 461.

SHAKESPEARE, Sonnet XXXI, "Thy Bosom Is Endeared with All Hearts"
H. W. PIPER, "Shakespeare's Thirty-First Sonnet,"

Times Literary Supplement (April 13, 1951), p. 229.

SHAKESPEARE, Sonnet XXXIII, "Full Many a Glorious Morning Have I Seen"

LEONARD DEAN, *English Masterpieces*, Vol. III, *Renaissance Poetry*, p. 10.

RANSOM, *The World's Body*, pp. 279-282.

SHAKESPEARE, Sonnet XXXV, "No More be Grieved at That Which Thou Hast Done"

L. C. KNIGHTS, "Shakespeare's Sonnets," *Scrutiny*, III (Sept., 1934), 142-143. Reprinted Brooks and Warren, *Understanding Poetry*, pp. 292-293.

Revised edition, pp. 152-153.

KNIGHTS, *Explorations*, pp. 64-66.

SHAKESPEARE, Sonnet XLVI, "Mine Eye and Heart Are at a Mortal War"

P. S. CLARKSON and C. T. WARREN, "Pleading and Practice in Shakespeare's Sonnet XLVI," *MLN*, LXII (Feb., 1947), 102-110.

SHAKESPEARE, Sonnet LI, "Thus Can My Love Excuse the Slow Offence"

A. DAVENPORT, "Shakespeare's Sonnet 51 Again," *Notes and Queries*, CXCVIII (Jan., 1953), 15-16

SHAKESPEARE, Sonnet LV, "Not Marble, nor the Gilded Monuments"

SMITH, *Elizabethan Poetry*, pp. 178-181.

SHAKESPEARE, Sonnet LX, "Like as The Waves Make Towards the Pebbled Shore"

DOUGLAS, LAMSON, SMITH, *The Critical Reader*, pp. 56-59.

JOHN CROWE RANSOM, "Shakespeare's Sonnets," *The Southern Review*, III (Winter, 1938), 548-549.

RANSOM, *The World's Body*, pp. 296-297.

SHAKESPEARE, Sonnet LXIV, "When I Have Seen by Time's Fell Hand Defaced"

VAN DOREN, *Introduction to Poetry*, pp. 117-120.

SHAKESPEARE, Sonnet LXV, "Since Brass, nor Stone,

nor Earth, nor Boundless Sea"
MILLETT, *Reading Poetry,* pp. 60-61.
SHAKESPEARE,   Sonnet LXXI, "No Longer Mourn for
Me When I Am Dead"
VAN DOREN, *Introduction to Poetry,* pp. 117-120.
SHAKESPEARE,   Sonnet LXXIII, "That Time of Year
Thou May'st in Me Behold"
ROBERT BERKELMAN, "The Drama in Shakespeare's
Sonnets," *College English,* X (Dec., 1948), 139.
KREUZER, *Elements of Poetry,* pp. 150-151.
R. M. LUMIANSKY, *The Explicator,* VI (June, 1948),
55.
WINIFRED LYNSKEY, "A Critic in Action: Mr. Ran-
som," *College English,* V (Feb., 1944), 244-245.
CARLISLE MOORE, *The Explicator,* VIII (Oct., 1949),2.
EDWARD F. NOLAN, *The Explicator,* VII (Nov., 1948),
13.
RANSOM, *The World's Body, pp.* 297-298.
ROSENTHAL and SMITH, *Exploring Poetry,* pp. 91-94.
SMITH, *Elizabethan Poetry,* pp. 182-185.
THOMAS and BROWN, *Reading Poems: An Introduc-
tion to Critical Study,* pp. 744-748.
SHAKESPEARE,   Sonnet LXXIV, "But Be Contented
When That Fell Arrest"
LONGWORTH CHAMBRUN, "The Rival Poet," *Times
Literary Supplement* (Feb. 2, 1951), p. 69.
SHAKESPEARE,   Sonnet LXXVII, "Thy Glass Will
Show Thee How Thy Beauties Wear"
YVOR WINTERS, "The Sixteenth Century Lyric in Eng-
land," *Poetry,* LIV (April, 1939), 49-51.
SHAKESPEARE,   Sonnet LXXXI, "Or I Shall Live Your
Epitaph to Make"
EMPSON, *Seven Types of Ambiguity,* pp. 69-70; (1947
ed.), pp. 53-54.
SHAKESPEARE,   Sonnet LXXXIII, "I Never Saw That
You Did Painting Need"

EMPSON, *Seven Types of Ambiguity*, pp. 168-175; (1947 ed.), pp. 133-139.

SHAKESPEARE, Sonnet LXXXVI, "Was It the Proud Full Sail of His Great Verse"

FRANKENBERG, *Invitation to Poetry*, pp. 94-95.

SHAKESPEARE, Sonnet LXXXVII, "Farewell! Thou Art Too Dear for My Possessing"

DANIELS, *The Art of Reading Poetry*, p. 212.

SHAKESPEARE, Sonnet XCIII, "So Shall I Live Supposing Thou Art True"

EMPSON, *English Pastoral Poetry*, pp. 89-101.

SHAKESPEARE, Sonnet XCIV, "They That Have Pow'r to Hurt and Will Do None"

EMPSON, *English Pastoral Poetry*, pp. 89-101.

L. C. KNIGHTS, "Shakespeare's Sonnets," *Scrutiny*, III (Sept., 1934), 147-149.

KNIGHTS, *Explorations*, pp. 69-70.

SMITH, *Elizabethan Poetry*, pp. 188-191.

SHAKESPEARE, Sonnet XCV, "How Sweet and Lovely Dost Thou Make the Shame"

EMPSON, *English Pastoral Poetry*, pp. 89-101.

SHAKESPEARE, Sonnet XCVII, "How Like a Winter Hath My Absence Been"

KREUZER, *Elements of Poetry*, pp. 10-11.

SHAKESPEARE, Sonnet CVII, "Not Mine Own Fears, Nor the Prophetic Soul"

F. W. BATESON, "Elementary, My Dear Hotson," *Essays in Criticism*, I (Jan., 1951), 81-88.

LAWRENCE MICHEL, "Shakespeare's Sonnet CVII," *Journal of English and Germanic Philology*, LIV (Apirl, 1955), 301-305.

RANSOM, *The World's Body*, pp. 298-299.

SHAKESPEARE, Sonnet CXIII, "Since I Left You, Mine Eye Is in My Mind"

DONIPHAN LOUTHAN, "Sonnet 113," *Times Literary Supplement* (July 6, 1951), p. 421.

SHAKESPEARE, Sonnet CXVI, "Let Me Not to the Marriage of True Minds"

SIGURD BURCKHARDT, "The Poet as Fool and Priest," *Journal of English Literary History*, XXIII (Dec., 1956), 289-298.

FRANKENBERG, *Invitation to Poetry*, pp. 398-399.

SMITH, *Elizabethan Poetry*, pp. 172-176.

SHAKESPEARE,   Sonnet CXX, "That You Were Once Unkind Befriends Me Now"

FRANKENBERG, *Invitation to Poetry*, p. 285.

SHAKESPEARE,   Sonnet CXXI, " 'Tis Better to be Vile Than Vile Esteemed"

L. C. KNIGHTS, "Shakespeare's Sonnets," *Scrutiny*, III (Sept., 1930), 155-156.

SHAKESPEARE,   Sonnet CXXIII, "No, Time, Thou Shalt Not Boast That I Do Change"

L. C. KNIGHTS, "Shakespeare's Sonnets," *Scrutiny*, III (Sept., 1934), 158-160.

KNIGHTS, *Explorations*, pp. 79-80.

SHAKESPEARE,   Sonnet CXXIV, "If My Dear Love Were But the Child of State"

ARTHUR MIZENER, "The Structure of Figurative Language in Shakespeare's Sonnets," *The Southern Review*, V (Spring, 1940), 734-747.

SHAKESPEARE,   Sonnet CXXIX, "The Expense of Spirit in a Waste of Shame"

C. W. M. JOHNSON, *The Explicator*, VII (April, 1949), 41.

RIDING and GRAVES, *A Survey of Modernist Poetry*, pp. 63-75, 78-80.

SMITH, *Elizabethan Poetry*, pp. 187-188.

KARL F. THOMPSON, *The Explicator*, VII (Feb., 1949), 27.

SHAKESPEARE,   Sonnet CXLII, "Love Is My Sin, and Thy Dear Virtue Hate"

T. WALTER HERBERT, *The Explicator*, XIII (April, 1955), 38.

SHAKESPEARE,   Sonnet CXLIV, "Two Loves I Have of Comfort and Despair"

JOHN M. STEADMAN, "'Like Two Spirits': Shakespeare and Ficino," *Shakespeare Quarterly,* X (Spring, 1959), 244-246.

SHAKESPEARE,   Sonnet CXLVI, "Poor Soul, the Center of My Sinful Earth"

ROBERT BERKELMAN, "The Drama in Shakespeare's Sonnets," *College English,* X (Dec., 1948), 139-141.

CHARLES A. O. Fox, "Shakespeare's Sonnet 146," *Notes and Queries,* I, n.s. (Feb., 1954), 83.

KREUZER, *Elements of Poetry,* pp. 91-92.

DONALD A. STAUFFER, *et al.,* "Critical Principles and a Sonnet," *American Scholar,* XII (Winter, 1942), 52-62.

Abridged in *The Case for Poetry,* pp. 317-319.

SHAKESPEARE,   Sonnet CXLVII, "My Love Is as a Fever, Longing Still"

SMITH, *Elizabethan Poetry,* pp. 186-187.

SHAKESPEARE,   Sonnet CLIII, "Cupid Laid by His Brand and Fell Asleep"

JAMES HUTTON, "Analogues of Shakespeare's Sonnets 153-54," *Modern Philology,* XXXVIII (May, 1941), 399-403.

SHAKESPEARE,   Sonnet CLIV, "The Little Love-God Lying Once Asleep"

JAMES HUTTON, "Analogues of Shakespeare's Sonnets 153-54," *Modern Philology,* XXXVIII (May, 1941), 399-403.

SHAKESPEARE,   "Take Oh Take Those Lips Away" (*Measure for Measure*)

EMPSON, *Seven Types of Ambiguity,* pp. 229-230; (1947 ed.), pp. 180-182.

STAUFFER, *The Nature of Poetry,* p. 107.

SHAKESPEARE,   "What Shall He Have That Kill'd the Deer?" (*As You Like It*)

PETER J. SENG, "The Foresters' Song in *As You Like It,*" *Shakespeare Quarterly,* X (Spring, 1959), 246-249.

SHAKESPEARE, "When Daisies Pied and Violets Blue" (*Love's Labour's Lost*)
BERTRAND H. BRONSON, "Daisies Pied and Icicles," *MLN*, LXIII (Jan., 1948), 35-38.

SHAKESPEARE, "When Icicles Hang by the Wall" (*Love's Labour's Lost*)
BERTRAND H. BRONSON, "Daisies Pied and Icicles," *MLN*, LXIII (Jan., 1948), 35-38.
DANIELS, *The Art of Reading Poetry*, pp. 50-51.
PERRINE, *Sound and Sense*, pp. 7-8.

SHAKESPEARE, "Who is Silvia? What is She" (*The Two Gentlemen of Verona*)
CLEANTH BROOKS, "Irony and 'Ironic' Poetry," *College English*, IX (Feb., 1948), 234-235; *The English Journal*, XXXVII (Feb., 1948), 60-61.
Reprinted Zabel, *Literary Opinion in America*, revised edition, pp. 733-734.
PAUL R. SULLIVAN, "Untheological Grace," *College English*, X (Dec., 1948), 164-165.

SHAPIRO, "Christmas Eve: Australia"
DAVID DAICHES, "The Poetry of Karl Shapiro," *Poetry*, LXVI (August, 1945), 267-269.
Reprinted Engle and Carrier, *Reading Modern Poetry*, pp. 250-251.

SHAPIRO, "The Dome of Sunday"
EDWIN FUSSELL, "Karl Shapiro: The Paradox of Prose and Poetry," *The Western Review*, XVIII (Spring, 1954), 240-242.

SHAPIRO, "Elegy for a Dead Soldier"
PAUL ENGLE, "Five Years of Pulitzer Poets," *The English Journal*, XXXVIII (Feb., 1949), 62-63.
EDWIN FUSSELL, "Karl Shapiro: The Paradox of Prose and Poetry," *The Western Review*, XVIII (Spring, 1954), 239-240.

SHAPIRO, "Poet"
MICHEL VINAVERT, *The Explicator*, IV (Dec., 1945), 23.

SHELLEY, "Adonais"

DAICHES and CHARVAT, *Poems in English,* p. 704.

HUNGERFORD, *Shores of Darkness,* pp. 216-239.

MICHAEL MACKLEM, "The Elegiac Theme in Housman," *Queens Quarterly,* LIX (Spring, 1952), 47-48.

JOHN P. O'NEILL and STEWART C. WILCOX, *The Explicator,* XII (Oct., 1953), 5.

TILLYARD, *Poetry Direct and Oblique,* pp. 172-173.

EARL R. WASSERMAN, " 'Adonais': Progressive Revelation as a Poetic Mode," *Journal of English Literary History,* XXI (Dec., 1954), 278-326.

WASSERMAN, *The Subtler Language,* pp. 305-361.

S. C. WILCOX, *The Explicator,* VIII (Nov., 1949), 13.

STEWART C. WILCOX, *The Explicator,* IX (April, 1951), 39.

SHELLEY, "Alastor"

LEONARD BROWN, "The Genesis, Growth, and Meaning of 'Endymion,' " *Studies in Philology,* XXX (Oct., 1933), 623-653 *passim.*

KENNETH NEILL CAMERON, "*Rasselas* and *Alastor:* A Study in Transmutation," *Studies in Philology,* XL (Jan., 1943), 58-78.

A. E. DuBois, "Alastor: The Spirit of Solitude," *Journal of English and Germanic Philology,* XXXV (1936), 530-545.

ALBERT GERARD, "Alastor, or the Spirit of Solopsism," *Philological Quarterly,* XXXIII (April, 1954), 164-177.

EVAN K. GIBSON, "Alastor: a Reinterpretation," *PMLA,* LXII (Dec., 1947), 1022-1045.

RAYMOND D. HAVENS, "Shelley's 'Alastor,' " *PMLA,* XLV (Dec., 1930), 1098-1115.

A. M. D. HUGHES, " 'Alastor, or the Spirit of Solitude' " *Modern Language Review,* XLIII (Oct., 1948), 465-470.

F. L. JONES, "The Inconsistency of Shelley's *Alastor*," *English Literary History*, XIII (Dec., 1946), 291-298.

F. L. JONES, "The Vision Theme in Shelley's *Alastor* and Related Works," *Studies in Philology*, XLIV (Jan., 1947), 108-125.

MARCEL KESSEL, PAUL MUESCHKE and E. L. GRIGGS, "The Poet in Shelley's *Alastor:* A Criticism and a Reply," *PMLA*, LI (March, 1936), 302-312.

ROBERT A. WICKERT, *The Explicator*, XII (Nov., 1953), 11.

SHELLEY,   "The Cloud"

BROOKS, PURSER, WARREN, *An Approach to Literature*, pp. 471-473.

MIGNONETTE E. HARRISON, *The Explicator*, XII (Nov., 1953), 10.

KNIGHT, *The Starlit Dome*, pp. 198-199.

SHELLEY,   "Epipsychidion"

K. N. CAMERON, "The Planet-Tempest Passage in Epipsychidion," *PMLA*, LXIII (Sept., 1948), 950-972.

JOHN HAWLEY ROBERTS, *The Explicator*, I (April, 1943), 49.

VIVANTE, *English Poetry*, pp. 174-177.

SHELLEY,   "Ginevra"

BEN W. GRIFFITH, JR., "Shelley's 'Ginevra,'" *Times Literary Supplement* (Jan. 15, 1954), p. 41.

SHELLEY,   "Hymn to Intellectual Beauty"

F. L. JONES, "Shelley's *On Life*," *PMLA*, LXXII (Sept., 1947), 775-778.

ELIZABETH NITCHIE, *PMLA*, LXIII (June, 1948), 752-753.

SHELLEY,   "The Indian Serenade"

BROOKS and WARREN, *Understanding Poetry*, pp. 320-323.

Revised edition, pp. 174-176.

SHELLEY,   "Julian and Maddalo"
CARLOS BAKER, "Shelley's Farrarese Maniac," *English Institute Essays 1946,* pp. 41-73.
SHELLEY,   "Lamia"
J. H. ROBERTS, "The Significance of *Lamia,*" *PMLA,* L (June, 1935), 550-561.
SHELLEY,   "Lines: When the Lamp is Shattered"
BEACH, *A Romantic View of Poetry,* pp. 76-81.
LOUISE SCHUTZ BOAS, *The Explicator,* I (April, 1943), 48.
R. H. FOGLE, "Romantic Bards and Metaphysical Reviewers," *English Literary History,* XII (Sept., 1945), 234-235.
ROBERT M. GAY, *The Explicator,* II (Oct., 1943), 6.
DANIEL GIBSON, F. A. PHILBRICK, and GILBERT MACBETH, *The Explicator,* I (May, 1943), 51.
MARCEL KESSEL, *The Explicator,* III (Nov., 1944), 13.
F. R. LEAVIS, "*Shelley* (Revaluations VIII)," *Scrutiny,* IV (Sept. 1935), 168-171. Reprinted *Revaluation,* pp. 216-220, and *Critiques,* pp. 169-172.
NORMAN NATHAN, "Shelley's 'Eagle Home,'" *Notes and Queries,* I, n.s., (Jan., 1954), 30.
ALLEN TATE, "Understanding Modern Poetry," *College English,* I (April, 1940), 570-571.
TATE, *Reason in Madness,* pp. 96-97.
TATE, *On the Limits of Poetry,* pp. 126-127.
RENÉ WELLEK, "A Letter," *The Importance of Scrutiny,* p. 28. First published in *Scrutiny,* 1937.
SHELLEY,   "Lines Written Among the Euganean Hills"
LOUISE SCHUTZ BOAS, *The Explicator,* III (Nov., 1944), 14.
J. P. KIRBY, *The Explicator,* I (Oct., 1942), 5.
SHELLEY,   "Mont Blanc"
I. J. KAPSTEIN, "The Meaning of Shelley's 'Mont Blanc,'" *PMLA,* LXII (Dec., 1947), 1046-1060.
LEAVIS, *Revaluation,* pp. 212-214. Reprinted *Critiques,* pp. 167-168.

F. R. LEAVIS, "A Reply," *The Importance of Scrutiny,* p. 39. First published in *Scrutiny,* 1937.

WASSERMAN, *The Subtler Language,* pp. 195-240.

RENÉ WELLEK, "A Letter," *The Importance of Scrutiny,* pp. 27-28. First published in *Scrutiny,* 1937.

YEATS, *Essays,* pp. 104-107.

SHELLEY,   "Music, When Soft Voices Die"

BOULTON, *The Anatomy of Poetry,* pp. 123-125.

JOHN CROSSETT, *The Explicator,* XIV (Feb., 1956), 32.

BEN W. GRIFFITH, JR., *The Explicator,* XV (Jan., 1957), 26.

WILLIAM HOWARD, *The Explicator,* XV (Jan., 1957), 26

F. R. LEAVIS, " 'Thought' and Emotional Quality," *Scrutiny,* XIII (Spring, 1945), 66-67.

JOHN UNTERECKER, *The Explicator,* XV (Jan., 1957), 26.

SHELLEY,   "Ode to the West Wind"

BATESON, *English Poetry,* pp. 213-217.

Abridged in *The Case for Poetry,* pp. 325-327.

R. H. FOGLE, "Romantic Bards and Metaphysical Reviewers," *English Literary History,* XII (Sept., 1945), 236-238, 249-250.

R. H. FOGLE, "The Imaginal Design of Shelley's 'Ode to the West Wind,' " *English Literary History,* XV (Sept., 1948), 219-226.

Abridged in *The Case for Poetry,* pp. 323-325.

I. J. KAPSTEIN, "The Symbolism of the Wind and the Leaves in Shelley's 'Ode to the West Wind,' " *PMLA,* LI (Dec., 1936), 1069-1079.

F. R. LEAVIS, "Shelley (Revaluations VIII)," *Scrutiny,* IV (Sept., 1935), 159-163 *et passim*. Reprinted *Revaluation,* pp. 204-206, and *Critiques,* pp. 162-163.

F. R. LEAVIS, "A Reply," *The Importance of Scrutiny,* p. 38. First published in *Scrutiny,* 1937.

DOUGLASS S. MEAD, *The Explicator*, V (May, 1947), Q20.

TATE, *Reactionary Essays on Poetry and Ideas*, pp. 95-97 *et passim*.

VIVANTE, *English Poetry*, pp. 164-169.

RENÉ WELLEK, "A Letter," *The Importance of Scrutiny*, pp. 26-27. First published in *Scrutiny*, 1937.

STEWART C. WILCOX, "Imagery, Ideas, and Design in Shelley's 'Ode to the West Wind,'" *Studies in Philology*, XLVII (Oct., 1950), 634-649. Abridged in *The Case for Poetry*, p. 325.

ARTHUR WORMHOUDT and K. H. FOGLE, *The Explicator*, VI (Oct., 1947), 1.

SHELLEY,   "Ozymandias"

ROBERT B. HEILMAN, "Poetic and Prosaic: Program Notes of Opposite Numbers," *Pacific Spectator*, V (Autumn, 1951), 456-457.

KIRK and McCUTCHEON, *An Introduction to the Study of Poetry*, pp. 37-39. Reprinted *Readings for Liberal Education*, II, 309-310.

SHELLEY,   "The Sensitive Plant"

FREDERICK L. JONES, "Shelley and Spenser," *Studies in Philology*, XXXIX (Oct., 1942), 667-669.

ELIZABETH NITCHIE, *The Explicator*, XV (Dec., 1956), 15.

WASSERMAN, *The Subtler Language*, pp. 251-284.

SHELLEY,   "To Ianthe"

BROOKS, PURSER, WARREN, *An Approach to Literature*, p. 463.

Reprinted third edition, pp. 333-334.

SHELLEY,   "To Jane, the Recollection"

VIVANTE, *English Poetry*, pp. 177-181.

SHELLEY,   "To Night"

DANIELS, *The Art of Reading Poetry*, pp. 354-358.

SHELLEY,   "To a Skylark"

JAMES V. BAKER, "The Lark in English Poetry," *Prairie Schooner*, XXIV (Spring, 1950), 71-74.

EMPSON, *Seven Types of Ambiguity*, pp. 197-202; (1947 ed.), pp. 156-159.

FRANKENBERG, *Invitation to Poetry*, pp. 82-83.

A. E. HOUSMAN in Grant Richards, *Housman, 1897-1936*, p. 246. First printed *Times Literary Supplement*, Dec. 20, 1927.

KNIGHT, *The Starlit Dome*, pp. 199-200.

E. WAYNE MARJARUM, "The Symbolism of Shelley's 'To a Skylark,' " *PMLA*, LII (Sept., 1937), 911-913.

T. S. MOORE, "Mr. T. S. Eliot and Shelley's Skylark," *Times Literary Supplement*, Nov. 16, 1928, p. 991; Jan. 3, 1929, p. 12.

TILLYARD, *Poetry Direct and Oblique*, pp. 163-166.

VIVANTE, *English Poetry*, pp. 169-174.

S. C. WILCOX, "The Sources, Symbolism, and Unity of Shelley's *Skylark*," *Studies in Philology*, XLVI (Oct., 1949), 560-576.

SHELLEY,   "The Triumph of Life"

WILLIAM CHERUBINI, "Shelley's 'Own Symposium': 'The Triumph of Life,' " *Studies in Philology*, XXXIX (July, 1942), 559-570.

YEATS, *Essays*, pp. 92-94.

SHELLEY,   "The World's Great Age Begins Anew" (from *Hellas*)

EMPSON, *Seven Types of Ambiguity* (1947 ed.), pp. 159-160.

SHIRLEY,   "The Glories of Our Blood and State" (*The Contention of Ajax and Ulysses for the Armor of Achilles*)

BOULTON, *The Anatomy of Poetry*, pp. 165-167.

E. SYDNOR OWNBEY, *The Explicator*, X (Feb., 1952), 30.

TILLYARD, *Poetry Direct and Oblique*, pp. 122-124.

SIDNEY,   "Because I Oft in Dark Abstracted Guise" (*Astrophel and Stella*, 28)

TUVE, *Elizabethan and Metaphysical Imagery*, p. 320.

SIDNEY,   "Cupid, Because Thou Shin'st in Stella's Eyes" (*Astrophel and Stella*, 12)

ROBERT S. KINSMAN, *The Explicator*, VIII (June, 1950), 56.

SIDNEY, "Dear, Why Make You More of a Dog Than Me" (*Astrophel and Stella,* 59)

TUVE, *Elizabethan and Metaphysical Imagery*, p. 321.

SIDNEY, "Having this Day My Horse, My Hand, My Lance" (*Astrophel and Stella*, 41)

RICHARD B. YOUNG, "English Petrarke: A Study of Sidney's *Astrophel and Stella*," *Three Studies in the Renaissance*, pp. 15-16.

SIDNEY, "High Way Since You My Chief Parnassus Be" (*Astrophel and Stella*, 84)

CURTIS DAHL, *The Explicator*, VI (May, 1948), 46.

YVOR WINTERS, "The Sixteenth-Century Lyric in England," *Poetry*, LIII (April, 1939), 328-329.

SIDNEY, "I Never Drank of Aganippe Well" (*Astrophel and Stella*, 74)

RICHARD B. YOUNG, "English Petrarke: A Study of Sidney's *Astrophel and Stella*," *Three Studies in the Renaissance*, pp. 7-8.

SIDNEY, "It Is Most True that Eyes Are Formed to Serve" (*Astrophel and Stella*, 5)

DE MOURGUES, *Metaphysical Baroque & Precieux Poetry*, pp. 14-15.

ROBERT L. MONTGOMERY, JR., "Reason, Passion, and Introspection in *Astrophel and Stella*," *University of Texas Studies in English*, XXXVI (1957), 132-133.

SIDNEY, "Leave Me, O Love, Which Reachest But to Dust" (*Astrophel and Stella*, 110)

HAROLD S. WILSON, *The Explicator*, II (April, 1944), 47.

Reprinted Locke, Gibson, and Arms, *Introduction to Literature*, third edition, pp. 23-24.

SIDNEY, "A Litany"

BROOKS and WARREN, *Understanding Poetry*, pp. 342-345.

Revised edition, pp. 206-210.

SIDNEY, "Love By Sure Proof I May Call Thee Unkind" (*Astrophel and Stella*, 65)
RICHARD B. YOUNG, "English Petrarke: A Study of Sidney's *Astrophel and Stella*," *Three Studies in the Renaissance*, pp. 18-20.

SIDNEY, "Loving in Truth and Fain in Verse My Love to Show" (*Astrophel and Stella*, 1)
ADAMS, *Strains of Discord*, pp. 4-6.
ARTHUR DICKSON, *The Explicator*, III (Oct., 1944), 3.
HENRY PETTIT and GERALD SANDERS, *The Explicator*, I (Feb., 1943), 26.

SIDNEY, "No More, My Dear, No More These Counsels Try (*Astrophel and Stella*, 64)
ROBERT L. MONTGOMERY, JR., "Reason, Passion, and Introspection in *Astrophel and Stella*," *University of Texas Studies in English*, XXXVI (1957), 137.

SIDNEY, "O How the Pleasant Airs of True Love Be" (*Astrophel and Stella*, 78)
HAROLD S. WILSON, *The Explicator*, II (Nov., 1943), 17.

SIDNEY, "*Phoebus* was Judge Between *Jove, Mars,* and *Love*" (*Astrophel and Stella*, 13)
RICHARD B. YOUNG, "English Petrarke: A Study of Sidney's *Astrophel and Stella*," *Three Studies in the Renaissance*, pp. 20-22.

SIDNEY, "Queen *Virtue's* Court, Which Some Call Stella's Face" (*Astrophel and Stella*, 9)
RICHARD B. YOUNG, "English Petrarke: A Study of Sidney's *Astrophel and Stella*," *Three Studies in the Renaissance*, p. 11.

SIDNEY, "Rich Fools There Be, Whose Base and Filthy Heart" (*Astrophel and Stella*, 24)
RICHARD B. YOUNG, "English Petrarke: A Study of Sidney's *Astrophel and Stella*," *Three Studies in the Renaissance*, pp. 29-30.

SIDNEY, "Stella, the Only Planet of My Light" (*Astrophel and Stella*, 68)

RICHARD B. YOUNG, "English Petrarke: A Study of Sidney's *Astrophel and Stella*," *Three Studies in the Renaissance*, pp. 35-36.

SIDNEY,   "Thou Blind Man's Mark, Thou Fool's Self-Chosen Snare" (*Astrophel and Stella*, 119)

DAN G. HOFFMAN, *The Explicator*, VIII (Feb., 1950), 29.

SIDNEY,   "*Virtue* Alas, Now Let Me Take *Some Rest*" (*Astrophel and Stella*, 4)

RICHARD B. YOUNG, "English Petrarke: A Study of Sidney's *Astrophel and Stella*," *Three Studies in the Renaissance*, pp. 33-34.

SIDNEY,   "What Have I Thus Betrayed My Liberty" (*Astrophel and Stella*, 47)

ROBERT L. MONTGOMERY, JR., Reason, Passion, and Introspection in *Astrophel and Stella*," *University of Texas Studies in English*, XXXVI (1957), 136-137.

RICHARD B. YOUNG, "English Petrarke: A Study of Sidney's *Astrophel and Stella*," *Three Studies in the Renaissance*, pp. 23-24.

SIDNEY,   "When Far Spent Night Persuades Each Mortal Eye" (*Astrophel and Stella*, 99)

RICHARD B. YOUNG, "English Petrarke: A Study of Sidney's *Astrophel and Stella*," *Three Studies in the Renaissance*, p. 85.

SIDNEY,   "When My Good Angel Guides Me to the Place" (*Astrophel and Stella*, 60)

DE MORGUES, *Metaphysical Baroque & Precieux Poetry*, pp. 15-16.

SIDNEY,   "With How Sad Steps, O Moon, Thou Climb'st the Skies" (*Astrophel and Stella*, 31)

RICHARD B. YOUNG, "English Petrarke: A Study of Sidney's *Astrophel and Stella*," *Three Studies in the Renaissance*, pp. 49-50.

SIDNEY,   "You Goat-Herd Gods, That Love the Grassy Mountains"

EMPSON, *Seven Types of Ambiguity*, pp. 45-50; (1947 ed.), pp. 34-38.

RANSOM, *The New Criticism*, pp. 108-114.

SITWELL, EDITH,   "Aubade"
EASTMAN, *The Literary Mind*, pp. 73-76 (quoting from Sitwell).
STAGEBERG and ANDERSON. *Poetry as Experience*, pp. 497-498.

SITWELL, EDITH,   "Fantasia for Mouth Organ"
RIDING and GRAVES, *A Survey of Modernist Poetry*, pp. 247-249.

SITWELL, EDITH,   "Gold Coast Customs"
SISTER M. JEREMY, "Clown and Canticle: The Achievement of Edith Sitwell," *Renascence*, III (Spring, 1951), 133-134.

SITWELL, EDITH,   "The Shadow of Cain"
SISTER M. JEREMY, "Clown and Canticle: The Achievement of Edith Sitwell," *Renascence*, III (Spring, 1951), 135-136.
JACK LINDSAY, "The Poetry of Edith Sitwell," *Life and Letters*, LXIV (Jan., 1950), 51-52.

SITWELL, EDITH,   "The Sleeping Beauty"
DEUTSCH, *Poetry in Our Time*, pp. 223-225.

SITWELL, EDITH,   "Spring Morning"
SISTER M. JEREMY, "Clown and Canticle: The Achievement of Edith Sitwell," *Renascence*, III (Spring, 1951), 136-137.

SITWELL, EDITH,   "When Sir Beelzebub"
DANIELS, *The Art of Reading Poetry*, pp. 400-401.

SITWELL, EDITH,   "The Winds Bastinado Whipt on the Calico"
RIDING and GRAVES, *A Survey of Modernist Poetry*, pp. 231-233.

SITWELL, SACHEVERELL,   "Doctor Donne and Gargantua: The First Six Cantos"
R. P. BLACKMUR, "A Poet's Lent," *Poetry*, XXXVIII (June, 1931), 162-166.

SITWELL, SACHEVERELL, "The Lady and the Rooks"
JOSEPH WARREN BEACH, "Rococo: The Poetry of Sacheverell Sitwell," *Poetry*, LXXIV (July, 1949), 229-231.

SITWELL, SACHEVERELL, "New Water Music"
JOSEPH WARREN BEACH, "Rococo: The Poetry of Sacheverell Sitwell," *Poetry*, LXXIV (July, 1949), 227.

SKELTON, JOHN, "Speak, Parrot"
WILLIAM NELSON, "Skelton's 'Speak, Parrot,' " *PMLA*, LI (March, 1936), 59-82.

SKELTON, JOHN, "With Lullay, Lullay, Like a Child"
FRANKENBERG, *Invitation to Poetry*, pp. 151-152.

SKELTON, ROBIN, "The Shell"
SKELTON, *The Poetic Pattern*, pp. 152-153.

SKELTON, ROBIN, "Temple Flower"
SKELTON, *The Poetic Pattern*, pp. 150-152.

SMART, "The Circumcision"
DARINA WILLIAMSON, "Christopher Smart's *Hymns and Spiritual Songs*," *Philological Quarterly*, XXXVIII (Oct. 1959), 416-422.

SMART, "Song to David"
R. D. HAVENS, "The Structure of Smart's *Song to David*," *Review of English Studies*, XIV (April, 1938), 178-182.

SOUTHEY, "His Books"
BROOKS, PURSER, WARREN, *An Approach to Literature*, pp. 464-467.
Reprinted third edition, pp. 337-340.

SOUTHWELL, "A Fancy Turned to a Sinner's Complaint"
MARTZ, *The Poetry of Meditation*, pp. 189-191.

SOUTHWELL, "At Home in Heaven"
MARTZ, *The Poetry of Meditation*, pp. 188-189.

SOUTHWELL, "Mary Magdalen's Complaint at Christ's Death"
MARTZ, *The Poetry of Meditation*, pp. 191-193.

SOUTHWELL, "Saint Peter's Complaint"

MARTZ, *The Poetry of Meditation,* pp. 193-197.

SOUTHWELL, "A Vale of Tears"

MARTZ, *The Poetry of Meditation,* pp. 207-210.

SPENDER, "Abrupt and Charming Mover"

RUDOLF ARNHEIM, "Psychological Notes on the Poetical Process," *Poets at Work,* pp. 150, 158-160.

SPENDER, "Awaking"

BERNARD KNIEGER, *The Explicator,* XII (March, 1954), 30.

SPENDER, "An Elementary School Class Room in a Slum"

PHYLLIS BARTLETT, *Poems in Process,* pp. 217-219.

SPENDER, "The Express"

DOUGLAS, LAMSON, SMITH, *The Critical Reader,* pp. 134-136.

KARL SHAPIRO, "The Meaning of the Discarded Poem," *Poets at Work,* pp. 94-101.

SPENDER, "The Funeral"

WILLIS D. JACOBS, "The Moderate Poetical Success of Stephen Spender," *College Enblish,* XVII (April, 1956), 376.

KARL SHAPIRO, "The Meaning of the Discarded Poem," *Poets at Work,* pp. 101-105.

SPENDER, "I Think Continually of Those"

HALLETT SMITH, *The Explicator,* II (Feb., 1944), 33.

DONALD A. STAUFFER, "Genesis, of the Poet as Maker," *Poets at Work,* pp. 76-80.

SPENDER, "The Landscape Near an Aerodrome"

WILLIS D. JACOBS, "The Moderate Poetical Success of Stephen Spender," *College English,* XVII (April, 1956), 375-376.

C. C. WALCUTT, *The Explicator,* V (March, 1947), 37. Reprinted Engle and Carrier, *Reading Modern Poetry,* pp. 85-86.

SPENDER, "Not Palaces"

WILLIS D. JACOBS, "The Moderate Poetical Success of Stephen Spender," *College English,* XVII (April, 1956), 376-377.

SPENDER,   "Oh What Is the Use Now of Our Meeting and Speaking"

RUDOLF ARNHEIM, "Psychological Notes on the Poetical Process," *Poets at Work*, pp. 146-147.

SPENDER,   "Oh Young Men Oh Young Comrades"

RALPH LYNN, JR., *English "A" Analyst*, No. 13, pp. 1-5.

SPENDER,   "The Pylons"

CHARLES D. ABBOTT, "Poetry in the Making," *Poetry*, LV (Feb., 1940), 262-266.

SPENDER,   "Rolled Over on Europe"

DANIELS, *The Art of Reading Poetry*, pp. 293-294.

SPENDER,   "Seascape"

BARBARA GIBBS, " 'Where Thoughts Lash Tail and Fin,' " *Poetry*, LXXXVI (July, 1955), 239-240.

DAY LEWIS, *The Poetic Image*, pp. 136-140 (with quotations from Spender's remarks).

SPENDER,   "There Are Some Days the Happy Ocean Lies"

STEPHEN SPENDER, "The Making of a Poem," *Partisan Review*, XIII (Summer, 1946), 297-300. Reprinted *Criticism*, pp. 189-190, and *Critiques*, pp. 20-22.

SPENDER,   "Tom's A-Cold"

J. F. NIMS, *A Critical Supplement to "Poetry,"* Oct., 1948, pp. 1-7.

SPENSER,   "*Amoretti*, Sonnet XV: Ye Tradeful Merchants, That with Weary Toil"

TUVE, *Elizabethan and Metaphysical Imagery*, pp. 64-65.

SPENSER,   "*Amoretti*, Sonnet XXIII: Penelope for Her Ulysses' Sake"

KREUZER, *Elements of Poetry*, pp. 83-84.

SPENSER,   "Amoretti, Sonnet XXXIV: Like as a ship That Through the Ocean Wide"

UNGER and O'CONNOR, *Poems for Study*, pp. 60-62.

SPENSER,   "*Amoretti*, Sonnet XLI: Is It Her Nature, or Is It Her Will"

TUVE, *Elizabethan and Metaphysical Imagery*, pp. 63-64.

SPENSER, *"Amoretti,* Sonnet XLVI: When My Abodes Prefixed Time Is Spent"
TUVE, *Elizabethan and Metaphysical Imagery*, pp. 325-327.

SPENSER, *"Amoretti,* Sonnet LVI: Fair Ye Be Sure, But Cruel and Unkind"
WINIFRED LYNSKEY, "A Critic in Action: Mr. Ransom," *College English*, V (Feb., 1944), 244-245.

SPENSER, *"Amoretti,* Sonnet LIX: Thrice Happy She, That Is So Well Assured"
BATESON, *English Poetry and the English Language*, pp. 32-33.

SPENSER, *"Amoretti,* Sonnet LXXII: Oft When My Spirit Doth Spread Her Bolder Wings"
W. B. C. WATKINS, "The Kingdom of Our Language," *The Hudson Review*, II (Autumn, 1949), 343-344.

SPENSER, "Muiopotmos"
DON CAMERON ALLEN, "On Spenser's *Muiopotmos*," *Studies in Philology*, LIII (April, 1956), 141-158.

SPENSER, "Prothalamion"
GEORGE ARMS, *The Explicator*, I (March, 1943), 36.
DAICHES and CHARVAT, *Poems in English*, pp. 650-652.
DAN S. NORTON, "Queen Elizabeth's 'Brydale Day,'" *Modern Language Quarterly*, V (1944), 149-154.

STEIN, "Lipschitz"
HARRY R. GARVIN, *The Explicator*, XIV (Dec., 1955), 18.

STEPHENS, "Little Things"
NAT HENRY, *The Explicator*, IX (Dec., 1950), 20.
LYSANDER KEMP, *The Explicator*, VIII (May, 1950), 50.

STEPHENS, "The Main Deep"
BROOKS and WARREN, *Understanding Poetry*, pp. 170-173.
Revised edition, pp. 74-77.

STEPHENS,   "The Rivals"
FRANKENBERG, *Invitation to Poetry*," p. 58.

STEVENS,   "Academic Discourse at Havana"
FRIAR and BRINNIN, *Modern Poetry*, p. 537.

STEVENS,   "Anecdote of the Jar"
HOWARD BAKER, "Wallace Stevens and Other Poetry,"
The Southern Review, I (Autumn, 1935), 376-377.
DON GEIGER, "Wallace Stevens' Wealth," *Perspective*,
VII (Autumn, 1954), 160.
J. P. KIRBY, *The Explicator*, III (Nov., 1944), 16.
CHARLES C. WALCUTT, "Interpreting the Symbol,"
College English, XIV (May, 1953), 449-451.
T. WEISS, "The Nonsense of Winters' *Anatomy*,"
Quarterly Review of Literature, I (Spring, 1944),
228.
WINTERS, *Anatomy of Nonsense*, pp. 93-95. Also *In
Defense of Reason*, pp. 435-437.

STEVENS,   "Anecdote of Men by the Thousand"
QUINN, *The Metamorphic Tradition.* p. 77.

STEVENS,   "The Apostrophe to Vincentine"
FRANK DOGGETT, "Wallace Stevens and the World We
Know," *The English Journal*, XLVIII (Oct., 1959),
369-370.
QUINN, *The Metamorphic Tradition*, pp. 75-76.
SISTER M. BERNETTA QUINN, O.S.F., "Metamorphosis
in Wallace Stevens," *The Sewanee Review*, LX
(Spring, 1952), 243-244.

STEVENS,   "Asides on the Oboe"
HI SIMONS, "The Genre of Wallace Stevens," *The
Sewanee Review*, LIII (Autumn, 1945), 570-579.

STEVENS,   "The Auroras of Autumn"
DONALD DAVIE, " 'The Auroras of Autumn,' " *Per-
spective*, VII (Autumn, 1954), 125-136.
C. ROLAND WAGNER, "The Idea of Nothingness in
Wallace Stevens," *Accent*, XII (Spring, 1952), 116-
117.

STEVENS,   "The Auroras of Autumn" I

RALPH J. MILLS, JR., "Wallace Stevens: The Image of the Rock," *Accent*, XVIII (Spring, 1958), 84.

STEVENS, "The Auroras of Autumn" II
JOSEPH BENNETT, "Five Books, Four Poets," *Hudson Review*, IV (Spring, 1951), 134-136.

STEVENS, "Bantams in Pine-Woods"
MARIUS BEWLEY, "The Poetry of Wallace Stevens," *Partisan Review*, XVI (Sept., 1949), 898-905.

R. P. BLACKMUR, "Wallace Stevens," *Hound and Horn*, V (Jan.-March, 1932), 247-248.
Reprinted *Language as Gesture*, pp. 242-243.

WILLIAM VAN O'CONNOR, "Wallace Stevens on 'The Poems of Our Climate,'" *University of Kansas City Review*, XV (Winter, 1948), 106-107.

FRED H. STOCKING, *The Explicator*, III (April, 1945), 45.

STEVENS, "Bouquet of Roses in Moonlight"
J. F. NIMS, *Poetry: A Critical Supplement*, Oct., 1947, p. 9.

STEVENS, "Certain Phenomena of Sound"
WILLIAM W. HEATH, *The Explicator*, XII (Dec., 1953), 16.

STEVENS, "Chocorua to Its Neighbor"
ROBERT PACT, "The Abstracting Imagination of Wallace Stevens: Nothingness and the Hero," *Arizona Quarterly*, XI (Autumn, 1955), 206-208.

STEVENS, "The Comedian as the Letter C"
- HOWARD BAKER, "Wallace Stevens," *The Southern Review*, I (Autumn, 1935), 377-381.

R. P. BLACKMUR, "Wallace Stevens," *Hound and Horn*, V (Jan.-March, 1932), 248-255. Reprinted *The Double Agent*, pp. 94-102.
Reprinted *Language as Gesture*, pp. 243-249.

J. V. CUNNINGHAM, "The Poetry of Wallace Stevens," *Poetry*, LXXV (Dec., 1949), 151-159.
Reprinted *Modern Literary Criticism*, pp. 356-360.

GUY DAVENPORT, "Spinoza's Tulips: A Commentary

on 'The Comedian as the Letter C,'" *Perspective,*
VII (Autumn, 1954), 147-154.

FRANKENBERG, *Pleasure Dome,* pp. 210-215.

DON GEIGER, "Wallace Steven's Wealth," *Perspective,*
VII (Autumn, 1954), 165.

HOFFMAN, *The Twenties,* pp. 183-185.

WILLIAM VAN O'CONNOR, "Wallace Stevens on 'The
Poems of Our Climate,'" *University of Kansas City
Review,* XV (Winter, 1948), 109.

O'CONNOR, *Sense and Sensibility in Modern Poetry,*
pp. 141-142.

HI SIMONS, "'The Comedian as the Letter C'; Its
Sense and Its Significance," *The Southern Review,*
V (Winter, 1940), 453-468.

FRED H. STOCKING, *The Explicator,* III (March, 1945),
43.

T. WEISS, "The Nonsense of Winters' *Anatomy,*"
Quarterly Review of Literature, I (Spring, 1944),
229.

WINTERS, *Anatomy of Nonsense,* pp. 98-103. Also *In
Defense of Reason,* pp. 439-444.

STEVENS,   "Cortége for Rosenbloom"

RICHARD ELLMAN, "Wallace Stevens' Ice Cream," *The
Kenyon Review,* XIX (Winter, 1957), 90-92.

STEVENS,   "The Course of a Particular"

ROBERT PACK, "The Abstracting Imagination of Wallace Stevens: Nothingness and the Hero," *Arizona
Quarterly,* XI (Autumn, 1955), 198-199.

STEVENS,   "Credences of Summer"

BERNARD HERINGMAN, "The Poetry of Synthesis,"
Perspective, VII (Autumn, 1954), 171-174.

RALPH J. MILLS, JR., "Wallace Stevens: The Image of
the Rock," *Accent,* XVII (Spring, 1958), 77-78, 81.

HAROLD H. WATTS, "Wallace Stevens and the Rock
of Summer," *The Kenyon Review,* XIV (Winter,
1952), 122-124.

STEVENS,   "The Death of a Soldier"

R. P. BLACKMUR, "Wallace Stevens," *Hound and Horn*, V (Jan.-March, 1932), 229-230. Reprinted *The Double Agent*, pp. 74-75.

STEVENS,   "Description Without Place"

ROBERT PACK, "The Abstracting Imagination of Wallace Stevens: Nothingness and the Hero," *Arizona Quarterly*, XI (Autumn, 1955), 199-200.

STEVENS,   "Disillusionment of Ten O'Clock"

R. P. BLACKMUR, "Examples of Wallace Stevens," *Hound and Horn*, V (Jan.-March, 1932), 228-229. Reprinted *The Double Agent*, pp. 73-74.

Reprinted, *Language as Gesture*, pp. 226-227.

RANDALL JARRELL, "Reflections on Wallace Stevens," *Partisan Review*, XVIII (May-June, 1951), 337-338.

STEVENS,   "Domination of Black"

WILLIAM J. ROONEY, " 'Spelt from Sibyl's Leaves'— A Study in Contrasting Methods of Evaluation," *Journal of Aesthetics and Art Criticism*, XIII (June, 1955), 512-514.

STEVENS,   "The Dwarf"

ROBERT PACK, "The Abstracting Imagination of Wallace Stevens: Nothingness and the Hero," *Arizona Quarterly*, XI (Autumn, 1955), 197-198.

STEVENS,   "Earthly Anecdote"

FRANKENBERG, *Pleasure Dome*, pp. 198-199.

STEVENS,   "The Emperor of Ice-Cream"

R. P. BLACKMUR, "Wallace Stevens," *Hound and Horn*, V (Jan.-March, 1932), 230-232. Reprinted *The Double Agent*, pp. 75-77.

Reprinted *Language as Gesture*, pp. 227-229.

DREW and SWEENEY, *Directions in Modern Poetry*, pp. 227-231.

Abridged in *The Case for Poetry*, p. 341.

RICHARD ELLMANN, "Wallace Stevens' Ice Cream," *The Kenyon Review*, XIX (Winter, 1957), 92-95.

FRIAR and BRINNIN, *Modern Poetry*, p. 538.

MAX HERZBERG and WALLACE STEVENS, *The Explicator*, VII (Nov., 1948), 18.

KENNETH LASH and ROBERT THACKABERRY, *The Explicator*, VI (April, 1948), 36.

Abridged in *The Case for Poetry*, p. 342.

RALPH NASH, "About 'The Emperor of Ice-Cream,' " *Perspective*, VII (Autumn, 1954), 122-124.

ELDER OLSON, "The Poetry of Wallace Stevens," *College English*, XVI (April, 1955), 397-398.

T. WEISS, "The Nonsense of Winters' *Anatomy*," *Quarterly Review of Literature*, I (Spring, 1944), 226.

STEVENS,   "Esthétique du Mal"

RICHARD ELLMANN, "Wallace Stevens' Ice Cream," *The Kenyon Review*, XIX (Winter, 1957), 100-101.

FRANKENBERG, *Pleasure Dome*, pp. 249-251.

LOUIS L. MARTZ, "The World of Wallace Stevens," *Modern American Poetry*, B. Rajan, ed., p. 106.

WYLIE SYPHER, "Connoisseur of Chaos: Wallace Stevens," *Partisan Review*, XIII (Winter, 1946), 84-86.

STEVENS,   "Esthétique du Mal" VII

RALPH J. MILLS, JR., "Wallace Stevens: The Image of the Rock," *Accent*, XVIII (Spring, 1958), 82-83.

STEVENS,   "Evening Without Angels"

FRIAR and BRINNIN, *Modern Poetry*, p. 537.

STEVENS,   "Flyer's Fall"

HAROLD H. WATTS, "Wallace Stevens and the Rock of Summer," *The Kenyon Review*, XIV (Winter, 1952), 133-134.

STEVENS,   "Frogs Eat Butterflies"

DON GEIGER, "Wallace Stevens' Wealth," *Perspective*, VII (Autumn, 1954), 158-160.

STEVENS,   "The Glass of Water"

DAVID H. OWEN, " 'The Glass of Water,' " *Perspective*, VII (Autumn, 1954), 181-183.

ERIC SELLIN, *The Explicator*, XVII (Jan., 1959), 28.

STEVENS,   "A High-Toned Old Christian Woman"

WILLIAM VAN O'CONNOR, "Wallace Stevens on 'The Poems of Our Climate,'" *University of Kansas City Review*, XV (Winter, 1948), 110.

STEVENS,   "Holiday in Reality"

BERNARD HERINGMAN, "The Poetry of Synthesis," *Perspective*, VII (Autumn, 1954), 169-171.

STEVENS,   "Homunculus et La Belle Étoile"

NORMAN SILVERSTEIN, *The Explicator*, XIII (May, 1955), 40.

STEVENS,   "The House Was Quiet and the World Was Calm"

J. V. CUNNINGHAM, "The Poetry of Wallace Stevens," *Poetry*, LXXV (Dec., 1949), 164-165.

Reprinted *Modern Literary Criticism*, pp. 365-366.

QUINN, *The Metamorphic Tradition*, p. 76.

STEVENS,   "How to Live. What to Do"

RALPH J. MILLS, JR., "Wallace Stevens: The Image of the Rock," *Accent*, XVIII (Spring, 1958), 76-77.

STEVENS,   "The Idea of Order at Key West"

DEUTSCH, *Poetry in Our Time*, pp. 248-250.

FRANK DOGGETT, "Wallace Stevens and the World We Know," *The English Journal*, XLVIII (Oct., 1959), 370-371.

DREW, *Poetry*, pp. 261-262.

FRIAR and BRINNIN, *Modern Poetry*, pp. 537-538.

LOUIS L. MARTZ, "Wallace Stevens: The World as Meditation," *Yale Review*, XLVII (Summer, 1958), 521-522.

LOUIS L. MARTZ, "The World of Wallace Stevens," *Modern American Poetry*, B. Rajan,, ed., pp. 101-103.

STEVENS,   "In a Bad Time"

C. ROLAND WAGNER, "The Idea of Nothingness in Wallace Stevens," *Accent*, XII (Spring, 1952), 119.

STEVENS,   "Infanta Marina"

MARIUS BEWLEY, "The Poetry of Wallace Stevens," *Partisan Review*, XVI (Sept., 1949), 906.

STEVENS, "Landscape with Boat"
WATTS, *Hound and Quarry*, pp. 48-49.
HAROLD H. WATTS, "Wallace Stevens and the Rock of Summer," *The Kenyon Review*, XIV (Winter, 1952), 128-130.

STEVENS, "Large Red Man Reading"
FRANK DOGGETT, "Wallace Stevens and the World We Know," *The English Journal*, XLVIII (Oct., 1959), 371-373.

STEVENS, "Less and Less Human, O Savage Spirit"
C. ROLAND WAGNER, "The Idea of Nothingness in Wallace Stevens," *Accent*, XII (Spring, 1952), 113-114.

STEVENS, "Life Is Motion"
ELDER OLSON, "The Poetry of Wallace Stevens," *College English*, XVI (April, 1955), 396-397.

STEVENS, "Life on a Battleship"
FRANKENBERG, *Pleasure Dome*, pp. 240-242.
WILLIAM VAN O'CONNOR, "The Politics of a Poet," *Perspective*, I (Summer, 1948), 206-207.

STEVENS, "The Load of Sugar-Cane"
DON GEIGER, "Wallace Stevens' Wealth," *Perspective*, VII (Autumn, 1954), 157-158.

STEVENS, "Looking Across the Fields and Watching the Birds Fly"
MARIUS BEWLEY, "The Poetry of Wallace Stevens," *Commonweal*, LXII (Sept. 23, 1955), 620-621.

STEVENS, "The Man Whose Pharynx Was Bad"
MARIUS BEWLEY, "The Poetry of Wallace Stevens," *Partisan Review*, XVI (Sept., 1949), 908-910.
T. WEISS, "The Nonsense of Winters' *Anatomy*," *Quarterly Review of Literature*, I (Spring, 1944), 230.

STEVENS, "The Man With the Blue Guitar"
FRANKENBERG, *Pleasure Dome*, pp. 222-227.
HI SIMONS, "The Genre of Wallace Stevens," *The Sewanee Review*, LIII (Oct.-Dec., 1945), pp. 571-574.

STEVENS,   "The Men that are Falling"

RALPH J. MILLS, JR., "Wallace Stevens: The Image of the Rock," *Accent*, XVIII (Spring, 1958), 78-79.

STEVENS,   "Metamorphosis"

QUINN, *The Metamorphic Tradition*, pp. 57-58.

SISTER M. BERNETTA QUINN, O.S.F., "Metamorphosis in Wallace Stevens," *The Sewanee Review*, LX (Spring, 1952), 235-236.

STEVENS,   "Metaphors of a Magnifico"

MARIUS BEWLEY, "The Poetry of Wallace Stevens," *Partisan Review*, XVI (Sept., 1949), 903-904.

DON GEIGER, "Wallace Stevens' Wealth," *Perspective*, VII (Autumn, 1954), 156.

STEVENS,   "Le Monocle de Mon Oncle"

R. P. BLACKMUR, "Wallace Stevens," *Hound and Horn*, V (Jan.-March, 1932), 232-233, 245-246. Reprinted *The Double Agent*, pp. 77-78, 91-93.

Reprinted *Language as Gesture*, pp. 229-230.

DONALD DAVIE, " 'Essential Gaudiness': The Poems of Wallace Stevens," *Twentieth Century*, CLIII (June, 1953), 455-462.

RICHARD ELLMANN, "Wallace Stevens' Ice Cream," *The Kenyon Review*, XIX (Winter, 1957), 97-99.

WILLIAM A. FAHEY, *The Explicator*, XV (Dec., 1956), 16.

FRANKENBERG, *Pleasure Dome*, pp. 205-207.

R. M. GAY, *The Explicator*, VI (Feb., 1948), 27.

EARL ROY MINER, *The Explicator*, XIII (March, 1955), 28.

ROBERT PACK, "Wallace Stevens: The Secular Mystery and the Comic Spirit," *The Western Review*, XX (Autumn, 1955), 57-59.

DELMORE SCHWARTZ, "In the Orchards of Imagination," *New Republic*, CXXXI (Nov. 1, 1954), 17.

T. WEISS, "The Nonsense of Winters' *Anatomy*," *Quarterly Review of Literature*, I (Spring, 1944), 225-226.

STEVENS, "The Motive for Metaphor"
JOHN CROWE RANSOM, "The Concrete Universal:
Observations on the Understanding of Poetry, II,"
The Kenyon Review, XVII (Summer, 1955), 400-402.

STEVENS, "Mrs. Alfred Uruguay"
FRIAR and BRINNIN, *Modern Poetry*, p. 536.

STEVENS, "Notes Toward a Supreme Fiction"
FRANK DOGGETT, *The Explicator*, XV (Feb., 1957), 30.
FRANKENBERG, *Pleasure Dome*, pp. 257-267.
FRIAR and BRINNIN, *Modern Poetry*, pp. 535-536.
BERNARD HERINGMAN, "The Poetry of Synthesis,"
Perspective, VII (Autumn, 1954), 167-168.
LOUIS L. MARTZ, "The World of Wallace Stevens,"
Modern American Poetry, B. Rajan, ed., pp. 98-101.

STEVENS, "Oak Leaves Are Hands"
QUINN, *The Metamorphic Tradition*, p. 85.
SISTER M. BERNETTA QUINN, O.S.F., "Metamorphosis
in Wallace Stevens," *The Sewanee Review*, LX
(Spring, 1952), 250-251.

STEVENS, "Of Hartford in a Purple Light"
NORMAN SILVERSTEIN, *The Explicator*, XVIII (Dec., 1959), 20.

STEVENS, "Of the Manner of Addressing Clouds"
R. P. BLACKMUR, "Examples of Wallace Stevens,"
Hound and Horn, V (Jan.-March, 1932), 225-227.
Reprinted *The Double Agent*, pp. 70-72.
Reprinted *Language as Gesture*, pp. 223-224.

STEVENS, "Of Modern Poetry"
WILLIAM VAN O'CONNOR, "Wallace Stevens on 'The
Poems of Our Climate,'" *University of Kansas City
Review*, XV (Winter, 1948), 108-109.

STEVENS, "An Ordinary Evening in New Haven"
C. ROLAND WAGNER, "The Idea of Nothingness in
Wallace Stevens," *Accent*, XII (Spring, 1952), 120-121.

STEVENS, "The Ordinary Women"

> R. P. BLACKMUR, "Examples of Wallace Stevens," *Hound and Horn*, V (Jan.-March, 1932), 227-228. Reprinted *The Double Agent*, pp. 72-73. Reprinted *Language as Gesture*, pp. 225-226.

> DON GEIGER,, "Wallace Stevens' Wealth," *Perspective*, VII (Autumn, 1954), 160-163.

> FRED H. STOCKING, *The Explicator*, IV (Oct., 1945), 4.

STEVENS, "The Owl and the Sarcophagus"

> RALPH J. MILLS, JR., "Wallace Stevens: The Image of the Rock," *Accent*, XVIII (Spring, 1958), 83.

> C. ROLAND WAGNER, "The Idea of Nothingness in Wallace Stevens," *Accent*, XII (Spring, 1952), 115-116.

STEVENS, "Owl's Clover"

> FRANKENBERG, *Pleasure Dome*, pp. 227-231.

> LOUIS L. MARTZ, "Wallace Stevens: The World as Meditation," *Yale Review*, XLVII (Summer, 1958), 523-526.

STEVENS, "Peter Quince at the Clavier"

> COOPER and HOLMES, *Preface to Poetry*, p. 63.

> WENDELL S. JOHNSON, "Some Functions of Poetic Form," *Journal of Aesthetics and Art Criticism*, XIII (June, 1955), 501-503.

> WILLIAM VAN O'CONNOR, "Tension and Structure of Poetry," *The Sewanee Review*, LI (Autumn, 1943), 559.

> O'CONNOR, *Sense and Sensibility in Modern Poetry*, pp. 149-150.

> FRED H. STOCKING, *The Explicator*, V (May, 1947), 47.

> MARY JANE STORM, *The Explicator*, XIV (Nov., 1955), 9.

STEVENS, "The Plot Against the Giant"

> FRANKENBERG, *Pleasure Dome*, p. 201.

> ALBERT W. LEVI, "A Note on Wallace Stevens and the Poem of Perspective," *Perspective*, VII (Autumn, 1954), 138-139.

STEVENS, "The Poems of Our Climate"
FRIAR and BRINNIN, *Modern Poetry,* p. 537.

STEVENS, "A Primitive Like an Orb"
MARIUS BEWLEY, "The Poetry of Wallace Stevens,"
Partisan Review, XVI (Sept., 1949), 913-914.
WATTS, *Hound and Quarry,* pp. 54-55.

STEVENS, "The Red Fern"
LOUIS L. MARTZ, "The World of Wallace Stevens,"
Modern American Poetry, B. Rajan, ed., pp. 97-98.

STEVENS, "Repetition of a Young Captain"
BERNARD HERINGMAN, "The Poetry of Synthesis,"
Perspective, VII (Autumn, 1954), 168-169.

STEVENS, "Restatement of Romance"
WATTS, *Hound and Quarry,* pp. 52-53.

STEVENS, "The Rock"
RALPH J. MILLS, JR., "Wallace Stevens: The Image of
the Rock," *Accent,* XVIII (Spring, 1958), 85-89.

STEVENS, "Sad Strains of a Gay Waltz"
MATTHIESSEN, *The Responsibilities of the Critic,*
pp. 15-16.

STEVENS, "Sea Surface Full of Clouds"
R. P. BLACKMUR, "Wallace Stevens," *Hound and
Horn,* V (Jan.-March, 1932), 233-235. Reprinted
The Double Agent, pp. 79-80.
Reprinted *Language as Gesture,* pp. 230-232.
DAVID R. FERRY, *The Explicator,* VI (June, 1948), 56.
ALBERT W. LEVI, "A Note on Wallace Stevens and
the Poem of Perspective," *Perspective,* VII (Au-
tumn, 1954), 141-142.
RANSOM, *The World's Body,* pp. 58-60.
JOSEPH N. RIDDEL, " 'Disguised Pronunciamento':
Wallace Stevens, 'Sea Surface Full of Clouds,' "
University of Texas Studies in English, XXXVII
(1958), 177-186.

STEVENS, "Six Significant Landscapes"
ALBERT W. LEVI, "A Note on Wallace Stevens and
the Poem of Perspective," *Perspective,* VII (Autumn, 1954), 142-144.

CHARLES MOORMAN, *The Explicator,* XVII (Oct., 1958), 1.

STEVENS,   "The Snow Man"

R. P. BLACKMUR, "Wallace Stevens," *Hound and Horn,* V (Jan.-March, 1932), 242-243. Reprinted *The Double Agent,* pp. 87-89.
Reprinted *Language as Gesture,* pp. 237-238.

C. ROLAND WAGNER, "The Idea of Nothingness in Wallace Stevens," *Accent* XII (Spring, 1952), 118.

STEVENS,   "So-and-So Reclining on Her Couch"

ROBERT M. FARNSWORTH, *The Explicator,* X (June, 1952), 60.

STEVENS,   "Sonatina to Hans Christian"

FRANK DOGGETT, "Wallace Stevens and the World We Know," *The English Journal,* XLVIII (Oct., 1959), 367.

STEVENS,   "Study of Images"

WARREN CARRIER, "Wallace Stevens' Pagan Vantage," *Accent,* XIII (Summer, 1953), 165-168.
Reprinted Engle and Carrier, *Reading Modern Poetry,* pp. 361-364.

STEVENS,   "Sunday Morning"

R. P. BLACKMUR, "Wallace Stevens," *Hound and Horn,* V (Jan.-March, 1932), 240-241, 244. Reprinted *The Double Agent,* pp. 85-87, 90.

Reprinted *Language as Gesture,* pp. 236-237.

J. V. CUNNINGHAM, "The Poetry of Wallace Stevens," *Poetry,* LXXV (Dec., 1949), 159-164.

Reprinted *Modern Literary Criticism,* pp. 360-365.

DREW, *Poetry,* pp. 217-221.

RICHARD ELLMAN, "Wallace Stevens' Ice Cream," *The Kenyon Review,* XIX (Winter, 1957), 95-97.

FRANKENBERG, *Pleasure Dome,* pp. 215-217.

DON GEIGER, "Wallace Stevens' Wealth," *Perspective,* VII (Autumn, 1954), 164-165.

LOUIS L. MARTZ, "The World of Wallace Stevens," *Modern American Poetry,* B. Rajan, ed., pp. 107-108.

ROBERT PACK, "Wallace Stevens: The Secular Mystery and the Comic Spirit," *The Western Review,* XX (Autumn, 1955), 53-55.

T. WEISS, "The Nonsense of Winters' *Anatomy,*" *Quarterly Review of Literature,* I (Spring, 1944), 232-233.

WINTERS, *The Anatomy of Nonsense,* pp. 88-91, 105-108. Also *In Defense of Reason,* pp. 431-434, 447-456. Reprinted *Readings for Liberal Education,* II, 530-533.

Reprinted Locke, Gibson, and Arms, *Introduction to Literature,* third edition, pp. 193-196.

STEVENS,   "Tattoo"

R. P. BLACKMUR, "Wallace Stevens," *Hound and Horn,* V (Jan.-March, 1932), 235-236. Reprinted *The Double Agent,* pp. 81-82.

Reprinted *Language as Gesture,* pp. 232-233.

STEVENS,   "That Which Cannot Be Fixed"

MARIUS BEWLEY, "The Poetry of Wallace Stevens," *Partisan Review,* XVI (Sept., 1949), 910-911.

STEVENS,   "Things of August"

JOHN BERRYMAN, *A Critical Supplement to "Poetry,"* Dec., 1949, pp. 1-9.

STEVENS,   "Thirteen Ways of Looking at a Blackbird"

FRANK DOGGETT, "Wallace Stevens and the World We Know," *The English Journal,* XLVIII (Oct., 1959), 368.

ALBERT W. LEVI, "A Note on Wallace Stevens and the Poem of Perspective," *Perspective,* VII (Autumn, 1954), 144-146.

UNGER and O'CONNOR, *Poems for Study,* pp. 608-616.

STEVENS,   "To the One of Fictive Music"

RICHARD E. AMACHER, *The Explicator,* XI (April, 1953), 43.

LOUIS L. MARTZ, "The World of Wallace Stevens," *Modern American Poetry,* B. Rajan, ed., p. 95.

STEVENS,   "Two Figures in Dense Violet Light"

ROBERT W. BUTTEL, *The Explicator,* IX (May, 1951), 45.

STEVENS, "Two Tales of Liadoff"
FRANKENBERG, *Pleasure Dome,* pp. 254-256.
STEVENS, "The Ultimate Poem Is Abstract"
J. F. NIMS, *Poetry: A Critical Supplement,* Oct., 1947, pp. 7-9.
STEVENS, "The Virgin Carrying a Lantern"
HOWARD BAKER, "Wallace Stevens and Other Poets," *The Southern Review,* I (Autumn, 1935), 374-376.
STEVENS, "The World as Meditation"
LOUIS L. MARTZ, "Wallace Stevens: The World as Meditation," *Yale Review,* XLVII (Summer, 1958), 517-518, 534.
SURREY, "Love That Doth Reign and Live within My Thought"
MILES, *Major Adjectives in English Poetry,* pp. 326-327.
HALLETT SMITH, "The Art of Sir Thomas Wyatt," *Huntington Library Quarterly,* IX (August, 1946), 334-337.
SURREY, "The Means to Attain Happy Life"
GEORGE ARMS, *The Explicator,* I (Nov., 1942), 10.
SWIFT, "Description of the Morning"
BATESON, *English Poetry,* pp. 175-178.
SWIFT, "Ode to Sancroft"
DAVID P. FRENCH, "Swift, the Non-Jurors, and Jacobitism," *MLN,* LXXII (April, 1957), 258-264.
SWINBURNE, "Autumn in Cornwall"
J. P. KIRBY, *The Explicator,* I (May, 1943), 56.
SWINBURNE, "Between the Sunset and the Sea"
DANIELS, *The Art of Reading Poetry,* pp. 450-453.
SWINBURNE, "A Cameo"
BROOKS WRIGHT, *The Explicator,* XII (Nov., 1953), 13.
SWINBURNE, "The Garden of Proserpine"
WILLIAM EMPSON, "Basic English and Wordsworth," *The Kenyon Review,* II (Autumn, 1940), 450-452.
WILLIAM FROST, *English Masterpieces,* Vol. VI, *Romantic and Victorian Poetry,* pp. 19-20.

THOMAS and BROWN, *Reading Poems: An Introduction to Critical Study*, pp. 640-641.

SWINBURNE, "Hertha"

C. C. CUNNINGHAM, *Literature as a Fine Art: Analysis and Interpretation*, pp. 101-106.

TILLYARD, *Five Poems, 1470-1870*, pp. 87-103.

SWINBURNE, "The Hounds of Spring"

LEAVIS, *Revaluation*, pp. 238-240. Reprinted *Critiques*, pp. 179-180.

UNGER and O'CONNOR, *Poems for Study*, pp. 555-556.

SWINBURNE, "Hymn to Proserpine"

CURTIS DAHL, "A Double Frame for Tennyson's Demeter?" *Victorian Studies*, I (June, 1958), 360-361.

SWINBURNE, "Laus Veneris"

EMPSON, *Seven Types of Ambiguity*, pp. 205-207.

SWINBURNE, "Nephelidia"

CIARDI, *How Does a Poem Mean?* pp. 934-936.

SWINBURNE, "A Nympholept"

PAULL F. BAUM, "Swinburne's 'A Nympholept,'" *South Atlantic Quarterly*, LVII (Winter, 1958), 58-68.

TAGGARD, "The Four Songs"

DONALD A. STAUFFER, "Genesis, or the Poet as Maker," *Poets at Work*, pp. 63-70.

TATE, "Again the Native Hour"

AUGUST H. MASON, *The Explicator*, VII (Dec., 1948), 23.

SAMUEL H. MONK, *The Explicator*, VI (June, 1948), 58.

TATE, "Causerie"

VIVIENNE KOCH, "The Poetry of Allen Tate," *The Kenyon Review*, XI (Summer, 1949), 366-367. Reprinted *The Kenyon Critics*, pp. 174-175. Reprinted *Modern American Poetry*, B. Rajan, ed., pp. 20-21.

TATE, "The Cross"

SISTER MARY BERNETTA, O.S.F., "Allen Tate's Inferno," *Renascence*, III (Spring, 1951), 118.

FREDERICK MORGAN, "Recent Verse," *The Hudson Review*, I (Summer, 1948), 263-264.

CHARLES C. WALCUTT, *The Explicator*, VI (April, 1948), 41.

TATE,　"Death of Little Boys"

VIVIENNE KOCH, "The Poetry of Allen Tate," *The Kenyon Review*, XI (Summer, 1949), 357-360.

Reprinted *The Kenyon Critics*, pp. 172-174.

Reprinted *Modern American Poetry*, B. Rajan, ed., pp. 12-14.

SOUTHWORTH, *More Modern American Poets*, p. 97.

WINTERS, *The Anatomy of Nonsense*, pp. 198-202.

Also *In Defense of Reason*, pp. 529-533.

TATE,　"Fragment of a Meditation"

VIVIENNE KOCH, "The Poetry of Allen Tate," *The Kenyon Review*, XI (Summer, 1949), 363-364.

Reprinted *Modern American Poetry*, B. Rajan, ed., pp. 17-18.

TATE,　"Last Days of Alice"

SISTER MARY BERNETTA, O.S.F., "Allen Tate's Inferno," *Renascence*, III (Spring, 1951), 117.

BROOKS, *Modern Poetry and the Tradition*, p. 104.

DELMORE SCHWARTZ, "The Poetry of Allen Tate," *The Southern Review*, V (Winter, 1940), 427-430.

TATE,　"The Meaning of Death"

BROOKS, *Modern Poetry and the Tradition*, pp. 106-108.

HOWARD NEMEROV, "The Current of the Frozen Stream," *Furioso*, III (Fall, 1948), 55-56.

HOWARD NEMEROV, "The Current of the Frozen Stream," *The Sewanee Review*, LXVII (Autumn, 1959), 590-592.

TATE,　"The Meaning of Life"

BROOKS, *Modern Poetry and the Tradition*, pp. 105-106.

HOWARD NEMEROV, "The Current of the Frozen Stream," *Furioso*, III (Fall, 1948), 54-55.

HOWARD NEMEROV, "The Current of the Frozen Stream," *The Sewanee Review*, LXVII (Autumn, 1959), 589-592.

TATE, "The Mediterranean"

LOUIS D. RUBIN, JR., "The Concept of Nature in Modern Southern Poetry," *American Quarterly*, IX (Spring, 1957), 64-65.

TATE, "Message from Abroad"

VIVIENNE KOCH, "The Poetry of Allen Tate," *The Kenyon Review*, XI (Summer, 1949), 364-365.

Reprinted *The Kenyon Critics*, p. 174.

Reprinted, *Modern American Poetry*, B. Rajan, ed., pp. 18-20.

TATE, "Mother and Son"

SISTER MARY BERNETTA, O.S.F., "Allen Tate's Inferno," *Renascence*, III (Spring, 1951), 114-115.

SOUTHWORTH, *More Modern American Poets*, p. 99.

TATE, "Mr. Pope"

MARGARET MORTON BLUM, "Allen Tate's 'Mr. Pope': A Reading," *MLN*, LXXIV (Dec., 1959), 706-709.

DANIELS, *The Art of Reading Poetry*, pp. 312-314.

JAMES EDWARD TOBIN, *The Explicator*, XV (March, 1957), 35.

TATE, "The Oath"

BROOKS, *Modern Poetry and the Tradition*, pp. 108-109.

TATE, "Ode to the Confederate Dead"

DENIS DONOGHUE, "Technique in Hopkins," *Studies*, XLIV (Winter, 1955), 449-450.

HOFFMAN, *The Twenties*, pp. 151-153.

VIVIENNE KOCH, "The Poetry of Allen Tate," *The Kenyon Review*, XI (Summer, 1949), 370-372.

Reprinted *Modern American Poetry*, B. Rajan, ed., pp. 24-26.

Louis D. Rubin, Jr., "The Concept of Nature in Modern Poetry, *American Quarterly,* IX (Spring, 1957), 70-71.

Schlauch, *Modern English and American Poetry,* pp. 97-78.

Southworth, *More Modern American Poets,* pp. 100-101.

Allen Tate in Friar and Brinnin, *Modern Poetry,* pp. 538-539.

Allen Tate, "Narcissus as Narcissus," *Virginia Quarterly Review,* XIV (Jan., 1938), 108-122.

Tate, *Reason in Madness,* pp. 136-151. Reprinted *On the Limits of Poetry,* pp. 248-262.
Reprinted Engle and Carrier, *Reading Modern Poetry,* pp. 207-219.

Tate, "Ode to Our Young Pro-Consuls of the Air"
Hoffman, *The Twenties,* pp. 385-388.

Tate, "Retroduction to American History"
Southworth, *More Modern American Poets,* pp. 99-100.

Tate, "Seasons of the Soul"
Richmond C. Beatty, "Allen Tate as a Man of Letters," *South Atlantic Quarterly,* XLVII (April, 1948), 233-234.

Alwyn Berland, "Violence in the Poetry of Allen Tate," *Accent* XI (Summer, 1951), 165-171.

Deutsch, *Poetry in Our Time,* pp. 199-202.

Vivienne Koch, "The Poetry of Allen Tate," *The Kenyon Review,* XI (Summer, 1949), 374-378.
Reprinted *The Kenyon Critics,* pp. 177-181.
Reprinted *Modern American Poetry,* B. Rajan, ed., pp. 28-30.

Tate, "Shadow and Shade"
Southworth, *More Modern American Poets,* pp. 97-98.

Tate, "Sonnet at Christmas: This Is the Day His Hour of Life Draws Near"

DELMORE SCHWARTZ, "The Poetry of Allen Tate," *The Southern Review*, V (Winter, 1940), 425-427.

TATE,   "The Subway"

DEUTSCH, *Poetry in Our Time*, pp. 198-199.

JOE HORRELL, "Some Notes on Conversion in Poetry," *The Southern Review*, VII (Summer, 1941), 119-122.

JOHN CROWE RANSOM, *The New Criticism*, pp. 222-225.

Reprinted in part *The Critic's Notebook*, pp. 252-253.

LOUIS D. RUBIN, JR., "The Concept of Nature in Modern Poetry," *American Quarterly*, IX (Spring, 1957), 66-67.

YVOR WINTERS, *Primitivism and Decadence*, pp. 4-5. Also *In Defense of Reason*, pp. 19-20.

Reprinted in part *The Critic's Notebook*, pp. 250-252.

TATE,   "The Wolves"

RICHMOND C. BEATTY, "Allen Tate as a Man of Letters," *South Atlantic Quarterly*, XLVII (April, 1948), 232.

TAYLOR,   "The Accusation of the Inward Man" (from *God's Determinations*)

SIDNEY E. LIND, "Edward Taylor: A Revaluation," *The New England Quarterly*, XXI (Dec., 1948), 525-527.

TAYLOR,   "An Address to the Soul Occasioned by a Rain"

WILLE T. WEATHERS, "Edward Taylor, Hellenistic Puritan," *American Literature*, XVIII (March, 1946), 24-25.

TAYLOR,   "The Experience"

W. C. BROWN, "Edward Taylor: An American 'Metaphysical,'" *American Literature*, XVI (Nov., 1944), 191, 196-197.

TAYLOR,   "The Glory of and Grace in the Church Set Out"

G. GIOVANNINI, *The Explicator*, VI (Feb., 1948), 26.

TAYLOR, "God's Determinations"

AUSTIN WARREN, "Edward Taylor's Poetry: Colonial Baroque," *The Kenyon Review,* III (Summer, 1941), 362-365.

WARREN, *Rage for Order*, pp. 8-12.

TAYLOR, "Huswifery"

ANONYMOUS, *"More Than Enough There,"* *Times Literary Supplement*, Special number (Nov. 6, 1959), p. XIV.

TAYLOR, "Meditation 1: What Love is This of Thine, That Cannot Be"

W. C. BROWN, "Edward Taylor: An American 'Metaphysical,'" *American Literature*, XVI (Nov., 1944), 194-195.

TAYLOR, "Meditation 6: Am I Thy Gold? or Purse, Lord, for Thy Wealth"

ANNE MARIE MCNAMARA, *The Explicator*, XVII (Oct. 1958), 3.

ROY HARVEY PEARCE, "Edward Taylor: The Poet as Puritan," *New England Quarterly*, XXIII (March, 1950), 34-35.

TAYLOR, "Meditation 8: I Kenning Through Astronomy Divine"

ROY HARVEY PEARCE, "Edward Taylor: The Poet as Puritan," *The New England Quartelry,* XXIII (March, 1950), 44-45.

AUSTIN WARREN, "Edward Taylor's Poetry: Colonial Baroque," *The Kenyon Review,* III (Summer, 1941), 365-368.

WARREN, *Rage for Order*, pp. 12-16.

TAYLOR, "Meditation 28: When I, Lord, Send Some Bits of Glory Home"

W. C. BROWN, "Edward Taylor: An American 'Metaphysical,' " *American Literature,* XVI (Nov., 1944), 192-193.

TAYLOR, "Meditation 33: My Lord, My Life, Can Envy Ever Be"

W. C. Brown, "Edward Taylor: An American 'Metaphysical,'" *American Literature,* XVI (Nov., 1944), 193.

TAYLOR,   "Meditation 56: Should I with Silver Tooles Delve Through the Hill"

Robert R. Hodges, "Edward Taylor's 'Artificiall Man,'" *American Literature,* XXXI (March, 1959), 76-77.

TAYLOR,   "Prologue" to "God's Determinations"

W. C. Brown, "Edward Taylor: An American 'Metaphysical,'" *American Literature,* XVI (Nov., 1944), 195-196.

TAYLOR,   "The Reflection"

Austin Warren, "Edward Taylor's Poetry: Colonial Baroque," *The Kenyon Review,* III (Summer, 1941), 368-370.

Warren, *Rage for Order,* pp. 16-17.

TENNYSON,   "The Ancient Sage"

Elizabeth Hellman Waterston, "Symbolism in Tennyson's Minor Poems," *University of Toronto Quarterly,* XX (July, 1951), 378-380.

TENNYSON,   "Break, Break, Break"

Brooks, *The Well Wrought Urn,* pp. 160-162.

Daiches and Charvat, *Poems in English,* pp. 712-713..

Daniels, *The Art of Reading Poetry,* p. 272.

Kreuzer, *Elements of Poetry,* pp. 41-43.

O'Connor, *Sense and Sensibility in Modern Poetry,* pp. 151-152.

TENNYSON,   "The Bugle Song"

Brooks, Purser, Warren, *An Approach to Literature,* pp. 458-459.

Reprinted third edition, pp. 311-312.

TENNYSON,   "Crossing the Bar"

Thomas J. Assad, "Analogy in Tennyson's 'Crossing the Bar,'" *Tulane Studies in English,* VIII (1958), 153-164.

Lord Dunsany, "The Food of Imagination," *Poetry Review,* XLI (July-Aug., 1950), 197-198.

FREDERICK L. JONES, *The Explicator,* X (Dec., 1951), 19.

G. GEOFFREY LANGSAM, *The Explicator,* X (April, 1952), 40.

HARRY W. RUDMAN, *The Explicator,* VIII (April, 1950), 45.

TENNYSON,   "Demeter and Persephone"

CURTIS DAHL, "A Double Frame for Tennyson's Demeter?" *Victorian Studies,* I (June, 1958), 356-362.

G. ROBERT STRANGE, "Tennyson's Mythology: A Study of *Demeter and Persephone,*" *Journal of English Literary History,* XXI (March, 1954), 67-80.

TENNYSON,   "A Dream of Fair Women"

ARTHUR J. CARR, "Tennyson as a Modern Poet," *The University of Toronto Quarterly,* XIX (July, 1950), 368-369.

CLYDE DE L. RYALS, "The 'Fatal Woman' Symbol in Tennyson," *PMLA,* LXXIV (Sept., 1959), 441.

TENNYSON,   "The Eagle"

BROOKS, PURSER, WARREN, *An Approach to Literature,* pp. 447-448.

Reprinted third edition, pp. 302-303.

TENNYSON,   "Eleanore"

CLYDE DE L. RYALS, "The 'Fatal Woman' Symbol in Tennyson," *PMLA,* LXXIV (Sept., 1959), 439.

TENNYSON,   "The Epic"

J. S. LAWRY, "Tennyson's 'The Epic': A Gesture of Recovered Faith," *MLN,* LXXIV (May, 1959), 400-404.

TENNYSON,   "The Hesperides"

G. ROBERT STRANGE, "Tennyson's Garden of Art: A Study of *The Hesperides,*" *PMLA,* LXVII (Sept., 1952), 732-743.

TENNYSON,   "In Memoriam, XI"

BROWER, *The Fields of Light,* pp. 34-35.

BEN W. FUSON, *The Explicator,* IV (March, 1946), 34.
RIDING and GRAVES, *A Survey of Modernist Poetry,* p. 49.

TENNYSON, "In Memoriam, XLIII"
KILBY, *Poetry and Life,* p. 150.

TENNYSON, "In Memoriam, LVI"
LAURENCE PERRINE, *The Explicator,* XII (March, 1954), 29.

TENNYSON, "In Memoriam, CXXII, CXVIII, LV, LVI"
WALKER GIBSON, "Behind the Veil: A Distinction Between Poetic and Scientific Language in Tennyson, Lyell, and Darwin," *Victorian Studies,* II (Sept., 1958), 61-67.

TENNYSON, "Lady Clara Vere de Vere"
CLYDE DE L. RYALS, "The 'Fatal Woman' Symbol in Tennyson," *PMLA,* LXXIV (Sept., 1959), 440.

TENNYSON, "The Lady of Shalott"
JOHNSON, *The Alien Vision of Victorian Poetry,* p. 9.
LIONEL STEVENSON, "Tennyson, Browning, and a Romantic Fallacy," *The University of Toronto Quarterly,* XIII (Jan., 1944), 184.
ELIZABETH H. WATERSTON, "Symbolism in Tennyson's Minor Poems," *The University of Toronto Quarterly,* XX (July, 1951), 375-376.

TENNYSON, "The Lotus-Eaters"
JOHNSON, *The Alien Vision of Victorian Poetry,* pp. 9-10.

TENNYSON, "Lucretius"
JOHNSON, *The Alien Vision of Victorian Poetry,* pp. 31-34.

TENNYSON, "Mariana in the South"
ELIZABETH H. WATERSTON, "Symbolism in Tennyson's Minor Poems," *The University of Toronto Quarterly,* XX (July, 1951), 376.

TENNYSON, "Maud"

page 265

Roy P. Basler, "Tennyson the Psychologist," *South Atlantic Quarterly*, XLIII (1944), 143-159.

Basler, *Sex, Symbolism, and Psychology in Literature*, pp. 73-93.

E. D. H. Johnson, "The Lily and the Rose: Symbolic Meaning in Tennyson's *Maud*," *PMLA*, LXIV (Dec., 1949), 1222-1227.

TENNYSON, "Merlin and the Gleam"

Gordon S. Haight, "Tennyson's Merlin," *Studies in Philology*, XLIV (July, 1947), 560-566.

TENNYSON, "Oenone"

Arthur J. Carr, "Tennyson as a Modern Poet," *The University of Toronto Quarterly*, XIX (July, 1950), 371.

Elizabeth H. Waterston, "Symbolism in Tennyson's Minor Poems," *The University of Toronto Quarterly* XX (July, 1951), 376.

TENNYSON, "The Palace of Art"

A. C. Howell, "Tennyson's 'Palace of Art'—An Interpretation," *Studies in Philology*, XXXIII (July, 1936), 507-522.

Clyde de L. Ryals, "The 'Fatal Woman' Symbol in Tennyson," *PMLA*, LXXIV (Sept., 1959), 440-441.

Lionel Stevenson, "Tennyson, Browning, and a Romantic Fallacy," *The University of Toronto Quarterly*, XIII (Jan., 1944), 182-184.

Elizabeth H. Waterston, "Symbolism in Tennyson's Minor Poems, "*The University of Toronto Quarterly*, XX (July, 1951), 376-377.

TENNYSON, "The Poet"

T. O. Mabbott, *The Explicator*, III (Oct., 1944), 9.

W. D. Paden, *The Explicator*, II (June, 1944), 56.

TENNYSON, "Sir Galahad"

George Arms, " 'Childe Roland' and 'Sir Galahad,' " *College English*, VI (Feb., 1945), 258-262.

Mary J. Donahue, "The Revision of Tennyson's

Sir Galahad," *Philological Quarterly*, XXVIII (April, 1949), 326-329.

TENNYSON, "The Splendor Falls on Castle Walls" DAICHES and CHARVAT, *Poems in English*, p. 713.

TENNYSON, "Tears, Idle Tears"
BATESON, *English Poetry*, pp. 225-233.

CLEANTH BROOKS, "The New Criticism: A Brief for the Defense," *American Scholar*, XIII (Summer, 1944), 286-293.

BROOKS, *The Well Wrought Urn*, pp. 153-162. Reprinted *Readings for Liberal Education*, II, 122-126. Abridged in *The Case for Poetry*, p. 355.
Reprinted Locke, Gibson, and Arms, *Introduction to Literature*, third edition, pp. 125-129.

WILLIAM EMPSON, "Thy Darling in an Urn," *The Sewanee Review*, LV (Autumn, 1947), 691-692.

F. R. LEAVIS, " 'Thought' and Emotional Quality," *Scrutiny*, XIII (Spring, 1945), 59.

JOHN CROWE RANSOM, "The Tense of Poetry," *The Southern Review*, I (Autumn, 1935), 221-222.

RANSOM, *The World's Body*, pp. 233-234.

FRED H. STOCKING, *The Explicator*, V (June, 1947), 54.
Abridged in *The Case for Poetry*, p. 355.

W. K. WIMSATT, JR. and M. C. BEARDSLEY, "The Affective Fallacy," *The Sewanee Review*, LVII (Winter, 1949), 46-47.

HERBERT G. WRIGHT, "Tennyson and Wales," *Essays and Studies*, XIV (1928), 75.

TENNYSON, "Tithonus"
MARY J. DONAHUE, "Tennyson's *Hail, Briton!* and *Tithon* in the Heath Manuscript," *PMLA*, LXIV (June, 1949), 400-415.

DOUGLAS, LAMSON, SMITH, *The Critical Reader*, pp. 96-100.

CARL ROBINSON SONN, "Poetic Vision and Religious Certainty in Tennyson's Earlier Poetry," *Modern Philology*, LVII (Nov., 1959), 88-90.

TENNYSON, "The Two Voices"

WENDELL S. JOHNSON, "Some Functions of Poetic Form," *Journal of Aesthetics and Art Criticism*, XIII (June, 1955), 504.

TENNYSON, "Ulysses"

ROY P. BASLER and WILLIAM FROST, *The Explicator*, IV (May, 1946), 48.

E. J. CHAISSON, "Tennyson's 'Ulysses'—A Reinterpretation," *The University of Toronto Quarterly*, XXIII (July, 1954), 402-409.

ROYAL A. GETTMANN and JOHN ROBERT MOORE, *The Explicator*, I (Feb., 1943), 33.

LANGBAUM, *The Poetry of Experience*, pp. 90-92.

PERRINE, *Sound and Sense*, pp. 172-174.

R. ROPPEN, " 'Ulysses' and Tennyson's Sea-Quest," *English Studies*, XL (April, 1959), 77-90.

CARL ROBINSON SONN, "Poetic Vision and Religious Certainty in Tennyson's Earlier Poetry," *Modern Philology*, LVII (Nov., 1959), 87-88.

CHARLES C. WALCUTT, *The Explicator*, IV (Feb., 1946), 28.

THOMAS, DYLAN, "After the Funeral (*In Memory of Ann Jones*)"

DAICHES and CHARVAT, *Poems in English*, pp. 744-745.

DEUTSCH, *Poetry in Our Time*, p. 342.

FRIAR and BRINNIN, *Modern Poetry*, p. 541.

DAY LEWIS, *The Poetic Image*, pp. 123-125.

MYRON OCHSHORN, "The Love Song of Dylan Thomas," *New Mexico Quarterly Review*, XXIV (Spring, 1954), 51.

MARSHALL W. STEARNS, *The Explicator*, III (May, 1945), 52.

Reprinted Engle and Carrier, *Reading Modern Poetry*, pp. 313-314.

THOMAS, DYLAN, "All All and All the Dry Worlds Lever"

JACOB KORG, "Imagery and Universe in Dylan

Thomas's '18 Poems,'" *Accent*, XXII (Winter, 1957), 12-15.

THOMAS, DYLAN, "Altar-Wise by Owl Light"
ERHARDT H. ESSIG, *The Explicator*, XVI (June, 1958), 53.
BREWSTER GHISELIN, "The Extravagant Energy of Genius," *The Western Rievew*, XVIII (Spring, 1954), 248.
BERNARD KNIEGER, *The Explicator*, XV (Dec., 1956), 18.
RALPH N. MAUD, *The Explicator*, XIV (Dec., 1955), 16.
SCHLAUCH, *Modern English and American Poetry*, pp. 84-85.

THOMAS, DYLAN, "Among Those Killed in the Dawn Raid Was a Man Aged a Hundred"
PHYLLIS BARTLETT, *The Explicator*, XII (Dec., 1953), 21.
ELMER L. BROOKS, *The Explicator*, XII (June, 1954), 49.

THOMAS, DYLAN, "The Ballad of the Long-Legged Bait"
RICHARD A. CONDON, *The Explicator*, XVI (March, 1958), 37.
ELDER OLSON, "The Poetry of Dylan Thomas," *Poetry* LXXXIII (Jan., 1954), 214-215.

THOMAS, DYLAN, "Because the Pleasure-Bird Whistles"
ELDER OLSON, "The Poetry of Dylan Thomas," *Poetry* LXXXIII (Jan., 1954), 218.

THOMAS, DYLAN, "Ceremony After a Fire Raid"
MYRON OCHSHORN, "The Love Song of Dylan Thomas," *New Mexico Quarterly Review*, XXIV (Spring, 1954), 46-65.

THOMAS, DYLAN, "The Conversation of Prayer"
ROBERT C. JONES, *The Explicator*, XVII (April, 1959), 49.
MARY ELLEN RICKY, *The Explicator*, XVI (Dec., 1957), 15.

THOMAS, DYLAN, "Death Is All Metaphors, Shape in One History"

BERNARD KNIEGER, *The Explicator*, XVIII (Nov., 1959), 14.

THOMAS, DYLAN, "And Death Shall Have No Dominion"

THOMAS E. CONNOLLY, *The Explicator*, XIV (Feb., 1956), 33.

THOMAS, DYLAN, "The Empty Purse"

JULIAN SYMOUR, "Obscurity and Dylan Thomas," *The Kenyon Review*, II (Winter, 1940), 64-65.

THOMAS, DYLAN, "Fern Hill"

WILLIAM BLISSETT, "Dylan Thomas," *Queens Quarterly*, LXIII (Spring, 1956), 52-54.

SISTER M. LAURENTIA, C.S.J., *The Explicator*, XIV (Oct., 1955), 1.

MYRON OCHSHORN, "The Love Song of Dylan Thomas," *New Mexico Quarterly Review*, XXIV (Spring, 1954), 58-60.

THOMAS, DYLAN, "The Force That Through the Green Fuse Drives the Flower"

DREW, *Poetry*, pp. 181-183.

FRANKENBERG, *Pleasure Dome*, pp. 318-319.

G. GIOVANNINI, *The Explicator*, VIII (June, 1950), 59. Reprinted Locke, Gibson, and Arms, *Introduction to Literature*, third edition, pp. 260-263.

S. F. JOHNSON, *The Explicator*, VIII (June, 1950), 60.

S. F. JOHNSON, *The Explicator*, X (Feb., 1952), 26.

MYRON OCHSHORN, "The Love Song of Dylan Thomas," *New Mexico Quarterly Review*, XXIV (Spring, 1954). 51-53.

THOMAS, DYLAN, "From Love's First Fever to Her Plague"

SAM HYNES, *The Explicator*, IX (Dec., 1950), 18.

THOMAS, "Hold Hard, These Ancient Minutes in the Cuckoo's Month"

HOWARD NEMEROV, "The Generation of Violence,"
The Kenyon Review, XV (Summer, 1953), 478-
480.

THOMAS, DYLAN,   "The Hunchback in the Park"
DEUTSCH, *Poetry in Our Time,* pp. 340-341.
S. F. JOHNSON, *The Explicator,* X (Feb., 1952), 27.

THOMAS, DYLAN,   "In My Craft or Sullen Art"
FRANKENBERG, *Invitation to Poetry,* pp. 99-101.
D. R. HOWARD, *The Explicator,* XII (Feb., 1954), 22.
PATRICIA MEYER SPACKS, *The Explicator,* XVIII
(Dec., 1959), 21.

THOMAS, DYLAN,   "In the White Giant's Thigh"
WILLIAM T. MOYNIHAN, *The Explicator,* XVII (May,
1959), 59.

THOMAS, DYLAN,   "I See the Boys of Summer"
BREWSTER GHISELIN, "The Extravagant Energy of
Genius," *The Western Review,* XVIII (Spring,
1954), 246.
MYRON OCHSHORN, "The Love Song of Dylan
Thomas," *New Mexico Quarterly Review,* XXIV
(Spring, 1954), 47-49.

THOMAS, DYLAN,   "Light Breaks Where No Sun Shines"
BERNARD KNIEGER, *The Explicator,* XV (Feb., 1957),
32.
WILLIAM T. MOYNIHAN, *The Explicator,* XVI (Feb.,
1958), 28.
MARSHALL W. STEARNS, "Unsex the Skeleton," *The
Sewanee Review,* LII (July-Sept., 1944), 435-440.

THOMAS, DYLAN,   "Love in the Asylum"
BREWSTER GHISELIN, "Use of a Mango," *Rocky Mountain Review,* VIII (Spring, 1944), 112.

THOMAS, DYLAN,   "The Map of Love: No. 4"
HENRY GIBSON, "A Comment," *The Critic,* I (Au-
tumn, 1947), 20.
EDITH SITWELL, "Comment on Dylan Thomas," *The
Critic,* I (Autumn, 1947), 18.

THOMAS, DYLAN, "The Marriage of a Virgin"
DAICHES and CHARVAT, *Poems in English*, p. 745.
BREWSTER GHISELIN, "The Extravagant Energy of Genius," *The Western Review*, XVIII (Spring, 1954), 249.
S. F. JOHNSON, *The Explicator*, X (Feb., 1952), 27.

THOMAS, DYLAN, "Poem 40: Twenty-Fours Years Remind the Tears of My Eyes"
ANDREWS WANNING, "Criticism and Principles: Poetry of the Quarter," *The Southern Review*, VI (Spring, 1941), 806-809.

THOMAS, DYLAN, "Poem in October"
DAVID DAICHES, "The Poetry of Dylan Thomas," *College English*, XVI (Oct., 1954), 7. Reprinted in *The English Journal*, XLIII (Oct., 1954), 355.
DEUTSCH, *Poetry in Our Time*, pp. 332-333.

THOMAS, DYLAN, "A Refusal to Mourn the Death, by Fire, of a Child in London"
JOHN A. CLAIR, *The Explicator*, XVII (Dec., 1958), 25.
DAVID DAICHES, "The Poetry of Dylan Thomas," *College English*, XVI (Oct., 1954), 3-5. Reprinted in *The English Journal*, XLIII (Oct., 1954), 351-352.
DEUTSCH, *Poetry in Our Time*, pp. 335-337.
HENRY GIBSON, "A Comment," *The Critic*, I (Autumn, 1947), 19-20.
EDITH SITWELL, "Comment on Dylan Thomas," *The Critic*, I (Autumn, 1947), 18.
EDITH SITWELL, "The Love of Man, the Praise of God," *Herald Tribune Book Review*, XXIX (May 10, 1953), 14.
EDITH SITWELL, "Dylan Thomas," *Atlantic*, CXCIII (Feb., 1954), 44-45.

THOMAS, DYLAN, "This Was the Crucifixion on the Mountain"
MARSHALL W. STEARNS, "Unsex the Skeleton: Notes

on the Poetry of Dylan Thomas," *The Sewanee Review*, LII (July-Sept., 1944), 430-433.

THOMAS, DYLAN,   "To-day, This Insect"
BILL CASEY, *The Explicator*, XVII (March, 1959), 43.

THOMAS, DYLAN,   "The Tombstone Told When She Died"
IHAB H. HASSAN, *The Explicator*, XV (Nov., 1956), 11.

THOMAS, DYLAN,   "Under Milk Wood"
GEOFFREY TAYLOR, "Studied Wood-notes," *Time and Tide*, XXXV (April, 24, 1954), p. 550.

THOMAS, DYLAN,   "Vision and Prayer"
DAVID DAICHES, "The Poetry of Dylan Thomas," *College English*, XVI (Oct., 1954), 6-7. Reprinted in *The English Journal*, XLIII (Oct., 1954), 354-355.
FRIAR and BRINNIN, *Modern Poetry*, pp. 540-541.
ROBIN MAYHEAD, "Dylan Thomas," *Scrutiny*, XIX (Winter, 1952-3), 146.

THOMAS, DYLAN,   We Lying by Seasand"
EDITH SITWELL, "Dylan Thomas," *Atlantic*, CXCIII (Feb., 1954), 44-45.
EDITH SITWELL, "The Love of Man, the Praise of God," *Herald Tribune Book Review*, XXIX (May 10, 1953), 1.

THOMAS, DYLAN,   "A Winter's Tale"
FRANKENBERG, *Pleasure Dome*, pp. 321-323.
ROBIN MAYHEAD, "Dylan Thomas," *Scrutiny*, XIX (Winter, 1952-3), 143-145.

THOMAS, EDWARD,   "Cock-Crow"
F. R. LEAVIS, "Imagery and Movement," *Scrutiny*, XIII (Sept., 1945), 133-134.

THOMAS, EDWARD,   "October"
B. RAJAN, "Georgian Poetry: A Retrospect," *The Critic*, I (Autumn, 1947), 13.

THOMAS, EDWARD,   "Tears"
B. RAJAN, "Georgian Poetry: A Retrospect," *The Critic*, I (Autumn, 1947), 11-12.

THOMAS, ROSEMARY, "The Big Nosed Adolescent Boys"
WARREN CARRIER, "A Facade of Modernity, and a
Personal Poet," *The Western Review,* XVI (Spring,
1952), 251.

THOMAS, ROSEMARY, "St. Francis of Assisi"
WARREN CARRIER, "A Facade of Modernity, and a
Personal Poet," *The Western Review,* XVI (Spring,
1952), 252.

THOMPSON, FRANCIS, "Grace of the Way"
TERENCE L. CONNOLLY, S.J., *The Explicator,* IX
(June, 1951), 56.
GEORGE G. WILLIAMS, *The Explicator,* IX (Nov.,
1950), 16.

THOMPSON, FRANCIS, "The Hound of Heaven"
BROOKS and WARREN, *Understanding Poetry,* revised
edition, pp. 283-285.

THOMPSON, FRANCIS, "New Year's Chimes"
W. G. WILSON, "Francis Thompson's Outlook on
Science," *Contemporary Review,* CXCII (Nov.,
1957), 266.

THOMPSON, FRANCIS, "The Nineteenth Century"
W. G. WILSON, "Francis Thompson's Outlook on
Science," *Contemporary Review,* CXCII (Nov.,
1957), 264.

THOMPSON, FRANCIS, "Sad Semele"
MYRTLE PIHLMAN POPE, *The Explicator,* XVII (Feb.,
1959), 35.

THOMSON, "The City of Dreadful Night"
DAVID DeCAMP, *The Explicator,* VII (Feb., 1949),
29.

THOMSON, "The Vine"
ALLEN TATE, "Tension in Poetry," *The Southern
Review,* IV (Summer, 1938), 104-108.
TATE, *Reason in Madness,* pp. 66-71. Reprinted *On
the Limits of Poetry,* pp. 78-82, and *Critiques,* pp.
57-60.

THOREAU, "Smoke"
DELMER RODABAUGH, *The Explicator,* XVII (April,
1959), 47.

THOREAU, "Smoke in the Winter"
MATTHIESSEN, *The American Renaissance,* pp. 165-166.

TODD, RUTHVEN, "Rivers: On Living in Brooklyn"
J. F. NIMS, *Poetry: A Critical Supplement,* May, 1948, pp. 18-20.

TREECE, HENRY, "Bardic Poem"
J. F. NIMS, *Poetry: A Critical Supplement,* Dec., 1947, pp. 15-20.

TYLER, "The Granite Butterfly"
WILLIAM CARLOS WILLIAMS, (Review), *Accent,* VI (Winter, 1946), 203-206.

VAN DOREN, MARK, "January Chance"
DEUTSCH, *Poetry in Our Time,* pp. 68-69.

VAUGHAN, "Cock-Crowing"
DON CAMERON ALLEN, "Vaughan's 'Cock-Crowing' and the Tradition," *Journal of English Literary History,* XXI (June, 1954), 94-106.

VAUGHAN, "I Walked the Other Day (to Spend My Hour)"
MARTZ, *The Poetry of Meditation,* pp. 64-67.

VAUGHAN, "Man"
KESTER SVENDSEN, *The Explicator,* II (June, 1944), 58.

VAUGHAN, "The Morning-Watch"
CONRAD HILBERRY, *The Explicator,* XIV (April, 1956), 44.

VAUGHAN, "The Night"
FERN FARNHAM, "The Imagery of Henry Vaughan's 'The Night,'" *Philological Quarterly,* XXXVIII (Oct., 1959), 425-435.
BAIN TATE STEWART, "Hermetic Symbolism in Henry Vaughan's 'The Night,'" *Philological Quarterly,* XXIX (Oct., 1950), 417-422.

VAUGHAN, "Peace"
L. G. LOCKE, *The Explicator,* I (April, 1943), 43.

VAUGHAN, "The Queer"

MACDONALD EMSLIE, *The Explicator*, XIII (March, 1955), 29.

LAURENCE PERRINE, *The Explicator*, XIII (March, 1955), 29.

CELESTE TURNER WRIGHT, *The Explicator*, XIII (March, 1955), 29.

VAUGHAN, "Quickness'
DREW, *Poetry*, pp. 244-245.

E. C. PETTET, "A Simile in Vaughan," *Times Literary Supplement* (Jan. 27, 1956), p. 53.

VAUGHAN, "Regeneration"
ROBERT ALLEN DURR, "Vaughan's Theme and Its Pattern: 'Regeneraton,' " *Studies in Philology*, LIV (Jan., 1957), 14-28.

VAUGHAN, "The Retreat"
M. Y. HUGHES, "The Theme of Pre-Existence and Infancy in *The Retreate*," *Philological Quarterly*, XX (July, 1941), 484-500.

KREUZER, *Elements of Poetry*, pp. 159-161.

VAUGHAN, "The Search"
MARTZ, *The Poetry of Meditation*, pp. 86-90.

VAUGHAN, "Vanity of Spirit"
MARTZ, *The Poetry of Meditation*, pp. 150-152.

VAUGHAN, "The Waterfall"
W. NELSON FRANCIS, *The Explicator*, XIV (June, 1956), 57.

VERY, "The Hand and Foot"
WINTERS, "Jones Very: A New England Mystic," *American Review*, VII (May, 1936), 161-163.

WINTERS, *Maule's Curse*, pp. 127-129. Also *In Defense of Reason*, pp. 264-266.

VERY, "The Lost"
WINTERS, "Jones Very: A New England Mystic," *American Review*, VII (May, 1936),171-172.

WINTERS, *Maule's Curse*, pp. 138-139. Also *In Defense of Reason*, pp. 274-276.

VIERECK, PETER, "Better Come Quietly"

J. F. Nims, *Poetry: A Critical Supplement*, Dec., 1947, pp. 1-4.

VIERECK, PETER,   "Blindman's Buff"
J. F. Nims, *Poetry: A Critical Supplement*, Dec., 1947, pp. 6-8.

VIERECK, PETER,   "Crass Times Redeemed by Dignity of Souls"
Ciardi, *How Does a Poem Mean?* pp. 952 -953.

VIERECK, PETER,   "Game Called on Account of Darkness"
J. F. Nims, *Poetry: A Critical Supplement*, Dec., 1947, pp. 9-10.

VIERECK,   "Like a Sitting Breeze"
Peter Viereck, "Correspondence Relating to 'Like a Sitting Breeze,' " *American Scholar*, XX (Spring, 1951), 216-217.

VIERECK, PETER,   "Six Theological Cradle Songs"
Peter Viereck, "My Kind of Poetry," *Mid-Century American Poets*, pp. 24-26.

VIERECK, PETER,   "Some Lines in Three Parts"
Peter Viereck, "My Kind of Poetry," *Mid-Century American Poets*, pp. 26-27.

VIERECK, PETER,   "Vale from Carthage (Spring, 1944)"
Kreuzer, *Elements of Poetry*, pp. 93-96.

WALLER,   "Go, Lovely Rose"
Kreuzer, *Elements of Poetry*, pp. 157-158.
Rosenthal and Smith, *Exploring Poetry*, pp. 695-697.

WALLER,   "On a Girdle"
L. G. Locke, *The Explicator*, I (May, 1943), 52.

WALLER,   "The Story of Phoebus and Daphne Applied"
Bateson, *English Poetry*, pp. 169-170.

WARREN,   "Aged Man Surveys the Past Time"
Brooks, *Modern Poetry and the Tradition*, pp. 78-79.
W. P. Southard, "Speculation," *The Kenyon Review*, VII (Autumn, 1945), 666-667.

WARREN,   "The Ballad of Billie Potts"

DEUTSCH, *Poetry in Our Time*, pp. 202-203.

RUTH HERSCHBERGER, "Poised Between the Two Alarms . . . ,' " *Accent*, IV (Summer, 1944), 245.

SAM HYNES, "Robert Penn Warren: The Symbolic Journey," *The University of Kansas City Review*, XVII (Summer, 1951), 280-281.

W. P. SOUTHARD, "Speculation," *The Kenyon Review*, VII (Autumn, 1945), 670-673.

JOHN L. STEWART, "Robert Penn Warren and the Knot of History," *Journal of English Literary History*, XXVI (March, 1959), 117, 120-122.

JOHN L. STUART, "The Achievement of Robert Penn Warren," *South Atlantic Quarterly*, XLVII (Oct., 1948), 570-574.

WARREN,   "Bearded Oaks"

BROOKS, *Modern Poetry and the Tradition*, pp. 81-82. Reprinted Engle and Carrier, *Reading Modern Poetry*, pp. 106-108.

O'CONNOR, *Sense and Sensibility in Modern Poetry*, pp. 154-155.

WARREN,   "The Child Next Door"

JAMES WRIGHT, "The Stiff Smile of Mr. Warren," *The Kenyon Review*, XX (Autumn, 1958), 648-655.

WARREN,   "Crime"

W. P. SOUTHARD, "Speculation," *The Kenyon Review*, VII (Autumn, 1945), 661-662.

WARREN,   "The Garden"

W. P. SOUTHARD, "Speculation," *The Kenyon Review*, VII (Autumn, 1945), 668.

WARREN,   "History"

BROOKS, *Modern Poetry and the Tradition*, pp. 85-87.

WARREN,   "History Among the Rocks"

BROOKS, *Modern Poetry and the Tradition*, pp. 77-78.

WARREN,   "Letter from a Coward to a Hero"

BROOKS, *Modern Poetry and the Tradition*, pp. 82-85.

W. P. SOUTHARD, "Speculation," *The Kenyon Review*, VII (Autumn, 1945), 659-660.

WARREN, "Love's Parable"
HOWARD NEMEROV, "The Phoenix in the World,"
Furioso, III (Spring, 1948), 36-46.

WARREN, "Man Coming of Age"
W. P. SOUTHARD, "Speculation," *The Kenyon Review,*
VII (Autumn, 1945), 657-658.

WARREN, "The Mango on the Mango Tree"
FREDERICK BRANTLEY, "The Achievement of Robert
Penn Warren," *Modern American Poetry,* B. Rajan,
ed., pp. 78-79.

WARREN, "Mexico Is a Foreign Country"
W. P. SOUTHARD, "Speculation," *The Kenyon Review,*
VII (Autumn, 1945), 668-670.

WARREN, "Monologue at Midnight"
FREDERICK BRANTLEY, "The Achievement of Robert
Penn Warren," *Modern American Poetry,* B. Rajan,
ed., pp. 76-77.

WARREN, "Original Sin: A Short Story"
RICHARD E. AMACKER, *The Explicator,* VIII (May,
1950), 52.
FREDERICK BRANTLEY, "The Achievement of Robert
Penn Warren," *Modern American Poetry,* B. Rajan,
ed., pp. 77-78.
CLIFFORD M. GORDON, *The Explicator,* IX (Dec.,
1950), 21.

WARREN, "Pursuit"
WILLIAM FROST, *The Explicator,* XI (Feb., 1953), 22.
W. P. SOUTHARD, "Speculation," *The Kenyon Review,*
VII (Autumn, 1945), 662-665.
ROBERT PENN WARREN in Friar and Brinnin, *Modern
Poetry,* p. 542.

WARREN, "The Return: An Elegy"
FREDERICK BRANTLEY, "The Achievement of Robert
Penn Warren," *Modern American Poetry,* B. Rajan,
ed., pp. 75-76.
BROOKS, *Modern Poetry and the Tradition,* pp. 79-80.

WARREN, "Revelation"
ROBERT PENN WARREN in Friar and Brinnin, *Modern Poetry*, pp. 541-542.

WARREN, "Terror"
ROBERT PENN WARREN in Friar and Brinnin, *Modern Poetry*, pp. 542-543.

WATKINS, VERNON, "Arakhova and the Daemon"
J. F. NIMS, *Poetry: A Critical Supplement*, March, 1947, pp. 1-3.

WATKINS, VERNON, "Ballad of the Mari Lwyd"
ROBERT GORHAM DAVIS, "Eucharist and Roasting Pheasant," *Poetry*, LXXIII (Dec., 1948), 171.

WATKINS, VERNON, "Music of Colours: The Blossom Scattered"
JOHN BERRYMAN, *A Critical Supplement to "Poetry,"* Dec., 1949, pp. 14-16.

WATTS, "Come, Holy Spirit, Heavenly Dove"
DANIELS, *The Art of Reading Poetry*, pp. 207-208.
HELEN S. and J. D. THOMAS, *The Explicator*, X (April, 1952), 39.

WELLESLEY, "Poem"
W. B. YEATS, *Letters on Poetry from W. B. Yeats to Dorothy Wellesley*, pp. 170-175.

WHEELWRIGHT, JOHN BROOKS, "Father"
AUSTIN WARREN, *New England Saints* (Ann Arbor: University of Michigan Press, 1956), pp. 174-175.

WHITMAN, "By Blue Ontario's Shores" ("Poem of Many in One")
WILLIE T. WEATHERS, "Whitman's Poetic Translations of His 1855 Preface," *American Literature*, XIX (March, 1947), 24-27.

WHITMAN, "Calamus"
JAMES E. MILLER, JR., "Whitman's 'Calamus': The Leaf and the Root," *PMLA*, LXXII (March, 1957), 249-271.

WHITMAN, "Chanting the Square Deific"
ALFRED H. MARKS, "Whitman's Triadic Imagery,"

American Literature, XXIII (March, 1951), 112-118.

G. L. Sɪxʙᴇʏ, " 'Chanting the Square Deific'—A Study in Whitman's Religion," *American Literature,* IX (May, 1937), 171-195.

WHITMAN, "Crossing Brooklyn Ferry"
Rɪcʜᴀʀᴅ P. Aᴅᴀᴍs, "Whitman: A Brief Revaluation," *Tulane Studies in English,* V (1955), 135-138.

WHITMAN, "The Mystic Trumpeter"
W. L. Wᴇʀɴᴇʀ, "Whitman's 'The Mystic Trumpeter' as Autobiography," *American Literature,* VII (Jan., 1936), 455-460.

WHITMAN, "A Noiseless, Patient Spider"
Vᴀɴ Dᴏʀᴇɴ. *Introduction to Poetry,* pp. 43-45.

WHITMAN, "On the Beach at Night"
Mᴀᴛᴛʜɪᴇssᴇɴ, *American Renaissance,* pp. 575-577.

WHITMAN, "Out of the Cradle Endlessly Rocking"
Rɪcʜᴀʀᴅ P. Aᴅᴀᴍs, "Whitman: A Brief Revaluation." *Tulane Studies in English,* V (1955), 138-140, 146-149

Rᴏʏ P. Bᴀsʟᴇʀ, *The Explicator,* V (June, 1947), 59.

C. C. Cᴜɴɴɪɴɢʜᴀᴍ, *Literature as a Fine Art: Analysis and Interpretation,* pp. 176-185.

C. W. M. Jᴏʜɴsᴏɴ, *The Explicator,* V (May, 1947), 52.

Aʟғʀᴇᴅ H. Mᴀʀᴋs, "Whitman's Triadic Imagery," *American Literature,* XXIII (March, 1951), 120-126.

Lᴏᴜɪsᴇ Pᴏᴜɴᴅ, "Note on Walt Whitman and Bird Poetry," *The English Journal,* XIX (Jan., 1930), 34-36.

Rᴏsᴇɴᴛʜᴀʟ and Sᴍɪᴛʜ, *Exploring Poetry,* 695-696.

Lᴇᴏ Sᴘɪᴛzᴇʀ, " 'Explication de Texte' Applied to Whitman's 'Out of the Cradle Endlessly Rocking,' " *English Literary History,* XVI (Sept., 1949), 229-249.

Fʟᴏʏᴅ Sᴛᴏᴠᴀʟʟ, "Main Drifts in Whitman's Poetry," *American Literature,* IV (March, 1932), 8-10.

CHARLES C. WALCUTT, "Whitman's 'Out of the Cradle Endlessly Rocking,'" *College English,* X (Feb., 1949), 277-279.

S. E. WHICHER, *The Explicator,* V (Feb., 1947), 28.

WHITMAN,   "Passage to India"

RICHARD P. ADAMS, "Whitman: A Brief Revaluation," *Tulane Studies in English,* V (1955), 141-143.

RICHARD E. AMACHER, *The Explicator,* IX (Dec., 1950), Q2.

S. K. COFFMAN, JR., "Form and Meaning in Whitman's 'Passage to India,'" *PMLA,* LXX (June, 1955), 337-349.

RUTH STAUFFER, *The Explicator,* IX (May, 1951), 50.

RANDALL STEWART, *The Literature of the United States,* II, 217.

FLOYD STOVALL, "Main Drifts in Whitman's Poetry," *American Literature,* IV (March, 1932), 1-21.

WHITMAN,   "Pioneers! O Pioneers!"

GAY WILSON ALLEN, "On the Trochaic Meter of 'Pioneers! O Pioneers!'" *American Literature,* XX (Jan., 1949), 449-451.

EDWARD G. FLETCHER, "Pioneers! O Pioneers!" *American Literature,* XIX (Nov., 1947), 259-261.

WHITMAN,   "Proud Music of the Storm"

SYDNEY J. KRAUSE, "Whitman, Music, and *Proud Music of the Storm,*" *PMLA,* LXXII (Sept., 1957), 707-716.

WHITMAN,   "The Sleepers"

MATTHIESSEN, *American Renaissance,* pp. 572-573.

WHITMAN,   "Song of the Broad-Axe"

STANLEY COFFMAN, JR., *The Explicator,* XII (April, 1954), 39.

WHITMAN,   "Song of Myself"

RICHARD P. ADAMS, "Whitman: A Brief Revaluation," *Tulane Studies in English,* V (1955), 144-145.

ERIC W. CARLSON, *The Explicator,* XVIII (Nov., 1959), 13.

MALCOLM COWLEY, "Walt Whitman's Buried Master-piece," *The Saturday Review*, XLII (Oct. 31, 1959), 11-13, 32-34.

T. J. KALLSEN, " 'Song of Myself': Logical Unity Through Analogy," *West Virginia University Philological Papers*, IX (June, 1953), 33-40.

JOHN KINNAIRD, "The Paradox of an American 'Identity,' " *The Partisan Review*, XXV (Summer, 1958), 385-394.

T. O. MABBOTT, *The Explicator*, XI (March, 1953), 34.

MATTHIESSEN, *American Renaissance*, pp. 535 ff., 547-549.

JAMES E. MILLER, JR., " 'Song of Myself' as Inverted Mystical Experience," *PMLA*, LXX (Sept., 1955), 636-661.

JAMES E. MILLER, JR., "Whitman and Eliot: The Poetry of Mysticism," *The Southwest Review*, XLIII (Spring, 1958), 114-123.

ROY HARVEY PEARCE, "Toward an American Epic," *The Hudson Review*, XII (Autumn, 1959), 366-370.

THOMAS J. ROUNDTREE, "Whitman's Indirect Expression and Its Application to 'Song of Myself,' " *PMLA*, LXXIII (Dec., 1958), 549-555.

CARL F. STRAUCH, "The Structure of Walt Whitman's 'Song of Myself,' " *English Journal* (college ed.), XXVII (Sept., 1938), 597-607.

WHITMAN, "Spontaneous Me"

HARRY R. WARFEL, "Whitman's Structural Principles in 'Spontaneous Me,' " *College English*, XVIII (Jan., 1957), 191-195.

WHITMAN, "To a Locomotive in Winter"

GEORGE ARMS, *The Explicator*, V (Nov., 1946), 14.

Reprinted Stageberg and Anderson, *Poetry as Experience*, p. 491.

F. J. Hoffman, "The Technological Fallacy in Contemporary Poetry," *American Literature,* XXI (March, 1949), 98.
Reprinted Stageberg and Anderson, *Poetry as Experience,* p. 491.

WHITMAN, "To Think of Time"
Matthiessen, *American Renaissance,* pp. 610-612.

WHITMAN, "Two Rivulets"
Alfred H. Marks, "Whitman's Triadic Imagery," *American Literature,* XXIII (March, 1951), 105-106.

WHITMAN, "When I Heard the Learn'd Astronomer"
Blair and Gerber, *Better Reading 2: Literature,* p. 114.

WHITMAN, "When Lilacs Last in the Dooryard Bloom'd"
Richard P. Adams, "Whitman's 'Lilacs' and the Tradition of Pastoral Elegy," *PMLA,* LXXII (June, 1957), 479-487.
Gay Wilson Allen, *The Explicator,* X (June, 1952), 55.
Calvin S. Brown, *Music and Literature* (Athens: University of Georgia Press, 1948). Reprinted Feidelson and Brodtkorb, *Interpretations of American Literature,* pp. 187-196.
Joseph Jones, *The Explicator,* IX (April, 1951), 42.
Matthiessen, *American Renaissance,* pp. 618-623. Reprinted *Readings for Liberal Education,* II, 543-547.
Ferner Nuhn, "*Leaves of Grass* Viewed as an Epic," *Arizona Quarterly,* VII (Winter, 1951), 335-336.
Floyd Stovall, "Main Drifts in Whitman's Poetry," *American Literature,* IV (March, 1932), 13-15.

WHITMAN "Whoever You Are Holding Me Now in Hand" (*Calamus*)
Frankenberg, *Invitation to Poetry,* pp. 97-99.

WHITTEMORE, REED,   "A Closet Drama"
HAYDEN CARRUTH, *A Critical Supplement to "Poetry,"*
Jan., 1949, pp. 1-10.
WHITTEMORE, REED,   *"The Primitives"*
J. F. NIMS, *Poetry: A Critical Supplement,* Oct., 1947,
pp. 13-14.
WHITTIER,   "Barbara Frietchie"
ARMS, *The Fields Were Green,* pp. 43-44.
WHITTIER,   "Birchbrook Mill"
ARMS, *The Fields Were Green,* pp. 37-38.
WHITTIER,   'Ichabod"
ARMS, *The Fields Were Green,* pp. 39-40.
WHITTIER,   "Maud Muller"
ARMS, *The Fields Were Green,* pp. 41-43.
WHITTIER,   "The Pennsylvania Pilgrim"
ARMS, *The Fields Were Green,* pp. 38-39.
WHITTIER,   "Skipper's Ireson's Ride"
ARMS, *The Fields Were Green,* pp. 40-44.
WHITTIER,   "Snow-Bound"
ARMS, *The Fields Were Green,* pp. 44-47.
WHITTIER,   "To S. P."
ABE C. RAVITZ, *The Explicator,* XIII (Feb., 1955),
22.
WILBUR, RICHARD,   "Castles and Distances"
THOMAS COLE, "Wilbur's Second Volume," *Poetry,*
LXXXII (April, 1953), 38-39.
WILBUR, RICHARD,   "Ceremony"
J. F. NIMS, *Poetry: A Critical Supplement,* Feb., 1948,
pp. 1-6.
WILBUR, RICHARD,   "The Death of a Toad"
ABBE, *You and Contemporary Poetry,* pp. 73-76.
WILBUR, RICHARD,   "Driftwood"
J. F. NIMS and RICHARD WILBUR, *A Critical Supplement to "Poetry,"* Dec., 1948, pp. 1-7.
WILBUR, RICHARD,   "Grasse: The Olive Trees"
THOMAS COLE, "Wilbur's Second Volume," *Poetry,*
LXXXII (April, 1953), 37-38.

WILBUR, RICHARD, "A Simile for Her Smile"
J. F. NIMS, *Poetry: A Critical Supplement,* Feb., 1948,
pp. 6-9.

WILBUR, RICHARD, *"To an American Poet Just Dead"*
J. F. NIMS and RICHARD WILBUR, *A Critical Supplement to "Poetry,"* Dec., 1948, pp. 7-9.

WILCOX, ELLA WHEELER, "After the Fierce Midsummer
All Ablaze"
RICHARDS, *Principles of Literary Criticism,* pp. 200-
202.

WILD, ROBERT, "An Epitaph for a Goodly Man's Tomb"
GUSTAV CROSS and R. P. DRAPER, *The Explicator,* XV
(May, 1957), 50.
WILLIAM BYSSHE STEIN, *The Explicator,* XVII (Dec.,
1958), 23.

WILDE, "The Ballad of Reading Gaol"
GEORGE ARMS and J. P. KIRBY, *The Explicator,* I
(March, 1943), 41.

WILLIAMS, OSCAR, "The Praying Mantis Visits a Pent-
house"
COOPER and HOLMES, *Preface to Poetry,* pp. 163-165.

WILLIAMS, WILLIAM CARLOS, "Burning the Christmas
Greens"
WILLIAM CARLOS WILLIAMS in Friar and Brinnin,
Modern Poetry, p. 546.

WILLIAMS, WILLIAM CARLOS, "By the Road to the Con-
tagious Hospital"
CHARLES V. HARTUNG, "A Poetry of Experience," *The
University of Kansas City Review,* XXV (Autumn,
1958), 67-68.
WINTERS, *Primitivism and Decadence,* pp. 67-70. Also
In Defense of Reason, pp. 78-82.

WILLIAMS, WILLIAM CARLOS, "The Clouds"
WILLIAM CARLOS WILLIAMS in Friar and Brinnin,
Modern Poetry, p. 545.

WILLIAMS, WILLIAM CARLOS, "The Cold Night"
CHARLES V. HARTUNG, "A Poetry of Experience," *The*

University of Kansas City Review, XXV (Autumn, 1958), 66-67.

WILLIAMS, WILLIAM CARLOS, "Flowers by the Sea"
ROSENTHAL and SMITH, *Exploring Poetry*, pp. 51-53.
A. J. M. SMITH, "Refining Fire: The Meaning and Use of Poetry," *Queens Quarterly*, LXI (Autumn, 1954), 355-356.

WILLIAMS, WILLIAM CARLOS, "A Flowing River"
MARSHALL W. STEARNS, "Syntax, Sense, Sound, and Dr. Williams," *Poetry*, LXVI (April, 1945), 36-37.

WILLIAMS, WILLIAM CARLOS, "Lear"
J. F. NIMS, *Poetry: A Critical Supplement*, May, 1948, pp. 1-7.

WILLIAMS, WILLIAM CARLOS, "Lines: Leaves Are Grey-green"
FREDERICK MORGAN, "William Carlos Williams: Imagery, Rhythm, Form," *The Sewanee Review*, LV (Autumn, 1947), 676 *et passim*.

WILLIAMS, WILLIAM CARLOS, "The Monstrous Marriage"
WILLIAM CARLOS WILLIAMS in Friar and Brinnin, *Modern Poetry*, pp. 545-546.

WILLIAMS, WILLIAM CARLOS, "Nantucket"
CHARLES V. HARTUNG, "A Poetry of Experience," *The University of Kansas City Review*, XXV (Autumn, 1958), 67.

WILLIAMS, WILLIAM CARLOS, "Philomena Andronico"
KARL SHAPIRO, "The Meaning of the Discarded Poem," *Poets at Work*, pp. 105-111.

WILLIAMS, WILLIAM CARLOS, "Queen-Ann's Lace"
WILLIAM VAN O'CONNOR, "Symbolism and the Study of Poetry," *College English*, VI (April, 1946), 378-379.
O'CONNOR, *Sense and Sensibility in Modern Poetry*, pp. 119-120.

WILLIAMS, WILLIAM CARLOS, "St. Francis Einstein of the Daffodils"

WILLIAM CARLOS WILLIAMS in Friar and Brinnin, *Modern Poetry*, p. 546.

WILLIAMS, WILLIAM CARLOS, "Struggle of Wings" RIDING and GRAVES, *A Survey of Modernist Poetry*, pp. 201-204.

WILLIAMS, WILLIAM CARLOS, "The Three Graces" FRANK JONES, *A Critical Supplement to "Poetry,"* Nov., 1949, pp. 16-17.

WILLIAMS, WILLIAM CARLOS, "To a Dog Injured in the Street" ABBE, *You and Contemporary Poetry*, pp. 35-38.

WILLIAMS, WILLIAM CARLOS, "To Waken an Old Lady" DEUTSCH, *Poetry in Our Time*, p. 101.

WILLIAMS, WILLIAM CARLOS, "Tract" WALTER GIERASCH, *The Explicator*, III (March, 1945), 35.

WILLIAMS, WILLIAM CARLOS, "The Yachts" DEUTSCH, *Poetry in Our Time*, pp. 102-104. RICHARD S. DONNELL, *The Explicator*, XVII (May, 1959), 52. UNGER and O'CONNOR, *Poems for Study*, pp. 9-10.

WILLIAMS, WILLIAM CARLOS, "The Yellow Chimney" MARSHALL W. STEARNS, "Syntax, Sense, Sound, and Dr. Williams," *Poetry*, LXVI (April, 1945), 38-39.

WILMOT, JOHN, EARL OF ROCHESTER, "Against Constancy" MACDONALD EMSLIE, "A New Song by Rochester," *Times Literary Supplement* (Feb. 26, 1954), p. 137. J. L. MACKIE, "A New Song by Rochester," *Times Literary Supplement* (Feb., 1954), p. 121.

WILMOT, JOHN, EARL OF ROCHESTER, "Epitaph on Charles II" COOPER and HOLMES, *Preface to Poetry*, pp. 169-170.

WILMOT, JOHN, EARL OF ROCHESTER, "Satire Against Mankind" THOMAS H. FIJIMURA, "Rochester's 'Satyr Against Mankind': An Analysis," *Studies in Philology*, LV (Oct., 1958), 576-590.

WINCHILSEA, LADY ANNE,   "An Affliction"
  REUBEN A. BROWER, "Lady Winchilsea and the Poetic
  Tradition of the Seventeenth Century," *Studies in
  Philology,* XLII (Jan., 1945), 65-66.
WINCHILSEA, LADY ANNE,   "An Invocation to Sleep"
  REUBEN A. BROWER, "Lady Winchilsea and the Poetic
  Tradition of the Seventeenth Century," *Studies in
  Philology,* XLII (Jan., 1945), 63-65.
WINCHILSEA, LADY ANNE,   "A Nocturnal Revery"
  REUBEN A. BROWER, "Lady Winchilsea and the Poetic
  Tradition of the Seventeenth Century," *Studies in
  Philology,* XLII (Jan., 1945), 78-80 *et passim.*
WINCHILSEA, LADY ANNE,   "The Spleen"
  REUBEN A. BROWER, "Lady Winchilsea and the Poetic
  Tradition of the Seventeenth Century," *Studies in
  Philology,* XLII (Jan., 1945), 67-70.
WINTERS,   "Before Disaster"
  CIARDI, *How Does a Poem Mean?* pp. 1005-1007.
WINTERS,   "The Invaders"
  DONALD F. DRUMMOND, "Yvor Winters: Reason and
  Moral Judgment," *Arizona Quarterly,* V (Spring,
  1949), 15-16.
WINTERS,   "The Old Age of Theseus"
  DONALD F. DRUMMOND, "Yvor Winters: Reason and
  Moral Judgment," *Arizona Quarterly,* V (Spring,
  1949), 11-14.
WINTERS,   "A Summer Commentary"
  ALAN SWALLOW, *The Explicator,* IX (March, 1951),
  35.
WORDSWORTH,   "The Brothers"
  STEPHEN M. PARRISH, "Dramatic Technique in the
  Lyrical Ballads" PMLA LXXIV (March, 1959), 92.
WORDSWORTH,   "Composed Among the Ruins of a
            Castle in North Wales"
  VIVANTE, *English Poetry,* p. 118.
WORDSWORTH,   "Composed upon Westminster Bridge"
  BEACH, *A Romantic View of Poetry,* pp. 64-71.

CLEANTH BROOKS, "The Language of Paradox," *The Language of Poetry*, pp. 39-42. Reprinted *Criticism*, p. 359.

BROOKS, *The Well Wrought Urn*, pp. 5-6. Reprinted *Critiques*, pp. 67-68. Reprinted *American Literary Criticism*, pp. 518-520.

DAICHES and CHARVAT, *Poems in English*, pp. 697-698.

CHARLES V. HARTUNG, "Wordsworth on Westminster Bridge: Paradox or Harmony?" *College English*, XIII (Jan., 1952), 201-203.

F. R. LEAVIS, "Imagery and Movement," *Scrutiny*, XIII (Sept., 1945), 127-130.

MILLET, *Reading Poetry*, pp. 19-20.

VAN DOREN, *Introduction to Poetry*, pp. 55-58.

WORDSWORTH,   "Elegiac Stanzas"

CHARLES I. PATTERSON, "The Meaning and Significance of Wordsworth's 'Peele Castle,'" *Journal of English and Germanic Philology*, LVI (Jan., 1957), 1-9.

CHARLES J. SMITH, "The Contrarieties: Wordsworth's Dualistic Imagery," *PMLA*, LXIX (Dec., 1954), 1188-1189.

WORDSWORTH,   "An Evening Walk"

POTTLE, *The Idiom of Poetry*, pp. 105-112; (1946 ed.), pp. 111-121.

WORDSWORTH,   "Goody Blake and Harry Gill"

JOHN E. JORDAN, "Wordworth's Humor," *PMLA*, LXXIII (March, 1958), 89.

WORDSWORTH,   "The Idiot Boy"

JOHN E. JORDAN, "Wordworth's Humor," *PMLA*, LXXIII (March, 1958), 88-89.

STEPHEN M. PARRISH, "Dramatic Technique in the *Lyrical Ballads*," *PMLA*, LXXIV (March, 1959), 87-88.

WORDSWORTH,   "I Thought of Thee, My Partner
and My Guide"
Stewart C. Wilcox, "Wordsworth's River Duddon
Sonnets," *PMLA*, LXIX (March, 1954), 139-141.

WORDSWORTH,   "I Travelled Among Unknown Men"
Walter Gierasch, *The Explicator*, I (June, 1943), 65.

WORDSWORTH,   "It Is a Beauteous Evening"
T. O. Beachcroft, "Nicholas Ferror and George Herbert," *The Criterion*, XII (Oct., 1932), 30-31.

Cleanth Brooks, "The Language of Paradox," *The
Language of Poetry*, pp. 38-39 *et passim*. Reprinted
Criticism, pp. 358-359.

Brooks, *The Well Wrought Urn*, pp. 4-5, 8-9. Reprinted *Critiques*, pp. 66-67, 70.

Reprinted *American Literary Criticism*, p. 518, 522.

F. R. Leavis, "Imagery and Movement," *Scrutiny*,
XIII (Sept., 1945), 125-127.

N. F. MacLean, "An Analysis of a Lyric Poem," *University Review*, VIII (Spring, 1942), 202-209.

WORDSWORTH,   "I Wandered Lonely As a Cloud"
Drew, *Poetry*, pp. 88-92.

Greene, *The Arts and the Art of Criticism*, pp. 114-
115.

Frederick A. Pottle, "The Eye and the Object in
the Poetry of Wordsworth," *Yale Review*, XL
(Sept., 1950), 29-40. Reprinted Locke, Gibson, and
Arms, *Introduction to Literature*, third edition, pp.
88-92.

Scott, *The Poet's Craft*, pp. 60-63.

Stageberg and Anderson, *Poetry as Experience*, pp.
194-195.

WORDSWORTH,   "Laodamia"
Wormhoudt, *The Demon Lover*, pp. 63-67.

WORDSWORTH,   "Lines Composed a Few Miles Above
Tintern Abbey"
James Benzigner, "*Tintern Abbey* Revisited," *PM-
LA*, LXV (March, 1950), 154-162.

FREDERICK M. COMBELLACK, *The Explicator,* XIV (June, 1956) , 61.

EMPSON, *Seven Types of Ambiguity,* pp. 192-194; (1947 ed.), pp. 151-154.

HARTMAN, *The Unmediated Vision,* pp. 3-12, 23-26.

LANGBAUM, *The Poetry of Experience,* pp. 43-45, 48.

FREDERICK A. POTTLE, *The Explicator,* XVI (March, 1958) , 36.

RANSOM, *The New Criticism,* pp. 115-119.

CHARLES J. SMITH, "The Contrarieties: Wordsworth's Dualistic Imagery," *PMLA,* LXIX (Dec., 1954) , 1184-1185.

ROY ARTHUR SWANSON, *The Explicator,* XIV (Feb., 1956) , 31.

RENÉ WELLEK, "A Letter," *The Importance of Scrutiny,* pp. 25-26. First published in *Scrutiny,* 1937.

WORMHOUDT, *The Demon Lover,* pp. 52-55.

WORDSWORTH,   "Lines Written in Early Spring"
KIRK and McCUTCHEON, *An Introduction to the Study of Poetry,* pp. 76-79.

WORDSWORTH,   "London, 1802"
BROOKS, PURSER, WARREN, *An Approach to Literature,* pp. 496-498.
Reprinted third edition, pp. 387-390.
M. J. WAGNER, *English "A" Analyst,* No. 1.
WALTER GIERASCH, *The Explicator,* II (April, 1944), 42.

WORDSWORTH,   "Lucy Gray, or Solitude"
UNGER and O'CONNOR, *Poems for Study,* pp. 363-365.

WORDSWORTH,   "The Mad Mother"
STEPHEN M. PARRISH, "Dramatic Technique in the *Lyrical Ballads,*" *PMLA,* LXXIV (March, 1959) , 96-97.

WORDSWORTH,   "Michael"
BROOKS and WARREN, *Understanding Poetry,* pp. 83-85.
Revised edition, pp. 36-37.

JAMES SMITH, Wordsworth: A Preliminary Survey," *Scrutiny*, VII (June, 1938), 52-55.

WORMHOUDT, *The Demon Lover*, pp. 55-58.

WORDSWORTH, "Mutability"

JOHN WAIN, "The Liberation of Wordsworth," *Twentieth Century*, CLVII (Jan., 1955), 72-73.

WORDSWORTH, "My Heart Leaps Up When I Behold"

RICHARD GREENLEAF, "Emerson and Wordsworth," *Science and Society*, XXII (Summer, 1958), 228-229.

ABBIE FINDLAY POTTS, "The Spenserian and Miltonic Influence in Wordsworth's 'Ode' and 'Rainbow,'" *Studies in Philology*, XXIX (Oct., 1932), 607-616.

WORDSWORTH, "A Night-Piece"

JAMES KISSANE, "'A Night-Piece': Wordsworth's Emblem of the Mind," *MLN*, LXXI (March, 1956), 183-186.

WORDSWORTH, "Ode: Intimations of Immortality"

BATESON, *English Poetry*, pp. 196-205.

BOWRA, *The Romantic Imagination*, pp. 76-102.

CLEANTH BROOKS, "The Intimations of the Ode (Reconsiderations V)," *The Kenyon Review*, VIII (Winter, 1946), 80-102.

BROOKS and WARREN, *Understanding Poetry*, revised edition, pp. 639-645.

BROOKS, *The Well Wrought Urn*, pp. 114-138, 163-165.

GILBERT R. DAVIS, *The Explicator*, XIII (May, 1955), 45.

WALLACE W. DOUGLAS, "The Professor and the Ode," *Western Review*, XIII (Autumn, 1948), 4-14. (Cleanth Brooks replies, *Ibid.*, 14-15.)

VICTOR M. HAMM, *The Explicator*, XII (April, 1954), 38.

HARTMAN, *The Unmediated Vision*, pp. 40-44.

KNIGHT, *The Starlit Dome*, pp. 37-49 *et passim*.

J. K. MATTHISON, "Wordsworth's *Ode,*" *Studies in Philology,* XLVI (July, 1949), 419-439.

GEORGE W. MEYER, "A Note on the Sources and Symbolism of the *Intimations Ode,*" *Tulane Studies in English,* III (1953), 33-46.

FREDERICK A. POTTLE, *The Explicator,* XIII (Feb., 1955), 23.

ABBIE FINDLAY POTTS, "The Spenserian and Miltonic Influence in Wordsworth's 'Ode' and 'Rainbow,'" *Studies in Philology,* XXIX (Oct., 1932), 607-616.

JOHN CROWE RANSOM, "William Wordsworth: Notes Toward an Understanding of Poetry," *The Kenyon Review,* XII (Summer, 1950), 514-518.

THOMAS M. RAYSOR, "The Themes of Immortality and Natural Piety in Wordworth's Immortality Ode," *PMLA,* LXIX (Sept., 1954), 861-875.

ROBERT L. SCHNEIDER, "Failure of Solitude: Wordsworth's Immortality Ode," *Journal of English and Germanic Philology,* LIV (Oct., 1955), 625-633.

CHARLES J. SMITH, "The Contrarieties: Wordsworth's Dualistic Imagery," *PMLA,* LXIX (Dec.., 1954), 1186-1188.

D. A. STAUFFER, "Cooperative Criticism," *The Kenyon Review,* IV (Winter, 1942), 133-144.

LIONEL TRILLING, "Wordsworth's 'Ode: Intimations of Immortality,'" *English Institute Annual 1941,* pp. 1-28.

WORMHOUDT, *The Demon Lover,* pp. 58-62.

WORDSWORTH,   "On the Extinction of the Venetian Republic"

Z. S. FINK, "Wordsworth and the English Republican Tradition," *Journal of English and Germanic Philology,* XLVII (April, 1948), 118-119.

WORDSWORTH,   "On the Power of Sound"

KNIGHT, *The Starlit Dome,* pp. 78-81.

WORDSWORTH,   "A POET!—He Hath Put His Heart to School"

PAUL FUSSELL, JR., "Some Observations on Wordsworth's 'A POET!—He Hath Put His Heart to School,' " *Philological Quarterly*, XXXVII (Oct., 1958) , 454-464.

WORDSWORTH,   "A Poet's Epitaph"
Brooks and Warren, *Understanding Poetry*, pp. 579-582.
Revised edition, pp. 423-427, 632.

WORDSWORTH,   "Resolution and Independence"
Langbaum, *The Poetry of Experience*, pp. 54-55.
W. W. Robson, *Interpretations*, John Wain, ed., pp. 117-128.
Charles J. Smith, "The Contrarieties: Wordsworth's Dualistic Imagery," *PMLA*, LXIX (Dec., 1954) , 1185-1186.

WORDSWORTH,   "The Sea Was Laughing at a Distance, All"
William Empson, "Basic English and Wordsworth," *The Kenyon Review*, II (Autumn, 1940), 450-457.

WORDSWORTH,   "She Dwelt Among the Untrodden
Edwin B. Burgum, "The Cult of the Complex in Poetry," *Science and Society*, XV (Winter, 1951) , 37-41.
Daniels, *The Art of Reading Poetry*, pp. 222-224.

WORDSWORTH,   "She Was a Phantom of Delight"
Walter Houghton, *The Explicator*, III (Dec., 1944), 20.
Monroe M. Stearns, *The Explicator*, I (June, 1943), 68.
J. E. Whitesell, *The Explicator*, I (April, 1943), 46.

WORDSWORTH,   "A Slumber Did My Spirit Seal"
Bateson, *English Poetry*, pp. 32-34.
Blair and Chandler, *Approaches to Poetry*, p. 262.
Cleanth Brooks, "Irony and 'Ironic' Poetry," *College English*, IX (Feb., 1948), 235-237; *The English Journal*, XXXVII (Feb., 1948), 61-63.
Reprinted Zabel, *Literary Opinion in America*, revised edition, pp. 735-737.
Drew, *Poetry*, pp. 132-133.

KREUZER, *Elements of Poetry*, pp. 200-204.

F. R. LEAVIS, " 'Thought' and Emotional Quality," *Scrutiny*, XIII (Spring, 1945), 53-55.
Reprinted Stallman and Watters, *The Creative Reader*, p. 851.

ROSENTHAL and SMITH, *Exploring Poetry*, pp. 89-90.

SKELTON, *The Poetic Pattern*, pp. 182-185.

THOMAS and BROWN, *Reading Poems: An Introduction to Critical Study*, pp. 642-643.

WORDSWORTH, "Sole Listener, Duddon! to the Breeze that Played"
RICHARDS, *Principles of Literary Criticism*, pp. 207-208.

WORDSWORTH, "The Solitary Reaper"
FREDERICK A. POTTLE, "The Eye and the Object in the Poetry of Wordsworth," *Yale Review*, XL (Sept., 1950), 29-40.

DONALD J. RYAN, "Scansion Scanned," *College English*, II (Jan., 1941), 390-393.

VAN DOREN, *Introduction to Poetry*, pp. 51-55.

W. K. WIMSATT, JR., "The Structure of the 'Concrete Universal' in Literature," *PMLA*, LXII (March, 1947), 274-275. Reprinted *Criticism*, pp. 399-400.

WIMSATT, *The Verbal Icon*, p. 80.
Reprinted Locke, Gibson, and Arms, *Introduction to Literature*, third edition, pp. 86-87.

WORDSWORTH, "Stepping Westward"
BEACH, *A Romantic View of Poetry*, pp. 74-75.

WORDSWORTH, "Strange Fits of Passion Have I Known"
LEAVIS, *Revaluation*, pp. 199-202.

WORDSWORTH, "Surprised by Joy—Impatient as the Wind"
BROWER, *The Fields of Light*, pp. 75-76.

DREW, *Poetry*, pp. 123-124.

F. R. LEAVIS, "Imagery and Movement," *Scrutiny*, XIII (Sept., 1945), 125-127.

WORDSWORTH,   "The Thorn"

STEPHEN M. PARRISH, " 'The Thorn': Wordworth's Dramatic Monologue," *Journal of English Literary History*, XXIV (June, 1957) , 153-163.

WORDSWORTH,   "Three Years She Grew in Sun and Shower"

FRANCIS CHRISTENSEN, *The Explicator*, IV (Dec., 1945), 18.

FRED A. DUDLEY, *The Explicator*, II (Feb., 1944), Q19.

CHARLES J. SMITH, "The Contrarieties: Wordsworth's Dualistic Imagery," *PMLA*, LXIX (Dec, 1954) , 1185.

J. E. WHITESELL, *The Explicator*, II (Nov., 1943), Q7.

WORDSWORTH,   "We Are Seven"

MARCEL KESSEL, *The Explicator*, II (April, 1944), 43.

ARTHUR K. MOORE, "A Folk Attitude in Wordsworth's 'We are Seven,' " *Review of English Studies*, XXIII (July, 1947), 260-262.

WORDSWORTH,   "The Winds Come to Me from the Fields of Sleep"

NOWELL SMITH, "Wordsworth's 'Fields of Sleep,' " *Times Literary Supplement* (Sept. 17, 1954) , 591.

WORDSWORTH,   "The World is Too Much With Us"

GEORGE ARMS, *The Explicator*, I (Oct., 1942), 4.

WORDSWORTH,   "Yew Trees"

GEORGE RYLANDS, "English Poets and the Abstract Word," *Essays and Studies*, XVI (1930), 64-65.

WOOTON,   "A Hymn to My God . . ."

DANIELS, *The Art of Reading Poetry*, pp. 438-442.

WYATT,   "At Last Withdraw Your Cruelty"

RUDOLPH GOTTFRIED, "Sir Thomas Wyatt and Pietro Bembo," *Notes and Queries*, I, n.s. (July, 1954) , 278-280.

WYATT,   "Behold Love, Thy Power How She Despiseth"

MILES, *Major Adjectives in English Poetry*, pp. 322-325.

WYATT,   "Desire, Alas, My Master and My Foe"

HALLETT SMITH, "The Art of Sir Thomas Wyatt," *Huntington Library Quarterly*, IX (August, 1946), 329-331.

WYATT, "Forget Not Yet the Tried Intent" DAICHES and CHARVAT, *Poems in English*, p. 642.

WYATT, "Heaven and Earth" HALLETT SMITH, "The Art of Sir Thomas Wyatt," *Huntington Library Quarterly*, IX (August, 1946), 342-344.

WYATT, "The Long Love That in my Thought Doth Harbor" MILES, *Major Adjectives in English Poetry*, pp. 325-326.

HALLET SMITH, "The Art of Sir Thomas Wyatt," *Huntington Library Quarterly*, IX (August, 1946), 333-337.

WYATT, "The Lover Compareth His State to a Ship in a Perilous Storm Tossed on the Sea" S. F. JOHNSON and WILLIAM P. ORWEN, *The Explicator*, V (April, 1947), 40.

WYATT, "The Lover Showeth How He Is Forsaken of Such as He Sometime Enjoyed" BATESON, *English Poetry and the English Language*, pp. 59-60.

BATESON, *English Poetry*, pp. 142-146.

FREDERICK M. COMBELLACK, *The Explicator*, XVII (Feb., 1959), 36.

DAICHES and CHARVAT, *Poems in English*, pp. 642-644.

LEONARD DEAN, *English Masterpieces*, Vol. III, *Renaissance Poetry*, pp. 3-4.

E. E. DUNCAN-JONES, *The Explicator*, XII (Nov., 1953), 9.

J. O. HAINSWORTH, "Sir Thomas Wyatt's Use of the Love Convention," *Essays in Criticism*, VII (Jan., 1957), 90-95.

S. F. JOHNSON, *The Explicator*, XI (April, 1953), 39.

ARTHUR K. MOORE, "The Design of Wyatt's *They Fle*

from Me," Anglia, LXXI (1953), 102-111.

ARNOLD STEIN, "Wyatt's 'They Flee From Me,'" *The Sewanee Review,* LXVII (Winter, 1959), 28-44.

WYATT,   "My Lute Awake"

HALLETT SMITH, "The Art of Sir Thomas Wyatt," *Huntington Library Quarterly,* IX (August, 1946), 344-345.

WYLIE,   "Castilian"

RICHARD E. AMACHER, *The Explicator,* VII (Nov., 1948), 16.

WYLIE,   "Cold-Blooded Creatures"

C. C. WALCUTT, "Critic's Taste or Artist's Intention," *University of Kansas City Review,* XII (Summer, 1946), 279-282.

WYLIE,   "This Corruptible"

DEUTSCH, *Poetry in Our Time,* p. 231.

WYLIE,   "Hymn to Earth"

W. NELSON FRANCIS, *The Explicator,* XVII (March, 1959), 40.

WYLIE,   "Sanctuary"

KREUZER, *Elements of Poetry,* pp. 165-166.

WYLIE,   "The Tortoise in Eternity"

RICHARD E. AMACHER, *The Explicator,* VI (March, 1948), 33.

WYLIE,   "Velvet Shoes"

LAURENCE PERRINE, *The Explicator,* XIII (Dec., 1954), 17.

MACKLIN THOMAS, "Analysis of the Experience in Lyric Poetry," *College English,* IX (March, 1948), 318-319.

YEATS,   "Adam's Curse"

STEPHEN SPENDER, "W. B. Yeats as a Realist," *The Criterion,* XIV (Oct., 1934), 18-19.

YEATS,   "After Long Silence"

ANONYMOUS, quoted in Fred B. Millett, *The Rebirth of Liberal Education* (New York: Harcourt, Brace, 1945), pp. 166-168.

BROOKS and WARREN, *Understanding Poetry,* pp. 224-230.

Revised edition, pp. 116-125.

W. C. BROWN, " 'A Poem Should Not Mean But Be,' " *The University of Kansas City Review,* XV (Autumn, 1948), 63.

T. O. MATTHIESSEN, "The Crooked Road," *The Southern Review,* VII (Winter, 1942), 462-463. Reprinted *The Responsibilities of the Critic,* pp. 32-33, 36.

JOHN CROWE RANSOM, "The Irish, the Gaelic, the Byzantine," *The Southern Review,* VII (Winter, 1942), 530-531.

YEATS,   "All Souls' Night"

BROOKS, *Modern Poetry and the Tradition,* pp. 29-30.

A. DAVENPORT, "W. B. Yeats and the Upanishads," *Review of English Studies,* III, n.s. (Jan., 1952), 58-60.

YEATS,   "Among School Children"

BOWRA, *The Heritage of Symbolism,* pp. 211-212.

BROOKS, *The Well Wrought Urn,* pp. 163-175.

RICHARD CHASE, "Myth As Literature," *English Institute Essays 1947,* pp. 18-21.

DEUTSCH, *Poetry in Our Time,* p. 269.

RICHARD ELLMANN, "The Art of Yeats: Affirmative Capability," *The Kenyon Review,* XV (Summer, 1953), 369-371.

KERMODE, *Romantic Image,* pp. 83-84.

L. C. KNIGHTS, "W. B. Yeats: The Assertion of Values," *The Southern Review,* VII (Winter, 1942), 436-438.

KNIGHTS, *Explorations,* pp. 200-202.

MAYNARD MACK, LEONARD DEAN, and WILLIAM FROST, *English Masterpieces,* Vol. III, *Modern Poetry,* p. 8.

ARTHUR MIZENER, "The Romanticism of W. B. Yeats," *The Southern Review,* VII (Winter, 1942), 618-620.

THOMAS PARKINSON, "The Individuality of Yeats," *Pacific Spectator,* VI (Autumn, 1952), 492-493, 496.

V. DE SOLA PINTO, *Crisis in English Poetry*, pp. 108-109.

CHARLES A. RAINES, "Yeats' Metaphors of Permanence," *Twentieth Century Literature*, V (April, 1959), 18-19.

JOHN CROWE RANSOM, "The Irish, the Gaelic, the Byzantine," *The Southern Review*, VII (Winter, 1942), 536-538.

DELMORE SCHWARTZ, "An Unwritten Book," *The Southern Review*, VII (Winter, 1942), 488-491.

DONALD A. STAUFFER, "The Reading of a Lyric Poem," *The Kenyon Review*, XI (Summer, 1949), 436-437.

JOHN WAIN, *Interpretations*, John Wain, ed., pp. 196-210.

CHARLES C. WALCUTT, *The Explicator*, VIII (April, 1950), 42.

YEATS,   "An Acre of Grass"
DREW, *Poetry*, 116-118.

YEATS,   "The Apparitions"
R. P. BLACKMUR, "Between Myth and Philosophy: Fragments of W. B. Yeats," *The Southern Review*, VII (Winter, 1942), 412-413.
Reprinted *Language as Gesture*, pp. 110-112.

YEATS,   "At Algeciras—A Meditation upon Death"
DEUTSCH, *Poetry in Our Time*, p. 267.

YEATS,   "The Ballad of Father Gilligan"
VAN DOREN, *Introduction to Poetry*, pp. 131-133.

YEATS,   "The Black Tower"
T. R. HENN, "The Accent of Yeats's *Last Poems*," *Essays and Studies*, IX (1956), 68-69.

YEATS,   "Blood in the Moon"
CLEANTH BROOKS, "The Vision of William Butler Yeats," *The Southern Review*, IV (Summer, 1938), 121-123.
DENIS DONOGHUE, "Notes Towards a Critical Method:

Language as Order," *Studies,* XLIV (Summer 1955) , 186-187.

YEATS, "Byzantium"

R. M. ADAMS, "Now That My Ladder's Gone—Yeats Without Myth," *Accent,* XIII (Summer, 1953) , 143-148.

R. A. AUTY, "Byzantium," *Times Literary Supplement* (Aug. 11, 1950) , p. 501.

BLACKMUR, *The Expense of Greatness,* pp. 98-99. Reprinted *Critiques,* pp. 372-373.

Reprinted *Language as Gesture,* pp. 98-99.

CLEANTH BROOKS, "The Vision of William Butler Yeats," *The Southern Review,* IV (Summer, 1938), 133-140.

BROOKS, *Modern Poetry and the Tradition,* pp. 192-200.

JOHN CHRISTOPHERSON, "Byzantium," *Times Literary Supplement* (Sept. 15, 1950) , p. 581.

DAICHES, *Poetry and the Modern World,* pp. 181-185.

DAICHES and CHARVAT, *Poems in English,* pp. 733-735.

A. DAVENPORT, "W. B. Yeats and the Upanishads," *Review of English Studies,* III, n.s. (Jan., 1952) , 59-60.

BONAMY DOBREE, "Byzantium," *Times Literary Supplement* (Sept. 22, 1950) , p. 597.

DREW and SWEENEY, *Directions in Modern Poetry,* pp. 166-171.

RICHARD ELLMANN, "The Art of Yeats: Affirmative Capability," *The Kenyon Review,* XV (Summer, 1953) , 360-366.

RICHARD ELLMANN in Locke, Gibson, and Arms, *Introduction to Literature,* third edition, pp. 168-170. Reprinted from Ellmann, *the Identity of Yeats* (New York: Oxford University Press, 1954) , pp. 219-222.

WILLIAM EMPSON, "Donne and the Rhetorical Tradition," *The Kenyon Review,* XI (Autumn, 1949), 576-577.

FRIAR and BRINNIN, *Modern Poetry,* pp. 552-554.

F. L. GWYNN, "Yeats's 'Byzantium' and Its Sources," *Philological Quarterly,* XXXII (Jan., 1953), 9-21.

A. N. JEFFARES, "The Byzantine Poems of W. B. Yeats," *Review of English Studies,* XXII (Jan., 1946), 49-52.

GWENDOLYN MURPHY, "Byzantium," *Times Literary Supplement* (Aug. 25, 1950), p. 533.

GWENDOLYN MURPHY, "Byzantium," *Times Literary Supplement* (Sept. 15, 1950), p. 581.

GWENDOLYN MURPHY, "Byzantium," *Times Literary Supplement* (Nov. 3, 1950), p. 693.

RICHARD MURPHY, "Byzantium," *Times Literary Supplement* (Sept. 1, 1950), p. 548.

STAUFFER, *The Nature of Poetry,* pp. 172-175.

THOMAS and BROWN, *Reading Poems: An Introduction to Critical Study,* pp. 714-715.

TSCHUMI, *Thought in Twentieth-Century English Poetry,* pp. 69-73.

LEONARD UNGER, "The New Collected Yeats," *Poetry,* LXXX (April, 1952), 47-48.

VERNON WATKINS, "Byzantium," *Times Literary Supplement* (Sept. 22, 1950), p. 597.

YEATS, "Cap and Bells"

BOWRA, *The Heritage of Symbolism,* pp. 192-193.

MORTON IRVING SEIDEN, "A Psychoanalytical Essay on William Butler Yeats," *Accent,* VI (Spring, 1946), 179-180.

YEATS, "The Cat and the Moon"

GROVER SMITH, "Yeats, Minnaloushe, and the Moon," *Western Review,* XI (Summer, 1947), 241-244.

VAN DOREN, *Introduction to Poetry,* pp. 86-89.

YEATS, "The Choice"

W. C. BROWN, " 'A Poem Should Not Mean But Be,' "

The University of Kansas City Review, XV (Autumn, 1948), 59-60.

YEATS,   "The Collar-Bone of a Hare"

HUGH KENNER, "The Sacred Book of the Arts," *The Sewanee Review*, LXIV (Autumn, 1956), 580-581.

MARION WITT, *The Explicator*, VII (Dec., 1948), 21.

YEATS,   "Coole and Ballylee, 1931"

D. S. CARNE-ROSS, "A Commentary on Yeats' 'Coole and Ballylee, 1931,' " *Nine*, No. 1 (Autumn, 1949), 21-24.

DONALD A. STAUFFER, "The Reading of a Lyric Poem," *The Kenyon Review*, XI (Summer, 1949), 437-438.

YEATS,   "Crazy Jane on God"

WALTER E. HOUGHTON, "Yeats and Crazy Jane," *Modern Philology*, XL (May, 1943), 326-327.

YEATS,   "Crazy Jane Talks With the Bishop"

R. P. BLACKMUR, "Between Myth and Philosophy: Fragments of W. B. Yeats," *The Southern Review*, VII (Winter, 1942), 423-424.

Reprinted *Language as Gesture*, pp. 121-122.

YEATS,   "Cuchulain Comforted"

T. R. HENN, "The Accent of Yeats's *Last Poems*," *Essays and Studies*, IX (1956), 67-68.

YEATS,   "Death"

R. P. BLACKMUR, "Between Myth and Philosophy: Fragments of W. B. Yeats," *The Southern Review*, VII (Winter, 1942), 118.

Reprinted *Language as Gesture*, p. 116.

YEATS,   "A Deep-Sworn Vow"

BROOKS and WARREN, *Understanding Poetry*, pp. 294-297.

Revised edition, pp. 148-152.

YEATS,   "The Delphic Oracle upon Plotinus"

DONALD PEARCE, "Yeats's 'The Delphic Oracle upon Plotinus,' " *Notes and Queries*, I, n.s. (April, 1954), 175-176.

YEATS,   "Demon and Beast"

CLEANTH BROOKS, "The Vision of William Butler Yeats," *The Southern Review,* IV (Summer, 1938), 129-130.

BROOKS, *Modern Poetry and the Tradition,* pp. 188-189.

YEATS,   "The Double Vision of Michael Robartes"

BOWRA, *The Heritage of Symbolism,* p. 207.

KERMODE, *Romantic Image,* pp. 59-60.

TSCHUMI, *Thought in Twentieth-Century English Poetry,* pp. 45-47.

THOMAS R. WHITAKER, "The Dialectic of Yeats's Vision of History," *Modern Philology,* LVII (Nov., 1959), 109-112.

YEATS,   "Easter, 1916"

BOWRA, *The Heritage of Symbolism,* pp. 202-203.

CHARLES A. RAINES, "Yeats' Metaphors of Permanence," *Twentieth Century Literature,* V (April, 1959), 13-14.

JOHN CROWE RANSOM, "The Irish, the Gaelic, the Byzantine," *The Southern Review,* VII (Winter, 1942), 535-536.

ARNOLD STEIN, "Yeats: A Study in Recklessness," *The Sewanee Review,* LVII (Autumn, 1949), 623-626.

YEATS,   "Ego Dominus Tuus"

TSCHUMI, *Thought in Twentieth-Century English Poetry,* pp. 38-40.

MARION WITT, "William Butler Yeats," *English Institute Essays 1946,* pp. 92-99.

YEATS,   "Father and Child"

DELMORE SCHWARTZ, "An Unwritten Book," *The Southern Review,* VII (Winter, 1942), 484-485.

YEATS,   "The Fisherman"

DEUTSCH, *This Modern Poetry,* pp. 201-203.

DEUTSCH, *Poetry in Our Time,* pp. 259-260.

YEATS,   "The Folly of Being Comforted"

PAUL R. MAIXNER, *The Explicator,* XIII (Oct., 1954), 1.

PETER J. SENG, *The Explicator*, XVII (April, 1959), 48.

YEATS,   "The Gyres"

ROBERT M. ADAMS, "Now That My Ladder's Gone—Yeats Without Myth," *Accent*, XIII (Summer, 1953), 141.

RICHARD ELLMANN, "Three Ways of Looking at a Briton," *The Sewanee Review*, LXI (Winter, 1953), 154.

A. NORMAN JEFFARES, "Yeats's 'The Gyres': Sources and Symbolism," *Huntington Library Quarterly*, XV (Nov., 1951), 88-97.

ELEANOR M. SICKLES, *The Explicator*, XV (June, 1957), 60.

DONALD A. STAUFFER, "W. B. Yeats and the Medium of Poetry," *English Literary History*, XV (Sept., 1948), 244-245.

TSCHUMI, *Thought in Twentieth-Century English Poetry*, pp. 53-55.

LEONARD UNGER, "The New Collected Yeats," *Poetry*, LXXX (April, 1952), 44-45.

YEATS,   "The Happy Townland"
BOWRA, *The Heritage of Symbolism*, pp. 190-191.

YEATS,   "He Thinks of His Past Greatness When a Part of the Constellation of Heaven"
QUINN, *The Metamorphic Tradition*, p. 229.

YEATS,   "The Hosting of the Sidhe"
KERMODE, *Romantic Image*, pp. 74-76.

YEATS,   "I Am of Ireland"
MARTHA GROSS, *The Explicator*, XVII (Nov., 1958), 15.

WALTER E. HOUGHTON, "Yeats and Crazy Jane," *Modern Philology*, XL (May, 1943), 324-325.

F. O. MATTHIESSEN, "The Crooked Road," *The Southern Review*, VII (Winter, 1942), 459-462.

Reprinted *The Responsibilities of the Critic*, pp. 30-32.

ELEANOR M. SICKELS, *The Explicator*, XV (Nov., 1956), 10.

YEATS, "I Wander by the Edge"
DEUTSCH, *This Modern Poetry*, pp. 201-203.

YEATS, "In Memory of Major Robert Gregory"
KERMODE, *Romantic Image*, pp. 30-42.

MARION WITT, "The Making of an Elegy: Yeats's 'In Memory of Major Robert Gregory,'" *Modern Philology*, XLVIII (Nov., 1950), 112-121.

YEATS, "Into the Twilight"
THOMAS PARKINSON, "The Sun and the Moon in Yeats's Early Poetry," *Modern Philology*, L (Aug., 1952), 55.

YEATS, "The Lake Isle of Innisfree"
KREUZER, *Elements of Poetry*, pp. 117-119.

JOHN CROWE RANSOM, "The Irish, the Gaelic, the Byzantine," *The Southern Review*, VII (Winter, 1942), 526-530.

YEATS, "Lapis Lazuli"
FRIAR and BRINNIN, *Modern Poetry*, pp. 551-552.

A. NORMAN JEFFARES, "Notes on Yeats's 'Lapis Lazuli,'" *MLN*, LXV (Nov., 1950), 488-491.

CHARLES A. RAINES, "Yeats' Metaphors of Permanence," *Twentieth Century Literature*, V (April, 1959), 15-16.

TSCHUMI, *Thought in Twentieth-Century English Poetry*, pp. 64-65.

YEATS, "Leda and the Swan"
R. P. BLACKMUR, "The Later Poetry of W. B. Yeats," *The Southern Review*, II (Autumn, 1936), 360-362.

BLACKMUR, *Expense of Greatness*, pp. 102-104. Reprinted *Critiques*, pp. 375-376.

Reprinted *Language as Gesture*, pp. 102-103.

KENNETH BURKE, "On Motivation in Yeats," *The Southern Review*, VII Winter, 1942), 554-555.

DEUTSCH, *Poetry in Our Time*, pp. 260-262.

DREW, *Poetry*, pp. 65-67.

DREW and SWEENEY, *Directions in Modern Poetry,* pp. 164-166.

JOSEPH MARGOLIS, *The Explicator,* XIII (April, 1955), 34.

QUINN, *The Metamorphic Tradition,* pp. 233-235.

CHARLES A. RAINES, "Yeats' Metaphors of Permanence," *Twentieth Century Literature,* V (April, 1959), 16-17.

JANE D. REID, "Leda, Twice Assaulted," *Journal of Aesthetics and Art Criticism,* XI (June, 1953), 378-389.

LEO SPITZER, "On Yeats's Poem 'Leda and the Swan,'" *Modern Philology,* LI (May, 1954), 271-276.

ARNOLD STEIN, "Yeats: A Study in Recklessness," *The Sewanee Review,* LVII (Autumn, 1949), 617-620.

HOYT TROWBRIDGE, "'Leda and the Swan': A Longinian Analysis," *Modern Philology,* LI (Nov., 1953), 120-129.

YEATS, "Line Written in Dejection"

THOMAS PARKINSON, "The Sun and the Moon in Yeats's Early Poetry," *Modern Philology,* L (Aug., 1952), 50, 53-55.

YEATS, "The Long-Legged Fly"

DAICHES and CHARVAT, *Poems in English,* pp. 735-736.

TSCHUMI *Thought in Twentieth-Century English Poetry,* pp. 61-63.

YEATS, "The Lover Mourns for the Change That Has Come upon Him and His Beloved and Longs for the End of the World"

STAUFFER, *The Nature of Poetry,* pp. 170-171.

YEATS, "The Magi"

THOMAS R. WHITAKER, "The Dialectic of Yeats's *Modern Philology,* LI (May, 1954), 271-276. 108.

YEATS, "The Man and the Echo"

THOMAS PARKINSON, "The Individuality of Yeats," *Pacific Spectator,* VI (Autumn, 1952), 497-498.

CHARLES A. RAINES, "Yeats' Metaphors of Permanence," *Twentieth Century Literature*, V (April, 1959), 14-15.

YEATS, "Men Improve with Years"

HUGH KENNER, "The Sacred Book of the Arts," *The Sewanee Review*, LXIV (Autumn, 1956), 578-580.

YEATS, "Meru"

RICHARD ELLMANN, "The Art of Yeats: Affirmative Capability," *The Kenyon Review*, XV (Summer, 1953), 373-376.

YEATS, "Michael Robartes and the Dancer"

KERMODE, *Romantic Image*, pp. 52-55.

YEATS, "Mohini Chatterjee"

MARION WITT, *The Explicator*, IV (June, 1946), 60.

YEATS, "The Moods"

MARION WITT, *The Explicator*, VI (Dec., 1947), 15.

YEATS, "Mother of God"

PETER ALLT, "Yeats, Religion, and History," *The Sewanee Review*, LX (Autumn, 1952), 647-651.

YEATS, "The New Faces"

A. N. JEFFARES, " 'The New Faces': A New Explanation," *Review of English Studies*, XXIII (Oct., 1947), 349-353.

YEATS, "News for the Delphic Oracle"

FRIAR and BRINNIN, *Modern Poetry*, pp. 550-551.

CHARLES A. RAINES, "Yeats' Metaphors of Permanence," *Twentieth Century Literature*, V (April, 1959), 12-13.

YEATS, "Nineteen Hundred and Nineteen"

FRAIR and BRINNIN, *Modern Poetry*, pp. 559-560.

DONALD A. STAUFFER, "The Reading of a Lyric Poem," *The Kenyon Review*, XI (Summer, 1949), 435-436.

TSCHUMI, *Thought in Twentieth-Century English Poetry*, pp. 55-56.

YEATS, "Old Tom Again"

DONALD A. STAUFFER, "W. B. Yeats and the Medium

of Poetry," *English Literary History*, XV (Sept., 1948), 241-242.

YEATS, "On a Picture of a Black Centaur by Edmund Dulac"

HARRY GOLDGAR, "Yeats and the Black Centaur in French," *Western Review*, XV (Winter, 1951), 113-122.

JOHN CROWE RANSOM, "The Irish, the Gaelic, the Byzantine," *The Southern Review*, VII (Winter, 1942), 522-524.

YEATS, "The Phases of the Moon"

TSCHUMI, *Thought in Twentieth-Century English Poetry*, pp. 42-45.

YEATS, "A Prayer for My Daughter"

WARREN BECK, "Boundaries of Poetry," *College English*, IV (March, 1943), 349-350.

BROOKS, PURSER, and WARREN, *An Approach to Literature*, third edition, pp. 368-371.

YEATS, "The Results of Thought"

RICHARD ELLMANN, "The Art of Yeats: Affirmative Capability," *The Kenyon Review*, XV (Summer, 1953), 368-369.

YEATS, "Ribh at the Tomb of Baile and Aillinn"

PETER URE, "Yeats's Supernatural Songs," *Review of English Studies*, VII, n.s. (Jan., 1956), 39-46.

YEATS, "Ribh Denounces Patrick"

PETER URE, "Yeats's Supernatural Songs," *Review of English Studies*, VII, n.s. (Jan., 1956), 46-48.

YEATS, "Ribh in Ecstasy"

PETER URE, "Yeats's Supernatural Songs," *Review of English Studies*, VII, n.s. (Jan., 1956), 40-41, 48-50.

YEATS, "The Rose"

HIRAM HAYDN, "The Last of the Romantics: An Introduction to the Symbolism of William Butler Yeats," *The Sewanee Review*, LV (Spring, 1947), 308-309.

YEATS, "The Rose of Battle"

THOMAS PARKINSON, "The Sun and the Moon in Yeats's Early Poetry," *Modern Philology*, L (Aug., 1952) , 55.

YEATS, "The Rose Tree"

BOWRA, *The Heritage of Symbolism*, p. 204.

YEATS, "Sailing to Byzantium"

BLACKMUR, *Expense of Greatness*, pp. 98-99.

Reprinted *Language as Gesture*, pp. 98-99.

CLEANTH BROOKS, "A Note on Symbol and Conceit," *The American Review*, III (May, 1934), 209-211.

CLEANTH BROOKS, "The Vision of William Butler Yeats," *The Southern Review*, IV (Summer, 1938), 131-133.

BROOKS, *Modern Poetry and the Tradition*, pp. 62-64, 190-192.

Abridged in *The Case for Poetry*, p. 401.

H. M. CAMPBELL, "Yeats's 'Sailing to Byzantium,' " *MLN*, LXX (Dec., 1955) , 585-589.

A. DAVENPORT, "W. B. Yeats and the Upanishads," *Review of English Studies*, n.s., III (Jan., 1952) , 56-57.

ALLAN DONALDSON, "A Note on W. B. Yeats' 'Sailing to Byzantium,' " *Notes and Queries*, I, n.s. (Jan., 1954) , 34-35.

DOUGLAS, LAMSON, SMITH, *The Critical Reader*, pp. 115-118.

DREW, *Poetry*, pp. 262-267.

FRANKENBERG, *Invitation to Poetry*, p. 383.

FRIAR and BRINNIN, *Modern Poetry*, pp. 554-555.

F. L. GWYNN, "Yeats's Byzantium and Its Sources," *Philological Quarterly*, XXXII (Jan., 1953) , 9-21.

A. N. JEFFARES, "The Byzantine Poems of W. B. Yeats," *Review of English Studies*, XXII (Jan., 1946), 44-49.

L. C. KNIGHTS, "W. B. Yeats: The Assertion of Values," *The Southern Review*, VII (Winter, 1942), 438-439.

KNIGHTS, *Explorations*, pp. 202-203.

MAYNARD MACK, LEONARD DEAN, and WILLIAM

FROST, *English Masterpieces,* Vol. VII, *Modern Poetry,* p. 7.

ELDER OLSON, *University of Kansas City Review,* VIII (Spring, 1942), 209-219. Reprinted in part, *Critiques,* pp. 284-288.
Reprinted Engle and Carrier, *Reading Modern Poetry,* pp. 139-149.
Abridged in *The Case for Poetry,* p. 401.

CHARLES A. RAINES, "Yeats' Metaphors of Permanence," *Twentieth Century Literature,* V (April, 1959), 18.

JOHN CROWE RANSOM, "The Irish, the Gaelic, the Byzantine," *The Southern Review,* VII (Winter, 1942), 518-522.

JOHN CROWE RANSOM, "Yeats and His Symbols," *The Kenyon Review,* I (Summer, 1939), 318-320.

WILLIAM O. RAYMOND, " 'The Mind's Internal Heaven' in Poetry," *The University of Toronto Quarterly,* XX (April, 1951), 231-232.

ROSENTHAL and SMITH, *Exploring Poetry,* pp. 577-582.

STAUFFER, *The Nature of Poetry,* pp. 243-246.
Abridged in *The Case for Poetry,* pp. 401-403.

THOMAS and BROWN, *Reading Poems: An Introduction to Critical Study,* pp. 712-714.

TSCHUMI, *Thought in Twentieth-Century English Poetry,* pp. 67-69.

W. K. WIMSATT, "Comment on 'Two Essays in Practical Criticism,' " *The University of Kansas City Review,* IX (Winter, 1952), 142.

YEATS,   "The Second Coming"

R. P. BLACKMUR, "The Later Poetry of W. B. Yeats," *The Southern Review,* II (Autumn, 1936), 343-347. Reprinted *Language as Gesture,* pp. 84-89.

BLACKMUR, *Expense of Greatness,* pp. 79-85. Reprinted *Critiques,* pp. 361-364.

EDWARD A. BLOOM, "Yeats' 'Second Coming': An Experiment in Analysis," *The University of Kansas City Review,* XXI (Winter, 1954), 103-110.

BOWRA, *The Heritage of Symbolism,* pp. 208-209.

DAICHES and CHARVAT, *Poems in English,* pp. 732-733.

DEUTSCH, *Poetry in Our Time,* pp. 273-274.

HIRAM HAYDN, "The Last of the Romantics: An Introduction to the Symbolism of William Butler Yeats," *The Sewanee Review,* LV (Spring, 1947), 314-315.

JOE HORRELL, "Some Notes on Conversion in Poetry," *The Southern Review,* VII (Summer, 1942), 123-126.

WENDELL S. JOHNSON, "Some Functions of Poetic Form," *Journal of Aesthetics and Art Criticism,* XIII (June, 1955), 505.

JEROME L. MAZZARO, *The Explicator,* XVI (Oct., 1957), 6.

JOHN CROWE RANSOM, "Yeats and His Symbols," *The Kenyon Review,* I (Summer, 1939), 317-318.

D. S. SAVAGE, "Two Prophetic Poems," *Western Review,* XIII (Winter, 1949), 67-78.

THOMAS and BROWN, *Reading Poems: An Introduction to Critical Study,* pp. 715-716.

TSCHUMI, *Thought in Twentieth-Century English Poetry,* pp. 56-57.

UNGER and O'CONNOR, *Poems for Study,* pp. 582-584.

VAN DOREN, *Introduction to Poetry,* pp. 81-85.

DONALD WEEKS, "Image and Idea in Yeats' *The Second Coming,*" *PMLA,* LXIII (March, 1948), 281-292.

YEATS,   "The Secret Rose"

BOWRA, *The Heritage of Symbolism,* p. 191.

YEATS,   "The Song of the Happy Shepherd"

MARION WITT, "Yeats's 'The Song of the Happy Shepherd,'" *Philological Quarterly,* XXXII (Jan., 1953), 1-8.

YEATS,   "The Song of the Wandering Aengus"

BOWRA, *The Heritage of Symbolism,* pp. 189-190.

THOMAS PARKINSON, "The Sun and the Moon in Yeats's Early Poetry," *Modern Philology*, L (Aug., 1952), 55.

YEATS.   "The Sorrow of Love"

BARTLETT, *Poems in Process*, pp. 193-195.

HERBERT READ, "The Collected Poems of W. B. Yeats," *The Criterion*, XIII (April, 1934), 468-472.

YEATS,   "The Statues"

RICHARD ELLMANN, "Three Ways of Looking at a Briton," *The Sewanee Review*, LXI (Winter, 1953), 154.

YEATS,   "Symbols"

DAICHES, *The Place of Meaning in Poetry*, pp. 43-44.

YEATS,   "That the Night Come"

BROOKS, PURSER, WARREN, *An Approach to Literature*, pp. 469-471.

Reprinted third edition, pp. 319-321.

YEATS,   "There"

PETER URE, "Yeats's Supernatural Songs," *Review of English Studies*, n.s., VII (Jan., 1956), 50-51.

YEATS,   "The Three Bushes"

EDWARD B. PARTRIDGE, "Yeats's 'The Three Bushes'— Genesis and Structure," *Accent*, XVII (Spring, 1957), 67-80.

LEONARD UNGER, "The New Collected Yeats," *Poetry*, LXXX (April, 1952), 48-49.

YEATS,   "The Three Hermits"

DEUTSCH, *Poetry in Our Times*, pp. 269-270.

YEATS,   "A Thought from Propertius"

DELMORE SCHWARTZ, "An Unwritten Book," *The Southern Review*, VII (Winter, 1942), 487.

YEATS,   "To D. W."

YEATS, *Letters on Poetry from W. B. Yeats to Dorothy Wellesley*, pp. 93-95.

YEATS,   "To a Friend Whose Work Has Come to Nothing"

MALCOLM BROWN, "The Sweet Crystalline Cry," *The Western Review*, XVI (Summer, 1952), 265.

YEATS, "To His Heart, Bidding It Have No Fear"

MARION WITT, *The Explicator*, IX (March, 1951), 32.

YEATS, "The Tower"

A. DAVENPORT, "W. B. Yeats and the Upanishads," *Review of English Studies*, III, n.s. (Jan., 1952), 60-62.

RICHARD ELLMANN, "The Art of Yeats: Affrmative Capability," *The Kenyon Review*, XV (Summer, 1953), 364-366.

FRIAR and BRINNIN, *Modern Poetry*, pp. 557-559.

JOHN CROWE RANSOM, "The Irish, the Gaelic, the Byzantine," *The Southern Review*, VII (Winter, 1942) 542-543.

DONALD A. STAUFFER, "The Reading of a Lyric Poem," *The Kenyon Review*, XI (Summer, 1949), 434-435.

TSCHUMI, *Thought in Twentieth-Century English Poetry*, pp. 47-49.

TUVE, *Elizabethan and Metaphysical Imagery*, pp. 269-271.

SARAH YOUNGBLOOD, "A Reading of 'The Tower,'" *Twentieth Century Literature*, V (July, 1959), 74-84.

YEATS, "Two Songs from a Play"

CLEANTH BROOKS, "The Vision of William Butler Yeats," *The Southern Review*, IV (Summer, 1938), 123-124.

BROOKS and WARREN, *Understanding Poetry*, pp. 615-621.

Revised edition, pp. 458-464.

BROWER, *The Fields of Light*, pp. 84-88.

FRIAR and BRINNIN, *Modern Poetry*, pp. 555-557.

YEATS, "The Two Trees"

KERMODE, *Romantic Image*," pp. 96-99.

YEATS, "Under Ben Bulben"

R. P. Blackmur, "Between Myth and Philosophy: Fragments of W. B. Yeats," *The Southern Review,* VII (Winter, 1942), 415-417.

Curtis B. Bradford, "Journeys to Byzantium," *Virginia Quarterly Review,* XXV (Spring, 1949), 212-214.

Tschumi, *Thought in Twentieth-Century English Poetry,* pp. 59-61.

YEATS,   "Under the Moon"

Thomas Parkinson, "The Sun and the Moon in Yeats's Early Poetry," *Modern Philology,* L (Aug., 1952), 56.

YEATS,   "Under the Round Tower"

Thomas Parkinson, "The Sun and the Moon in Yeats's Early Poetry," *Modern Philology,* L (Aug., 1952), 55-56.

YEATS,   "The Valley of the Black Pig"

Thomas R. Whitaker, "The Dialectic of Yeats's Vision of History," *Modern Philology,* LVII (Nov., 1959), 101-102.

YEATS,   "A Vision"

Cleanth Brooks, "The Vision of William Butler Yeats," *The Southern Review,* IV (Summer, 1938), 116-142.

Drew and Sweeney, *Directions in Modern Poetry,* pp. 154-155.

Morton Irving Seiden, "A Psychoanalytical Essay on William Butler Yeats," *Accent,* VI (Winter, 1946), 189-190.

YEATS,   "The Wanderings of Oisin"

Russell K. Alspach, "Some Sources of Yeats's 'The Wanderings of Oisin,' " *PMLA,* LVIII (Sept., 1943), 849-866.

Morton Irving Seiden, "A Psychoanalytical Essay on William Butler Yeats," *Accent,* VI (Winter, 1946), 180-189.

YEATS,   "When You are Old"

Arthur Minton, *The Explicator,* V (May, 1947), 49.

ELISABETH SCHNEIDER, *The Explicator,* VI (May, 1948), 50.

MARION WITT, *The Explicator,* VI (Oct., 1947), 6.

YEATS,   "The White Birds"

DAICHES, *The Place of Meaning in Poetry,* pp. 42-43.

YEATS,   "Who Goes with Fergus?"

EMPSON, *Seven Types of Ambiguity,* pp. 238-240; (1947 ed.), pp. 187-190.

ANDREW RUTHERFORD, *The Explicator,* XIII (May, 1955), 41.

YEATS,   "The Wild Swans at Coole"

BROOKS, PURSER, WARREN, *An Approach to Literature,* pp. 456-457.

Reprinted third edition, pp. 314-315.

HUGH KENNER, "The Sacred Book of the Arts," *The Sewanee Review,* LXIV (Autumn, 1956), 581-582.

KARL SHAPIRO, "Prosody as the Meaning," *Poetry,* LXXIII (March, 1949), 340-341.

DONALD A. STAUFFER, "The Reading of a Lyric Poem," *The Kenyon Review,* XI (Summer, 1949), 428-440.

YEATS,   "The Withering of the Boughs"

DONALD A. STAUFFER, "The Reading of a Lyric Poem," *The Kenyon Review,* XI (Summer, 1949), 432-434.

MAIN SOURCES CONSULTED*

ABBE, GEORGE. *You and Contemporary Poetry.*
North Guilford, Connecticut: Author-Audience Publication, 1957.

Accent: A Quarterly of New Literature, I (Autumn, 1940)—XIX, No. 4 (Autumn, 1959).

ADAMS, ROBERT M. *Strains of Discord: Studies in Literary Openness.* Ithaca, New York: Cornell Univesrity Press, 1958.

American Literary Criticism, 1900-1950.
CHARLES I. GLICKSBERG, ed. New York: Hendricks House, Inc., 1951.

American Literature: A Journal of Literary History, Criticism, and Bibliography, I (1929)—XXXI, No. 3 (Nov., 1959).

The American Review, I (April-Oct., 1933)—IX (Oct., 1937).

Anniversary Lectures 1959: Robert Burns, 1759, by ROBERT

---

* When explication might generally be assumed to appear in a book that we have examined, we have listed that book even though no explication has been found in it. We have, however, added the parenthetical comment that it contains "no explication."

HILLYER; *Edgar Allen Poe, 1809,* by RICHARD
WILBUR; *Alfred Edward Housman, 1859,* by
CLEANTH BROOKS. Lectures Presented Under the
Auspices of the Gertrude Clarke Whittall Poetry
and Literature Fund. Washington: Reference De-
partment, Library of Congress, 1959.

ARMS, GEORGE. *The Fields Were Green: A New View
of Bryant, Whittier, Holmes, Lowell, and Longfellow, with a Selection of Their Poems.* Stanford,
California: Stanford University Press, 1953.

ARNSTEIN, FLORA S. *Adventure into Poetry.* Stanford,
California; Stanford University Press, 1951. (No
explication.)

BARTLETT, PHYLLIS. *Poems in Process.* New York:
Oxford University Press, 1951.

BASLER, ROY P. *Sex, Symbolism, and Psychology in Literature.* New Brunswick: Rutgers University Press,
1948.

BATESON, F. W. *English Poetry: A Critical Introduction,* London and New York: Longman's Green Co.,
1950.

BATESON, F. W. *English Poetry and the English Language: An Experiment in Literary History.* Oxford:
The Clarendon Press, 1934.

BEACH, JOSEPH WARREN. *A Romantic View of Poetry.*
Minneapolis: The University of Minnesota Press,
1944.

BELGION, MONTGOMERY. *Reading for Profit.* Chicago:
Henry Regnery Company, 1950.

BLACKMUR, R. P. *The Double Agent: Essays in Craft
and Elucidation.* New York: Arrow Editions, 1935.

BLACKMUR, R. P. *The Expense of Greatness.* New
York: Arrow Editions, 1940.

BLACKMUR, R. P. *Language as Gesture: Essays in Poetry.* New York: Harcourt, Brace and Company, 1952.

BLAIR, WALTER and W. K. CHANDLER. *Approaches to
Poetry.* New York: D. Appleton-Century Co., 1935.

BLAIR, WALTER and JOHN C. GERBER. *Better Reading 2: Literature.* Chicago: Scott, Foresman and Company, 1948.

BODKIN, MAUD. *Archetypal Patterns in Poetry.* London: Oxford University Press, 1934.

BOULTON, MARJORIE. *The Anatomy of Poetry.* London: Routledge & Kegan Paul, 1953.

BOWRA, C. M. *The Creative Experiment.* London: Macmillan & Co., Ltd., 1949.

BOWRA, C. M. *The Heritage of Symbolism.* London: Macmillan & Co. Ltd., 1947.

BOWRA, C. M. *The Romantic Imagination.* Cambridge, Mass.: Harvard University Press, 1949.

BROOKS, CLEANTH, JR. *Modern Poetry and the Tradition.* Chapel Hill: University of North Carolina Press, 1939.

BROOKS, CLEANTH, JR. *The Well Wrought Urn.* New York: Reynal and Hitchcock, 1947.

BROOKS, CLEANTH, JR., JOHN THIBAUT PURSER, ROBERT PENN WARREN. *An Approach to Literature.* Revised edition. New York: F. S. Crofts & Co., 1942. (Also, third edition, 1952.)

BROOKS, CLEANTH, JR., and ROBERT PENN WARREN. *Understanding Poetry: An Anthology for College Students.* New York: Henry Holt and Company, 1938. Revised edition, 1950.

BROWER, REUBEN ARTHUR. *The Fields of Light: An Experiment in Critical Reading.* New York: Oxford University Press, 1951.

BURKE, KENNETH. *Counter-Statement.* New York: Harcourt, Brace and Co., 1931.

BURKE, KENNETH. *Permanence and Change.* New York: New Republic, Inc., 1935. (No explication.)

BURKE, KENNETH. *The Philosophy of Literary Form.* Baton Rouge: Louisiana State University Press, 1941.

BURKE, KENNETH. *A Rhetoric of Motives.* New York: Prentice-Hall, Inc., 1950. (No explication.)

The Case for Poetry, FREDERICK L. GWYNN, RALPH W. CON-
DEE, ARTHUR O. LEWIS, JR., eds. Englewood Cliffs,
New Jersey: Prentice-Hall, Inc., 1954.

CIARDI, JOHN. *How Does a Poem Mean?* Boston:
Houghton Mifflin Company, 1959.

COFFMAN, STANLEY K. *Imagism: A Chapter for the
History of Modern Poetry.* Norman, Oklahoma: University of Oklahoma Press, 1951. (No explication.)

College English, I (Oct. 1939)—XXI, No. 3 (Dec., 1959).

COOPER, CHARLES W., and JOHN HOLMES. *Preface to
Poetry.* New York: Harcourt, Brace and Company,
Inc., 1946.

Criterion: A Quarterly Review, I (Oct., 1922)—XVIII (Jan.,
1939).

The Critic, I (Spring, 1947)—I, No. 2 (Autumn, 1947).

A Critical Supplement to "Poetry," Oct., 1948—Dec., 1949.
The listing in this checklist is incomplete and limited to
poems by widely recognized contemporaries. The poems ex-
plicated appear in the corresponding issues of *Poetry: A
Magazine of Verse.*

Criticism: A Quarterly for Literature and the Arts, I, No. 1
(Winter, 1959) — I, No. 4 (Fall, 1959).

Critics and Criticism: Ancient and Modern. R. S. CRANE, ed.
Chicago: University of Chicago Press, 1952. (No
explication.)

The Critic's Notebook. ROBERT WOOSTER STALLMAN, ed.
Minneapolis: The University of Minnesota Press,
1950.

Criticism: The Foundations of Modern Literary Judgment.
Mark Schorer, Josephine Miles, and Gordon McKen-
zie, eds. New York: Harcourt, Brace and Company,
1948.

Critiques and Essays in Criticism, 1920-1948. Selected by Robert Wooster Stallman. New York: The Ronald Press
Company, 1949.

CRUTWELL, PATRICK. *The Shakespearean Moment
and Its Place in the Poetry of the 17th Century.*

New York: Columbia University Press, 1955.

CUNNINGHAM, CORNELIUS CARMAN. *Literature as a Fine Art: Analysis and Interpretation.* New York: Thomas Nelson and Sons, 1941.

DAICHES, DAVID. *The Place of Meaning in Poetry.* Edinburgh and London: Oliver and Boyd, 1935.

DAICHES, DAVID and WILLIAM CHARVAT. *Poems in English, 1530-1940.* New York: The Ronald Press Company, 1950.

DAICHES, DAVID. *Poetry and the Modern World: A Study of Poetry in England Between 1900 and 1939.* Chicago: The University of Chicago Press, 1940.

DAICHES, DAVID. *A Study of Literature for Readers and Critics.* Ithaca: Cornell University Press, 1948.

DANIELS, EARL. *The Art of Reading Poetry.* New York: Farrar & Rinehart, Inc., 1941.

DAY LEWIS, C. *The Poetic Image.* London: Jonathan Cape, 1947.

DE MOURGES, ODETTE. *Metaphysical Baroque & Precieux Poetry.* Oxford: Oxford University Press, 1953.

Determinations: Critical Essays, by Twelve Contributors, with Introduction. F. R. Leavis, ed. London: Chatto and Windus, 1934.

DUETSCH, BABETTE. *Poetry in Our Time.* New York: Henry Holt and Company, 1952.

DEUTSCH, BABETTE. *This Modern Poetry.* New York: W. W. Norton and Company, Inc., 1935.

The Dial, LXXVIII (Jan., 1925)—LXXXVI (July, 1929).

DOUGLAS, WALLACE, ROY LAMSON, HALLETT SMITH. *The Critical Reader.* New York: W. W. Norton & Company, 1949.

DREW, ELIZABETH. *Discovering Poetry.* New York: W. W. Norton & Co., 1933.

DREW, ELIZABETH. *The Enjoyment of Literature.* New York: W. W. Norton & Co., Inc., 1935. (No explication.)

DREW, ELIZABETH, in collaboration with JOHN L. SWEENEY. *Directions in Modern Poetry.* New York: W. W. Norton & Co., Inc., 1940.

DREW, ELIZABETH. *Poetry: A Modern Guide to Its Understanding and Enjoyment.* New York: W. W. Norton & Company, Inc., 1959.

EASTMAN, MAX. *Enjoyment of Poetry* (Revised). New York: Charles Scribner's Sons, 1930. (No explication.)

EASTMAN, MAX. *The Literary Mind.* New York: Charles Scribner's Sons, 1931.

ELIOT, T. S. *Essays, Ancient and Modern.* New York: Harcourt, Brace and Company, 1936. (No explication.)

ELIOT, T. S. *The Sacred Wood: Essays on Poetry and Criticism.* London: Methuen and Co., Ltd., 1920. (No explication.)

ELIOT, T. S. *Selected Essays.* New York: Harcourt, Brace and Company, 1932. (No explication.)

ELIOT, T. S. *The Use of Poetry and the Use of Criticism.* New York: Harcourt, Brace and Company, 1933. (No explication.)

EMPSON, WILLIAM. *English Pastoral Poetry.* New York: W. W. Norton & Co., 1938.

EMPSON, WILLIAM. *Seven Types of Ambiguity.* London: Chatto and Windus, 1930. (Also revised edition, New York: New Directions, 1947.)

EMPSON, WILLIAM. *The Structure of Complex Words.* Norfolk, Connecticut: New Directions Books, 1951.

ENGLE, PAUL and WARREN CARRIER. *Reading Modern Poetry,* Chicago: Scott, Foresman and Company, 1955.

English "A" Analyst (Northwestern University), Nos. 1-17 (1947?-1949).

English Institute Annual 1939-1942; English Institute Essays. New York: Columbia University Press, 1940-1943, 1946-1948, 1947-1949, 1950-1952.

The English Journal (High School and College Editions), XIV (Jan. 1925) —XLVIII, No. 10 (Dec. 1959).

English Masterpieces: An Anthology of Imaginative Literature from Chaucer to T. S. Eliot. VII vols.: MAY-

NARD MACK, LEONARD DEAN, WILLIAM FROST, eds. New York: Prentice-Hall, Inc., 1950.

English Studies in Honor of James Southall Wilson, FRED-SON BOWERS, ed. University of Virginia Studies, Vol. 4. Charlottesville: University of Virginia Press, 1951.

English Studies (superseding *Essays and Studies* . . .), I (1948)—II (1949).

Essays and Studies by Members of the English Association. Oxford: The Clarendon Press, XI (1925)—XXXIII (1947). New Series III (1950)—XII (1959).

Essays in Modern Literary Criticism. RAY B. WEST, JR., ed. New York: Rinehart & Company, Inc., 1952.

The Explicator, I (Oct., 1942)—XVIII, No. 3, (Dec., 1959).

FRANKENBERG, LLOYD. *Invitation to Poetry.* New York: Doubleday & Company, Inc., 1956.

FRANKENBERG, LLOYD. *Pleasure Dome: On Reading Modern Poetry.* Boston: Houghton Mifflin Company, 1949.

FRIAR, KIMON and JOHN MALCOLM BRINNIN. *Modern Poetry, American and British.* New York: Appleton-Century-Crofts, 1951.

Furioso, I (Summer, 1939)—VIII (Spring, 1953).

GARDNER, HELEN. *The Business of Criticism.* Oxford: The Clarendon Press, 1959.

GOODMAN, PAUL. *The Structure of Literature.* Chicago: The University of Chicago Press, 1954.

GREENE, THEODORE M. *The Arts and the Art of Criticism.* Princeton: Princeton University Press, 1940.

HAMILTON, G. ROSTREVOR. *The Tell-Tale Article: A Critical Approach to Modern Poetry.* New York: Oxford University Press, 1950. (No explication.)

HARTMAN, GEOFFREY H. *The Unmediated Vision: An Interpretation of Wordsworth, Hopkins, Rilke, and Valéry.* New Haven: Yale University Press, 1954.

HOFFMAN, FREDERICK J. *The Twenties: American*

Writing in the Postwar Decade. New York: The Viking Press, 1955.

HOUGHTON, WALTER E. *The Victorian Frame of Mind, 1830-1870*. New Haven: Yale University Press, 1957. (No explication.)

Hound and Horn, I (Sept., 1927)—VII (July-Sept., 1934).

The Hudson Review, I (Spring, 1948) —XII, No. 4 (Winter, 1959-1960).

HUNGERFORD, EDWARD B. *Shores of Darkness*. New York: Columbia University Press, 1941.

The Importance of Scrutiny: Selections from Scrutiny: A Quarterly Review, 1932-1948. Eric Bentley, ed. New York: George W. Stewart, Publisher, Inc., 1948.

The Intent of the Critic. Donald A. Stauffer, ed. Princeton: Princeton University Press, 1941. (No explication.)

Interpretations: Essays on Twelve English Poems. JOHN WAIN, ed. London: Routledge and Kegan Paul, 1955.

Interpretations of American Literature. CHARLES FEIDELSON, JR., and PAUL BRODTKORB, JR., eds. New York: Oxford University Press, 1959.

JOHNSON, E. D. H. *The Alien Vision of Victorian Poetry*. Princeton, New Jersey: Princeton University Press, 1952.

The Kenyon Critics: Studies in Modern Literature from the "Kenyon Review." JOHN CROWE RANSOM, ed., Cleveland and New York: The World Publishing Company, 1951.

The Kenyon Review, I (Winter, 1939) —XXI, No. 4 (Autumn, 1959).

KERMODE, FRANK. *Romantic Image*. London: Routledge and Kegan Paul, 1957.

KILBY, CLYDE S. *Poetry and Life: An Introduction To Poetry*. New York: The Odyssey Press, 1953.

KIRK, RICHARD RAY, and ROGER PHILIP McCUTCHEON. *An Introduction to the Study of Poetry*. New York: American Book Co., 1934.

KNIGHT, G. WILSON. *The Burning Oracle: Studies in the*

Poetry of Action. London, New York, Toronto: Oxford University Press, 1939.

KNIGHT, G. WILSON.   *The Starlit Dome: Studies in the Poetry of Vision.* London, New York, Toronto: Oxford University Press, 1941.

KNIGHTS, L. C.   *Explorations: Essays in Criticism.* New York: George W. Stewart, 1947.

KREUZER, JAMES R.   *Elements of Poetry.* New York: The Macmillan Company, 1955.

KRIEGER, MURRAY.   *The New Apologists for Poetry.* Minneapolis: The University of Minnesota Press, 1956.

LANGBAUM, ROBERT.   *The Poetry of Experience: The Dramatic Monologue in Modern Literary Experience.* New York: Random House, 1957.

The Language of Poetry. Allen Tate, ed. Princeton: Princeton University Press, 1942.

LEAVIS, F. R.   *Education and the University: A Sketch for an 'English School.'* London: Chatto and Windus, 1943; New York: George W. Stewart, Publisher, Inc., 1948.

LEAVIS, F. R.   *New Bearings in English Poetry.* London: Chatto and Windus, 1932.

LEAVIS, F. R.   *Revaluation: Tradition and Development in English Poetry.* London: Chatto and Windus, 1936. (Also, same pagination, New York: George W. Stewart, 1947.)

LEISHMAN, J. B.   *The Metaphysical Poets: Donne, Herbert, Vaughan, Traherne.* Oxford: Oxford University Press, 1934.

Literary Opinion in America. M. D. Zabel, ed. New York: Harper & Brothers, 1937. Revised edition, 1951.

Literary Scholarship: Its Aims and Methods. Chapel Hill: University of North Carolina Press, 1941. (No explication.)

The Literature of the United States. Walter Blair, Theodore

Hornberger, and Randall Stewart, eds. Chicago: Scott, Foresman and Company, 1947.

LOCKE, LOUIS G., WILLIAM M. GIBSON, and GEORGE ARMS. *Introduction to Literature,* third edition. New York: Rinehart & Company, Inc., 1957.

MARTZ, LOUIS L. *The Poetry of Meditation: A Study in English Religious Literature.* New Haven: Yale University Press, 1954.

MATTHIESSEN, F. O. *American Renaissance: Art and Expression in the Age of Emerson and Whitman.* New York: Oxford University Press, 1941.

MATTHIESSEN, F. O. *The Responsibilities of the Critic.* JOHN RACKLIFFE, ed. New York: Oxford University Press, 1952.

Mid-Century American Poets. JOHN CIARDI, ed. New York: Twayne Publishers, Inc., 1950.

MILES, JOSEPHINE. *Major Adjectives in English Poetry: From Wyatt to Auden.* Berkeley and Los Angeles: University of California Press, 1946.

MILES, JOSEPHINE. *The Primary Language of Poetry in the 1640's.* Berkeley and Los Angeles: University of California Press, 1948.

MILLET, FRED B. *Reading Poetry: A Method of Analysis with Selections for Study.* New York: Harper & Brothers, 1950.

Modern American Poetry, B. RAJAN, ed. New York: Roy Publishers, 1950.

Modern Language Notes, XL (Jan., 1925) —LXXIV, No. 8, (Dec. 1959). (Abbreviated in checklist as *MLN.*)

Modern Literary Criticism. IRVING HOWE, ed. Boston: Beacon Press, 1958.

Modern Philology, XXII (August, 1924) — LVII, No. 2 (Nov., 1959).

MOORE, ARTHUR K. *The Secular Lyric in Middle English.* Lexington: University of Kentucky Press, 1951.

MURRY, JOHN MIDDLETON. *Aspects of Literature,* 2nd ed. London: W. Collins Sons and Company, Ltd., 1921. (No explication.)

MURRY, JOHN MIDDLETON. *Countries of the Mind: Essays in Literary Criticism*, First Series. London: Oxford University Press, Humphrey Milford, 1931 (New Edition). (No explication.)

MURRY, JOHN MIDDLETON. *Countries of the Mind: Essays in Literary Criticism*, Second Series. London: Oxford University Press, Humphrey Milford, 1931. (No explication.)

NICOLSON, MARJORIE HOPE. *The Breaking of the Circle*. Evanston: Northwestern University Press, 1950.

O'CONNOR, WILLIAM VAN. *Sense and Sensibility in Modern Poetry*. Chicago: The University of Chicago Press, 1948.

PALMER, HERBERT. *Post-Victorian Poetry*. London: J. M. Dent and Sons, Ltd., 1938.

PERRINE, LAURENCE. *Sound and Sense: An Introduction to Poetry*. New York: Harcourt, Brace and Company, 1956.

Perspective. I (Autumn, 1947) —XI, No. 3 (Autumn, 1959).

PINTÓ,VIVIAN DE SOLA. *Crisis in English Poetry 1880-1940*. London: Hutchinson's University Library, 1951.

Poetry: A Critical Supplement. March, 1947—May, 1948. See the note under *A Critical Supplement to "Poetry."*

Poetry: A Magazine of Verse, XXV (Jan., 1925) —XCV No. 3 (Dec., 1959).

Poets at Work. Charles D. Abbott, ed. New York: Harcourt, Brace and Co., 1948.

Politics and Letters (incorporating *The Critic*), I (Summer, 1947)—I, No. 4 (Summer, 1948).

POTTLE, FREDERICK A. *The Idiom of Poetry*. Ithaca: Cornell University Press, 1941. (Also, revised edition, 1946.)

Publications of the Modern Language Association of America, XL (March, 1925) —LXXIV, No. 5 (Dec., 1959). (Abbreviated in checklist as *PMLA*.)

Quarterly Review of Literature, I, No. 1 (Autumn, 1943); II
(Fall, 1944)—IV, No. 4.

QIUNN, SISTER M. BERNETTA. *The Metamorphic Tradition in Modern Poetry.* New Brunswick, New
Jersey: Rutgers University Press, 1955.

RANSOM, JOHN CROWE. *God Without Thunder.* New
York: Harcourt Brace and Co., 1930. (No explication.)

RANSOM, JOHN CROWE. *The New Criticism.* Norfolk,
Conn.: New Directions, 1941.

RANSOM, JOHN CROWE. *The World's Body.* New York:
Charles Scribner's Sons, 1938.

READ, HERBERT. *Collected Essays in Literary Criticism.*
London: Faber and Faber, Ltd., 1938. (No explication.)

Readings in Applied English Linguistics. HAROLD B. ALLEN,
ed. New York: Appleton-Century-Crofts, Inc., 1958.

Readings for Liberal Education, volume II, *Introduction to
Literature.* Louis G. Locke, William M. Gibson, and
George Arms, eds. New York: Rinehart & Company,
1948.

RICHARDS, I. A. *Coleridge on Imagination.* New York:
Harcourt, Brace and Co., 1935. (No explication.)

RICHARDS, I. A. *How to Read a Page.* New York: W. W.
Norton and Co., 1942. (No explication.)

RICHARDS, I. A. *The Philosophy of Rhetoric.* New
York: Oxford University Press, 1936. (No explication.)

RICHARDS, I. A. *Practical Criticism.* New York: Harcourt, Brace, and Co., 1929.

RICHARDS, I. A. *Principles of Literary Criticism.* 2nd
ed. London: Kegan Paul, Trench, Trubner & Co.,
Ltd., 1926.

RICHARDS, I. A. *Science and Poetry,* 2nd ed. London:
K. Paul, Trench, Trubner and Co., Ltd., 1935. (No
explication.)

RICHARDS, I. A., C. K. OGDEN, JAMES WOOD. *The*

Foundations of Aesthetics. 2nd ed. New York: Lear Publishers, 1948. (No explication.)

RIDING, LAURA, and ROBERT GRAVES. *A Survey of Modernist Poetry.* New York: Doubleday, Doran and Company, 1928.

ROSENTHAL, M. L. and A. J. M. SMITH. *Exploring Poetry.* New York: The Macmillan Company, 1955.

SAVAGE, D. S. *The Personal Principle: Studies in Modern Poetry.* London: George Routledge and Sons, Ltd., 1944.

SCHLAUCH, MARGARET. *Modern English and American Poetry: Techniques and Idealogies.* London: C. A. Watts & Co., Ltd., 1956.

SCHNEIDER, ELISABETH. *Aesthetic Motive.* New York: The Macmillan Co., 1939.

SCOTT, A. F. *The Poet's Craft.* Cambridge: Cambridge University Press, 1957.

SCOTT, NATHAN A., JR. *Rehearsals of Discomposure.* New York: King's Crown Press, 1952.

Scottish Poetry: A Critical Survey, JAMES KINSLEY, ed. London: Cassell and Company, Ltd., 1955.

Scrutinies, by Various Writers. 2 volumes. Edgell Rickword, ed. London: Wishart & Company, 1928 and 1931.

Scrutiny: A Quarterly Review, I (May, 1932) —XIX, No. 4 (Oct., 1953).

The Sewanee Review, XXXIII (Jan., 1925) — LXVII, No. 4 (Oct.-Dec., 1959).

SEWELL, ELIZABETH. *The Structure of Poetry.* London: Routledge and Kegan Paul, 1951.

SKELTON, ROBIN. *The Poetic Pattern.* Berkeley and Los Angeles: University of California Press, 1956.

SMITH, HALLETT. *Elizabethan Poetry: A Study in Conventions, Meaning, and Expression.* Cambridge: Harvard University Press, 1952.

The Southern Review, I (July, 1935)—VII (Spring, 1942).

SOUTHWORTH, JAMES G. *More Modern American*

Poets. New York: The Macmillan Company, 1954.

SOUTHWORTH, JAMES G. *Some Modern American Poets.* Oxford: Basil Blackwell, 1950.

SPITZER, LEO. *A Method of Interpreting Literature.* Northampton, Massachusetts: Smith College, 1949.

STAGEBERG, NORMAN C. and WALLACE ANDERSON. *Poetry as Experience.* New York: American Book Company, 1952.

STALLMAN, R. W. and R. E. WATTERS. *The Creative Reader: An Anthology of Fiction, Drama, and Poetry.* New York: The Ronald Press Company, 1954.

STAUFFER, DONALD A. *The Nature of Poetry.* New York: W. W. Norton & Co., Inc., 1946.

STEVENS, WALLACE. *The Necessary Angel.* New York: Alfred A. Knopf, 1951.

Studies in Honor of John Wilcox. A. DOYLE WALLACE and WOODBURN O. Ross, eds. Detroit: Wayne State University Press, 1958.

Studies in the Literature of the Augustan Age: Essays Collected in Honor of Arthur Ellicott Case. RICHARD C. Boys, ed. Ann Arbor: The George Wahr Publishing Co., 1952. (No explication.)

Studies in Philology, XXII (Jan., 1925) —XVI, No. 4 (Oct., 1959).

TATE, ALLEN. *On the Limits of Poetry.* New York: The Swallow Press and William Morrow & Company, 1948.

TATE, ALLEN. *Reactionary Essays on Poetry and Ideas.* New York: Charles Scribner's Sons, 1936.

TATE, ALLEN. *Reason in Madness.* New York: G. P. Putnam's Sons, 1941.

THOMAS, WRIGHT, and STUART GERRY BROWN. *Reading Poems:An Introduction to Critical Study.* New York: Oxford University Press, 1941.

Three Studies in the Renaissance: Sidney, Jonson, Milton. BENJAMIN CHRISTE NANGLE, ed. *Yale Studies in English,* Vol. 138. New Haven: Yale University Press, 1958.

TILLYARD, E. M. W.   *Five Poems, 1470-1870.* London: Chatto and Windus, 1948.

TILLYARD, E. M. W.   *The Metaphysicals and Milton.* London: Chatto and Windus, 1956.

TILLYARD, E. M. W.   *Poetry Direct and Oblique.* London: Chatto and Windus, 1934.

TSCHUMI, RAYMOND.   *Thought in Twentieth-Century English Poetry.* London: Routledge and Kegan Paul, Ltd., 1951.

TUVE, ROSEMOND.   *Elizabethan and Metaphysical Imagery.* Chicago: The University of Chicago Press, 1947.

[*The Harvard*] *Wake,* V (Spring, 1946); *Wake* VII (Autumn, 1948) —XII (1953).

UNGER, LEONARD.   *The Man in the Name: Essays on the Experience of Poetry.* Minneapolis: The University of Minnesota Press, 1956.

UNGER, LEONARD and WILLIAM VAN O'CONNOR. *Poems for Study.* New York: Rinehart & Company, Inc., 1953.

VAN DOREN, MARK.   *Introduction to Poetry.* New York: William Sloane Associates, Inc., 1951.

Victorian Studies, I, No. 1 (Sept., 1957) —III, No. 2 (Dec., 1959).

VIVANTE, LEONE.   *English Poetry and Its Contribution to the Knowledge of a Creative Principle.* New York: The Macmillan Company, 1950.

WAGGONER, HYATT HOWE.   *The Heel of Elohim: Science and Values in Modern American Poetry.* Norman: University of Oklahoma Press, 1950.

WARREN, AUSTIN.   *Rage for Order: Essays in Criticism.* Chicago: The University of Chicago Press, 1948.

WASSERMAN, EARL R.   *The Subtler Language: Critical Readings of Neoclassic and Romantic Poems.* Baltimore: The John Hopkins Press, 1959.

WATTS, HAROLD H.   *Hound and Quarry.* London: Routledge and Kegan Paul, 1953.

WEITZ, MORRIS.   *Philosophy of the Arts,* Cambridge: Harvard University Press, 1950.

WELLS, E. K.   *The Ballad Tree.* New York: Ronald Press, 1950.

WELLS, HENRY W.   *New Poets from Old: A Study in Literary Genetics.* New York: Columbia University Press, 1940.

The Western Review, XI (Autumn, 1946) —XXIII (Spring, 1959).

WHEELWRIGHT, PHILIP.   *The Burning Fountain: A Study in the Language of Symbolism.* Bloomington: Indiana University Press, 1954.

WILSON, EDMUND.   *Axel's Castle.* New York: Charles Scribner's Sons, 1931.

WIMSATT, W. K. JR.   *The Verbal Icon: Studies in the Meaning of Poetry.* Lexington: University of Kentucky Press, 1954.

WINTERS, YVOR.   *The Anatomy of Nonsense.* Norfolk, Conn.: New Directions, 1943.

WINTERS, YVOR.   *In Defense of Reason.* New York: The Swallow Press and William Morrow and Co., 1947; third ed. Denver: Alan Swallow, 1960.

WINTERS, YVOR   *The Function of Criticism: Problems and Exercises.* Denver: Alan Swallow, 1957.

WINTERS, YVOR.   *Maule's Curse.* Norfolk, Conn.: New Directions, 1938.

WINTERS, YVOR.   *Primitivism and Decadence.* New York: Arrow Editions, 1933.

WORMHOUDT, ARTHUR.   *The Demon Lover: A Psychoanalytical Approach to Literature.* New York: Exposition Press, 1949.

YEATS, W. B.   *Essays.* New York: The Macmillan Co., 1924.

YEATS, W. B.   *Letters on Poetry from W. B. Yeats to Dorothy Wellesley.* New York: Oxford University Press, 1940.